BEYOND REPAIR?

CENTER FOR THE STUDY OF
GENOCIDE
& HUMAN RIGHTS

GENOCIDE, POLITICAL VIOLENCE, HUMAN RIGHTS SERIES

Edited by Alexander Laban Hinton, Stephen Eric Bronner, and Nela Navarro

BEYOND REPAIR?

Mayan Women's Protagonism in the Aftermath of Genocidal Harm

ALISON CROSBY AND M. BRINTON LYKES

RUTGERS UNIVERSITY PRESS

New Brunswick, Camden, and Newark, New Jersey, and London

Library of Congress Cataloging-in-Publication Data

Names: Crosby, Alison, author. | Lykes, M. Brinton, 1949- author.
Title: Beyond repair? : Mayan women's protagonism in the aftermath of genocidal
    harm / Alison Crosby, M. Brinton Lykes.
Description: New Brunswick : Rutgers University Press, [2019] | Series: Genocide,
    political violence, human rights | Includes bibliographical references and index.
Identifiers: LCCN 2018022085| ISBN 9780813598970 (cloth) | ISBN 9780813598963
    (pbk.)
Subjects: LCSH: Maya women—Guatemala—Social conditions. | Women—Crimes
    against—Guatemala. | Guatemala—History—Civil War, 1960-1996—Social
    aspects. | Guatemala—History—Civil War, 1960-1996—Atrocities.
Classification: LCC F1435.3.W55 C76 2019 | DDC 305.4097281—dc23 LC record available
    at https://lccn.loc.gov/2018022085

A British Cataloging-in-Publication record for this book is available from
the British Library.

The painting featured on the cover, *Personajes* (People), is by José Colaj (1959–2011), a
Mayan artist from Comalapa, Chimaltenango. The yellows, reds, oranges, and blues
capture the earth tones of rural Guatemala; embodied sketches of peasants are
pictured from behind, obscuring their faces yet eliciting remembrances of the intensity
of life during Guatemala's genocidal violence. As described by his family, "The work of
the master artist José Colaj is always representative of the struggle, suffering and
resistance of our communities, but also hopes for the revindication of our rights and
worth as a people."

♾ The paper used in this publication meets the requirements of the American National
Standard for Information Sciences—Permanence of Paper for Printed Library
Materials, ANSI Z39.48-1992.

www.rutgersuniversitypress.org

Manufactured in the United States of America

To the next generations of Maya who draw strength from their ancestors, and to those who walk in solidarity with them.

CONTENTS

ABBREVIATIONS

AJR	Asociación Justicia y Reconciliación [Association for Justice and Reconciliation]
APDHE	Asociación Pro Derechos Humanos de España [Spanish Human Rights Association]
ASA	Asociación Sororidad Activa [Active Sisterhood Association]
AVIHDESMI	Asociación de Víctimas, Viudas, Huérfanos y Desarraigados del Conflicto Armado Interno de la Sierra de las Minas [Association of Victims, Widows, Orphans, and People Displaced by the Internal Armed Conflict in the Sierra de las Minas]
CAFCA	Centro de Análisis Forense y Ciencias Aplicadas [Center for Forensic Analysis and Applied Sciences]
CALDH	Centro para la Acción Legal en Derechos Humanos [Center for Legal Action in Human Rights]
CEDAW	Convention on the Elimination of All Forms of Discrimination against Women
CEH	Comisión para el Esclarecimiento Histórico [Commission for Historical Clarification]
CICIG	Comisión Internacional contra la Impunidad en Guatemala [International Commission against Impunity in Guatemala]
COCODES	Consejos Comunitarios de Desarrollo [Community Development Councils]
CONAVIGUA	Coordinadora Nacional de Viudas de Guatemala [National Coordinating Committee of Widows of Guatemala]
CPR	Comunidades de Poblaciones en Resistencia [Communities of Populations in Resistance]
DIWN	Defensoría Indígena Wajxaqib' No'j [Wajxaqib' No'j Indigenous Legal Defense Organization]
ECAP	Equipo de Estudios Comunitarios y Acción Psicosocial [Community Studies and Psychosocial Action Team]
EGP	Ejército Guerrillero de los Pobres [Guerrilla Army of the Poor]
FAFG	Fundación de Antropología Forense de Guatemala [Foundation of Forensic Anthropology of Guatemala]
FIRE	Feminist International Radio Endeavor
IACHR	Inter-American Commission on Human Rights
ICC	International Criminal Court

ICCPG	Instituto de Estudios Comparados en Ciencias Penales de Guatemala [Institute for Comparative Studies in Criminal Sciences of Guatemala]
INACIF	Instituto Nacional de Ciencias Forenses [National Institute of Forensic Sciences]
INGUAT	Instituto Guatemalteco de Turismo [Guatemalan Tourism Institute]
INTA	Instituto Nacional de Transformación Agraria [National Institute of Agrarian Transformation]
LASA	Latin American Studies Association
MTM	Mujeres Transformando el Mundo [Women Transforming the World]
NGO	nongovernmental organization
ODHAG	Oficina de Derechos Humanos del Arzobispado de Guatemala [Human Rights Office of the Archbishopric of Guatemala]
OSJI	Open Society Justice Initiative
PACs	Patrullas de Autodefensa Civil [Civilian Self-Defense Patrols]
PAR	participatory action research
PCS	Project Counselling Service [Consejería en Proyectos]
PNR	Programa Nacional de Resarcimiento [National Reparations Program]
REMHI	Recuperación de la Memoria Histórica [Recovery of Historical Memory]
TRC	Truth and Reconciliation Commission
UN	United Nations
UNAMG	Unión Nacional de Mujeres Guatemaltecas [National Union of Guatemalan Women]
UNDP	United Nations Development Program
URNG	Unidad Revolucionaria Nacional Guatemalteca [Guatemalan National Revolutionary Unity]

BEYOND REPAIR?

INTRODUCTION

We felt happy to see that the court allowed us in, listened to us, especially us women, because we never thought that they would grant us that right or give us that space. We thank the judges who listened to us.... Then I felt calm, and at the same time I cried from the effort. I remembered those of us who were there sitting, watching, and listening. When we rejoiced the most is when the judge issued the ruling, because we fulfilled our struggle and I felt calmer because I heard how many years the culprits were sentenced to serve in jail ... when we heard it or when I heard it I felt calmer knowing that they will pay for what they did to us,

—Demecia Yat, plaintiff in the Sepur Zarco trial, as cited
in Impunity Watch and Alliance (2017, p. 45)

If violence, when it happens dramatically, bears some relation to what is happening repeatedly and unmelodramatically, then how does one tell this, not in a single narrative but in the form of a text that is being constantly revised, rewritten, and overlaid with commentary?

—Veena Das (2007, p. 80)

On February 26, 2016, the High Risk Court "A" in Guatemala City found both Esteelmer Reyes Girón, the former commander of the Sepur Zarco military outpost in El Estor, Izabal in northeastern Guatemala, and Heriberto Valdéz Asij, the former military commissioner in the region, guilty of crimes against humanity in the form of sexual violence and domestic and sexual slavery perpetrated against Maya Q'eqchi' women. This was the first time such a conviction for these particular crimes had been achieved in the country where they had been committed. The trial, its verdict, and the courage and determination of the 15 Q'eqchi' women plaintiffs in the case were celebrated widely in Guatemala and transnationally, with hashtags such as #WeAreAllSepurZarco and #IamSepur-Zarco trending. Demecia Yat, one of the plaintiffs, highlighted the enormous affective impact of the verdict, as well as the trial's toll, when she said, "I cried from the effort." In a country structured by centuries of colonial violence and dispossession resulting in the exclusion and marginalization of indigenous women, she added, "We never thought that they would grant us that right or give us that space."

This book traces the struggles for redress by 54 Mayan women protagonists, including the 15 Q'eqchi' plaintiffs in the Sepur Zarco case, all of whom survived sexual harm and many other violations perpetrated against them during the height of Guatemala's 36-year armed conflict. These protagonists argue that such harm is irreparable; "no one can take this thorn from my soul,"[1] one woman told the Tribunal of Conscience for Women Survivors of Sexual Violence in March 2010, a truth-telling forum organized as a precursor to the trial. Acknowledgment of a harm's irreparability does not, however, signify the impossibility of agency, but rather underlies these protagonists' engagement with mechanisms seeking truth, justice, and reparations, central elements of the paradigm of transitional justice (Teitel, 2000) within which many actions for redress in postgenocide Guatemala are now situated—and also contested.

We use the concept of protagonism to deconstruct dominant psychological discursive positionings of women as "victims," "survivors," "selves," "individuals," and/or "subjects." We argue that at different moments across the eight years of our research (2009–2017),[2] Mayan women were actively engaged as protagonists in constructivist and discursive performances through which they narrated new, mobile, embodied meanings of the "Mayan woman," repositioning themselves at the interstices of multiple communities and through their participation in actions seeking redress for harm suffered. Our conception of protagonism emphasizes the dialogic dimensions of knowledge construction through praxis; that is, the action-reflection processes through which a multiplicity of actors co-construct meanings and transformative possibilities. The term represents the person-in-context approach, invoking the Greek chorus within theater—that is, the dialogic rather than the individualized voice—and drawing on the call-and-response form within African American religious contexts.[3] We explore how Mayan women positioned themselves vis-à-vis other survivors, Mayan communities, and others who accompanied them, whom we refer to in this volume as "intermediaries" (Merry, 2006), wherein mutual relationality and empathy dialogically co-constitute the former's protagonism. Our understanding of protagonism invokes the performative (Taylor, 2003),[4] including the creative arts and embodied practices that were central methodological resources in the research and activism discussed in this book. It also recognizes two levels of struggle identified and discussed by Kaqchikel scholar Otzoy (2008) as "congruent and incongruent with the lived experiences of indigenous women today ... [that is] the socially and culturally intertwined struggles for the exercise of collective rights and for the enjoyment of individual rights" (p. 174). In her analysis of justice-seeking processes among the Maya, Otzoy examines the ways in which indigenous peoples' engagement with community customary laws in situ reflects their concern with "the effective functioning of the social order" (p. 176), while women's struggles for justice in the wake of sexual violence are focused more frequently on individual "needs, feelings, voice and dignity" (p. 178).

At its essence this book is about the relationship between Mayan women protagonists and those who have accompanied them in their struggles for more than a decade and who co-construct their protagonism. These intermediaries include Mayan, *ladinx*,[5] and transnational activists, interpreters, feminists, lawyers, psychologists, and researchers, ourselves included. Merry (2006) defines intermediaries as "the people in the middle . . . who translate the discourses and practices from the arena of international law and legal institutions to specific situations of suffering and violation" and "work at various levels to negotiate between local, regional, national and global systems of meaning" (p. 39). She and her coauthors (Goodale & Merry, 2007; Levitt & Merry, 2009; Merry & Levitt, 2017) have written extensively about how people, most particularly women, often appropriate the human rights discourse and practices in innovative ways, translating them into praxis that moves their local agendas forward. Drawing on their multiple years of ethnographic research with two urban women's nongovernmental organizations (NGOs) in each of four countries—China, India, Peru, and the United States— Merry and Levitt (2017) argue that "forms of translation differed depending on differences in funding and support, choice of issues, and local attitudes toward human rights" (pp. 225–226). We draw on this research and theorization to think through how intermediaries translate or "vernacularize" (Merry, 2006, 2009; Merry & Levitt, 2017) knowledge generated from national and international feminist and human rights domains in their work with protagonists; we also examine how such knowledge is transformed in that journey and, most importantly, the extent to which knowledge generated from below by protagonists travels up into and informs these transnational discourses and regimes of power (Grewal & Kaplan, 2000). The 54 Mam, Chuj, Poptí, Q'eqchi', and Kaqchikel protagonists came from three regions of the country—Huehuetenango, Alta Verapaz/Izabal,[6] and Chimaltenango—and their experiences of racialized gendered violence,[7] as well as of resistance and struggle, have been diverse, multifaceted, and context specific. The book traces how intermediaries accompanied Mayan protagonists in performing a "community of women" outside of their local geographically based community, creating a space within which to enact actions for redress within Western transitional justice mechanisms, and the implications for indigenous and place-based struggles.

CONTEXTUALIZING RACIALIZED GENDERED VIOLENCE

Mayan women were the targets of racialized gendered harm, including sexual harm, in the genocidal violence perpetrated by the Guatemalan state against its indigenous peoples during the 36-year armed conflict from 1960 to 1996 (CEH, 1999; Fulchiron, Paz, & López, 2009; Velásquez Nimatuj, 2012). At the roots of the armed conflict were deeply skewed inequities of economic and political power resulting from a colonial system that led to the dispossession of indigenous lands and the exclusion of the indigenous population from sociopolitical and economic life, which continued after Guatemala gained formal independence from Spain in 1821. In its final report, the *Comisión para el Esclarecimiento Histórico* [Commission for Historical Clarification] (CEH) (1999) estimated that, during the armed conflict, more than 200,000 people were murdered or disappeared (vol. 5, p. 21) and between 500,000 and 1.5 million people were displaced within the country or beyond its borders (vol. 3, pp. 37–38). The report documented massacres that destroyed 626 villages (vol. 3, p. 252) and concluded that, at the height of the armed conflict in the early 1980s, acts of genocide were committed against particular Mayan communities (vol. 3, p. 358).[8]

In the early 1990s, as international conditions and resources that had supported the armed conflict—including the direct and indirect intervention of the United States (Grandin, 2004; Grandin, Levenson, & Oglesby, 2011)—shifted, and the overt violence receded, the Guatemalan government and the umbrella guerrilla organization, the *Unidad Revolucionaria Nacional Guatemalteca* [Guatemalan National Revolutionary Unity] (URNG), began negotiations to bring the war to a close, concluding with the signing of the final Peace Accords in 1996 (Jonas, 2000). The 1995 Agreement on Identity and Rights of Indigenous Peoples included the recognition of the identity of indigenous peoples; respect for and the exercise of their political, cultural, economic, and spiritual rights; and proposals for changes in the Guatemalan constitution that would guarantee these rights. The rights of indigenous women were singled out in the Agreement, and both sides also agreed to work toward promoting and implementing the United Nations (UN) Convention on the Elimination of All Forms of Discrimination against Women (CEDAW) (1979). However, constitutional reforms to recognize indigenous customary law were rejected in a national referendum in May 1999, and these agreements have for the most part not been implemented in the postwar period.

The Catholic Church's Human Rights Office's *Recuperación de la Memoria Histórica* [Recovery of Historical Memory] (REMHI) project (see ODHAG, 1998) began its truth-telling process in 1995, and the UN-sponsored CEH started work in 1997. These initiatives collected individual and group testimonies from survivors about what had transpired, and scholars and human rights experts contributed chapters to each final report that documented the structural and systemic nature of the armed conflict, its historical and racialized underpinnings, and the gendered dimensions of these gross violations of human rights. The CEH report (1999) cited 1,465 cases of sexual violence (considered to be a fraction of the actual number of incidents), of whom 88.7% of the victims were Mayan women (vol. 3, p. 23). Fifty-two percent of women who testified to the CEH chose to focus "on what happened to others in their community" (Nolin & Shankar, 2000, p. 268), while 48% talked about their own experiences of violence, although not necessarily sexual violations (CEH, 1999, vol. 3, p. 28).

Despite these truth-telling processes that began soon after the cessation of armed conflict, for many women, particularly rural Mayan women, the traumatic effects of their racialized gendered experiences of the genocidal violence have persisted. They still live in "limit situations" in which the tensions and stressors occurring in the wake of war, including ongoing violence, poverty, and impunity, constitute a "normal abnormality" (Martín-Baró, 1994) of their everyday lives that is carried in their bodies (Hollander & Gill, 2014). Many women widowed in the armed conflict have lost access to land and community structures and supports (Green, 1999; Zur, 1998). Survivors often live in close proximity to perpetrators, generating conditions of insecurity and the ever-present possibility of revictimization. Many of those who were sexually abused have been ostracized by their own communities, accused of being "military women" (Fulchiron et al., 2009). The violence of everyday life in Guatemala—in particular the violence of indigenous women's extreme impoverishment—is a structural reality that has been exacerbated by decades of militarized violence (CEH, 1999).

Our emphasis in this volume on protagonism does not negate Mayan women's experiences of suffering. Indeed, they suffered deeply, and their pain and loss are not only individual but also interpersonal and structural: what Kleinman, Das, and Lock (1997) refer to as "social suffering." As they argue, social suffering can be thought of as "an assemblage of human problems that have their origins and consequences in the devastating injuries that social forces can inflict on human experience" (p. ix); its causes can be found in "what political, economic, and institutional power does to people and, reciprocally . . . how these forms of power themselves influence responses to social problems" (p. ix). Unlike many psychological theories on the effects of war and state violence that locate the problem within the individual (see, e.g., the vast literature on post-traumatic stress disorder), social suffering shifts "what we define as 'problems' off the backs of individuals and onto systems, structures, and policies, here focusing on the geopolitical-structures of state sanctioned surveillances and violence" (Stoudt et al., 2016, p. 4; see Lykes & Mersky, 2006). As such, in this volume we are concerned with the ways in which responses—in particular, those of human rights regimes—to protagonists' claims for acknowledgment of their pain and suffering can often in fact reinforce and contribute further to this suffering, pathologizing trauma as an individuated rather than a social phenomenon that is embodied in particular ways by each one marked by it (Martín-Baró, 1994). As Kleinman et al. (1997) argue, such responses "often transform the local idiom of victims into universal professional languages of complaint and restitution—thereby remak[ing] both representations and experiences of suffering" and are "inattentive to how the transformations they induce contribute to the suffering they seek to remedy" (p. x). The Sepur Zarco case, which we examine in detail in chapter 3, shows how Q'eqchi' women's experiences of violence are produced, mediated, and transformed by their engagement with the legal domain and the transnational human rights regime, whereby the imperative to prove the harm that was suffered—a key component of acknowledgment in the legal domain—affects the women's subjectivity. Das and Kleinman (2000) have explored how subjectivity—"the felt interior experience of the person that includes his or her position in a field of relational power" (p. 1)—is shaped both by the experience of violence and the transnational networks of people and power that "become entangled with local logics in identity formation" (p. 1). The micro- and macro-politics of these entanglements and how they inform protagonists' attempts to move beyond the experience of violence are of particular interest to us in this volume.

Thinking critically about the influence of rights discourses and the legal realm on Mayan protagonism neither negates nor precludes the agency and resilience of protagonists who engage with these domains and use them to their benefit. They are not objects who have been acted on in these processes; instead, they continuously resist and subvert the expectations laid on them to inhabit the category of victim in rigid and homogenizing ways. In thinking about the relationship of protagonism to agency, we adopt Carey's (2013) framing of the protagonism of Mayan and poor women as "the ways an individual's subjectivity both bounded and sustained their agency" (p. 8). One of the Q'eqchi' plaintiffs in the Sepur Zarco trial succinctly articulates how the survival of the self is a remarkable feat of agency, given what it has taken to live with the "poisonous knowledge" (Das, 2007, p. 54) of violence suffered when so many others denied it: "I am a miracle because I survived." The individual "I" is always bound to the social "we," the living to the dead, and the absence to the presence, which is all the more profound when the dead are disappeared, as was so often the case in Guatemala (Beristain, Paez, & González, 2000; Kistler, 2010; Otzoy, 2008; see also Rojas-Perez, 2017, for a discussion of this issue in the Peruvian context, and Esteva & Parkash, 1998/2014, for similar discussions in the Mexican and Indian contexts).

Das (2007) addresses the challenge of reconciling the living and the dead when she speaks about "the complex relationship between speaking and hearing, between building a world that the living can inhabit with their loss and building a world in which the dead can find a home" (p. 58). These border zones that the living and the dead inhabit are framed in particular ways by the Mayan cosmovision or worldview, and they facilitate and constrain gendered and racialized social subjectivities. García Ixmatá et al. (1993/2017) suggest further that the Mayan languages "encircle this cosmovision, or philosophy of life, that can neither be expressed nor translated exactly in another language" (p. 137).[9] As such, the challenges for local and international intermediaries accompanying these Mayan women protagonists are complex.

TRANSITIONAL JUSTICE AND SEXUAL HARM

The Sepur Zarco trial exemplifies the increasingly transnational turn taken over the past few decades by what has come to be known as "transitional justice" in its effort to address the harms of the past and ensure they will not be repeated in societies emerging from periods of state repression, armed conflict, genocidal violence, and mass violations of human rights (Hayner, 2011; Kritz, 1995; Minow, 1998; Teitel, 2000; Wilson, 2001). The assumption underlying the transitional justice paradigm is that the transition in question is to Western liberal democracy. This paradigm was solidified in the 1990s with the South African Truth and Reconciliation Commission (TRC) and the formation of the International Criminal Court (ICC). Transitional justice mechanisms typically include prosecutions, truth commissions, and reparations programs—forms of which have all been undertaken in postgenocide Guatemala (including the aforementioned CEH and REMHI truth-telling processes)—as well as international war crimes tribunals. The issue of protagonism is a central preoccupation within transitional justice endeavors, provoking questions such as the following: Who gets to decide how these processes are shaped and how they will unfold? What is the relationship between protagonists and those who accompany them within these processes? What does it mean to tell stories of harm, including sexualized harm, to audiences who as bystanders may not have suffered such racialized gendered violence? When the state is the perpetrator of violence, as in Guatemala, what effect does this have on national transitional justice processes aimed at redressing said violence? How do women and men differentially experience racialized gendered violence and what does it mean to redress such harms? Despite the many experiences of transitional justice processes over the past two decades and the transnational circulation of "lessons learned" and "best practices," the answers to these questions remain contested, revealing the continuation of fraught relationships among survivors, perpetrators, bystanders, beneficiaries, and the state itself (see Kesselring, 2017; Ross, 2003; Theidon, 2012, among many others).

As such, despite their acknowledged ground-breaking and necessary attempts to confront the wrongs of the past—the Sepur Zarco trial did produce a guilty verdict against the two defendants—transitional justice mechanisms have been critiqued by many scholars as being overly prescriptive, failing to adapt to historical, gendered, and cultural particularities and to take local actors, particularly survivors themselves, seriously as protagonists (Bell, 2009; Lambourne, 2009; Lykes & Mersky, 2006; McEvoy & McGregor, 2008; Ní Aoláin & Rooney, 2007; Shaw, Waldorf, & Hazan, 2010). They rarely build on local practices and indigenous knowledge and resources; all too frequently these mechanisms are mediated—and controlled—by transnational actors who shape the human rights discourses deployed, couching them in the liberal language of individual rights. When these mechanisms do include women's experiences, they often position local protagonists as victims whose voices are included through testimonies of harm, such as rape, torture, and/or disappearance: these mechanisms hypervisibilize them as victims, embedding them in deep colonial histories that continue to construct the racialized gendered other (Henry, 2009; Kapur, 2002). The victim becomes an absent presence required to bring into being such "spectacles of suffering" (Clarke, 2009, p. 13; see Hesford, 2011). These spectacles, rooted in histories of oppression of the racialized other, can often reinforce the subjectivity of those who are witness to another's pain. In her analysis of slavery and self-making in the United States in the 19th century, Hartman (1997) points to "the precariousness of empathy," arguing that "only more obscene than the brutality unleashed at the whipping post is the demand that this suffering be materialized and evidenced by the display of the tortured body or endless recitations of the ghastly and the terrible." She asks, "How does one give expression to these outrages without exacerbating the indifference to suffering that is the consequence of the benumbing spectacle or contend with the narcissistic identification that obliterates the other or the prurience that is too often the response to such displays" (p. 7)?

In agreeing to participate in our research, Mayan protagonists made clear that they were not interested in retelling their stories of the "ghastly and the terrible"; indeed they made a condition of their participation that they not be required to provide "spectacles of suffering," and this was reflected in the informed consent process that we initiated. Yet their engagement with the legal domain, with truth-telling projects, and the state-sponsored *Programa Nacional de Resarcimiento* [National Reparations Program] (PNR) continuously required them to do precisely that. This book is, at least partially, an exploration of how protagonists participated in, yet resisted and subverted, the demands and expectations of their interlocutors, including their intermediaries, through their engagements in these and other actions. Their decision, for example, to conceal their identities in the Tribunal of Conscience that we discuss in chapter 2, as well as in the Sepur Zarco trial that we analyze in chapter 3, was made not only because of security concerns. It also undermined what Hesford (2011, p. 29) terms the "ocular epistemology" (i.e., "seeing-is-believing") that lies at the heart of human rights spectacles. As we explore in chapter 2, the spectators' inability to see the other and confirm her identity caused great discomfort among many of them, disrupting their authorial privilege to consume the other's pain and their discursive construction of the "good victim."

The spectacularization of harm through the abjection of "the victim" is particularly prevalent in attempts to address sexual harm within transnational rights regimes, in what Marcus refers to as "the gendered grammar of violence" (as cited in Buss, 2009, p. 155), which is inherently racialized (Grewal, 2005; Kapur, 2002). The conflicts in the former Yugoslavia and Rwanda in the 1990s led to an increased recognition within international feminist, human rights, and legal discourse that

sexual violence is instrumental to war and genocide, rather than an isolated or individuated event or byproduct (Copelon, 2003; Halley, 2005; MacKinnon, 2006).
As the result of sustained organizing and pressure by international feminist activists, rape and sexual violence were prosecuted as genocide and crimes against
humanity in the ad hoc tribunals for both these countries, and these violations
were subsequently incorporated into the Rome Statute of the International Criminal Court (1998) that came into effect in 2002. Today, reports on the atrocities
of sexual violence perpetrated in ongoing and emerging conflicts are pervasive
within international media and human rights campaigns.[10] And the opening of
this transnational space to address sexual harm has led to in-country prosecutions
such as the Sepur Zarco case and the Manta y Vilca case in Peru involving soldiers from an army base in a Quechua community in Huancavelica (Bueno-
Hansen, 2016).

While breaking the silence about sexual harm as an integral component of
war and genocide is recognized as a significant advance in combating the causes
and consequences of gendered violence, the feminist literature has raised many
questions about the impact of this increased visibility on the women protagonists themselves as they search for justice and redress within the international
rights regime (Buss, 2009; Engle, 2005; Henry, 2009; Jaleel, 2013). As we discuss
in this volume, narrating sexual harm within transitional justice processes,
from truth commissions to tribunals, court cases, and reparations programs, can
be problematic. Survivors are often asked to retell individuated and event-based
accounts of sexualized pain in what Theidon (2007) refers to as "a pornography
of violence," a narrative burden that perpetrators are not asked to carry (p. 455;
see also Al-Kassim, 2008). As Henry (2009) argues, within the legal domain,
"rape is an identity-producing practice. Subjectivity is often contingent on narratives of injury and victimization" (p. 131). The "raped woman" is thus often a
product of these processes (p. 131). And despite the consensus that women need
and are increasingly receiving psychological support in these processes, Nowrojee
(2005), among others, has documented not only the many ways in which current
international procedures provide insufficient support to women who have experienced rape but also the multiple threats, stigmatization, and ostracism that many
women experience on return to the spaces in which the violations occurred. The
legitimacy of many transitional justice processes (i.e., their being seen to be inclusive of women) may increasingly rely on women delivering these "prized rape
scripts" (Buss, 2009, p. 115), at the expense of what protagonists themselves may
want to say and do about their many experiences and/or multiple violations.

In seeking to elucidate the meaning and significance of the increasing recognition of the issue of sexual harm within the international legal regime, Jaleel (2013)
traces the leadership role played by U.S. and transnational feminists, arguing that
the gendered discourse they use "retreads and reconfigures the heated 1980s
U.S. Sex Wars debates on workings of gender, sex, race and power" (p. 115). In the

international domain we can see the influence of the second-wave feminist position that universalizes "both 'woman-as-a-category' and 'rape-as-act,'" as revealed in declarative statements such as the one by Brownmiller that rape "is nothing more or less than a conscious process of intimidation by which *all men* keep *all women* in a state of fear" (as cited in Smith, 2005, p. 7; emphasis added). The effect of such categorizations, Jaleel (2013) argues, "is to place these terms on a theoretically pristine plane untouched by socio-historical context, or competing, interrelated iterations of violence" (p. 115; see Grewal, 2005; Mohanty, 2003). What is occluded is an understanding of the historical and material specificities "through which gender and race gain cultural meaning" (Jaleel, 2013, p. 115). As such, it is important to pay attention to the transnational circulations of power both in the constitution and promulgation of discourses of gendered harm and in human rights activists' efforts to address such harm; it is also important to note how discourses and actions are vernacularized or contested (Clarke, 2009) by protagonists within localized contexts.

The underlying assumption "of women as a group united through shared sexual vulnerability" (Jaleel, 2013, p. 115) serves to erase structures and practices of colonization, imperialism, and white supremacy that continue to this day. For example, Smith (2005) points to a statement made by MacKinnon (a key player in shaping international jurisprudence on rape as a weapon of war and genocide) in reference to the war in Bosnia: "the world has *never* seen sex used this consciously, this cynically, this elaborately, this openly, this systematically, as a means of destroying a whole people" (as cited in Smith, 2005, p. 28; emphasis added by Smith). Smith (2005) notes that such statements not only erase the pervasive and systemic perpetration of sexual violence against indigenous women in, for example, the Guatemalan armed conflict and in Chiapas, Mexico, but also within MacKinnon's own country, the United States, where "millions of Native people were raped, sexually mutilated, and murdered" (p. 28) during colonization, with this violence reproducing itself into the present (Arvin, Tuck, & Morrill, 2013).

Sexual harm is, of course, not the only way in which war and genocide are gendered, even for those who have experienced sexual harm, as was the case with the Mayan protagonists in our research; in addition, its reification within human rights, legal, and feminist discourses can preclude a broader understanding of how violence is structured through gender in an intersection with other relations of power, including "race" (Sieder, 2017; Theidon, 2012; Velásquez Nimatuj, 2012, 2016). The positioning of women as victims erases longer histories of agency that preceded and followed experiences of harm. It is also important to continue to challenge the notion that gender equals woman and instead explore the complex relationships of masculinities to militarization from positions of victim and perpetrator, with the two subjectivities often intertwined for some men within war and colonial violence (Eichler, 2014; Mama, 2013). In Guatemala, indigenous men were forced to patrol their own communities as part of *Patrullas de Autodefensa Civil* [Civilian Self-Defense Patrols] (PACs) implemented as a counterinsurgency tactic that created "the enemy within," and young indigenous boys were often forcibly conscripted into the army (CEH, 1999; Nelson, 2009; Remijnse, 2002). In many places the PACs were identified as the direct perpetrators of war crimes, although local participants were often forced to commit such crimes under threat of death from the army. The binaries of gender in relation to constructions of "victims" and "perpetrators" remain disturbingly intact within feminist understandings of war and violence, and in our work with Mayan women protagonists we have been challenged to subvert, not replicate, them.

Within contexts of colonial dispossession, it is crucial to center indigenous ways of knowing and conceptions of justice, which may in fact be incommensurate with the individual, rights-based underpinnings of Western feminist and human rights discourses (Esteva & Prakash, 1998/2014). In Guatemala, Mayan women activists and theorists emphasize the importance of collectivity, autonomy, and self-determination in their experiences of family and community (Chirix García, 2003); suffering, loss, and healing (Álvarez Medrano, 2016; AVANCSO, 2017; CALDH, 2014); and in their struggles for justice (Ajxup Pelicó, 2000; Álvarez Medrano, 2006; AVANCSO, 2016; CALDH, 2014; Curruchich, 2000; Hernández Castillo, 2016; Jocón, 2005; Velásquez Nimatuj, 2012). They note that gender oppression cannot be separated from colonial oppression, and they have sought "to find a decolonized language or their own language to talk about rights, dignity and moral and ethical behavior, and gender relations" (Sieder & Macleod, 2009, p. 55). Yet, as Otzoy (2008) suggests, "while the complex 'I' of indigenous women struggling for our rights carries differential angles to the cultural values of nonindigenous women, a complex 'us' is relevant in collective efforts such as in feminist struggles or in the struggles of indigenous people" (p. 183). Or, as Hernández Castillo (2016) confirms, based on her activist scholarship in Mexico, indigenous women's analysis "conceive[s] their experiences of violence not as individual but as part of a collective history that has been characterized by a *continuum* of violence against indigenous peoples" (pp. 52–53; emphasis in the original); these women's demand for compensation before the Inter-American Commission of Human Rights (IACHR), among other actions, reflects "the cultural construction of a sense of personhood that is constituted mutually by the individual and the collective" (p. 53; see also Sieder, 2017). Our eight-year feminist participatory action research (PAR) documents some of the complex movements of a small group of Mayan protagonists accompanied by Mayan, ladinx, and North American intermediaries, who engaged in praxis at the interstices of decolonial feminisms, Mayan customary beliefs, and transitional justice mechanisms, through which they came together, moved away from each other, and were distanced.

Our disturbance of the reification and spectacularization of racialized gendered harm required us to excavate and claim both the everyday and the structural dimensions of violence, issues that protagonists in our research continuously emphasized. Indeed, as was articulated in one participatory workshop we facilitated, for many protagonists, violence against women signified "carrying the heavy load" of ongoing impoverishment. Miller (2008) among others has critiqued a tendency of rights-based regimes such as the transitional justice paradigm to relegate to the background structures of violence and histories of colonization and dispossession "in favor of more obvious concerns about physical violence . . . . Although a nuanced understanding of context is crucial to understanding the power and politics of rights, poverty and inequality tend to be depicted merely as the landscape against which murder, disappearance, torture and other gross human rights violations are committed" (p. 267). As an example, she describes the experience of South Africa following the TRC process, in which apartheid became "a story about racism or about specific, individual rights violations rather than about long-term, systemic abuse born of a colonial project with economic objectives" (p. 280; see also Ross, 2003). Thus, she argues, apartheid was seen as "the background to particular violations rather than the violation itself" (Miller, 2008, p. 277). What was absent in these discussions, as in most Guatemalan transitional justice processes, was the challenge of redistributing resources, in particular the return of land stolen through colonial dispossession.

In thinking through representations of colonial violence, their impact on indigenous peoples and their communities, and particularly outsiders' engagement with them, indigenous scholar Tuck (2009) has called for a moratorium on what she calls "damage-centered research" (p. 413), in which the pain and loss of indigenous and other communities that have been the targets of structural repression are the central focus of inquiry. As Tuck argues, the danger of such research "is that it is a pathologizing approach in which the oppression singularly defines a community"; such research "operates, even benevolently, from a theory of change that establishes harm or injury in order to achieve reparation" (p. 413). An analysis of the contexts of colonization and structural racism that is necessary to understand such harm is often "submerged . . . and all we're left with is the damage" (p. 413). This critique of research parallels and complements the earlier cited critiques of victim-centered rights regimes.

Tuck (2009) emphasizes the implications of such framing for communities, which often come to see themselves as damaged: "even when communities are broken and conquered, they are so much more than that—so much more that this incomplete story is an act of aggression" (p. 416). Instead, Tuck argues for a "desire-based framework," which is "concerned with understanding complexity, contradiction, and the self-determination of lived lives" (p. 416). As she elaborates, "desire, yes, accounts for the loss and despair, but also the hope, the visions, the wisdom of lived lives and communities" (p. 417). Within such a framing, Tuck argues, damage and desire are not in binary opposition; it is not a question of either/or, but rather of complex, multifaceted assemblages of power, complicity, and resistance.

We took up Tuck's (2009) challenge to the deeply colonizing tendencies of many research and human rights practices that seek to document harm and that often pathologize colonized communities in the process. We avoided a hyper-reductionist focus on sexual harm by using the concept of protagonism to make visible Mayan women's multifaceted agency and subjectivity in narrating and contesting the wake of violence and its aftermath (as opposed to seeking to represent the content of the violence itself): we examined their spoken and embodied performances, as well as their preservation of certain silences, and their complex and conflictive struggles to create new social relations within the families, communities, and society in which they live. As such, our research did not aim to "give voice" to women, but rather to create spaces in which to listen to Mayan women's voices in context; that is, in the communities in which they lived and acted, as well as in the community of women they developed. Thus, we strove to hear their complex, intersectional stories of resistance, contestation, and cooptation within everyday life (Butalia, 2000; Das, 2007; Ross, 2003; Theidon, 2012). Rather than directing the narratives in a linear process, we engaged feminist PAR as a methodology, using creative techniques and in-depth interviews to elicit the complexities of protagonists' own stories and emotional responses to the issues under discussion, as well as those of the intermediaries who accompanied them. In the following section we detail some of feminist PAR techniques and identify some of its antecedents, as well as those of other methodologies with similar goals.

FEMINIST PAR

The roots of PAR have been traced to the work of Fals-Borda and Rahman (1991) in the Global South and to that of Lewin (1946, 1951), among others, working within the U.S. context (see also Reason & Bradbury, 2008). Within Guatemala, applied or activist anthropologists, including Noval (1960; see also Adams, 2000; Dary, 2014), Mack (AVANCSO, 1990, 1992), and Falla (1994, 2011), worked alongside the Maya in their rural communities or in refuge, often at the height of the genocidal violence, risking their lives to listen to and document the social suffering of these Mayan protagonists and to defend their rights to self-determination.

Despite disparate origins and varied articulations, many who engage in activist scholarship draw on a shared set of values, including democratic or participatory knowledge production, ethical fairness in the benefits of knowledge generation and use, and researcher reflexivity, as they facilitate participatory and transformative change processes with those most directly affected by social disparities and oppressions in sites of humanitarian disaster, armed conflict, and postwar transitions (Lykes & Hershberg, 2012). Humanitarian workers, psychosocial service providers, researchers, and human rights activists are among those who have looked to PAR and other community-based research and action processes in search of methodological resources (Lykes, 2013) that can help position themselves in "pragmatic solidarity" (Farmer, 2003) alongside survivors of war, unnatural disasters, and gross violations of human rights who are engaged in "the everyday work of repair" (Das, 2007, p. 62) in the aftermath of violence. And here we are mindful of Tuck and Yang's (2012) assertion that solidarity is always necessarily an "uneasy, reserved, and unsettled matter that neither reconciles present grievances nor forecloses future conflict" (p. 5).

As feminists engaging with PAR, we have positioned ourselves with "just enough trust" (Maguire, 1987) alongside those who have suffered gendered violations of their rights. Feminist PARers have critiqued psychologists' tendencies to speak over participants' voices (Fine, 1992); to focus exclusively or primarily on their experiences of damage rather than on their resistance and resilience; or to reduce complex and intersectional circulations of power that rupture community to intraindividual symptoms while ignoring systems and "circuits of dispossession" (Lykes & Mersky, 2006; Weis & Fine, 2012). Feminist PARers strive to facilitate knowledge construction that recognizes the particularities and historical situatedness of those with whom we partner and that emphasizes researcher reflexivity. The latter approach contributes to our ability as feminists who are white, highly educated, and beneficiaries of economic resources to critically interrogate our privileges as we accompany those with whom we collaborate as coresearchers. Through creating safe-enough spaces, feminist PARers listen deeply to the experiences of participants, their families, and communities at the intersections of gendered, racialized, classed and heterosexist violations and facilitate processes through which we can together document those experiences, analyze their root causes, and generate collaborative actions to redress harm and create change (Lykes & Crosby, 2014b).

We also draw on the work of postcolonial feminist theorists such as Grewal and Kaplan (2000) to infuse our feminist PAR with a transnational (as opposed to global or international) lens as a way to "destabilize rather than maintain boundaries of nation, race and gender" (para. 3). Grewal and Kaplan conceptualize transnational feminist practices as "forms of alliance, subversion and complicity within which asymmetries and inequalities [of power] can be critiqued" (para. 4); analyzing those practices requires attention to how knowledge is produced and by whom, as well as to the dissemination of discourses and power across national borders. Categorizations of "race," gender, sexuality, and class, enmeshed in colonial and imperial histories and neoliberal structures of globalization, are "concepts that travel," because they "circulate and work in different and linked ways in different places and times" (para. 5).

More recently, social science researchers and Latin Americanists engaged in activist scholarship, among whom are a growing number of latinx and activist scholars from the Global South, including Guatemala, have described an "encounter of knowledge(s)." They seek to emphasize the horizontal engagements between community-based organizers and organizations and "outsider" or research-centered and university-based researchers (AVANCSO, 2016, 2017) and focus on partnerships between activists and researchers that strive to generate activist scholarship for social change (Hale, 2008; Sieder, 2017). Latin Americanists have established a section of the Latin American Studies Association (LASA), *Otros Saberes* [Other Knowledges] that "promotes collaborative, transformative research and exchange between academics and civil society knowledge producers to further social justice" (LASA, 2018). Each of these initiatives challenges researchers from and/or educated in the Global North who have racial, gender, class, and/or heteronormative privileges, among others, to humbly position themselves to listen to the knowledge(s) produced by those whom they all too often marginalize or speak for or over.

The feminist PAR processes we designed and facilitated with our research partner, the *Unión Nacional de Mujeres Guatemaltecas* [National Union of Guatemalan Women] (UNAMG), included participatory workshops, creative activities (e.g., drawing, body movement, storytelling, dramatization, and image theater), and Mayan beliefs and practices (Asociación Médicos Descalzos Chinique, 2012; Grupo de Mujeres Mayas Kaqla, 2010). Through iterative feminist action-reflection processes we documented how these Mayan women protagonists performed and made meaning of their engagements in reparation(s), truth-telling, and justice-seeking actions in dialogical relationships with one another, as well as with those who accompanied them. Mayan women's ways of knowing are voiced and performed in and through these relational processes, recovering previously repressed beliefs and practices that contribute to personal and social transformation.

Our research was the next iteration of UNAMG's earlier work facilitated with this same group of Mayan women survivors between 2003 and 2008 as part of the *Consorcio Actoras de Cambio* [Actors for Change Consortium]—herewith referred to as "the Consortium." The Consortium addressed gendered absences within the formal truth-telling processes in Guatemala (CEH, 1999; ODHAG, 1998), generating both spaces in which Mayan women could tell their truths, particularly in relation to the perpetration of sexual violence, and audiences who would listen. It brought together individual feminists and Mayan women, as well as two NGOs—UNAMG and the *Equipo de Estudios Comunitarios y Acción Psicosocial* [Community Studies and Psychosocial Action Team] (ECAP)—to accompany women survivors in these processes. The Consortium described its goals as "generat[ing] healing processes, empowerment, reconstruction of historical memory and the struggle for justice" to enable women survivors "to construct themselves as subjects of their own lives" (Fulchiron et al., 2009, p. 5). It provided individual and group psychosocial accompaniment, as well as workshops in women's rights and the arts. The women participated in regional mutual support groups and occasionally came together as a broader group. In the support groups facilitated by the Consortium, Mayan women were asked to share their own knowledge and capacities in relation to their wartime experiences, focusing on how they had resisted, struggled, and survived. Women who were midwives, healers, or spiritual guides shared their knowledge with others in the groups. Many workshops would begin with a Mayan ceremony led by the spiritual guides. The incorporation of Mayan ceremonies and of knowledge from the Mayan cosmovision became increasingly central to the group processes, emphasizing the group members' shared and recovered history. The sharing of these abilities and of knowledge "created conditions that enabled women to see themselves from a perspective other than that of victim" (p. 386). Such representations stand in sharp contrast to the repression of the self described by Chirix García (2003) in her discussion of societies characterized by racism and oppression where "it is much easier to be the other than to be oneself. To be the other is to be accepted and valued, at the price of negating one's own identity" (p. 135). The Consortium structured workshop performances and representations in a way that invited the 54 Mayan protagonists to engage with these experiences of self over time and to highlight any changes that they might have noted in themselves as individuals and as a community of women. The Consortium also conducted a four-year research project documenting Mayan women's experiences of the war, which resulted in the book *Tejidos que lleva el alma: Memoria de las mujeres Mayas sobrevivientes de violación sexual durante el conflicto armado* [Weavings of the Soul: Memories of Mayan women Survivors of Sexual Violence during the Armed Conflict] (Fulchiron et al., 2009).

When the Consortium came to an end in 2008, its various constituents continued their work with this group of 54 Mayan women, following a range of different perspectives and approaches (see Fulchiron, 2017, for a description of the work of the *Colectivo Actoras de Cambio* [Actors for Change Collective], which was created as a separate organization after 2008). In 2008 we negotiated a partnership with UNAMG and in 2009 initiated a feminist PAR process with the 54 women. A member of UNAMG's research staff worked alongside us (Crosby, Lykes & Caxaj, 2016); additional UNAMG staff and professionals working with two other Guatemalan NGOs—ECAP and the feminist lawyers' collective *Mujeres Transformando el Mundo* [Women Transforming the World] (MTM)— participated in many of the processes. We accompanied Mayan protagonists in creative exercises and reflective processes through which they narrated and performed loss, suffering, and resistance, positioning themselves within the complex "circuits of dispossession" (Fine & Ruglis, 2009) generated by the armed conflict and persisting into the present, as well as demonstrating new possibilities for themselves as Mayan women. We use the term "accompaniment" to signify sustaining long-term relationships of common cause and mutual accountability with protagonists, through a shared commitment to effecting social change, albeit from differing social locations and positionings (Crosby, 2009; see also Watkins, 2015).

Protagonists' performances, as well as their own and our analyses of their creative outputs, were informed by "critical bifocality" (Weis & Fine, 2012): the naming and documenting of complex social structures and systems that produce and impinge on their lives, as well as the identification of multiple ways in which they make sense of (and resist) these systems of oppression. The repeated iterations of suffering and resistance in protagonists' stories, actions, and embodied representations can best be understood through this critical analysis of the complex interface of racism, gender violence, entrenched impoverishment, and the ongoing extraction of natural resources and occupation of indigenous lands: structural forces that protagonists themselves identified and resisted in their narratives and performances (see also AVANCSO, 2016, for a discussion of extractive practices in Alta Verapaz and their impact on the lives of Q'eqchi' women there).

Our feminist PAR project emerged in part as an effort to understand how Mayan women protagonists engaged with the multiple truth- and justice-seeking transitional justice processes underway in Guatemala in the post–Peace Accord era; in particular, we wanted to understand how they conceived of reparation(s) under the shadow of the state-sponsored PNR that began in 2003 and at the time of writing in 2017 was still being implemented, although in a modified, truncated, and frequently stalled form. Drawing on Hamber's work (2009), we used the concept of reparation(s) to refer both to victims' psychological experience of "adequate amend" (p. 97) having been made for the harm suffered ("reparation") and the various sets of measures through which this amend is sought ("reparations"). We created spaces through which we could listen to and document their understandings of the transitional justice actions in which they as Mayan women protagonists from diverse ethnolinguistic and geographic regions and the NGOs accompanying them were engaging; we were particularly interested in what reparation(s) for an irreparable harm (Hamber, 2009) meant from their standpoint and in relation to the PNR process. As we discuss in detail in chapter 4, our research uncovered their palpable feeling of bitterness toward the PNR; "*nos engañaron* [they deceived us]" was a constant refrain, further articulated by participants in statements such as the following: "It's just to distract; treating you like a child so you don't complain"; "It's to shut you up, cover your mouth"; "It's not right, not valid"; "this government lies"; "while the government lives happily, we live in poverty"; "As indigenous women they continue to use us through deception." The fraught relationship between survivors and the PNR was confirmed in an interview we conducted with senior PNR staff in 2013, in which they implied that community members manipulated women to invent stories of sexual harm in order to receive reparations.

In our collaboration with UNAMG, the organization identified several goals that included both strengthening its institutional research capacities and supporting interdisciplinary collaboration through the *Alianza Rompiendo el Silencio y la Impunidad* [Breaking the Silence and Impunity Alliance]— the "Alliance." The

Alliance was a three-party collaboration of UNAMG, ECAP, and MTM that coordinated the accompaniment of the 54 Mayan women protagonists as they engaged in these actions for redress: the Tribunal of Conscience, preparation and prosecution of the Sepur Zarco case, and a petition for integral reparation(s) for presentation to the IACHR (which argued for a more holistic understanding of reparation(s) in both its symbolic and material dimensions, including redress for loss of land and livelihoods).[11] We also facilitated multiple workshops with staff from each of these organizations using similar creative resources to those deployed with Mayan protagonists, and we conducted in-depth interviews with selected members of the Alliance, as well as with some women involved in the Consortium. Several of these workshops functioned as didactic "training of the trainers" sites (Hope & Timmel, 2014) through which Alliance staff critically reflected on their praxis—and creatively represented their understandings of the transitional justice mechanisms that they were deploying with Mayan protagonists. For example, in 2010 we facilitated a PAR training workshop for the UNAMG research team, which included some of the Mayan women interpreters who were working with the 54 women protagonists: it provided an important opportunity for team building and skill development. In 2010 and 2011, we worked with UNAMG to design creative workshops with Mayan interpreters and to plan gatherings in which members of the Alliance staff, including the interpreters, integrated local and professional knowledge systems through PAR processes to generate cross-organizational exchanges about participants' meaning-making relating to integral reparation(s). These gatherings with Alliance staff also afforded us opportunities to practice peer data collection and interpretation with our research collaborators and to explore the ways in which these processes might both contribute to reparation(s) and justice-seeking actions among the 54 Mayan protagonists and inform actions taken by the participating NGOs. At several points during the eight years, drawings and collages produced by the Alliance staff were presented to the Mayan women protagonists, who then had the opportunity to interpret the meanings made of reparation(s) and represented through the creative productions of their accompaniers, and vice versa.

In June 2013, we held a *Conversatorio* [Dialogue] during which we shared the Spanish versions of two papers we had written on the first three years of collaboration to that date (Crosby & Lykes, 2011; Lykes & Crosby, 2015a) and UNAMG staff shared a draft paper on reparation(s) (Caxaj, Chutan, & Herrera, 2013). We were seeking more formal feedback from the Alliance, as well as from other feminists and indigenous and other activists and practitioners we had previously interviewed as key informants. This—and other meetings and individual interviews we had with leaders within the Alliance—constituted "member checks," opportunities to assess our ongoing iterative interpretations that we were collaboratively developing and documenting in multiple workshops and that we or UNAMG staff had systematized in individual and collaborative publications. Thus, the circulation of more formal writing went beyond ourselves as the outsider researchers and authors, facilitating not only a greater diversity of ideas in the co-construction of knowledge but also ensuring that we remained accountable to Mayan and ladina protagonists and intermediaries. The Dialogue, which was audio recorded, constituted one of many records of local Guatemalan intermediaries' contributions to these iterative data analytic processes informed by a triangulation of data from multiple sources. These multilayered interpretive exercises formed part of our meaning-making about Mayan women's struggles seeking truth, justice and, more particularly, integral reparation(s), its promise, and the challenge of delivery.

Situating Ourselves as Northern White Feminist Coresearchers

Both of us have engaged with local actors in responding to genocidal violence in Guatemala in feminist and critical PAR for nearly three decades (Blacklock & Crosby, 2004; Cabrera Pérez-Armiñan & Lykes, 2008; Crosby, 1999, 2000, 2009; Lykes, 1994, 2001, 2010; Lykes, Beristain, & Cabrera Pérez-Armiñan, 2007; Melville & Lykes, 1992; Women of PhotoVoice/ADMI & Lykes, 2000). As feminist PARers and as a sociologist (Crosby) and community-cultural psychologist (Lykes), currently employed by universities in two countries of the Global North (Canada and the United States, respectively), we have positioned ourselves alongside Mayan women—and with local organizations such as UNAMG with which we have partnered—to facilitate transformative actions and critical and iterative reflections on those actions toward co-constructing knowledge that will inform future action. This praxis engages fundamental epistemological and methodological challenges that are present in contexts overshadowed by ever-present histories of colonization and imperial intervention, including our hegemonic power as North American academics who seek to "know" the Guatemalan other.

Critical reflexivity—which is a means through which researchers can deconstruct and then reconstruct their actions and knowledge generation—has been a key aspect of our feminist PAR action-reflection processes (Hickson, 2016; Riessman, 2015). It facilitates our accessing and critically deconstructing the multiple and complex micro and macro sociopolitical and economic contexts in which we make meaning of the observable processes that we accompany—and in which we are implicated as white North American feminists; it then enables us to deploy our "particular selves" within dialogic and collective knowledge co-constructive processes. Yet, as Shaw (2010) cautions, it is critical that as researchers we not reinsert ourselves at the center, displacing the narratives of those whom we accompany (see also Crosby, Lykes, & Doiron, 2018). And without the relinquishment of "land, power or privilege," critical reflexivity can also be seen as a "move to innocence" that reinscribes settler colonial power (Tuck & Yang, 2012, p. 10).

As women who are white, we bring similar yet distinctive experiences of "the ascendancy of whiteness" (Chow, quoted in Arvin et al., 2013, p. 10).[12] As such, we are both informed by and resist our location of white and class privilege within settler colonial contexts in Canada and the United States, as well as the power and benefits that come with "whitestream feminism" (Arvin et al., 2013; Grande, 2004). Central to whitestream feminism is the colonial imperative to rescue the racialized gendered other, both within white settler societies and in relation to countries of the Global South: this is the "saving brown women from brown men" (Spivak, 1998) rescue narrative that has informed Western feminist and human rights discourses. We have sought to develop "traitorous identities"; that is, to undermine what Harding (1991) has termed the epistemic foundations of whiteness, to learn how not to know and to tolerate self-doubt. Sholock (2012) argues that "a methodology of the privileged should not resolve the self-doubt of white antiracists but rather strategically deploy epistemic uncertainty as a treasonous act against the cognitive privileges that support white Western hegemonies" (p. 709).

Given this positionality, we have examined our situated subjectivities and engaged collaboratively with intermediaries alongside protagonists in accompanying their actions and in inviting them into parallel processes of reflexivity about their praxis. Through critically reflecting on the knowledge(s) generated through these action-reflection processes, we have co-constructed "third voices" (Lykes, TerreBlanche, & Hamber, 2003) reflected in this volume and grounded in "onto-epistemologies" (Barad, 2007). The former concept posits that what is produced through accompaniment processes within circulations of power that privilege some voices and marginalize others is neither exclusively the voice of the privileged committed to decolonizing their privilege nor of the marginalized who dare to break the silence, but is rather a dialogic co-construction. The latter construct captures the dynamic relationship between being and knowing that characterizes Barad's concept of agential realism. This stance, a critical component of antiracist feminist and critical PAR, not only facilitates working with and alongside women who have survived sexual violence in wartime but also critically problematizes an essentialized "woman-centered" focus in much conflict-focused research and activism, a focus that fails to emphasize the particularities of racialized gendered violence and to develop an anticolonial social science (Cannella & Manuelito, 2008). In addition, through this methodology we were deeply challenged to, in the words of Hernández Castillo (2016), "critically analyze our own conceptualizations . . . and to do away with the idea of the existence of a 'false consciousness' (which sometimes underlies the conception of popular education as a 'conscienticizing' tool), and to learn to listen and understand the experiences of the women participating in the workshop[s]" (p. 47).

Feminist PAR is a methodological resource through which multiple actors can engage as collaborative coresearchers. As outsiders, we positioned ourselves in pragmatic solidarity alongside protagonists and local activists and healers, engaging in processes designed to enhance critical awareness and shared leadership capacities through collaborations and to co-construct new ways of knowing that inform and are informed by collective actions aimed at improving conditions in local coresearchers' lives in order to bring about a more just and equitable society (Reason & Bradbury, 2008). As noted earlier, the 54 Mayan protagonists and the Alliance were engaged in a series of transitional justice actions prior to our collaboration. Thus we entered a process in which Guatemalan intermediaries and Mayan protagonists were already taking action; we sought to accompany them in creative workshops that served as reflexive spaces for documenting their work and for co-constructing ways of knowing that reflected their local understandings and meaning-making processes. This repositioning of multiple collaborators has been dialogic, a mobile co-construction in which a diverse group of intermediaries recognize that education, status, citizenship, and whiteness facilitate and constrain their collaborations and thus their accompaniment in border spaces. The antiracist feminist PAR accompaniment processes (Lykes & Hershberg, 2012) we have deployed therefore center racialized gender as an analytic tool and locate and frame the identified social issue or problem intersectionally making visible the interlocking power of gender, "race," sexuality, and social class that deeply informs and constrains the knowledge developed herein (Bannerji, 1995; Combahee River Collective, 1983; Crenshaw, 1991; Hill Collins & Bilge, 2016).

MULTIPLE STRATEGIES FOR COLLABORATING WITH MAYAN PROTAGONISTS

During the eight-year feminist PAR process, the 54 Mayan women protagonists participated in regional and national workshops and in a series of truth-telling, reparation(s), and justice-seeking processes organized by the Alliance. One such action was the aforementioned Tribunal of Conscience held in Guatemala City in March 2010, at which a small group of Mayan women narrated their experiences of violence during the armed conflict and their demands for justice publicly for the first time. They spoke before an audience of more than 800, including members of the Guatemalan judiciary, state institutions, civil society organizations, and the international community (Mendia Azkue & Guzmán Orellana, 2012). Additionally, MTM interviewed most of the group of 54 women to prepare their formal demand for integral reparation(s) before the IACHR in Washington, DC, arguing that the Guatemalan government had not delivered on its promises for reparation(s). Finally, in 2013, a subgroup of 15 Q'eqchi' women initiated criminal proceedings against two of the men they identified as responsible for their rapes and enforced "service" at the Sepur Zarco military camp after many of their husbands were killed or disappeared over a land dispute.

In each of these actions—and in earlier and subsequent reflections on their actions—Mayan women protagonists were accompanied by the Alliance and other organizations. We documented many of these processes. Data for this project included field notes, minutes, artwork and other creative productions from 10 workshops we conducted between 2010 and 2017. Workshop participants included some members of the Alliance, the Mayan women interpreters who played such a key intermediary role, and many of the 54 Mayan protagonists. The protagonists' participation in these workshops varied, depending on individual schedules and weather that sometimes prohibited their travel to the capital where most were held. Data also included transcripts of the earlier mentioned 48 individual interviews with women protagonists conducted by MTM and of individual and/or small group interviews with leaders of Alliance organizations and of other key informants, some of whom were interviewed at several points during the eight years. Key informants included feminist activists; Mayan activists from the indigenous women's organization *Grupo de Mujeres Mayas Kaqla* [Kaqla Women's Group—herewith, Kaqla, a Q'eqchi' word for rainbow]; PNR staff, including its director; and directors and/or leaders within a number of other human rights NGOs within Guatemala working in the area of transitional justice. Our research team also took ethnographic field notes during the Tribunal (discussed in chapter 2) and the Sepur Zarco trial (the focus of chapter 3).[13]

Data Generation and Analysis: Iterative Processes within and across Performances

The workshops we facilitated preceded—and followed—some of these more formal justice- and reparation(s)-seeking and truth-telling actions. As such, we were able to document Mayan women's less linear narratives and performances of suffering, survival, and protagonism (Bueno-Hansen, 2015). The workshops also created a space in which protagonists could voice their resistance to the "official" justice-seeking mechanisms that frequently constrained, rather than facilitated, their sharing their own experiences; and they articulated demands drawn from their everyday experiences since the genocidal violence. And, as reported by many of the women in a workshop in 2011, the workshops contributed to strengthening the community of women formed during earlier work with the Consortium, increasing trust in each other and achieving new forms of communication despite being from diverse ethnolinguistic groups and geographic areas of the country (as discussed in chapter 1).

Creative resources—including dramatic play, such as image theater (Boal, 1985) and dramatic multiplications (Pavlovsky, Martinez Bouquet, & Moscio, 1985); creative storytelling (Rodari, 1996); and individual and collective drawings and other constructions outside the self with images (e.g., collage, murals) (Lykes, 1994, 2001)—were resources through which nonlinguistically similar participants could, with the help of interpreters, share increasingly complex sets of representations and meanings made up of loss, suffering, survival, resilience, and resistance, as well as demands for a better future for themselves and their families and communities. Protagonists infused the creative workshops with practices and beliefs from their cosmovision: "the entirety of knowledges and practices that strengthen our communion with ourselves, each other and our surroundings" (Grupo de

Mujeres Mayas Kaqla, 2010, p. 23). These included scientific discoveries in the realms of astronomy, mathematics, and the calendar, as well as values and ceremonies or rituals that strengthen the community and its relations with the universe. They performed rituals such as lighting colored tapers and situating flowers in the center of the workshop space, which reminded all present of the four cardinal points, the sacredness of all life, and the significance of color, the earth, and spiritual and physical interconnections (Chirix García, 2003). The performance of these rituals at the beginning of many of the workshops we facilitated—at the suggestion of the protagonists and/or Mayan facilitators—confirmed that many of the Mayan protagonists valued and had internalized connections between these participatory embodied workshops and the Mayan cosmovision; it reflected processes of "Mayanization" (Bastos, Cumes, & Lemus, 2007; Grupo de Mujeres Mayas Kaqla, 2006, 2010), which had been an explicit focus of the work they did with the Consortium. And the workshops we conducted with Alliance staff facilitated their critical reflections on the methodological contributions of many of the creative resources they were using and provided opportunities for them to represent their onto-epistemological assumptions about transitional justice through performances that were more accessible to the 54 Mayan protagonists they were accompanying.

Triangulating Findings toward Knowledge Generation

The data analyzed and triangulated in this feminist PAR process included observations from the Tribunal of Conscience and the Sepur Zarco trial, as well as notes, minutes, art work, and photographs from all of the workshops and transcriptions of in-depth interviews conducted with Alliance staff and other key informants over the course of the eight-year process. We drew on our ethnographic field notes and structured follow-up interviews after the Tribunal and trial to contextualize our analyses of protagonists' performances and the accompaniment processes of the intermediaries. The multiple meanings the actors made of these actions and the potential and limitations of these transitional justice mechanisms for meeting protagonists' demands were explored through the creative workshops.

We drew on a grounded theory analysis of 12 in-depth interviews that we conducted with 6 Mayan and 6 ladina intermediaries to analyze further the ways in which the intermediaries positioned themselves through multiple performances alongside the Mayan protagonists. Through constructivist grounded theory (Charmaz, 2014) we sought to understand how the intermediaries situated themselves in their multiple diversities and to interrogate the discursive use of the term "intermediary." We explored how human rights discourse and transitional justice praxis may obscure rather than clarify local Mayan knowledge systems and constrain rather than facilitate what might be a more integral and/or Mayan bottom-up praxis of redress. Through iterative participatory data analysis processes and the triangulation of data from these reflection-action processes, we sought to critically interrogate transnational transitional justice processes and to generate alternative knowledge(s) and praxis co-constructed by the multiple diversely positioned protagonists and intermediaries who collaborated in these processes—while recognizing the ongoing challenges and limitations of the partial knowledge(s) and ongoing doubts generated therein.

ORGANIZATION OF THE BOOK

Chapter 1, "Documenting Protagonism: 'I Can Fly with Large Wings,'" situates the 54 Mayan protagonists within their local rural communities, drawing in part on their testimonies and in-depth interviews during their work with the Consortium, as well as on later interviews conducted by MTM. It focuses on the contributions of the creative and participatory workshops in facilitating protagonists' self-reflections over time of (1) their experiences of the continuities of violence embodied in an ever-present past; (2) their representations of violence as a heavy load from the past, in the present, and anticipated in their futures; and (3) their movements within and between home communities and a multilingual, pluriethnic community of women. We draw on their performances and interpretations of these diverse self-understandings and self-positionings to further analyze their individual and communal transformative changes as shown through the creative workshops.

Chapter 2, "Recounting Protagonism: 'No One Can Take This Thorn from My Soul,'" examines the conditions under which indigenous women whose identities are deeply situated within local Mayan communities narrate and perform truth outside of those contexts, as well as how the multiple spectators, in the presence of whom they recount their truth, relate to "the pain of others" (Razack, 2007; Sontag, 2003). Central to the chapter is an analysis of the Tribunal of Conscience, in which we participated as honorary witnesses. We argue that truth-telling is both a necessarily complex, gendered, racialized social construction and an inherently relational process. The chapter reflects on the constitutive meaning of harm, taking into consideration the implications of how truth-telling processes tend to be framed within the liberal language of rights and to emphasize the experience of individuated harm, particularly bodily harm. These processes also tend to focus on this harm as a particular racialized gendered "event," rather than as part of the broader structural relations of power that shape and inform the construction of the subject within her social context. The chapter considers how, in the Guatemalan context, the historically specific and multifaceted experiences of Mayan women are sometimes occluded within such gendered racialized essentialisms, potentially eliding their protagonism.

Chapter 3, "Judicializing Protagonism: 'What Will the Law Say?'" situates the Sepur Zarco trial within the current "turn to the law" (Engle, 2015) in Guatemala to combat impunity for crimes of the past; it also locates the trial historically in terms of Mayan women's access to the formal legal system and of heterogeneous practices of indigenous or customary law rooted in the Mayan cosmovision. Our analysis of the Sepur Zarco trial, which took place in February 2016, focuses on three aspects that illuminate the liminality of the courtroom space and of justice itself: (1) the reliance of the legal domain on spectacles of suffering, (2) the meaning and content of justice as always in translation between protagonists and their interlocutors, and (3) Mayan men's testimonies of their experiences of gendered racialized harm. We also examine reflections from the plaintiffs after they returned home in the wake of this historic decision. We argue in the chapter that retributive or carceral justice is an integral but not sufficient aspect of the struggle for redress. In situations of massive human rights violations such as occurred in Guatemala's genocidal war, prosecuting individual perpetrators for structural and systemic state-sponsored crimes falls far short of responding to the desire for redress, including what protagonists term transformative or integral reparation(s).

Chapter 4, "Repairing Protagonism: 'Carrying a Heavy Load,'" examines the implementation of the state-sponsored PNR from the standpoint of the Mayan protagonists. The PNR was established by the Guatemalan government in 2003 with a 13-year mandate and has been a source of continued controversy, with constant turnovers in staff and a generally perceived failure to fulfill its overall mandate to provide integral reparation(s), instead mainly handing out checks to some victims. We triangulate data on and from the PNR itself with 48 individual interviews and a number of participatory workshops with Mayan women on what reparation(s) means to them, as well as with interviews with reparations stakeholders. Analysis of these data confirms that protagonists have woven their understanding of reparation(s) from three main threads: (1) their experiences of loss and harm, (2) their recognition of the Guatemalan state's duplicity, and (3) their protagonism in justice-seeking processes. The chapter concludes by arguing that "the everyday work of repair" (Das, 2007) that protagonists desire requires attention to the deep-seated impoverishment that they highlight as the heavy load of racialized gendered violence they carry with them.

Chapter 5, "Accompanying Protagonism: 'Facing Two Directions,'" examines how, through their engagement in struggles for truth, justice, and reparation(s), Mayan women are differentially positioning themselves not only within but also at the border of their geographic communities and a community of women. The chapter analyzes how the boundaries of community, as well as the concept of protagonism itself, were, at least in part, shaped by those intermediaries or accompaniers who walked alongside Mayan protagonists: local NGOs staff comprised of ladina and Mayan professionals and nonprofessionals, indigenous interpreters, indigenous leaders within local communities, and international feminist and participatory action researchers, ourselves included. This diverse set of intermediaries collaborated in but also complicated the processes described in this volume and the resulting social constructions of community. We draw on Lykes et al.'s

(2003) theorization of a third voice and Fine's (1992) earlier work on ventrilo-quism and "working the hyphen" to rethink some of what have become core concepts within community-based PAR. Data for this chapter include interviews and participatory workshops with intermediaries and Mayan protagonists. Particular emphasis is placed on the in-between role played by indigenous women interpreters, some of whom are survivors of violence themselves, in the vernacularization of human rights and feminist discourses. We explore both the transformative potential of this work and the limits of reflexivity encountered in the everyday praxis of transitional justice. The pragmatics of tribunals, trials, and reparation(s) processes all too frequently silence the challenge to decolonize Western theory and praxis through which those schooled in such knowledge reposition themselves alongside, in this case, racialized gendered knowledge(s) of the Maya.

The conclusion to this volume provides an opportunity to revisit the overall goals of this research and to interrogate the multiple performances of accompaniment, intermediarity, and pragmatic solidarity represented over eight years of research. We examine the possibilities and constraints of privileged ladinas' and transnational feminists' vernacularization of international norms as performed in struggles for justice, to ask whether we engage in deep listening and responsiveness to what protagonists desire as integral or transformative reparation(s). Are we willing to turn toward indigenous women's ways of knowing and being? In what ways did the Guatemalan NGOs' decisions to engage with and through existing transitional justice mechanisms as best practices in accompanying protagonists with whom they partnered over a decade ago facilitate or constrain actions for redress? How might this reflect Mayan protagonists' willingness to risk entering the intermediaries' worlds and the contrasting inability we face as predominantly ladina and white Spanish-speaking intermediaries to enter into their worlds? And how do we foreground the role of Mayan intermediaries who look both ways? In the conclusion, drawing on Anzaldúa's conception of *nos-otras* (Torre, 2009), we identify the contributions and contradictions experienced through these feminist PAR processes, as well as some of their implications for ourselves and other anti-racist feminist activists committed to decolonial praxis in working with communities in the wake of genocidal violence toward building more just and equitable futures for all.

1 · DOCUMENTING PROTAGONISM

"I Can Fly with Large Wings"

[I am] old, without suffering, without fear and without shame. Today I am capable of doing all that I can. I am like a bird. I can fly with large wings.

—Chuj protagonist, participant in a July 2011 workshop

We recognize that [culture] is not a static structure, [rather it] is a social process that can be transformative and creative, that permits us to deal with new challenges and thus respond to the specific needs of the constitutive social groups.... The challenge is to claim the right to affect in order to change the structure of oppressions. This challenge implies ... the need to put forward a new cosmovision and political culture.

—Emma Delfina Chirix García (2003, p. 206)

This chapter situates the 54 Mayan protagonists from Alta Verapaz/ Izabal, Chimaltenango, and Huehuetenango within their ethnolinguistic communities and then examines their performances as a community of women outside those spaces, as facilitated by intermediaries. When work with these protagonists began in 2003, the Consortium decided that it was neither feasible nor safe to help Mayan women break nearly three decades of silence about their experiences of sexual violence in the local communities where many of their alleged perpetrators continued to live and hold power. Yet it was in these spaces that they grew up and experienced the armed conflict; it was from their own geographically based communities that they emerged to develop a community of women; and it is within these local communities and their families of origin that they embody and perform the outcomes of their collective struggles for redress. An emphasis on speaking out in the ladino-dominated public sphere risks weakening local, place-based, indigenous relationality and collective struggles for redress, and decentering indigenous knowledge systems. In tracing protagonists' construction of a community of women, we examine their perceptions and performances of their struggles for redress through a series of creative workshops. These creative resources facilitated intermediaries' "psychosocial accompaniment" (Watkins, 2015) of the protagonists and provided opportunities to document protagonists' embodied performances of their understandings of transitional justice praxis.

Critical feminist PAR has contributed to our deepening recognition that iterative and co-constructive processes are complex and that knowledge about racialized gendered violence and social suffering and its wake is neither unidimensional nor linear. Researchers trained in post-positivist top-down processes have benefited from epistemological assumptions and research methods that prioritize random assignment and control, limiting what can be known to what can be constructed through hypothesis testing. In contrast, bottom-up processes, including feminist PAR, strive for equal rigor but have less rigid constraints, which contribute to the generation of messy, iterative, and complex representations of what may never be fully known. Those who developed this latter praxis suggest that we need to engage in dialogic processes of knowledge construction and that a better representation of what can be known across the chasms of differences traversed by the Mayan protagonists and those who accompany them might be that reflected in the conception of a third voice.

This is not to suggest that the knowledge constructed through these feminist PAR processes is not also facilitated and constrained by human rights discourse and, more particularly, as documented in this volume, by transitional justice processes. The lawyers, psychologists, feminist activists, interpreters, and researchers who accompanied the 54 survivors of racialized gendered violence—the protagonists of the stories reported herein—are human rights activists committed to redressing the long-standing injustices that gave rise to the Guatemalan armed conflict. Thus the processes and practices that have come to define transitional justice frame or, minimally, inform the knowledge(s) generated through the dialogic relationships between the 54 protagonists and the professional and paraprofessional accompaniers. As discussed by Merry and Levitt (2017), translation or vernacularization means that human rights and transitional justice processes take different forms in local contexts and are read and performed in relation to local power structures and cultural dynamics. Moreover, these intermediaries draw on a set of disciplinary theories and practices grounded in Western assumptions that privilege speech-acts constitutive of individual healing and justice. The Mayan cosmovision and customary law are concerned about the functioning of the social order and prioritize the interrelationships among the individual, the collective, and the natural environment (Chirix García, 2003; Otzoy, 2008), suggesting that neither healing nor justice is exclusively individually constituted or performed. This is further complicated by the particularity of each of the different ethnolinguistic groups to which the 54 women belong and the multiple ways in which the Maya are racialized, classed, and gendered, with women's socialization and lived experiences repressing and marginalizing them in ways that all too often reflect intragroup privileging of Mayan men (Chirix García, 2003; Hernández Castillo, 2016).

The multiple linguistic groups to which the 54 protagonists belong and the limited language capacities of the intermediaries—most of whom spoke Spanish, some of whom spoke English, and only the Mayan interpreters and one other among them spoke one or more Mayan languages—generated additional challenges for all. The Mayan interpreters were particularly burdened by the complex range of processes engaged in during these eight years. For these reasons—and in light of previous work within Mayan communities that had survived massacres and gross violations of human rights (Lykes, 1994)—as we sought to more deeply understand the contextualized and local meaning-making systems of the 54 protagonists, we turned to more embodied and creative practices, such as theater, drawing, and storytelling, to generate other forms of knowledge.

In this chapter, we first position the 54 Mayan protagonists within the particular ethnolinguistic community to which each belongs and vis-à-vis the narratives each has shared of experiences of violation and loss before, during, and after the armed conflict. Our decision to eschew the reproduction of damage-centered research does not negate the importance of situating protagonists within the deeply racialized and gendered ethnolinguistic local communities where they positioned themselves and where many experienced multiple forms of violence. Thus, although all of the work that we facilitated with the 54 Mayan protagonists took place in collective creative workshops that sought to tap into women's protagonisms, each has been personally marked by a particular set of experiences before, during, and in the postgenocide struggles for truth, justice, and reparation(s). These brief portraits of women from different ethnolinguistic and geographic communities illuminate some of their personal experiences of violence, and the ethnolinguistic group summaries shed light on their gendered, geographic, linguistic, and/or religious particularities. Second, we describe the creative and Mayan resources and strategies deployed through the participatory workshops, identifying antecedents within Guatemala and beyond, and describing in more detail the workshops' structure, including the iterative data analytic processes used through this feminist PAR. Third, we describe protagonists' engagement through creative workshops in 2011 and 2012, examining their meaning-making processes and their developing subjectivities and positionalities in situ in relation to their (1) sense and performance of selves before and after their engagement with creative methodologies, (2) representations of violence, and (3) representations of community. We explore the ways in which the protagonists' creative engagement with each other within the workshops illuminate local understandings and critically contest internationally driven performances of transitional justice processes in which they participated. We conclude the chapter with a brief discussion of some of the multiple challenges encountered in collaborations between Mayan protagonists and those who accompanied them, including ourselves, as we performed our positionalities as intermediaries between them and the wider transitional justice mechanisms through which the women sought redress, and as facilitators of these workshops.

SITUATING PROTAGONISTS REGIONALLY, HISTORICALLY, AND SOCIALLY

When we began our research, protagonists were clear that they were not interested in retelling their stories of harm suffered. Rather than reinterviewing them individually to develop these portraits, we drew on data previously collected by MTM, the feminist lawyers' collective, which conducted individual interviews with 48 of the 54 protagonists in 2009 in preparation for a reparations brief to the IACHR; they generously shared these interviews with us. Each interview included the woman's narratives about life before the war, as well as her experience of the armed conflict and its aftermath. They are presented here by region and ethnolinguistic group and analyzed further in chapters 3 and 4. During the interviews, protagonists often spoke in their maternal Mayan language, through a local interpreter, and sometimes in Spanish. The interviewers from MTM were monolingual Spanish speakers (the complexities of the issue of interpretation and the role of interpreters as intermediaries are discussed further in chapter 5). We also draw extensively on published research that documented this group of protagonists' experiences of the war (Fulchiron et al., 2009), the CEH report (1999), and some of the nine life story interviews developed as part of the Consortium research process and redacted and published by the Colectivo Actoras de Cambio (2011). In these life story interviews, nine protagonists—three Q'eqchi', three Kaqchikel, one Mam, one Chuj, and one Poptí/returnee—situated themselves within their families and/or communities of origin. Each of these nine women talked about rigid gendered roles, including significant restrictions on girls interacting with boys when they were growing up. Some described the marked preference for boys over girls, with many stating that they had little to no formal education in part due to gender but also to the family's poverty, noting that there were few to no schools in their villages. Some were physically beaten as children and many described their fathers'—and then their spouses'—drinking as an ongoing family problem. Work began for many when they were only 6 years old, and some traveled to *fincas* [estates] with their fathers when they were 10 years old. Several described being "sold" into marriage as young as age 10. Most received no sexual education from their mothers, and many noted that they had no idea what to expect or how to behave the first night in their husband's bed. Others noted their deep sadness when forced to leave their mother's home when they got married and the multiple challenges they faced in living with in-laws. Life for most of these 54 women reflected the realities of racialized gendered violence in Guatemala before, during, and after the armed conflict. In participatory research with Mayan and ladina women in highland communities who used a photovoice methodology, Duffy (2018) documented similar experiences of lifelong gendered oppression. Individual names are replaced by pseudonyms and placed inside quotation marks.

Alta Verapaz/Izabal

Twenty-one of the 54 protagonists are Q'eqchi' women from the Polochic Valley in northeastern Guatemala; all are rural peasant women, and all who were married lost their husbands during the war. Although a number of them remarried, they all self-identify as widows (Fulchiron et al., 2009). In the late 1990s, the United Nations Development Program (UNDP) noted that the department of Alta Verapaz had one of the highest levels of social exclusion (including reported rates of deaths of those under 40 years old, adult illiteracy, malnutrition in children under age 5, and access to basic services; CEH, 1999, vol. 1). Yet most of the women in the Q'eqchi' group related lives of relative comfort before the war: they lived in simple *manaca* [cornstalk and thatched roof] houses, described by one as large with a separate kitchen (one woman had two *lámina* [metal] houses, plus a manaca kitchen, beds, and armoires; another had both a lámina and manaca house). Several spoke of growing enough corn, beans, or rice to sell as part of the surplus harvest. They also grew chile, oranges and mandarins, pineapples, sweet potatoes, yucca, garden vegetables, sugar cane, cilantro, *güiscil* [chayote squash], cocoa, and squash. Most kept chickens, turkeys, pigs, and ducks, and a few had cows and a horse. A couple of women made a bit of extra money stocking a small storefront in their homes.

Fulchiron et al. (2009) describe the women from this region as the most cohesive of the three regional groups. They are from communities that are relatively close to each other geographically, and many share family ties; they generally make group decisions, which hold preeminence over those of individuals. Religion and tradition are important elements of daily life for the protagonists, who find religious or spiritual meaning in every aspect of life (Fulchiron et al., 2009). The Catholic Church played a central role in the colonization of the departments of Alta Verapaz and Baja Verapaz (known collectively as the Verapaces) as did Protestant Christianity (Adams, 2001); Judeo-Christian values and norms related to virginity and women's monogamy are also rigid moral codes (Fulchiron et al., 2009). The rupture in the daily offerings to the *culto al cerro* [cult to the mountain] deities *Tzuultaq'a* also deeply informed women's experiences of violence during the internal armed conflict, and many Q'eqchi' understood this rupture as one source of community problems (Adams, 2001; Colectivo Actoras de Cambio, 2011; Fulchiron et al., 2009). The Tzuultaq'a deities are integrally linked to the land, contributing to the territory itself playing a greater identity-defining role for the Q'eqchi' than ethnolinguistic characteristics (Fulchiron et al., 2009). Relatedly, Méndez and Carrera (2004) argue that these women's identities are very much shaped by the history of Q'eqchi' people's "continual dispossession . . . and permanent search for new land on which to sow and live" (p. 24), factors that had led the Q'eqchi' people to move farther into the lowlands of the Polochic Valley.

The Liberal government of General Justo Rufino Barrios (1873–1885) passed national laws that usurped indigenous lands, converting them into large private estates dedicated to commercial agriculture of export crops (coffee, bananas, cardamom) in the late 19th century. German farmers installed a system of labor exploitation of indigenous people under a *mozo colono* [colonial servitude] model (CEH, 1999, vol. 6; Fulchiron et al., 2009). Almost a century later, in the 1950s, the Guatemalan government encouraged peasant settlement in the Polochic Valley on land that had been abandoned when its German owners had been expelled during World War II (Fulchiron et al., 2009; Méndez & Carrera, 2014). Many Q'eqchi' families settled in the area to escape the harsh conditions they faced as mozos on coffee and cardamom estates in other parts of the department. However, as the Guatemalan government's Northern Transversal Strip project brought renewed economic interest in this mineral- and oil-rich region in the 1960s and 1970s, military men, large landowners, and transnational companies rapidly accumulated large plots of land through questionable processes—often using the courts to get land registered in their own names (AVANCSO, 2016; Fulchiron et al., 2009; Méndez & Carrera, 2014).

As Q'eqchi' peasant leaders started forming more and more Land Committees in the 1970s to initiate processes to obtain title to their lands, the large landowners called on the military, with whom they enjoyed a close relationship, to help them protect the "status quo of land accumulation" (Fulchiron et al., 2009, p. 61). Indeed, although several of the women described their husband's or father's murders or disappearances as due to their participation in guerrilla activity (Colectivo Actoras de Cambio, 2011), others suggested that insurgent or guerrilla organizations did not have a significant presence in this region in the 1970s (Fulchiron et al., 2009). Méndez and Carrera (2014) argue instead that "the army used the armed conflict to put an end to *campesino* [peasant] organization and mobilization for access to land . . . putting into practice the entire counterinsurgency arsenal, kidnapping, torturing, and assassinating campesinos, razing communities, forcibly displacing the population and sexually abusing the women" (p. 60). Whether or not their husbands participated in the guerrilla organizations, all the women in the group were very clear about the link between their husbands' struggles to obtain titles to their land and the violence that they experienced. Indeed, as one woman explained, "Her husband was [on the] Land Committee; in the past you asked for land, requested land, at that time it was the *Instituto Nacional de Transformación Agraria* [National Institute of Agrarian Transformation] (INTA), and they saw her husband and heard that he was [on the] committee, and that's why they went to take him from the house." And another woman states, "There was a massacre for the land, because they started looking for the leaders who were going to request land" (Méndez & Carrera, 2014, p. 57).

The Panzós massacre in May 1978, in which 53 Q'eqchi' peasants were killed and another 47 were wounded, is the exemplar of the lengths to which the Guatemalan Army was willing to go to protect the economic interest of landowners in the region. According to the CEH, the Panzós massacre marked both the beginning of large-scale, indiscriminate violence throughout the country and of "selective repression against community leaders who were reclaiming land as well as against Mayan priests" in the Polochic Valley (CEH, 1999, vol. 6, p. 19; see also Grandin, 2004; Sanford, 2009).

Many of the women interviewed by MTM spoke of the army patrolling in their community regularly before taking their husbands, who were kidnapped and disappeared because of the land disputes. Most of the women were raped in their homes when the soldiers came to get their husbands or soon thereafter. Almost all of these women had their homes, possessions, and crops destroyed or stolen during the armed conflict (Méndez & Carrera, 2014). Several of them described their participation in the *Coordinadora Nacional de Viudas de Guatemala* [National Coordinating Committee of Widows of Guatemala] (CONAVIGUA) and other organizations as sources of sustenance and sites through which they were able to participate in exhumations and/or secure some resources for rebuilding homes during the postgenocide years. Despite their involvement for many years in this widows' rights organization, most noted that they had not yet shared the stories of rape and sexual violation with anyone until they started working with the Consortium in 2005 or 2006.

In addition to the presence of permanent army patrols, Méndez and Carrera (2014) cite the recruitment of men from the community to serve as military commissioners and the establishment of PACs [civilian defense patrols] as elements of the counterinsurgent operations put in place in the region. To control the rural indigenous peasant population, the army also established a series of military outposts in the area, many located on private plantations: Sepur Zarco, Tinajas, Sa'quiha', Panacté, and Pataxte (Méndez & Carrera, 2014). It is clear from the MTM interviews and from additional sources that the fact that their husbands had been taken and that they were "alone" not only left the women unprotected but was also used by the military commissioners as the justification for them "serving" at the military outpost: their husbands were not participating in the PACs so they were expected to work in their place (Méndez & Carrera, 2014). The military outpost at Sepur Zarco was built in mid-1982 as a recreational center where troops were sent to relax and have their clothes washed (Hernández, 2012; Méndez & Carrera, 2014). Méndez and Carrera (2014), however, argue that the use of this outpost for the purpose of raping women was deliberate and planned by the army: there was a "constant and massive rotation of soldiers" at the outpost (p. 59), and they quote one woman survivor as describing soldiers arriving by the thousands.

Twelve of the women interviewed by MTM spoke of having been ordered to "serve" at the Sepur Zarco outpost. The other women in the group suffered experiences of being raped after their husbands were kidnapped and disappeared, but then fled to the mountains to escape the fate of being brought to Sepur Zarco: one woman spent six years in the mountains with her children, three of whom died; another also spent six years in the mountains where she also lost three children; and a third spent two years in the mountains, and after she descended, settled in Sepur Zarco where she was made to bring tortillas to the outpost, but was never brought inside. The abuses against women at the Sepur Zarco military outpost are the focus of the legal case discussed in detail in chapter 3.

Chimaltenango

Fourteen protagonists in this study are Kaqchikel women from the department of Chimaltenango, located in Guatemala's central plateau between the Western Highlands and Guatemala City. The distances between the villages in this department are larger than in other regions, thus influencing the group dynamic, which is "much more marked by individualism" (Fulchiron et al., 2009, p. 41). That individualist character may also be reflected in the significant number of women in the group who owned their own land and worked outside the home for cash income.

Until the 1980s, the Catholic Church had a strong presence in the region and, since the 1960s, had participated in community organization processes with the Mayan people, including through Catholic Action; this socially conservative movement within the church was formed to resist the spread of communism, but evolved to support social and economic change, as reflected in the liberation theology of the 1970s and later (Falla, 2001). As in many other regions of the country, evangelical churches gained entry into Chimaltenango communities in the aftermath of the internal armed conflict during which many Mayan Catholic catechists were persecuted (ODHAG, 1998). Today, 75% of these 14 previously Catholic Kaqchikel women are evangelical (Fulchiron et al., 2009). While many of these women remember a history of Mayan spiritual practices that some continue to seek out (e. g., *comadronas* [midwives] and those who use traditional medicinal plants), these traditions are no longer part of their daily lives (Fulchiron et al., 2009). Additionally, some scholars have found that evangelical churches engage in a "counter-insurgent discourse of forgetting. Thus many evangelical women speak of not wanting to remember the past and of not promoting justice, [which is] an ambivalent discourse since they are the same women who have promoted exhumations in their communities" (p. 45).

The department's proximity to Guatemala City and the relatively easy access to markets shaped the socioeconomic context of these Kaqchikel women's experiences of the internal armed conflict and its aftermath. While UNDP figures from 1996 placed the overall level of social exclusion in the department of Chimaltenango at an intermediate level (CEH, 1999), the conditions in some municipalities in the department, such as San José Poaquil where some of these women live, were of extreme poverty at the time (Fulchiron et al., 2009). The Kaqchikel women grew up in rural households that depended mostly on subsistence agriculture; some families relied on seasonal migration to work in cotton plantations on Guatemala's southern coast, migration that persists today (Fulchiron et al., 2009). Others benefited from the diversification of the regional economy, creating new, albeit often precarious, income-generating opportunities (Fulchiron et al., 2009).

Eight of the 14 protagonists were married but are now widowed, and 6 were single and living with their parents at the time the violence began. They ranged in age from 11 to 27 years of age (three were between 11 and 13 years old). Overall the Kaqchikel protagonists seem to have, on average, a higher prewar socioeconomic level than women from the other regions. Most owned their own land that they inherited from their father or husband and also worked outside the home as midwives, domestic workers, buying/selling at markets, or running small stores. Additionally, many have used the agricultural skills they learned as children to commercialize their crops, selling garden vegetables and fruit to generate income for their families. Many were cultivating fairly diverse crops: in addition to corn and beans, some grew coffee, sugarcane, wheat, and a variety of garden vegetables and fruits (cauliflower, broccoli, cabbage, summer squash, carrots, peas, tomatillos, passion fruit). All but one of the women mentioned keeping at least some small animals before the armed conflict (chickens, hens, ducks, pigs), and most also had larger animals: cows, horses, goats, and rams. Many had adobe and wood houses, and a few lived in concrete blockhouses, while some had cornstalk houses with straw roofs.

Chimaltenango was a strategic location for the guerrilla forces, allowing them to control the InterAmerican highway that crosses the department; it acted as a "first line of defense" between the capital, Guatemala City, and the Western Highlands (CEH, 1999, vol. 2). All three major insurgent groups operated there at some point during the 36-year internal armed conflict. The *Ejército Guerrillero de los Pobres* [Guerrilla Army of the Poor] (EGP), which had begun its political work in the department as early as 1976, increased its presence from mid-1981, particularly in San Martín Jilotepeque (CEH, 1999, vol. 6), one of the municipalities in the department hardest hit by government repression in this period. In the early 1980s, the violent regime of General Romeo Lucas García launched the first of a series of military task forces that would sweep through the highlands of Guatemala, bringing indiscriminate violence, massacres, and scorched-earth campaigns that targeted entire villages (CEH, 1999).

Most of the women interviewed by MTM described having experienced sexual violence in the context of mass violence or massacres in their communities or their places of refuge; they often spoke of continued harassment and pursuit by the armed forces. Several of the women were raped when their husbands had to leave the house to hide from the military or had been killed or disappeared. In many cases survivors of massacres in rural areas were forced by the army to relocate into nearby towns; not doing so attracted the suspicion of the urban populations and accusations from the army of being supporters of the guerrillas (CEH, 1999, vol. 4). However, as many of the women interviewed by MTM echoed, people in "receiving" communities were often wary of refugees and the possibility that their presence might attract military violence to their communities: "That good woman sheltered us, we stayed in the courtyard, but the man [her husband] didn't want [us there] he was saying, 'Get them out of here; they'll come throw us out because of them.'" Indeed, this woman, who was 20 years old and 6 months pregnant when she fled her community after the army raped her, found it quite difficult to find a safe place to stay: after leaving the "good woman's" house, she, her mother-in-law, sister-in-law, and her sister-in-law's six children spent a week sleeping out in the open before being reunited with her husband and brother-in-law and finding shelter together in a *galera* [a covered, open-air pen] in the middle of a coffee field where they stayed for a few months.

While this specific combination of events is particular to this woman's story, its elements are in no way exceptional. All of the women interviewed by MTM had to flee their homes at least temporarily—many hiding in the mountains or trying to find shelter in neighboring communities, and fleeing to estates, the nearest village, and even as far as Antigua and Guatemala City. Most had to move several times, many family members got separated along the way, and only a lucky few were able to reunite after a few days, a few months, or even a few years. For some women, living in a new community meant no longer wearing their own *traje* [dress] so as not to be recognized.

Many of the women spoke about how hard they had to work to meet their children's needs and to make sure they had enough to eat. The women's failing health—for many a consequence of the violence they suffered—also exacerbated past and current challenges: "We have lost many things and besides that we gained many illnesses." One woman explained that because of her health problems, her children had to start working at very young ages. Today, many are dependent on their children, which makes some uncomfortable or fearful that their children will one day get tired of supporting them. While many women were widowed when their husbands were killed or disappeared, some later remarried, and some described husbands as having left when they found out or heard rumors about them having been raped.

Huehuetenango

The group of 19 protagonists from Huehuetenango is the most diverse, consisting, in fact, of three ethnolinguistic subgroups: six Chuj women from the municipality of Nentón and its villages; seven Mam women from Colotenango communities; and six returnee Spanish-speaking women from Chaculá (including three Mam, one Chuj, and two Poptí), whose current identities are shaped more by their experience of exile and refuge in Mexico than by their ethnicity (Fulchiron et al., 2009). According to the CEH (1999, vol. 2, p. 395), "the conditions of extreme poverty and the imposition of migrations to the South Coast generated a permanent state of tension in the communities of northern Huehuetenango"; this led the state to perceive the Chuj and Q'anjob'al people of the region as rebellious, "antagonistic to authority," and "very hard to penetrate . . . [because of] language, origins and customs," and to define them as one of the army's most stigmatized "internal enemies," along with the people of the Ixil and Ixcán Grande regions of the northern Quiché (CEH, 1999, vol. 2, pp. 396–397). The army's scorched-earth campaign was most intense in northern Huehuetenango between June and August 1982. Human rights organizations and activists conducting multiple investigations between 1982 and 2007 estimated that 373 women, men, children, and elderly were killed in the San Francisco massacre on July 17, 1982; this widespread violence, which alerted the local population to the reality that the army was willing to kill entire communities, sparked a mass exodus of approximately 9,000 Chuj and ladinxs into Mexico (Falla, 2011). In addition to those who fled over the border to Mexico as refugees, another significant proportion of the population in northern Huehuetenango was forcibly displaced for periods ranging between 4 to 6 weeks and up to 12 years in a few cases (CEH, 1999, vol. 3, p. 408). Indeed, some of the women spoke of hiding in caves or in the mountains when the bombing would start, resulting in their losing animals that they could not feed and crops that they could not harvest.

These women are from rural peasant families, and most lived in conditions of extreme impoverishment before the war, migrating to Guatemala or Mexico's Pacific Coast with their families to work on coffee plantations (Fulchiron et al., 2009). The Chuj women illustrated their significant prewar poverty by noting that they did not have nice *huipiles* [blouses] or full *cortes* [skirts], and so wore pieces of corte that were barely big enough to wrap around themselves, and that their families could not buy everyday necessities such as *panela* [unrefined cane sugar], sugar, coffee, or salt. They had received no formal schooling and worked in the fields with their parents at very young ages (Fulchiron et al., 2009). A few women spoke of not even having corn, of having to eat flour tortillas filled only with plants gathered from the surrounding hills. They remembered their mothers earning a bit of money making *petates* [straw mats]; their families lived in straw or thatched houses, with their small corn fields often located a long trek from where they lived.

Several of them talked of making petates themselves to earn a bit of money and of raising small animals (mostly chickens and a few pigs). By the time the armed conflict broke out in their communities, most of the women in this group were married—most seeming to have married quite young (i.e., at 14 to 15 years old). One Chuj woman reported that her father had sold her into marriage to an older man when she was only 10, but also added, "In my community there is no problem in separating from someone if one has been living together. It was just a union; if one wants to stay together one can, . . . if not, no one can obligate a woman to stay together as it is her life. She can decide to leave if the man is bad" (Actoras de Cambio, 2011, "Julia," p. 23). And decide to leave she did, when she was 15. She and the Mam and Poptí women from Huehuetenango who shared their life stories spoke repeatedly of alcoholic fathers and spouses and of family violence both when they were growing up and in their own marriages.

From what the Chuj women described—and from Falla's (2011) descriptions of the periods before and after the San Francisco and related massacres—it does not seem as if their village in Nentón was directly targeted by the army's scorched-earth campaign. One woman explained that it was hearing about the massacres in nearby communities that prompted them to leave their homes and seek refuge in caves in the mountain. These women talked about violence at the hands of both soldiers and guerrillas. Two of the women in the group identified the men that raped them as being guerrilla fighters: Chuj men from a village of San Mateo Ixtatán. Another woman was not sure if the three men who raped her were the soldiers or guerrillas, explaining that both had the same style of dress and carried guns.[1] All but one of the women specified that they were raped while their husbands were on patrol. Indeed, their husbands' absence from their homes and community marks most of these testimonies and frames their experience. As one woman stated in an interview with MTM, "[When they] took the men to patrol then we were left behind, we couldn't even go out to gather *hierbitas* [plants to eat] since we were surrounded by soldiers. . . . We suffered. We couldn't even go gather firewood with the man [husband] gone." The community was occupied "by soldiers during day and guerrillas at night," and, as one woman explained, both expected the population to feed and support them, which people did out of fear. As the interpreter described during this woman's interview with MTM, "she was afraid because she didn't know who to obey, the guerrillas or the soldiers, so she had the same fear of the two groups because both were obligating them to do things they didn't want to."

In contrast, most of the Mam women recounted being attacked in what seemed to have been part of a larger "sweep" of their village by the Guatemalan Army. In fact, one woman mentioned the same thing having happened to women in neighboring villages on the same day. Three of the women specified having been attacked in 1982, which was during the most intense period of genocidal violence in Huehuetenango: they were quite young and single when they were attacked (between 10 and 14 years old) and were raped along with their mothers. In every case several soldiers came together to each house. Two women mentioned being asked where the guerrillas were or being accused of being guerrillas themselves; two others said that their male kin were also murdered, and some noted that family members were participating in the guerrilla activities. There were also references to soldiers pillaging and burning their houses and stealing their animals. For most of these women, the violence forced them to leave their homes, at least temporarily.

Protagonists in the Huehuetenango group all have histories of community and collective organizing, but these histories differ by ethnolinguistic group. The Chuj women's experiences are more similar to those of the Q'eqchi' group from the Polochic Valley than to the Mam group. With northern Huehuetenango being quite isolated geographically, kinship systems remain strong, and collective interests prevail over women's individual decisions (Fulchiron et al., 2009). The Mayan cosmovision and *la costumbre* [customs] are still very much a part of daily life, as is their connection to nature, land, plants, and energies (Fulchiron et al., 2009). Several of the women were midwives, describing themselves as practicing Catholics and as Mayan spiritualists. One of the Chuj summarized the armed conflict as a time when "many people died because of poverty. Soldiers were sent by the rich to kill the poor; in the war there was a good relation between the indigenous and the guerrillas, we protected each other. But the suffering and sadness that I still have has to do with being raped" (Actoras de Cambio, 2011, "Julia," p. 31). Mam women from Colotenango, whose communities were a base for the guerrillas, reported a clearer understanding of campesino struggles against the state and the oligarchy: their "world vision is more political than religious" (Fulchiron et al., 2009, p. 48). Yet, despite these understandings a Mam woman from Colotenango, "Carmela," concluded her life story with a critique of the guerrillas, remembering those from Chimaltenango and El Quiché who "were together with us around the fire, who ate with us—and now, who knows where they are—perhaps they were successful but they don't even ask about us, nothing—not even to ask us how we are today; they don't even look at us . . . not about the people with whom they lived or the villages where they were. What happened to us—perhaps we will only forget it when we are dead" (Actoras de Cambio, 2011, "Carmela," p. 29).

While the Mam remember Mayan spirituality, they generally do not practice it nor does the church have much of a presence in their communities (Fulchiron et al., 2009). Some abandoned their ancestral practices, dress, and language after they fled to Mexico (Fulchiron et al., 2009). In addition to learning Spanish and participating in literacy programs and rights and gender trainings while in Mexico, many continued to participate in rights and gender trainings on their return to Guatemala—largely through the refugee-returnee women's organization, Mamá Maquín—which Fulchiron et al. (2009) credit for the Mam's greater awareness of gender issues than other groups of women in the project. After returning to Guatemala, many returnee women became active with the Catholic parish in Nentón, with some even becoming catechists (Fulchiron et al., 2009).

Conditions of life in the postwar period have not been easy for any of these groups, and migration to the United States, through Mexico, has increased significantly in this region in recent years; some of the returnees to Guatemala after the armed conflict were among those migrants (Fulchiron et al., 2009). Many women continue to travel to work on coffee plantations for three months a year and engage in subsistence agriculture and raise small animals the rest of the time. This migration, despite the hard conditions in which the women work, has given them more mobility, and the complementary income that they earn has allowed them to improve their living conditions and gain a better position within their households (Fulchiron et al., 2009). Chuj and returnee women have succeeded in getting their own names on land titles, and most now own their own land, some as co-owners with their husbands (Fulchiron et al., 2009).

Despite their many individual, ethnolinguistic, and geographic differences, each of the women in all three groups was raped, that is, all 54 women—most multiple times—during the armed conflict. Most noted that these experiences took place in their homes after their husbands had been forced to collaborate with the military or had been kidnapped or disappeared. Some were pregnant at the time; many others were raped in the presence of their young children or were themselves still children and were violated while their mothers were forced to watch. Most explained that they spoke to no one after this experience, fearful about the consequences of sharing this information. Their fears and anxieties included concerns about *chismes* [rumors]: that women and/or men in their communities would say that they "had asked for it" or were "soldiers' whores." A few told their mothers or partners, but more common were those like "Beatriz" in Chimaltenango who noted, "I think that [my sons] now know what happened to me during that time, but I have never spoken to them about it and they don't ask: 'Why did they do that to you?' Or 'have you told papa?' Anyway, I prefer to continue as if it were a secret. . . . Although I have organized struggles in my community, I still am afraid of my husband and I can't tell him what I lived through" (Colectivo Actoras de Cambio, 2011, "Beatriz," p. 36). Yet most of the women defend their right "to speak about how they feel and to denounce before the authorities what happened to us. Justice for me is to make a claim for the suffering and pain that we experienced and that they punish those who are guilty" (Colectivo Actoras de Cambio, 2011, "Julia," p. 33). Their gendered racialized, ethnolinguistic relationships and communities continue to be constrained by patriarchal and deeply violent relationships that marginalize them as Mayan women. As Chirix García (2003) writes, "In this system of domination, Mayan women have suffered and survived ethnic-racial, gendered and class oppression" (p. 129). An Ixil woman who sought refuge in Mexico and was interviewed there by Hooks (1991) in the late 1980s, echoed a similar analysis of these intersecting systems of oppression in describing her experiences in Guatemala: "The Indian woman suffers from a triple exploitation by virtue of being a woman, being Indian and being poor. We have to find a way of combating these three problems simultaneously" (p. 72).

It is within the community of women informed by human rights discourse and infused with their ever-developing protagonism as Mayan women that they dare not only to speak their truth but also to demand justice. According to Chirix García (2003), Mayan women's lived experiences of such oppression contribute to their experiencing devaluation, disapproval, contempt, and humiliation. That said, she emphasizes the importance of not speaking rationally about these experiences but rather facilitating processes through which Mayan women, based on their experiences, "focus on themselves as active subjects, as actors in resistance" (p. 130). This need is similar to that acknowledged by the Ixil woman, mentioned earlier, who noted that her experiences participating in a women's group with other Mayan refugee women in Mexico contributed to her realization "that women themselves, Indian women included, reproduce their own oppression—in the way they bring up their children, for example. There are many things, which if they are not questioned, will reproduce the same oppression" (Hooks, 1991, p. 72). The next section focuses on a range of experiences through which the 54 Mayan protagonists and the intermediaries who accompanied them engaged in such questioning, dialogically constructing knowledge(s) and performing multiple subjectivities—and describes some of the limitations of those activities.

CREATIVITY, MAYAN HEALING PRACTICES, AND PARTICIPATORY WORKSHOPS

The creative arts (drawing, collage, storytelling), embodied practices (massage, human sculptures, role plays, theater), and the Mayan cosmovision and spirituality (e.g. ceremonies and rituals) were resources through which Mayan protagonists reflected on their experiences of the armed conflict, their struggle for redress, and the multiple personal shifts they made as they interrogated themselves and these processes over time. Although the particular combination of resources was adapted to the goals of this project, creative techniques have been used in earlier work with Mayan communities (Caja Lúdica, 2000; Duffy, 2018; Grupo de Mujeres Mayas Kaqla, 2006; Lykes, 1994, 2001; Women of Photovoice/ADMI & Lykes, 2000). Similarly, healing practices within indigenous communities and First Nations in other parts of the world (Archibald & Dewar, 2010; Castellano, 2006) and in the wake of contemporary genocides and state-sponsored violence (Lykes, Rosales et al., 1994; Taylor, 2003; Yuyachkani, n.d.), as well as that within Guatemala (Asociación Médicos Descalzos Chinique, 2012, 2014, 2016; Grupo de Mujeres Mayas Kaqla, 2004, 2009, 2011, 2014), were resources drawn on by this work with Mayan protagonists who survived racialized gendered violence.

As Taylor (2003) argues, many acts of oppression—including lynching, torture, and forced disappearances—are themselves "embodied performances" that have "contributed to the maintenance of a repressive social order" (p. 22; see also Kesselring, 2017, for an examination of the relationship between violence and what she refers to as "bodily memory"). Rape during war is deeply embodied, and as such, efforts to address its effects must engage the body. Thus, in the workshops facilitated by the Consortium between 2003 and 2008 with the 54 Mayan protagonists, which complemented more orally based support groups that it had organized, emphasis was placed on women's relationships to their bodies (Fulchiron et al., 2009). Locally based Mayan and ladina intermediaries drew on a range of eclectic practices, many of which originated beyond Guatemala's borders. Techniques such as massage and dance were used to develop trust among the women and help them become more comfortable with each other's bodies and with their own. As discussed further in chapter 5, rural Mayan campesina women were slow to embrace their own and each other's bodies, and interpreters and Mayan healers with whom they worked sought to respect their hesitancies while adopting strategies that would slowly introduce them to the embodied pain they were carrying— and to participatory resources for healing. For example, the women were asked to draw pictures of their own bodies and to discuss different body parts using colored paint: "this is how guilt began to fade: talking, drawing and freely expressing everything related to their body and sexuality" (Fulchiron et al., 2009, p. 383).

In 2009, the Peruvian theater group *Yuyachkani* [I Am Thinking/I Am Remembering] facilitated participatory workshops in Guatemala with these women survivors of sexual violence. Women engaged in body mapping and group performances representing their journeys in search of redress. The use of these body-centered approaches helped create new reference points in relation to the embodiment of their suffering, challenging silences, shame, and guilt, as well as taboos and myths about the body and sexuality deeply grounded in religious beliefs, while contributing to transformations in Mayan women's relationship to their own bodies and in their embodied relationships with others (Fulchiron et al., 2009; Grupo de Mujeres Mayas Kaqla, 2011).

Multiple resources from the Mayan cosmovision and traditional practices reported in the *Popol Vuh* [Council book], as well as a range of other Mayan texts, complemented these embodied practices. The *Popol Vuh* is referred to frequently as the "K'iche' Bible" and is described as "a creation story believed to be the single most important source documenting Mayan culture" (Grandin et al., 2011, p. 13). Kaqla and the *Asociación Médicos Descalzos Chinique* [Barefoot Doctors Association—henceforth, Médicos Descalzos] are two local Guatemalan NGOs whose work draws on many of these knowledge systems and informed that of the Mayan intermediaries who collaborated with this eight-year project. Kaqla (2006, 2011) sought to deconstruct social and personal oppression and develop women-based Mayan healing processes, while Médicos Descalzos (2012, 2014) systematized Mayan illness narratives and healing practices performed by Mayan spiritual guides or *Ajq'ijab*.

Kaqla (2011) situates its work in a critical analysis of colonial power, delineating how colonization and patriarchy have shaped present-day Mayan–ladinx relationships, as well as many within Mayan communities themselves. Kaqla members engage in group processes through which they explore and document their own and other Mayan women's internalization of feelings of inferiority, including a "victim syndrome" of blaming and shaming (Grupo de Mujeres Mayas Kaqla, 2004) that has contributed to a loss of identity and what Fanon (1963/2004) described as the internalization of their own oppression. The women of Kaqla have developed an eclectic healing process that incorporates not only Mayan traditions but also Western integrative therapies and alternative therapies, including meditation and massage, to address the embodied nature of racialized gendered oppression and its intergenerational marking of women's genetic, corporeal, and historical memory (Grupo de Mujeres Mayas Kaqla, 2014).

Healing then is holistic, rooted in Mayan cosmology (Grupo de Mujeres Mayas Kaqla, 2014), and integrating emotional, cognitive, and embodied processes that can only be fully realized through balancing one's positive and negative selves, one's light and shadow. It begins at the personal level and moves out to the collective and through generations (Grupo de Mujeres Mayas Kaqla, 2010). Mayan women analyze their own communities, their country, and the planet, specifying how each affects the generation of a politics of transformation through which they as Mayan women create new subjectivities (Grupo de Mujeres Mayas Kaqla, 2010). The collective intergenerational identifications engaged through these healing processes are sites through which grandmothers, daughters, and granddaughters generate interactive forms of resistance and transformative relationships (Grupo de Mujeres Mayas Kaqla, 2014).

Médicos Descalzos (2012) has documented Mayan traditional therapies found in Guatemala's El Quiché department. Working closely with 12 Mayan spiritual guides, Ajq'ijab, they analyzed the six most common Mayan illnesses, processes defined by their causes rather than by symptoms. These core illnesses are characterized by interdependent emotional and physical dimensions (Médicos Descalzos, 2012). Plants, herbs, and Mayan ceremonies at sacred sites are used to return those possessed by illness to harmony or to achieve forgiveness. According to Chirix García (2003), "the Mayan cosmovision fosters a holistic vision of things, does not divide events, but rather emphasizes the interrelations among the psychosocial, the environmental, and the cosmic towards an integral approach to people and reality" (p. 23). These beliefs and practices—understood and subscribed to in varying ways by the 54 Mayan protagonists within and through a deeply particularized and fractured community life—were deployed by intermediaries in the collaborative work of the creative workshops within the feminist PAR processes described in this volume.

The creative workshops were designed to offer resources that resonated with and enhanced the women's cultural, linguistic, and educational capacities to address some of the effects of their experiences of violence and to reflect on the transitional justice processes in which they were engaged. They were organized along three axes: (1) corporal expression, including role playing or dramatic play, and dramatic multiplication (Pavlovsky et al., 1985), and image theater (Boal, 1985); (2) drawing and other forms of physical creativity "outside of ourselves," including creating models made with newspapers or other materials and collages (Butler-Kisber & Poldma, 2010; Lykes, 1994; Lykes et al., 1994); and (3) verbal techniques: playing with words in ways that reveal their liberating character (Rodari, 1996; Zipes, 1995; see also Goudvis, 1991, for a video presentation and discussion of the intersection and application of these techniques). Additional participatory documentation included women's narratives, storytelling, and the research team's ethnographic observations, as well as iterative analyses of creative performances in the workshops and subsequent analyses of drawings and photographs of and from these activities. The analyses of the artwork and photos afforded multiple opportunities for protagonists' critical meaning-making about some of the many ways in which they and the intermediaries were shaped by and are shaping the truth-, justice-, and reparations-seeking mechanisms of transitional justice.

The workshops were conducted in Guatemala City, in public spaces outside of the women's local communities, in the country's official language, Spanish. Although all protagonists understand at least some Spanish, some linguists suggest that many Maya access it primarily for "instrumental" purposes, given that most are more comfortable speaking in their own Mayan language (García Ixmatá et al., 1993/2017). The workshops' facilitation of affective or socioemotional responses to experiences of violation, as well as their focus on meaning-making, make it likely that the participants would have preferred the use of their Mayan languages. Given our and the ladina intermediaries' linguistic limitations, we relied on Mayan interpreters from the Alliance to facilitate the active participation of all protagonists.

The structure and content of each workshop were shaped by the number of participants, the context in which it was carried out, language considerations, and the specific thematic focus. The methods of each of the workshops that we facilitated over these eight years differed slightly (for example, in the use of dramatizations or drawings) according to the participants' own preferences or emotional reactions to the issues under discussion and to the goals sought through their participation. Despite this variation, a general format was designed that facilitated participants' creative performances of and participatory reflections on the redress processes in which they were engaged and, as importantly, their identification of individual transformations and seeds and/or actions toward social transformation. Most workshops opened with a Mayan ritual or ceremony. As one of the Mayan women interviewed by Chirix García (2003) suggested, "The ceremonies help to connect to one's emotional equilibrium, strengthening one's understanding of oneself and others. In the wake of so much aggression, [Mayan] spirituality is a solid rootedness in life and in resistance" (p. 199). Either a Mayan protagonist or a Mayan intermediary facilitated the Mayan ceremony, which included ceremonial candles and flowers organized in a way to represent the four cardinal directions, each with a distinct energy and direction. The facilitator frequently incorporated mention of the *nawal*[2] [protective spirit] of the day on which we were gathered; she might then invite participants to kneel in front of the red, yellow, white, blue, and green candles; light the smaller candles they were holding; and place them on the floor while she explained the significance of the different colors: "red = sun; black = sunset; yellow = asking for thanks if we have animals, money, corn, children; white = water, clouds, giving strength to the harvests (of corn, beans, plants, and animals); blue = sky and moon; green = mountains, forests, the air that circulates through the trees and mountains" (see also Grupo de Mujeres Mayas Kaqla, 2009, 2010). The ceremony was followed by a brief description of the feminist PAR process and the purpose of the gathering, an explanation of the need for anonymity and confidentiality, a request for permission to take photos and record the workshops, and an introduction of the facilitators. In most workshops this introduction was followed by some "warm-up" exercises that engaged the body in movement and play.

Analyses of data from the workshop were undertaken collaboratively and iteratively. They began with scaffolded interpretive exercises within the workshops that we complemented with further inductive thematic coding (Charmaz, 2014). Thus, the first iterations involved participants' engagement with a technique— drawing, collage, dramatization, storytelling, etc.—around a topic selected as the workshop focus (e.g., experiences of community, meanings made from the use of creative techniques, understanding of reparation(s)). Working either individually or in small groups—and frequently within her own language group—each protagonist generated and then shared her creations with the group. The larger group was asked to describe what they perceived in the performance or image, and then the creator(s) explained what she or they had hoped to communicate.

Drawings were sometimes exchanged between groups, which were then asked to multiply the previous analyses through dramatizations. Participants engaged or performed each other's representations through this multiplication process, generating additional interpretations based on their own experiences. These activities were frequently followed by a large-group discussion of why this particular technique was chosen and what was learned from it. Each step of the process was documented through photographs, field notes, and/or audio recordings that were later transcribed. The group analyses generated within the workshop were treated as "first-level content analyses" within a larger analytic process informed by Charmaz's (2014) constructivist grounded theory. Each workshop included a shared meal and ended with a brief evaluation.

PROTAGONISTS' MEANING-MAKING THROUGH CREATIVE WORKSHOPS

In 2011 and 2012 we facilitated workshops with some of the 54 Mayan protagonists. Five women from Huehuetenango (three Chuj women, and two Mam women) and six Kaqchikel women from Chimaltenango participated in the 2011 workshop. Additional participants included a Chuj woman who served as an interpreter (the two Mam women spoke Spanish); four UNAMG staff, including a Kaqchikel member of the research team who served as interpreter for the women from Chimaltenango; another international member of our research team; and ourselves. The women from the Polochic Valley were unable to participate because heavy rains had made the roads from their communities impassable. Sixteen protagonists—five Q'eqchi' women from Alta Verapaz/Izabal, seven Mam and Chuj women from Huehuetenango, and four Kaqchikel women from Chimaltenango—participated in the 2012 workshop. Two UNAMG interpreters and two additional UNAMG staff attended as well.

Central activities in these workshops were the creation of collective drawings focusing on how they saw themselves today, after their years of working together, in comparison to how they saw themselves before participating in their work in the Consortium and the Alliance; representations of their understandings of "community"; collages depicting their experiences with and understandings of reparation(s); dramatizations; and varied brainstorming exercises. The remainder of this chapter summarizes the iterative analyses of these creative performances in terms of the protagonists' (1) sense and performance of selves before and after their engagement with creative methodologies, (2) representations of violence, and (3) representations of community—and the ways in which they perceive these as having developed or been negatively affected over their years of collaborating in transitional justice processes.

Performance of Selves: Before and After

Using an individual or collective "draw myself/ourselves" creative technique, participants were invited to represent themselves and their feelings in the present and to compare and contrast them with how they remembered themselves before their engagement in the work of the Consortium and the Alliance. Their creations reflected particularities of context, language, time, and localized experiences of the war within each ethnolinguistic subgroup, but all included images of trees, flowers, fruit, and seeds to represent themselves today. The images reflect the women's attachment to nature through which they identify themselves as com-

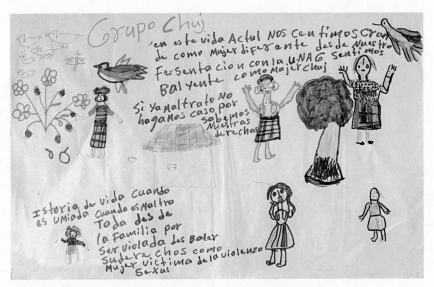

FIGURE 1. Chuj women represent life during the war and today.

ing from and/or living in rural communities wherein seeds are signs of new life and new beginnings. One of the Chuj women talked about herself as "old, without suffering, without fear and without shame. Today I am capable of doing all that I can. I am like a bird. I can fly with large wings." Another Chuj woman, referring to Figure 1, described herself as a tree whose roots are "sad" because "I have been humiliated" but the "branches are growing." A third described feeling "happiness. I can do many things, including speak to the authorities in the community. I can sign my name." Talking about the Chuj women's drawing, Mam women noted the "sun coming out" and their reflections of themselves as "happy" now.

Although asked to represent themselves today, each ethnolinguistic group responded by combining their present and their pasts in a single collective drawing. The drawings suggest an ever-present past in which the past and the present merge, a lived experience that some identify in words as having been "humiliated." The earlier reference to "sad roots" also testifies to the past's centrality in these women's present experiences. One Chuj woman talked about the "humiliations we've experienced" as "over," whereas a Kaqchikel woman spoke explicitly and openly about her sexual violation within the armed conflict beginning in 1980, stating that "we lived sexual violence and the disappearances of our husbands" and it has left us alone with our children who are "malnourished, sad, afraid, without clothing and without food" (Figure 2). These images of the past sit alongside those of the present, suggesting that neither are linear stories and that the ever-presence of past violence is not erased by a different present. This is reflected further in the creation of the Chuj women who threaded words and visual representations of the past and present in a single drawing (Figure 1).

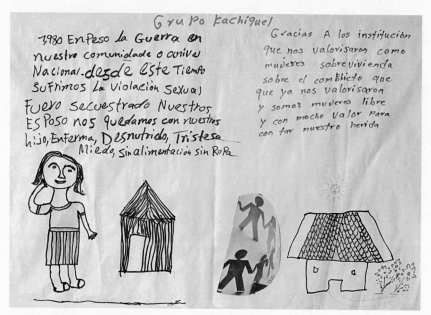

FIGURE 2. Kaqchikel women represent life during the war and today.

Similarly, the Mam group represented themselves along a path or journey that reflected both past and present in a single image; they centered their developing skills as leaders of an organization through which they were confronting discrimination, drawing on what they had learned/were learning from UNAMG. The tall figure in pants in the upper-right quadrant of their drawing (Figure 3) was of particular interest to all the other participants, generating wide-ranging interpretations that it represented the "military," "police," and the "president of Guatemala." The Mam women clarified that it was drawn to represent "us": the intermediaries with whom they had been working, who provided financial and psychoeducational resources, and whom they urged not to cease accompanying them. These echoed the words within the Kaqchikel representations of their present situation in which they thanked "the institutions who value them as survivors." The Mayan women protagonists thus represented themselves in a variety of roles and contexts, acknowledging explicitly the presence of the intermediaries and representing the dialogic relationality through which they were constructing knowledge(s) of themselves in the midst of the multiple struggles they confronted in the various transitional justice processes in which they were engaged. Of interest is the relative size of the intermediary figure in this drawing and the explicit plea not to discontinue the work.

Representations of Violence

These Mayan women protagonists' drawings reflected their representations of the discontinuities and continuities of impoverishment and everyday violence that

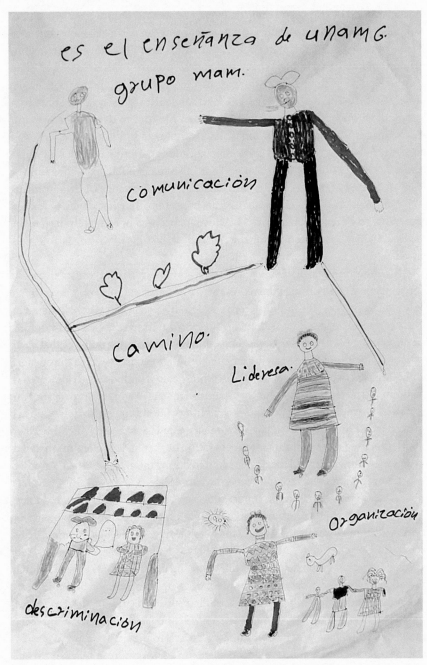

FIGURE 3. Mam women represent their—and our—teaching/learning.

are embedded in and frame their daily experiences. In Figure 2 the Kaqchikel women used words in their drawings to document the particular experiences of sexual violence, the kidnapping of their husbands, and the sadness, fear, malnutrition, and lack of clothing that were a consequence of these actions. They represented their homes in both sides of the drawing; it juxtaposes a single, lonely woman and a straw home with a thatched roof used in the past to a group of women and a concrete home with a tile roof to denote the present. Such images and descriptions contrasting wartime and postwar experiences of impoverishment also appeared in the dramatizations performed in the 2012 workshop. The discussions in both 2011 and 2012 also made reference to the current context of everyday violence in Guatemala and the presence of drug traffickers and gangs, as well as the women's fears concerning the presidency of former general Otto Pérez Molina. He has been widely accused of being responsible for many atrocities committed during the war and, at the time of writing in 2018, was in jail awaiting trial on corruption charges.

This understanding of violence and its effects in Mayan protagonists' lives was further complicated through the representations of reparation(s) processes in the July 2012 workshop (the findings from this activity are also presented in detail in chapter 4 as part of our discussion of the protagonists' conception of reparation(s) in the context of the PNR). Of particular interest here are the collages that each ethnolinguistic group created after a brainstorming exercise in which they generated a long list of concepts that for them represented definitions—as interpreted to them by the translators—for the Spanish-language terms for reparation(s): *reparación, reparación integral*, and *resarcimiento*. Of the approximately 20 ideas evoked by the three terms, which the women seemed to use interchangeably, one-quarter focused on reparation(s) as recognition or acknowledgment of what had been stolen from them and the damage caused during the armed conflict. Another quarter of the comments recapitulated the harm done, with descriptions of their houses, land, animals, husbands, culture, and their health before the armed conflict. Most of the remaining ideas or themes focused on the impossibility of repairing the devastation caused by the war and the multiple ways in which the government's reparation(s) efforts were failing, themes that had also been expressed and performed earlier in the day in their drawings and dramatizations. Those failures included unkept promises, efforts to put a price on that which is beyond financial remuneration (e.g., their bodies and their husbands' lives), and the use of money to "shut you up" or "distract you," representing in their minds the government's treatment of them as children. Each ethnolinguistic group was then asked to get together and develop a collage, using images from magazines and newspapers in the room to "re-present the many meanings of reparation(s)" that they as a group felt best reflected their experiences as particular ethnolinguistic Maya. Each of the four groups completed a collage and, because of time limitations, presented its collage to the whole, explaining how each hoped to represent reparation(s) for their community.

All four collages included images of land and/or homes, with the collages completed by the Chuj and the Kaqchikel women also placing emphasis on what was inside the home: furniture, household goods, and so on. In describing their collages, they spoke about basic needs, broken promises, homes half-completed by the government, or a lack of funds for them to complete the work themselves. The Q'eqchi' and Kaqchikel groups represented in images and in words that loss extended beyond material goods to their own and their children's health. Some of the latter were born as a result of rape, and all the children were malnourished and needed health care, as did the women. As in the brainstorming exercise, the collages of the Mam (see Figure 4) and the Kaqchikel represented and addressed racialized gendered violence. They labeled and verbally described the photo of a woman who was forced to carry a heavy load as "violence against women" and that of a woman crouched and photographed from behind as representative of the ongoing violence against women today (we return to this issue in chapter 4). The Kaqchikel group spoke of women as widows and as having survived rape, and of the continuities of violence against women today with that of the past.

In stark contrast to the brainstorming exercises that elicited stories of the past and condemnations of the government for its manipulative use of reparations processes, the collages included multiple pictures of women's resistance. As can be seen in Figure 4, the Mam included several images of protests, as well as photos of Ríos Montt and Pérez Molina, heads of state whom they held responsible for the violence of the armed conflict and the poverty, violence, and broken promises of today. But rather than focus on how these leaders manipulated them, the collages included representations of men and women demonstrating against violence and violations, as well as demanding their rights. This was also clear in the Q'eqchi' collage that addressed more explicitly past and present movements to defend land rights, while the Kaqchikel emphasized their demand for justice. The Kaqchikel collage also included a picture of a woman whom they described as working to form a cooperative; in the group discussion they spoke of their efforts as widows to develop cooperatives to ensure the well-being of their children—and their demands for capital from the government to support their organizing efforts. This creative resource facilitated women's elaborations of the previously noted understandings of reparation(s) generated through the brainstorming exercise, a dynamic that seemed to encourage slightly more individualized stories reflecting testimonies of damage and of further victimization and government manipulation. The collage generated spaces for the creative expression of their collective protagonism and resistance.

It is important to note that the brainstorming exercise was done in the larger group and required calling out individual responses across language groups—

FIGURE 4. Mam collage: integral reparation(s).

responses that were then translated for each individual language subgroup—whereas the collages were developed in ethnically linguistically similar subgroups in an atmosphere of small-group sharing. Thus the differences noted earlier may reflect both the creative and the more collective and linguistically homogeneous context in which these activities were performed. Significantly, the meanings made of "reparation(s)" were complex and included clarity about the impossibility of ever repairing the war's consequences, the absolute demand for economic or material repair ranging from land and houses to health care, and the clear representation of their ability to organize themselves as women to demand what was rightfully and justly theirs. Unlike the legal and linear constraints of the truth-telling, justice-seeking, and reparation(s) processes analyzed in the next three chapters, this feminist PAR process, which integrated creative workshops, opened spaces through which some of the 54 protagonists participating in the broader transitional justice processes could re-present themselves as activists demanding justice while organizing with other indigenous community members to speak their truth to power.

Representing Community

As we argue throughout this volume, the 54 Mayan protagonists were being differently positioned and were differently positioning themselves at the intersection or border between a community of women and a local, geographically based community. The creative methodologies facilitated our exploration of the dynamism of such border spaces and of the intermediaries' engagement with these women not only as they were positioned as survivors but also as they positioned themselves as protagonists in their increasingly diverse communities. Reflexively interrogating this positioning illuminates and clarifies some of the diverse ways in which intermediaries facilitate and constrain the knowledge(s) co-constructed through the transitional justice and feminist PAR processes described in this volume. To develop a better understanding of how the protagonists experienced the border between their developing community of women and their local, geographically based communities, we facilitated a series of activities with them in 2012.

Following introductions, the 16 Mayan protagonists and their interpreters were asked to gather in language-specific groups to discuss the term "community." Each group then shared their understandings of what they meant by this concept. The four Kaqchikel women spoke of the family and workplace as community, clarifying that the latter was only a community if and when it was organized to facilitate working together and sharing. Another woman noted that the community was "the place where we live, our village," that is, a geographic location. They spoke about diverse religious groups coexisting in a single community and also mentioned that as women they were frequently "not taken into account." Another participant added that "we are no longer afraid of the men, we can deal with them now" and exemplified this by sharing a recent experience in which she challenged a bus driver who was not willing to drive her all the way home, demanding her money back if he refused to honor her right for passage to her village, for which she had paid. The Mam group reported that their meetings with UNAMG were community gatherings, where "we meet with different groups, regions, languages; we are a community because we get to know each other." They later added that when they returned "to where we live, our community, we share what we learn. When we are together here, we are a community; when we are there we are another community," adding that when they went to a community where they are not known that it is "complicated . . . they don't know what we know. We can only share if they will let us." The Q'eqchi' women emphasized the intergenerational and familial nature of community in which people perform different roles and work together to request something, such as a school, if it is needed. They characterized a community as reflecting "unity and communication," a site where "a sick person can be taken to be healed"—and added that UNAMG was organized and had members and thus was "like a community."

The women were then asked to draw a picture representing their community's gains and losses, advances or setbacks, over the previous six years during which they had been working with UNAMG, a key member of the Alliance (and convener of the workshop). Each group was asked to share its drawing, asking others in the workshop to tell them what they perceived the drawing to be about and then sharing what they had hoped to represent with their community drawings. All four drawings highlighted the experience of coming together as women thanks to the work of UNAMG. Women described themselves as afraid to talk before participating in the workshops. A Kaqchikel woman described her first experiences of being invited to a workshop: "When I went there my problems were still guarded in my heart. I didn't trust enough to tell my stories from the war; we each had different problems. But when I started talking in the group I saw I was not alone, not the only one. . . . It was in these workshops that I have come to understand that I am a woman. I have rights, that after everything, my life can recover."

Both groups from Huehuetenango focused on their accomplishments and remaining or persistent challenges. The larger group analyzed the Chuj women's drawing (see Figure 5) along similar lines to those later articulated by the subgroup that had drawn it, and the subgroup added further details from their experiences as refugees in Mexico. This subgroup noted that they were "in bad shape, did not go to school, did not understand" when they began their journey during the war and then as refugees in Mexico, experiences represented by the roots in their picture. They encountered Mamá Maquín and learned how to build an organization while in Chiapas, and then, after returning to Guatemala, UNAMG had helped them. They spoke of starting as only two people, then three, and then growing in number, as represented by the flowering tree with many blossoms and the many women who worked as organizers: "Then we got a group together, we were able to get a house. Now we are like this tree, we have learned, we know our rights, we are no longer afraid of the men." Others in the group described how some women did not join the group and were sometimes prevented by men from being in it. In contrast, another member of their group noted, "When a man says 'you can't go,' we duck under their arm and go anyway." Another woman added that when the war started she was afraid, but now even President Pérez Molina does not frighten her: "Even if he is standing in front of me, I will speak and say what his soldiers did to us." Another woman noted that the organization [UNAMG] gives them help "to travel and get our room and board."

The Mam women, also from Huehuetenango, also included trees and plants in their drawing, but more clearly differentiated the "women's group" and the community from the wider national panorama beyond them. Again, there was considerable overlap between what the larger group described when looking at the Mam drawing (see Figure 6) and what the Mam women noted in their description. Yet, the women from the subgroup again added details, noting that the group that they had been able to organize was not typical of women in all communities and that it had been created with the help of UNAMG. The trees were described as representing not only the environment that they were nurturing in their village but also the importance of protecting the forests and waterways of Guatemala, particularly from those seeking to extract resources from them today. One woman noted that the "big man" represented Otto Pérez Molina, describing him as a "threatening leader" who was not a menace to them, but threatened other women. His outstretched hand represented a gesture that "indicated that he does not want these women, they bother him"; she added, "We have to get him to give

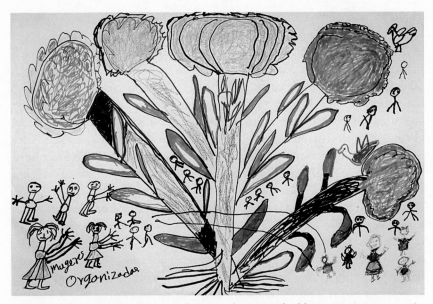

FIGURE 5. Chuj women represent challenges and successes building community.

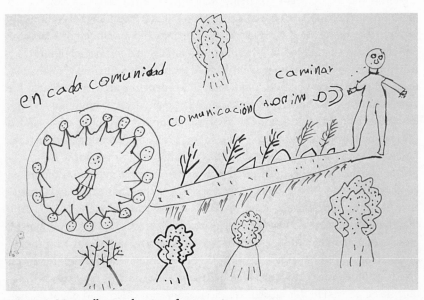

FIGURE 6. Mam collective drawing of community.

us our freedom, let us be." Another member of the subgroup added, "We will gather, organize, to demonstrate against Otto Pérez Molina."

The larger group then explored the continuing challenges facing them as multiple communities of women. The exercise was an opportunity to engage with each other from their own experiences and to better understand the ways in which they saw themselves as belonging to and moving between a community of women organized by UNAMG, among other NGOs, and women in geographically based communities who organize themselves and others in their local context. They noted how the workshops facilitated by UNAMG and other NGOs had contributed to their personal and collective change as women who now understood themselves to be bearers of rights who could ask for what they needed, speak truth to power, and organize to demonstrate against the then-head of state (Pérez Molina), whom they described as responsible for many of the violations of their rights. In the subsequent larger group discussion some elaborated on current challenges facing those whose lands were being occupied by multinational corporations, supported by government forces, who were seeking to extract minerals or cultivate single-plant crops for export, rather than supporting local agriculture. In contrast to transitional justice actions of truth, reparation(s), and justice seeking that ask them to revisit their pasts—all too frequently constraining them to victim positions—this exercise among others in these workshops tapped into their protagonism and their current leadership skills and expertise moving toward a better future. It contributed to the co-construction of understandings of community wherein they represented themselves through plants and flowers, emphasizing the importance of women-in-local community—and distinctive imaginaries through which these women additionally positioned themselves as members of an organized and nationally engaged community of women. The activity facilitated the visualization and documentation of the diverse experiences of community of each ethnolinguistic group during the years of armed conflict. For some, this included the experience of being in refuge, while for others it entailed being forced to survive within their geographic communities under military occupation.

Many of the challenges identified by the women were situated during the armed conflict before their participation in workshops with the Consortium and the Alliance. It is noteworthy, as suggested by García Ixmatá and colleagues (1993/2017), that the initial iterations of this performance took place within ethnolinguistic groups that facilitated the use of their Mayan languages and thereby expressive or affective communication—resulting in a more integral representation. Each group critiqued the current president (Pérez Molina) and his resistance to their organizing efforts. In the subsequent discussion, some identified ongoing challenges with some men in their communities who continue to refuse to let women participate. Others expressed ongoing sadness and illnesses stemming from their experiences during the armed conflict, while some pointed to current political challenges, with a focus on ongoing poverty and local politicians betraying their communities through selling land rights to hydroelectric and mining companies or to plantation owners who were ruining local lands through cultivating African palm crops. Each group was then invited to pick one of the many setbacks that had been identified and to dramatize the problem—and a possible solution to it.

The Q'eqchi', Kaqchikel, and Chuj women selected setbacks that were more directly related to their experiences as survivors of racialized gendered violence during the armed conflict, whereas the Mam women focused on a current political challenge relating to the extractive industry's incursions on their local lands. The Mam represented a showdown between a mining company, representatives from the government, and local community activists. The activists refuse to move when the company and government seek to drive them off their lands and call on members of neighboring communities to help them resist the mining company. The vignette ends with the activists' success: they are able to gather such a large crowd that government representatives and the company have to leave. As mentioned, each of the other three dramatizations represented a challenge facing women who had survived sexual violence during the armed conflict. The Q'eqchi' women dramatized a conflict between spouses over women's responsibilities in the home. Someone representing a husband asserts angrily, "He married her to have his children and care for them, and to cook for the family." Other women intervene, urging this woman to talk to her husband and to help him understand that she "really wants to participate, to know her rights." His anger subsides, and he responds positively to her reasoning, giving her permission to attend meetings with other women in the community.

A Chuj woman dramatized sadness and loss, as well as physical ailments, that resulted from her having been raped by armed men during the war. One woman urges her to seek reparations from the PNR, but she replies that money will not heal her head, heart, or bodily ailments. The visitor acknowledges that whatever money she might receive cannot take away her sadness, but the organizations can help her with that (she is referencing the counseling and mutual support groups initiated by UNAMG and ECAP). The suffering woman reports that husbands do not allow their wives to participate "because they think that if women go to a woman's group they will go with other men who touch and caress them." The visitor urges her to come to a meeting and reminds her of the Mayan rituals in which they participated earlier in the morning and of their healing properties, and how they will "bring her energies." The woman agrees to accompany her visitor to the next gathering of UNAMG and ECAP.

The Kaqchikel dramatization also addressed the legacies of rape from the armed conflict, but it was focused more on the unkept promises made by the government and its continual failure to pay reparations to the women. One woman represents Otto Pérez Molina and defends the government, arguing that there are limited resources and that he must pay the ex-PAC first. He urges the woman to leave her paperwork with him and assures her that he will take care of it. She once again demands assurance from him that he will repair the damage inflicted on her. He repeats his promise, but adds: "But I don't want you protesting, coming to the city to protest, that I don't want."

The discussions following this exercise focused on what participants were feeling while they enacted their oppressors: husbands who refused to let them participate and/or spread chismes about them as women, or government officials who continued to lie to them about providing reparations. Some mentioned being afraid when they were pressuring other women and felt relieved when they were being pressured by those enacting men's roles and other women came to their aid. The dramatic representations enabled them to experience another's feelings, including those of men who are more powerful. They noted gendered differences in the enactment of power and suggested that dramatic play enabled them not only to see a different reality but also to access different feelings. Some women argued that both are necessary to learn how to organize to defend their rights. They suggested that the exercise allowed them to explore the diverse dimensions of any conflict and that dramatizations are good teaching rubrics for their children and others in their communities, particularly because the issues addressed are present there. Finally, several suggested that the experience introduced them to new ideas for trying to bring about change and that the embodied performances gave them a more integrated feel for what that change might be like.

In both the drawings and in their dramatizations, these Mayan protagonists represented a broad range of understandings of community. They represented the community of women that they were creating as including other Mayan protagonists and the intermediaries. Their local, geographically based communities continue to be dominated by circuits of dispossession in which women are relegated to serving men within their homes, with limited access to participation outside the home. That said, violence was notably absent from the family site, and some men were represented as open to dialogue. This stands in sharp contrast to most of the lived experiences they reported from their childhoods and their lives during the armed conflict. Alcoholism was also absent. Despite the fact that each of the drawings and dramatizations represented changes attendant to the establishment of communities of women, they also represented state power as the protagonists experience it; that is, as controlled by the oligarchy and military and dominated by unfulfilled promises. That said, the Mam community dramatized a locally based community organizing success that included both men and women—and others from neighboring communities—who came together across diversities to resist mining extraction. Juxtaposing their drawing and their dramatization one can read across the two experiences to imagine an integration of a community of women and a geographically based ethnolinguistic community whose organizing not only transcends gender but also local community. Moreover, the Mam women have recourse to the constitution to defend their rights, while the Q'eqchi' women represented negotiation and communication as resources to convince husbands of their wives' rights. This echoes the affirmation of the importance of communication in both of the Mam's women's collective drawings (see Figure 3 and Figure 6), a process that they complement with representations of leadership. In one of their drawings the leadership is positioned in the intermediaries, whereas in the other and in their dramatization it is located within themselves. Within and across these creative productions these Mayan women protagonists perform themselves as they are becoming through their ongoing collaborations in and across community.

CONCLUDING REFLECTIONS

The findings from these participatory processes of engagement with Mayan women document the contributions of creative techniques and participatory workshops to protagonists' psychosocial well-being and to the various actions they have taken over the past decade in search of redress as a community of women and in local organizing in their communities. The workshops described in this and other chapters in this book provided spaces of contention, all too absent in the surrounding, deeply conflictive, and increasingly remilitarized social world of Guatemala. Fear and anxieties could be momentarily risked, enacted through an embodied character in the context of a performance, and anger could be directed against the perpetrator who is also present through performance and thus, in this imagined space, now under local control. The real is thus both more and less "really real," enabling the women to dare to experience and/or re-experience feelings that were rarely, if ever, expressed previously. Play and creative expression facilitated laughing at the unlaughable, connecting protagonists to potential alternative responses to ongoing fear. In the creations of the smaller, ethnolinguistically similar groups and in the broader "community's" (whether indigenous, women survivors, protagonists and intermediaries, or the broader Guatemalan public) recognition of what has been created, both its descriptive and analytic dimensions, participants play with forces that constrain and oppress—thus gaining some small degree of relief and control while developing potentially important resources for resistance and participation in wider, community, and/or national-level transformative processes.

Through their creative representations and embodied performances, Mayan protagonists also clarified that many of the truth-, justice-, and reparations(s)-seeking actions they had undertaken (and which are analyzed in more detail in chapters 2–4) would not have been possible without the accompaniment of the multiple intermediaries with whom they were engaged in rethreading the social fabric of the multiple communities in which they were performing increasing protagonism and in the diverse public spaces more typically controlled by ladinx and men that they were increasingly occupying. We documented how protagonists recognized and represented this engagement in a variety of creative exercises in the workshops throughout this multiple-year feminist PAR project. Dramatization, art, massage, storytelling, and theater were some of the creative resources used to facilitate protagonists' self-expressions and recognition of diverse but overlapping stories of survival and protagonism in each other's creative output. These resources facilitated important moments of self-discovery in the context of community and beyond. Protagonists performed their embodied understandings of the militarization of their communities to control the population and the particular strategies implemented by each branch of the military-civilian service, as well as the impoverishment that it gave rise to and that persists in the aftermath of genocidal violence. The iterative interpretations fostered dialogic engagement with past and current experiences, reflecting an emerging critical understanding of and engagement with racialized gendered circulations of power that continue to constrain Mayan women's protagonism.

As documented in this chapter and acknowledged repeatedly by the 54 Mayan protagonists, the role of intermediaries and accompaniers was key. Yet our positionalities within the work that unfolded during the armed conflict and in its aftermath were not without their contradictions and complications. As is discussed in more detail in chapters 2–4, the transitional justice mechanisms deployed more intentionally in the work of the Alliance constrained Mayan women's protagonism, often requiring them to tell and retell stories of harm in which they were victims of sexual violence. Merry (2006) and Merry and Levitt (2017) write about interpreters who straddle international and local contexts, translating international human rights norms into local languages and thus disseminating these norms and practices more widely. We argue in this chapter that the feminist PAR process and the use of creative methodologies enhance the probability that performances of more diverse, culturally and linguistically embedded local interpretations and understandings can "travel up" if intermediaries position themselves as listeners, declining to talk over local meaning-making. To that end, a significant number of Mayan, ladina, and international interpreters or intermediaries facilitated multiple participatory processes, which sought to generate spaces through which Mayan women performed their experiences and narrated their understanding of the causes and consequences of racialized gendered violence. The analysis presented in this chapter suggests that power circulates within and through "insider-outsider" relationships (Bartunek & Louis, 1996) wherein intermediaries seek to work the hyphen, generating a hybridized third voice. The latter is neither a singular, essentialized narrative of Mayan women survivors nor the work of a ventriloquist who facilitates or manipulates their creative and performative liberatory acts as protagonists. Feminist PAR processes facilitate the travel of hybridized voices, accompanied by embodied narratives that more easily journey beyond local communities to national and international listeners. These experiences, as well as the analysis presented in this chapter, argue for critical engagement with these hybridities, recognizing the primacy of Mayan women survivors' lived experiences while neither reifying nor essentializing what are rethreaded discourses and actions toward disrupting interlocking gendered, racialized, and class-based structures and creating shared struggles toward resistance and social transformation.

Although intermediaries have sought to engage with Mayan protagonists in ways that prioritized the cultural and educational capacities of participants and were sufficiently flexible to allow for the kinds of transformative practices described here, transitional justice mechanisms often force a different framing, serving as barriers to the women's more local and contextualized meaning-making processes. This chapter has emphasized the importance of creative methodologies as a resource for listening to indigenous meaning-making and facilitating Mayan women's protagonism. Specifically, these resources facilitated the active participation of rural, nonformally educated Mayan women in a wide range of processes that contributed to and documented their personal transformations. Mayan beliefs and practices—many of which were deployed by Mayan co-facilitators—preceded the performances using creative resources. They resonated with knowledge rooted in local experiences and reflected critical ways of retheorizing women's knowledge, embodying and complexifying earlier constructions and transitional justice mechanisms that risk essentializing "women's ways of knowing" (Belenky, Clinchy, Goldberger, & Tarule, 1997). Mayan women's knowledge is performed through their imaginings of a "new future," one that is rooted in the ever-present sadness attendant to the violations of the past, yet is performed through embodied protagonism.

These hybridities are not without their challenges, and as feminist antiracist PARers we seek to problematize and critically interrogate the presence and participation of ourselves and our Guatemalan-based ladina and Mayan intermediaries. Chapters 2–4 report on three performances through which the Mayan women protagonists, accompanied by the Alliance intermediaries, sought truth (chapter 2), justice (chapter 3), and reparation(s) (chapter 4) as survivors of racialized gendered violence. Chapter 5 explores the intermediary–Mayan protagonist relationships over time, listening more closely to the meanings made by intermediaries as they engaged with the 54 Mayan protagonists over many years of accompaniment.

2 · RECOUNTING PROTAGONISM

"No One Can Take This Thorn from My Soul"

I ask the members of this Tribunal of Conscience to listen to us. It may just be me speaking at this moment, but we are many, a majority in Guatemala, who were subjected to this type of constant violence. We need you to believe us, and for everything to be made public, so that everyone knows that here in Guatemala grave violations of our human rights were committed. There was a loss of respect for life and for our integrity, which is the most sacred thing to us ... I need to speak to those of you who make up this Tribunal, so that you hear our truth ... that you hear that this really happened, that it is not a fabrication, and that we did not ask for this.

—Q'eqchi' protagonist, Tribunal of Conscience, March 2010

It is often considered the task of historiography to break the silence that announces the zones of taboo. There is even something heroic in the image of empowering women to speak and to give voice to the voiceless. I myself have found this a very complicated task, for when we use such imagery as breaking the silence, we may end up using our capacity to "unearth" hidden facts as a weapon. Even the idea that we should recover the narratives of violence becomes problematic when we realize that such narratives cannot be told unless we see the relation between pain and language that a culture has evolved.

—Veena Das (2007, p. 57)

In March 2010, we were invited to participate as honorary witnesses in the Tribunal of Conscience for Women Survivors of Sexual Violence during the Armed Conflict in Guatemala, organized by the Alliance in coordination with CONAVIGUA and the feminist journalists' collective *La Cuerda*. The organizers had two main objectives: to create a public space for protagonists to testify about their experiences of violence and be heard by their fellow citizens and the state, and to lay the groundwork for a paradigmatic case of sexual violence as a weapon of war to be presented for prosecution in the Guatemalan courts. During the two-day event, five Mayan and two ladina protagonists testified, some for the first time in a public space, about their experiences of violence to an audience of approximately 800 people that included other women protagonists, survivors of the genocide and other experiences of violence during the armed conflict, members of Guatemalan civil society, state officials, and a cross section of the international community.[1]

Protagonists who testified to the Tribunal spoke from behind a curtain, hidden from view, to conceal their identities. In 2010, impunity for crimes of the past and present was widespread in Guatemala, and it was even more pervasive for gender-based crimes (Diez & Herrera, 2004; Impunity Watch, 2009; UDE-FEGUA, 2010). Some of the Mayan protagonists continued to live in the same community as their assailants and thus had very real concerns about their safety and security (Paz y Paz Bailey, 2006). Most had still not told their families about what had happened to them. But they came to speak publicly, to seek justice and social recognition for violations of their human rights. In this chapter, we make visible how Mayan women's protagonism has been shaped, at least in part, by their participation in truth-telling exercises such as the Tribunal of Conscience. As Ross (2003) argues within the context of the South African TRC, "Remembering and recounting harm is neither a simple nor a neutral act" (p. 162). Truth-telling is a necessarily complex, gendered, racialized, cultural, and political construction, and, as we argue throughout this volume, it is also an inherently relational process. We narrate or perform our truths in multiple and varied relations to and with others within particular historical contexts and over time (Falla, 2011; Jelin, 2003). In fact, the meaning of truth itself is constituted through such "dialogical interaction" (Bakhtin, 1984, p. 110). In foregrounding the Tribunal, we seek to clarify how local, national, and transnational webs of relationships that constitute truth-telling processes, and the speech-acts and silences that these webs of relationships simultaneously engender, inform processes of transitional justice but can also (often unintentionally) reinforce or reify victimization. Sexual harm is a particularly fraught terrain for gendered discourse. As Theidon (2007) notes, drawing on work with survivors in Peru, "women are routinely asked to narrate their experiences in an idiom of sexual vulnerability and degradation. What does it mean to narrate your life in an idiom that cannot possibly 'do you justice'?" (p. 473). We explore differing strategies that protagonists engaged to tell their stories in search of reparation(s) and justice and how others describe what it means to receive such stories. Specifically, we focus on what these stories of sexual harm signify to those who listen, who in fact co-constitute protagonists' narrative constructions through their self-positioning as observers of their pain.

In the first part of the chapter, we situate the Tribunal within a growing literature on gender and truth-telling within moments of transitional justice, as well as the more local, civil-society-initiated processes in Guatemala that were instrumental in enabling some protagonists to "break the silence" and publicly testify at the Tribunal. In the second part of the chapter, we examine the public presentation of the narrative of sexual harm in the Tribunal of Conscience through an analysis of protagonists' narratives, organized along four thematic dimensions that emerged from inductive content coding of their testimonies: (1) change (that is, the contrast they drew between life before, during, and after the violence); (2) violations and harm suffered; (3) demands; and (4) silence, voice, and witnessing. We examine these themes within and across two groups of protagonists who presented to the Tribunal: (1) three Mayan women who had been working with the Alliance (whom we refer to as the "Alliance Group")—a Q'eqchi' woman from Alta Verapaz/Izabal, a Kaqchikel woman from Chimaltenango, and a Chuj woman from Huehuetenango; and (2) the four others who testified (whom we refer to as the "External Group")—a K'iche' woman from El Quiché and a Mam woman from Huehuetenango, both members of the widows' organization CONAVIGUA; a ladina from El Quiché who was a member of the guerrillas; and a ladina from the department of Guatemala testifying about her sister's rape, torture, and disappearance. In drawing this distinction, we seek to understand the impact of differing organizational experiences (including the role of intermediaries) in shaping testimonial narratives, as well as to highlight commonalities across the five Mayan women's testimonies, given the central tension of a "community of women" versus a "local or geographically based community" that we are exploring throughout this volume. In the subsequent section, we discuss the dilemmas confronted in planning and carrying out such a public narrative across diverse cultural and linguistic national and transnational communities, including but not limited to the various demands of the multiple spectators. We then examine the social space of the local geographic community in which Mayan women protagonists live, where truth-telling about sexual harm was assumed to have been rarely possible or permissible. We reflect on whether and, if so, how spectators who receive truth-telling processes—the Guatemalan intermediaries and ourselves as researchers included—can or indeed should relate to and make meaning of the pain of others, and we conclude with what this means for future racialized gendered truth-telling processes. Data for this chapter include preparatory workshops conducted in the lead-up to the Tribunal, transcripts from the Tribunal itself (published in 2012 as an edited volume, see Mendia Azkue & Guzmán Orellana, 2012), our own field notes, and follow-up interviews and workshops we conducted with Tribunal participants.

SITUATING RACIALIZED GENDERED
TRUTH-TELLING IN THE WAKE OF ATROCITY

Guatemala's more than five centuries of colonial history is one of racialized dispossession and violence against the country's indigenous majority and the preservation of elite wealth and interests. During the 36-year armed conflict, Mayan women were seen as "the progenitors of future 'guerrillas,' unruly or rebellious Indians" (Velásquez Nimatuj, 2012, p. 125), and mass rapes were often committed preceding massacres in indigenous villages. Although mostly not told in the women's own voices, some stories about the violence perpetrated against Mayan women in Guatemala were related by (mostly male) informants in the reports of the Catholic Church's REMHI project (ODHAG, 1998) and the UN-sponsored CEH (1999), which were both released within three years of the signing of the Peace Accords in 1996. However, while the CEH and REMHI reports noted the violence targeted specifically against women—in particular rape—they underreported and underexamined the scope and scale of gender-based violence (Aguilar & Fulchiron, 2005; Nolin & Shankar, 2000; Patterson-Markowitz, Oglesby, & Marston, 2012).

These Guatemalan truth-telling processes are not unique in this respect. Because women are more likely to have survived armed conflict than men, they have made up the majority of those giving testimony in some of the more than 40 truth commissions set up to document massive violations of human rights in the second half of the 20th century and into the 21st, including in South Africa and Peru (Hayner, 2011). A prevalent understanding among those who design these processes, as well as those who analyze them, has been that women tend not to speak about what happened to themselves, but rather about what happened to their families, their husbands, their sons, and their communities or about the destruction of their homes, crops, and animals (Nolin & Shankar, 2000). Even where sexual violence was raised as an issue, as in the cases of Guatemala, South Africa, and Peru, women tended not to speak about it in the first person (Ross, 2003; Theidon, 2007). Shame—both personal and relating to the family and/or community—seemed to be at least partially responsible for this self-silencing. Spaces therefore needed to be constructed that enabled women to speak; for example, the women's hearings organized by the South African and Peruvian TRCs (Ross, 2003; Theidon, 2007). Moreover, impunity is a dominant feature of many postwar contexts, and indeed, amnesty is often a precondition for the setting up of truth commissions. This was the case in Guatemala, where some perpetrators and beneficiaries of racialized gendered violence continued to live near their victims in rural communities and to occupy high-level positions in political, economic, and social life, contributing to the local community-based silencing of women's stories (Paz y Paz Bailey, 2006).

In their work on South Africa and Peru, respectively, Ross (2003) and Theidon (2007) have challenged this assumption that women do not speak about themselves and their gendered experiences in truth-telling processes. They contend that the issue has more to do with what those who are listening consider to be gendered narratives, which are often reduced to stories of sexualized harm. So if women choose not to speak about sexual harm, the listeners assume they have not spoken about their gendered experiences. These researchers argue that we need to listen better to the stories women do tell. As Theidon (2007, p. 459; emphasis in the original) points out,

> When women talk about the suffering of family members and of their communities; when they recall the long daily walks to the river for water and the hours spent scrounging for bits of kindling; when they tearfully recall their children's gnawing hunger that they tried to calm with water and salt; when they remember with outrage how they were subjected to ethnic insults in the streets of the very cities in which they sought refuge—they *are* talking about themselves and the gendered dimensions of war. And, beyond the list of dangers that engulfed them, they have much to say about the actions they took in the face of those challenges.

Truth-telling processes, in which documentation relies on the personal testimonies of survivors who have been directly or indirectly affected by the violations under consideration, tend to be framed within the liberal language of rights and emphasize the experience of individuated harm, and for women this is most particularly bodily harm. Discourses of suffering and survival also tend to be framed within individuated psychological discourses of trauma (see Hamber & Gallagher, 2015, for a critique of such framings within psychology). These narratives also focus on harm as a particular and dramatic event, rather than as part of the broader structural relations of power or the microprocesses of survival and resistance that shape and inform the construction of the subject within her social context (Kapur, 2002; Ross, 2003; Theidon, 2007). Such rights-based discourse is rooted in the assumption that, as Ross (2003) puts it, "'violation' necessarily produce[s] 'victims'" and that this is a gendered relation (p. 12). Violence produces women victims, the underlying assumptions being that victims are gendered female, that women are all the same, and that, within the individuated framework of rights violations and bodily harm, the harm they experienced was sexual violence. Thus, sexual harm is reified as *the* gendered face of war. As Ross (2003) says with reference to the South African TRC, "Diverse identities, activities, and experiences were obscured through the emphasis on sexual difference and harm. The effect of essentializing suffering and gender in this way is to displace questions of resistance, class, race, age and cultural difference in the making of apartheid's subjects and their re-making in the post-apartheid era. An emphasis on the similarity of women's bodily experience comes at the expense of a historical understanding of the constitution of the subject" (p. 25).

In the Guatemalan context, the historically specific and multifaceted experiences of Mayan women are occluded within such racialized gendered essentialisms. Moreover, this highly individualistic Western rights-based discourse runs contrary to indigenous customary law, which, despite its heterogeneity as practiced in local communities, situates responses to violence against women within the Mayan cosmovision; that is, within processes that call for the reestablishment of community order or harmony and the maintenance of the stability and well-being of the collectivity, which includes not only human beings but also the wider natural environment and deities (Grupo de Mujeres Mayas Kaqla, 2004, 2009; Macleod, 2011; Otzoy, 2008). Context, culture, language, and historical practices are deeply implicated in the structures that give rise to sexual violence against women and are requisite components in truth- and justice-seeking processes (Hessbruegge & Ochoa, 2004).

It would seem that there is a tension within institutionalized truth-telling processes between, on the one hand, an occlusion of the cultural, historical, and structural gendered dimensions of violence and, on the other, the hypervisibility given to experiences of sexual violence. The seeming duality of occlusion and hypervisibility contributes to a continued monolithic representation of women, in particular racialized women, as victims (Kapur, 2002). As argued in the introduction to this book, the increasing focus on sexual harm within truth-telling processes is mirrored in other transitional justice mechanisms, in part due to efforts by feminist activists to raise awareness about sexual violence as a weapon of war and to end gross violations of women's rights, redress injustice, and repair harm.

In the absence of access to formal judicial or institutionalized truth-telling mechanisms, or in response to their perceived weaknesses, NGOs, women's groups, and indigenous activists have also been involved in a range of local, national, and international forums or popular tribunals that often mirror formal processes; these activists have accompanied survivors in telling their stories and seeking justice. Some trace the first of these popular tribunals to the 1966 International War Crimes Tribunal on the Vietnam War organized by Bertrand Russell (Terrell, 2005). In 1979, the Lelio Basso International Foundation for the Rights and Liberation of Peoples founded the Permanent Peoples' Tribunal, which continues to organize hearings on a range of conflicts. One of the first public testimonies on the massacres in Guatemala during the 1980s was before the Permanent Peoples' Tribunal on Guatemala in 1983 in Spain (Jonas, McCaughan, & Sutherland, 1984), although it did not focus on the gendered nature of these violations. Over the past 20 years, the number of popular tribunals with a particular gender and/or feminist perspective has been steadily growing. El Taller International (1995) supports World Courts of Women organized by NGOs in Africa, Asia, the Arab world, the Mediterranean region, and Latin America, which provide spaces where women can tell their stories about specific violations, as well as about the interlocking structural oppressions due to "race," gender, sexuality, and social class that sustain and generate gender violence and other violations of women's rights. Women in national and international leadership positions frequently serve as judges and advocates in these courts, rendering judgments on the basis of the testimonies presented and urging states to launch legally binding initiatives to reduce or end women's oppression.

The tribunal that most directly inspired the Guatemalan Tribunal of Conscience was the Women's International War Crimes Tribunal on Japan's Military Sexual Slavery, held in Tokyo on December 8–12, 2000, with a final judgment rendered in The Hague a year later. The Tokyo Tribunal was established to adjudicate Imperial Japan's use during the Asia-Pacific War of the so-called comfort station system between 1932 and 1945 that affected between 200,000 and 400,000 women and girls throughout the territories occupied by Japan; its aims were also to bring those responsible to justice and to end the ongoing cycle of impunity for wartime sexual violence against women (Qiu, Zhiliang, & Lifei, 2013; Yokiaki, 2002). In its preliminary judgment, the Tribunal found Emperor Hirohito guilty and Japan responsible for crimes of rape and sexual slavery that it deemed "crimes against humanity" (Sakamoto, 2001). The idea for the Guatemalan Tribunal of Conscience originated in part because one of the founders of the Consortium, Yolanda Aguilar, had participated in the Tokyo Tribunal. Moreover, one of the activists responsible for the Tokyo Tribunal, Shihoko Niikawa, joined the panel of judges in the Guatemalan Tribunal of Conscience. Aguilar also proposed the idea for the Tribunal of Conscience for Women's Human Rights, held in Guatemala in December 1998 and organized by a number of Guatemalan women's and human rights organizations, academics, and other civil society groups (González, 2011). This Tribunal highlighted, among other issues, sexual violence committed against women during the armed conflict, as well as state repression and violence against indigenous peoples (González, 2011).

Each of these popular tribunals is structured similarly to more formal international or state-sponsored bodies. Testimonies are given publicly, legal advocates ask questions, and judgments are rendered. Although the judgments are not legally binding, they create a public record of the past and, in some cases, opportunities for survivors to confront, albeit in tightly controlled environments, the perpetrators who appear and "acknowledge guilt." In some contexts, due to either the large number of perpetrators or the diverse cultural practices within the country, local communities have sought other justice mechanisms, ones that incorporate cultural practices from previous generations. The most widely known of these is *gacaca*, a form of local or community justice in Rwanda, where the genocide displaced approximately 1.7 million Hutus and left 400,000 widows, 500,000 orphans, and 130,000 imprisoned on suspicion of committing acts of genocide (Tiemessen, 2004). The UN estimated that between 250,000 and 500,000 Rwandan women were raped during the 1994 genocide (UN Office for the Coordination of Humanitarian Affairs, 2008). Exact figures will never be known, but some estimate that "'almost all' girls and women who survived the genocide were either 'direct victims of rape or other sexual violence, or were profoundly affected by it.' The United Nations Special Rapporteur on Rwanda found that during the genocide, 'rape was the rule and its absence the exception'" (UN Development Fund for Women, 2010, p. 84)

In its precolonial forms, gacaca was used to moderate disputes over land use and rights, cattle, marriage, and damage to property. Rwanda passed a law in 1996 seeking to facilitate reconciliation and restorative justice through the gacaca system in a context where perpetrators and victims lived side by side. Recent scholarship has explored some of the contradictions embedded in processes that interweave local cultural practices and centrally controlled state law. Through in-depth ethnographic observations of three forms of mediation in postgenocide Rwanda, Doughty (2016) identified the possibilities and limits of such grassroots legal practices grounded in local authority and mediation processes, finding that "framing law-based reconciliation in terms of interpersonal relationships . . . tends to ignore the political-economic forces, including deep power imbalances, that drove and continue to drive conflict" (p. 227).

The gacaca system has been even more problematic in delivering justice for women and, more particularly, in cases involving sexual violence. Women have participated in various levels of gacaca mediation, and the government has required that at least 30% of the judges be female, thus ensuring that women had an identity beyond that of victim. Further, the law categorized sexual violence as one of the most serious violations—that is, a category one crime—alongside planning the genocide. Thus, although individual testimonies were taken and evidence collected in communities through gacaca, the prosecution of alleged perpetrators of sexual violence took place in the formal judicial system, which was slower moving and more difficult for survivors to access. The seriousness of sexual violence was recognized, but the local community was cut out of both deliberations and ensuring accountability (UN Development Fund for Women, 2010; see also Tiemessen, 2004).

In Guatemala, following the signing of the Peace Accords, the Mayan rights movement and local indigenous community authorities worked for the "recuperation" and "revitalization" of indigenous customary law as part of efforts to rebuild a community fabric torn apart by war, as well as in response to the continued prevalence of racialized impunity within the formal legal system (Sieder & Macleod, 2009). These efforts have included the opening up of spaces to address violence against Mayan women, specifically the high levels of domestic violence (Sieder & Macleod, 2009). Easier access to local courts, the use of Mayan languages, the naming of a few women as local auxiliary mayors, the establishment of the *Defensoría de la Mujer Indígena* [Office for the Defense of Indigenous Women], and the racism of the formal judicial mechanisms of the Guatemalan state are all contributing to growing numbers of women in search of justice telling their stories through Mayan legal processes (Gómez, 1993; Otzoy, 2008; Sieder & Sierra, 2010). Professional Mayan women have also integrated gender and Mayan identity into their theory and practice, arguing that Mayan principles of complementarity, duality, and equilibrium are resources that can promote greater gender equity (Grupo de Mujeres Mayas Kaqla, 2004, 2009). However, despite these advances, the heterogeneity of local practices and long-standing patriarchal structures limit Mayan women's access to justice mechanisms, which has costly implications for women, their families, and their communities (Carey & Torres, 2010; Sieder & Sierra, 2010). As significantly, many of these initiatives have not tended to address the racialized gendered violence of the war, a key impetus for the Tribunal and the justice-seeking process it was intended to stimulate.

THE PUBLIC PERFORMANCE OF SEXUAL HARM

> I am the spokesperson for many who are asking to be heard, so that what happened is known and investigated. The state in particular must assume this responsibility, because the army came and marked our bodies forever, our lives were marked; they tortured us.
> —Q'eqchi' protagonist, Tribunal of Conscience, March 5, 2010

The 54 Mayan women protagonists who have been working since 2003 with UNAMG and ECAP, as well as other sets of intermediaries discussed in the introduction to this volume and in further detail in chapter 5, claim definitively that the state is responsible for the historical and structural destruction of their communities and that they want justice. They also demand social recognition and validation that these violations happened to them and that it was not their fault. In response to these demands, UNAMG, ECAP, and MTM, together with CONAVIGUA and *La Cuerda*, organized and facilitated the Tribunal of Conscience in March 2010. The organizers spent the year leading up to the Tribunal preparing the group of women protagonists for the process, as well as conducting a sensitization campaign, *Ni Olvido Ni Silencio* [Neither Forgetting nor Silence], with key sectors of Guatemalan civil society and with the general public.

As with other Peoples' Tribunals, the Guatemalan Tribunal of Conscience was structured as a mock trial, with prosecutors, judges, protagonists' testimonies, and expert witness reports. The judges were women survivors and activists, including Juana Méndez Rodríguez from Guatemala, Gladys Canales from Peru, Teddy Atim from Uganda, and Shihoko Niikawa from Japan. The proceedings were presided over by Lucía Morán, executive director of MTM at that time, with two prominent lawyers—María Eugenia Solís, who is Guatemalan, and Juana Balmaseda Ripero, who is Spanish—as the prosecutors. We were two of the approximately fifty invited national and international honorary witnesses.

Members of the Guatemalan Supreme Court and lawyers from the Public Prosecutor's Office, as well as the head of the *Comisión Internacional contra la Impunidad en Guatemala* [International Commission against Impunity in Guatemala]
(CICIG), were in the audience. For the first time ever in Guatemala, simultaneous interpretation was provided between Spanish and four Mayan languages
(Kaqchikel, Q'eqchi', Chuj, and Ixil); also provided was the less-novel interpretation between Spanish and English.

The first day of the Tribunal was dedicated to hearing protagonists' testimonies, while the second day focused on expert witness reports that aimed to provide the structural context for the use of sexual violence as a weapon of war and
to put forth the kind of evidence that could be used in a legal case. One of the
obstacles to successful legal action is the lack of physical evidence of sexual harm,
given that these crimes took place more than 30 years ago. Thus the expert witness reports aimed to provide other forms of proof, including those that could
be used in subsequent legal proceedings to demonstrate the systematic use of sexual violence during the armed conflict; for example, psychological reports and
forensic evidence of the perpetration of massacres gathered from exhumations of
mass graves collected by Guatemala's teams of forensic anthropologists. In contrast to proceedings in a trial, the expert witnesses were not interrogated about
their expertise or their findings. They testified to the historic racialized gendered
violence against Mayan women and to the continuities of these assaults against
them during the armed conflict. The judges read a symbolic sentence as a final
declaration of the Tribunal's proceedings, and all honorary witnesses signed a
written copy of this document (Mendia Azkue & Guzmán Orellana, 2012). The
Tribunal was live-streamed on MTM's website and broadcast by the Feminist
International Radio Endeavor (FIRE). UNAMG's radio station was present at
the event, with its broadcasters conducting live interviews with Tribunal participants throughout the two days.

On the first day, five Mayan women testified about their experiences of sexual
violence at the hands of the army in rural areas of Guatemala: they were the
Chuj, Q'eqchi', and Kaqchikel protagonists from the Huehuetenango, Alta Verapaz/
Izabal, and Chimaltenango regions, respectively, who were working with the
Alliance, and the K'iche' and Mam protagonists, from El Quiché and Huehuetenango, respectively, who were members of CONAVIGUA. These testimonies
were linear accounts of what occurred before, during, and after the experience of
sexual violence and described its impact on family and community, including
the loss of land, livestock, and homes. The Mayan protagonists were followed by
two ladina testifiers who spoke in Spanish about wartime violence against activists:
one talked about the experiences of violence that contributed to her decision to
join the guerrillas, while the other gave testimony about the disappearance of her
sister. This latter testimony differed from the others: it was a third-person testimony and was quite animated, in contrast to the other testimonies that seemed

more rehearsed. As a member of our research team described in her field notes, "I couldn't help but notice the stark difference in tone between the previous testimonies and this one. This one was clearly more politicized and performed in a very different manner: even the shadow of the woman who was speaking, who spoke standing up, added to this 'performance' as we could see her move behind the curtain as her voice rose and fell." The final testimony given on the first day was a report on women survivors' accounts of their rape by police, military, and private security forces during evictions of Mayan communities from their land and homes by a Canadian mining company in El Estor, Izabal, in January 2007 (see Russell, 2010 for a description of this case). This report aimed to show the continuity of sexual violence from the past to the present, highlighting global connections as well as structures of ongoing militarization, colonial economic power, and impunity in Guatemala.

We inductively content-coded the first seven testimonies (Charmaz, 2014). The mining case was not coded both because it discussed present-day violence and it was a report compiled by an organization (Rights Action), as opposed to testimony presented by direct victims or family members to the audience. We were interested in understanding how women constructed their testimonies about their or their relatives' experiences during the armed conflict: what they chose to talk about, how they performed the narrative, and what could be gleaned of the relationship between the testimony and the space in which it was presented—in this case, a public Tribunal of Conscience. In the next several sections, we discuss the identified thematic areas, assessing the similarities and differences within each theme across all of the testimonies, and between the testimonies of the three Mayan women from the Alliance Group and the four Mayan and ladina women from the External Group. We show the impact and influence of the accompaniment work by intermediaries that focused on the issue of sexual violence in shaping the testimonies presented to the Tribunal and indeed Mayan women's protagonism. Our analysis of the data also allows us to tease out some commonalities across the five Mayan women protagonists' testimonies that highlight the particularities of racialized gendered violence in rural indigenous communities in Guatemala during the war.

Change: Before, during, and after la Violencia

All five Mayan protagonists talked in similar ways about life before the war, describing it as tranquil and happy; despite their extreme poverty, they were able to live a "normal" life. The Q'eqchi' protagonist described the dreams she and her husband had for their children:

> I want to share with you that before, at the beginning, at 15 years old I married and started a life with a working man who gave everything to fight for a dream for his children. And we started to work together for this, to grow [crops], to work the

earth and to have more dignified land for the two of us, for our children. . . . As I was telling you, at the beginning we started our life together, with dreams for our children, working mother earth. And in this way we started to produce beans, corn; we started to have the fruits of our struggle together. Thinking about the dream to give our children education and a more just life. And I repeat, at the beginning, everything was a more normal life.

This sense of normality, and of being able to plan for a future for one's children, was contrasted to the loss of independence and autonomy once they came under military control during the war. Mayan protagonists described their communities being invaded by the army who built camps and controlled their lives. As the Kaqchikel protagonist from Chimaltenango put it, "When the war arrived, from then on, we didn't live so tranquilly. All the time, during the day, at night, we were afraid to see what day or at what time they were going to kill us. Why? Because the army arrived in the communities in which we lived." And the Q'eqchi' protagonist testified, "In Guatemala, they have committed grave violations of our human rights; they lost respect for life, respect for our integrity, which is the most sacred part of ourselves." This description differed from many of the other accounts of change that the violence brought, because it focused on the loss of something less material, which she described as "sacred." The reference to "that most sacred part of ourselves" suggests that the speaker was inflecting or invoking the Mayan holistic vision that all of life is interconnected and that human dignity, reflected through another's respect, is at the core of human subjectivity: both were attacked repeatedly during the armed conflict (Chirix García, 2003). This same protagonist later emphasized the gendered aspect of this loss: "There was no respect for life, even less for women." Finally, of the two ladina women from the External Group, the former URNG combatant talked about how her life changed completely when the war came and she decided to join the guerrillas.

Violations and Harm Suffered: "No One Can Take This Thorn from My Soul"

In their testimonies, protagonists talked about the violence/violations to which they and their family and community were subjected. All seven referred to sexual violence—six as a personal experience, with the seventh referring to her sister's experiences. They also described experiences of torture and, for some, the torture and/or forced disappearance of loved ones including husbands and siblings. Violence against children was also noted. All five of the Mayan women emphasized the innocence of those whose rights were violated—either of themselves as women, of their families, or of the community/indigenous people more broadly: they "didn't cause it" or "look for it." As the Mam protagonist from the External Group stated, "It wasn't because of anything else, it was because of the conflict that was occurring; it wasn't the fault of the [indigenous] peoples, it was the fault of the governments, which intended to spread this conflict to all of Guatemala, because this wasn't just happening in one department, but in all the departments."

The two ladinas' testimonies provided the most detailed descriptions of experiences of sexual violence. We learned from the organizers that one of these women, the former URNG combatant, was talking about her experience for the first time; unlike the other witnesses, she made a point of stating her name to the audience, an issue we come back to later in the chapter. The Q'eqchi', Chuj, K'iche', and Mam protagonists also emphasized the continuation of violence into the present, including the rape and assassinations of poor and indigenous women that have come to be defined as feminicide (Fregoso & Bejarano, 2010; Sanford, 2008).[2]

All the testimonies described the nature of the harm suffered as a consequence of the violence. All five of the Mayan women made repeated references to their pain and suffering, "putting up with so much pain in the heart, suffering in silence," which continued into the present: "I know that this pain will never ever be forgotten; it will never ever leave us." As the K'iche' protagonist from the External Group put it, "I also want to say: who can repair this harm in my heart? We know that no one can take this thorn from my soul. Because I have so much pain in my soul. No one can repair this harm." It is important to note here the reference to pain in the testifier's active voice. At the time of giving her testimony, this protagonist, unlike the Alliance testifiers, had not participated in any of the psychosocial processes developed to accompany survivors in a process to address the harm they suffered. The presence of suffering is palpable in her testimony.

The Chuj protagonist talked about her sense of isolation: "I was alone, enclosed, alone in my house, suffering with all this pain." She also referred to her shame and to the stigma she experienced in her community: "They always said to me, 'There goes the soldiers' woman,' and every time I heard that it pained me." The K'iche' protagonist stated that it was the army and the state instead that should feel shame: "The shame is theirs. The shame is not ours, but rather it is the shame of the army as well as the state. Now I want the state to be ashamed for what it has done." The ladina protagonist who testified about her sister referred to a productive quality to pain and suffering: how it motivated her to work for justice. She said, "It's good that pain exists, that despair exists, because this commits us; these feelings make us responsible for speaking out and contributing to there being justice in Guatemala." Testifiers' words thus revealed a range of emotional experiences: pain was articulated by an indirect victim of harm who had explored and voiced its productive possibilities, while direct victims spoke of the wound that would not heal or the thorn that cannot be removed from their hearts or souls.

There were also references in two of the External Group testimonies to how pain is gendered: both in terms of women's particular suffering and their collective suffering. As the Mam protagonist put it, "All this hurts us as women, because it is the women who suffered the most during the armed conflict. We were raped by the army, other women were assassinated, so there was a lot of suffering; we suffered during the armed conflict." And as the ladina protagonist testifying about her sister stated, "More than thirty years have passed for women to be able to express our feelings of pain, of despair." Although she was an indirect survivor of sexual violence, of her sister's rape and disappearance, this testifier stood in solidarity with other protagonists, naming "our" collective pain and despair. Our inductive coding allowed us to identify this collective claim against the state, as well as various particularities of social suffering named by direct survivors in the wake of these violations of human rights. Moreover, the varied experiences reported by participants in the Tribunal reflected protagonists' multiple strategies through which they sought to reposition themselves in relation to these violations, speaking back to the "psychosocial trauma" (Martín-Baró, 1994) that both marked them in particular ways and polarized some families.

All three of the Mayan protagonists from the Alliance Group, as well as the Mam protagonist and the former ladina guerrilla member from the External Group, spoke of fear alongside their articulations of pain. The Chuj protagonist stayed quiet after she was raped by soldiers, describing how "every time my husband went to work, I felt a lot of fear there in the house. I was afraid, because I thought that the army would come and rape me; I felt that they would attack me again, and I couldn't speak." The Kaqchikel protagonist commented, "All the time, during the day, at night, we were afraid to see which day and at what time they were going to kill us." She also said, "All these problems passed in our lives, in our bodies, all this *susto*[3] will never ever leave us, all these fears, all this."

The Mam protagonist from the External Group talked about her child born from the multiple rapes by soldiers (an issue that is rarely discussed in Guatemala, either publicly or privately), while several referred to the suffering of their children. Although several of the protagonists lost their husbands during the war, only one person—the Kaqchikel protagonist from the Alliance Group—mentioned the impact of the loss of her husband, both in terms of his labor and in caring for their children. There was little mention of economic hardship and impoverishment in protagonists' descriptions of the harm they suffered caused by these sexual violations, in marked contrast to the prominence of this issue in our own research with protagonists from the Alliance Group, which we discuss throughout this volume. This absence may be due to the Tribunal's overall structure and intent—to demonstrate sexual harm within a quasi-judicial setting—which shaped the form the testimonies took, how they were heard by the audience, and how they held no promise of repair. As such, testimonies were structured to recount the before, during, and after of the event of sexual harm, which perhaps precluded reference to ongoing economic impoverishment as a feature of colonial dispossession. As work with protagonists unfolded after the Tribunal, and our research project accompanied and documented this work, the definition and understanding of sexual harm by intermediaries themselves expanded, as protagonists increasingly emphasized structural harm *as* violence against women and integrated this understanding into conceptions of justice and reparation(s) (see chapters 3 and 4 for detailed discussion of this issue). However, as mentioned, the Kaqchikel protagonist did describe the economic impact of the loss of her husband. It is also notable that she invoked both the individual and collective dimensions of this loss: "We lost our animals, our homes, our food; we didn't have any clothing anymore. At the national level, they massacred us, they burned our homes, they burned our clothing, all that we had, the army arrived at our homes and robbed us, some of us had a few cents, some of us had a few things in our homes, and they took everything." This protagonist was also one of only two (along with the K'iche' protagonist) who mentioned reparation(s) directly, as we discuss later.

Demands

Protagonists put forth a number of demands in their testimonies. All seven testimonies demanded that the state assume responsibility for the violence. As the K'iche' protagonist put it, "Today the state knows that it did us much harm. Why did it do this? And why does it continue to do so?" Protagonists also demanded that they be heard by the state. As the Chuj protagonist said, "To the authorities that are present, I want them to hear me so that they understand the reality that women experienced in the communities." The Mam protagonist hoped "that our voice is heard by the government." The K'iche' protagonist's demand to be heard was more generalized, directed to the audience as a whole: "I want my pain to be known." This demand seemed more politicized, reflecting an activism that extended beyond those present and was perhaps reflective of her participation as a member of CONAVIGUA. The Mayan protagonists accompanied by the Alliance emphasized being heard and not being victimized, reflecting the influence of psychosocial healing discourses in the development of their protagonism. Our inductive analyses of protagonists' testimonies confirmed that they were deeply relational, reflecting a call-and-response form framed differentially vis-à-vis not only their individual experiences and ethnolinguistic communities but also the intermediaries who accompanied them within the organizations in which they participated or through the processes developed specifically to break the silence of sexual violence. The testimonies were the protagonists' story, but no story is unmediated. The feminist PAR accompaniment process within our research provided a set of methodological resources that enabled us to document and analyze this relationality, as well as the co-construction of their narratives and their demands, as is discussed in more detail in chapter 5.

As can be expected given the goals of the Tribunal, for most of the protagonists, justice was a key demand for themselves and for all women who have survived sexual violence. According to the Chuj protagonist, "I am here to ask for justice, justice in the name of all." She continued, "But I am here to ask for justice for those women who could not speak." She asked the state for justice "for all those who lost their lives in the war." The ladina protagonist testifying about her sister stated, "It's everyone's [women and men] commitment to move forward to clarify these violations, so that we can tell our children, our grandchildren, that there is justice in this country, because we opened our mouths to break the silence about impunity in this country." Protagonists urged that the violence of the war never be repeated and that justice be served for crimes in the present. As the Q'eqchi' protagonist put it, "What motivates me to express to you what I have lived through, is that it be used to visibilize [those who are guilty], so that there be a kind of punishment for the class of people who harm other human beings, because this keeps happening, with the assassinations of women." And as the Chuj protagonist said, "I don't want to go through what I went through during the war. No more. That's why I'm here. I don't want other children to go through what I went through. No more; that's why I'm asking the state for justice." The demand for justice was linked to the demand for the nonrepetition of harm and for peace. As the same Chuj protagonist from Huehuetenango put it, "I want peace for my municipality, for my department, and for the whole country. So that as Guatemalans, we can live in peace, because so much death, so many problems, and what is the state doing about it?"

Only the Kaqchikel and K'iche' protagonists explicitly referenced reparation(s), mostly to point out the failure of the state's reparations program. The K'iche' protagonist, who had emphasized that the thorn in her soul cannot be repaired, added, "With respect to reparations, I am asking that they see us, that they treat us with dignity, that they attend to the suffering that we experienced during the 1980s." She referenced their suffering "as women and as human beings," saying, "Perhaps the Reparations Program or even the government said in their report, perhaps saying that they are accomplishing all they are doing, but lamentably, at the national level they are not fulfilling [their mandate]. We are displaced. Well, now they are giving some projects, but there are many requirements. And lamentably, we are the ones who suffered, so, hopefully we will be attended to, we will be helped, that all these projects repair everything that we lost during those times." This same protagonist emphasized that money alone does not repair the harm: "Even if they gave us this [the money], it is not worth it. I say that my husband does not have a cost, money cannot replace him not being alive." We learned that this woman from Chimaltenango had not received any money from the PNR, the official reason being that she had received compensation for her husband being a member of the PAC (the relationship between payments to former PAC members and the PNR is discussed further in chapter 4).

All five Mayan protagonists' demands included that their rights as women—and specifically as indigenous women—be respected, and they called for an end to discrimination against them, which they linked to the violence of the war. As the

K'iche' protagonist put it, "Despite being a woman who has suffered, I know that I have my rights, I work to demand my rights. I am here today asking for the women who stayed behind, demand[ing] rights for us as women." As the Chuj protagonist said,

> I am only saying, only the men have work. They don't want to give work to women. Why? They only want to give work to men, and not to the poor women. There are women who want to be in the COCODES,[4] there are women who want to be mayors, there are women who want to work, to do the work men do. Not just men want to work; women do too. Why are women's rights not being met? Can only men speak and not women? That is why we want to speak here today; we are going to tell all here, so that women are given their rights, so that women have work.

It is interesting to note that this Chuj protagonist from Huehuetenango, who had been speaking through a translator to that point, switched to Spanish to make these points about the gendered nature of rights and work. Perhaps because she was drawing attention to the patriarchal nature of both the state and citizenship in terms of assumptions about work and rights, she took on the language of the hegemon to make her point. Regardless of her reasons, this was a notable assertion of protagonism by a bilingual protagonist who switched linguistic codes in order to directly engage with those in her audience representing the power system: the Spanish-speaking Guatemalan and international witnesses to the Tribunal. Departing from her earlier reliance on an interpreter to access the hegemon, she inserted herself directly into the dominant discursive domain of the Tribunal. In other parts of her testimony, she relied on her language of origin, reflecting psychologists' and psychiatrists' research and clinical findings (Woodman, 2011), as well as those of Mayan linguists (García Ixmatá et al., 1993/2017), that suggest that people are more likely to express affect generated from these harms in their native language. In these contexts, participants need to have the opportunity to express themselves in the language that they feel will most fully convey the depth and nuances of their lived experiences (García Ixmatá et al., 1993/2017).

Silence, Voice, and Witnessing

The testimony in Spanish given by the Chuj protagonist highlights the issue of speech and its significance, in particular the relationship among testifier, intermediaries, and the audience. In all the testimonies, protagonists made reference to voice and witnessing. We read these as relatively self-conscious statements or reflections by protagonists to explain their presence in the Tribunal: why they are speaking out, the fact that they are doing so as representatives of a larger group, and the impact that they hope their voice will have. Protagonists all addressed the

Tribunal audience directly in their testimonies. In six of the seven testimonies, protagonists thanked the audience for hearing them. As the K'iche' protagonist said, "I would like to thank everyone present; thank you for listening to me, this was my voice." The Kaqchikel protagonist put it this way: "We wanted to let everyone who is present know, they are hearing all these problems, all the pain that we have in our hearts."

The audience was implicated in the testimonies by being called to listen to and know what was being recounted in the testimonies: they were being called to act as witnesses, with its implication of bearing the responsibility of responding to what they heard, an issue we return to later in the chapter. This call to witnessing and to being heard was the most frequently repeated theme across the testimonies, mentioned 32 times across six of the seven testimonies. The K'iche' protagonist wanted the audience to hear about and know her pain. The Q'eqchi' protagonist said, "I need to tell the people who are visiting, and those who form the Tribunal, so they can hear our truth, so that . . . they know that this was real, that it was not an invention, and also that we did not deserve this." She added, "We need to be believed." Protagonists were calling the audience to make a response, performing the relationships that they recognized as necessary to facilitate truth-telling, justice seeking, and reparation(s).

Protagonists were aware of the different audiences who were present—representatives from the state, the international community, and the Guatemalan public—and addressed them both separately and collectively. Given protagonists' assertion of the state's responsibility for the crimes committed against them, the presence of the state was important: both to hear what happened and to ensure that justice was served. International audience members were given the responsibility of taking what they had heard back to their own countries. As the Kaqchikel protagonist requested, "Hopefully these people who are here from different countries; they will support us; they will do us the great favor of telling [people] in other places what happened in our country."

Six of the testimonies also emphasized the importance of the collective voice, of speaking on behalf of many survivors. The Chuj protagonist said,

> I am here to ask for justice for all the women who could not speak, for all the women who died; I am here so that all should know that many women died in the conflict without being able to speak out. In their name I am here to give my testimony, and before the [state] authorities who are present, I want them to hear me to learn about the realities that women lived through in the communities. So many women were marginalized, so many women suffered, but today it is time.

And the ladina protagonist testifying about her sister said, "Because it wasn't just my sister who was kidnapped and disappeared, there are more than 45,000 disappeared in Guatemala, 250,000 dead, tens of villages razed to the ground, thousands of women raped in the countryside."

The issue of silence is ever present in these testimonies, or perhaps more accurately, the acts of silencing—in killing, torturing, and disappearing people and in threatening survivors—pervade their accounts. As the Chuj protagonist put it, after she was raped by the soldiers, "When he [her husband] came home, I didn't tell him anything, because the army told me that if I went and talked they would kill my whole family; that is why I stayed quiet, putting up with so much pain in my heart. I suffered in silence, this is why I couldn't speak, I couldn't even [tell] my husband or even my mother. . . . I stayed silent." The ladina protagonist who testified about her sister also talked about self-silencing as being part of how her sister was "triply disappeared, because the whole society, we have kept silent, and with our silence we have disappeared our families, our *compañeros*, our martyrs." Protagonists saw breaking the silence as key to justice. As the ladina former URNG combatant said, "I am here to share this with all of you, because only this way can we fight for life and break down the wall of impunity that we have had for so many years in this country. I am calling on everyone to continue struggling to find the justice, truth, and peace we all need." At the same time, protagonists reminded the audience of the pain of speech and the toll it takes, something that those who listen to other people's pain must constantly keep in mind. The Q'eqchi' protagonist made repeated references in her testimony to how the act itself of remembering and recounting stories of harm to the Tribunal audience was painful and of the gap between sufferer and nonsufferer: "In truth, sharing this with you in this moment is painful, it is painful to remember, it affects me. I cannot tell you that I can act normally, because [the experience] left much fear, not only in my heart but also my mind. I am constantly vigilant that something may happen to me." Breaking silence and calling out impunity is not a monolithic experience and process and is not always necessarily transformative or liberatory for those who do so or for those who listen; as such the imperative to "break the silence" is not unconditional. Das reminds us in the chapter epigraph that the power of the historiographer to excavate and hear truth can become a weapon, widening the gulf between protagonist and nonsufferer, between the speaker and those who witness her testimony. Words are the weapons. As Das (2007) reflects on the violence experienced by women during the partition of India, "What 'right words' could have been spoken against the wrong that had been done them" (p. 57)? And in the Guatemalan context, McAllister (2013) also draws attention to how silence can be a strategy of resistance, "as something *withheld*, rather than something that cannot be said, as secrets rather than traumatic ruptures" (p. 106; emphasis in the original). Given the often incommensurability of pain and language, an issue we return to in later chapters, the reliance on words alone is not enough; it cannot reflect the multifaceted dimensions of protagonism and can in fact weaken the dialogue between protagonist and audience, sufferer and nonsufferer.

RECKONING WITH THE TRIBUNAL

In interviews and focus groups that we conducted in the months following the Tribunal with the 54 Mayan women protagonists from the Alliance who were all present as audience members and as testifiers, respondents emphasized the importance of hearing the testimonies of their fellow survivors from other regions of the country: "It wasn't just me. Before, I thought that this had only happened to me, but now I see that it happened in all of Guatemala." The presence of state officials was also important, generating significant expectations for follow-through. One respondent said, "I liked that the government could hear all the testimonies of the women and so that justice could be done." They also questioned the role of the state and whether or when it would fulfill protagonists' demands for reparation(s) and justice: "They haven't captured any of the culprits." Some participants described a visceral relationship to the absent presence of the perpetrator: "We were looking for him in the crowd to see if we could see his face, to see if he would admit it or not." They also remarked on the presence of international representatives, academics such as ourselves, as well as activists and embassy officials, and the witnessing role they played: "People came from other countries, showed solidarity." Others noted the fact that survivors from other countries were present and that sexual violence had occurred in other conflicts, not just in Guatemala. Protagonists repeatedly noted the importance of the judges being survivors and activists who work with survivors.

During the Tribunal, in addition to simultaneous interpretation between Spanish and Kaqchikel, Q'eqchi', Chuj, Ixil, and English, consecutive interpretation was provided to the Mam protagonist behind the curtain and to Achí women in the audience. Those we interviewed appreciated the interpretation: "I liked it because I understood what they were saying." Public speech in Guatemala is frequently incomprehensible to monolingual Mayan women because it takes place in Spanish. Several Tribunal participants also commented on the fact that this was one of the first major public events to address the issue of bidirectional interpretation and translation in multiple indigenous languages and Spanish in any systematic way.

Most of the interpreters were indigenous women *promotoras* [promoters]: local bi- or multilingual community members who worked alongside professional intermediaries and feminist activists to facilitate communication. Many had been working with the protagonists for several years. They had noted in the PAR workshops that we facilitated that concepts such as rape do not exist in some of the Mayan languages, and one of the Q'eqchi' translators in the post-Tribunal interview talked about challenges inherent in the interpretive process. She described translating the concept of rape as "they darkened my soul," because protagonists made statements such as the following: "They left the illness in all of my body and mind"; "It is too much pain that I carry in my soul"; and "Who can repair this damage in my heart?" (Muñoz, 2010, para. 4). Thus concepts that are captured by single, often abstract terms in Spanish or in English are rendered in Mayan languages in phrases or sentences that are frequently more materially grounded. Less clear to us given our limited capacities in any Mayan language were the complexities of moving from one indigenous language to another, particularly among those that do not share any roots (we discuss issues related to translation, interpretation, and language in more depth in subsequent chapters).

The fact that those who testified spoke from behind a curtain drew much attention from the audience. After some audience members questioned whether the women were actually speaking or whether the audience was hearing an audio recording, the organizers placed a spotlight behind the curtain so that the audience could see the women's profiles. The decision to conceal testifiers' identities was made at the last minute by the organizers because some of those who were to testify feared for their safety. However, not all of those testifying felt this way, and one of the ladinas named herself during her testimony. Another made direct reference to the fact that she was hidden, but insisted she was present, giving her testimony firsthand. And when it was noted during the planning process that Mayan women's style of dress would immediately identify the community from which they came, all the participants, including Mayan women protagonists who were members of the audience and not testifying, opted to wear white blouses.

Relatedly, one Tribunal participant argued that the organizers had not chosen "good victims," particularly from a legal standpoint in regard to future court cases: "You need to have good victims for any national or international case; a victim that you can put in front of the camera and who can dare to say what happened. And that's a survivor, someone who can talk about it." This comment suggests that these women who failed to show their faces had not gone through a process of moving from victim to survivor or protagonist. In this sense, public speech is not enough, but needs to be both aurally and visually identifiable to the audience: the listener needs to see the speaker, as well as hear her. Hesford (2011) refers to this notion of "seeing as believing" as "ocular epistemology" (p. 29), a fundamental component of the human rights spectacle and an issue we take up further in chapter 3. As this participant noted, "You cannot call these women who had to be hidden survivors. They have not overcome this situation, and it's not because they cannot, [but] it's because the context is completely unfavorable; work has not been done at the community level." She continued, saying that a survivor "is someone who shows their face to the sun, who can say, 'This happened to me, this is what they did to me, and my community did not support me, they stigmatized me, they were sexist.'" In response to this critique, one of the Tribunal organizers noted, "The women were really ready, and actually many of them wanted to show their faces. I think that many of them were frustrated about not showing their faces. But it's not them who weren't ready, it's the country." Some participants made comparisons to the Tokyo Tribunal discussed earlier in this chapter. As one international honorary witness who participated in both initiatives said, "The concept I have of a Tribunal of Conscience is that victims are front and center. The Japanese Tribunal was so successful because the victims were ready." In the Japanese case, preparation for the Tribunal took many years, so "when the women managed to talk they were ready to show their faces and be protagonists."

The hyperfocus on the issue of being hidden can turn attention away from the content of what women had to say and the multiple forms of resistance they engaged in when confronted by violence. Again this issue relates more to what we as witnesses or listeners choose to hear and see in these processes. Resistance took many everyday forms: the women described in their testimonies how they survived in the aftermath of atrocity (we return in more detail to these multiple forms of resistance and survival in later chapters), as well as the more overt form of resistance detailed by the woman who joined the guerrillas. As one of the Tribunal judges noted in an interview we conducted, this woman's participation in the insurgency was fueled by her "understanding of how the violence on their bodies was not just against them, but [also against] their children, husbands, their communities." This judge heard this testimony as a sign of collective struggle, not individuated abjection. The decision to include this woman's testimony that highlighted her participation in the guerrillas was important, given the tendency of truth-telling processes to emphasize stories of victimization, rather than organized resistance. In the South African context, Ross (2003) notes that women who actively resisted apartheid "seldom gave public testimony" (p. 17). In Guatemala's truth-telling processes, McAllister (2013) draws attention to the "reiteration of *testimonio* [testimony] as therapy" and the related subsuming of revolutionary testimonies where "the story does not end in suffering" but rather continues in the "call to 'go on'" (p. 97).

The lack of direct engagement between the testifiers and the audience was also a major point of discussion for audience members we interviewed. In addition, several participants remarked on the lack of community engagement in the process, focusing on the apparent absence of protagonists' family and community members and thus the seeming disconnection of this process from local struggles, an issue to which we return later. Both the use of the curtain and the court-like proceeding adapted for the Tribunal of Conscience concealed more than just protagonists' identities; they also occluded the dialogical nature of the truth-telling processes. Specifically, despite the testifiers' repeated invocations of their interlocutors, the particularities of the relationships between protagonists and the Tribunal organizers, the indigenous women interpreters, and the psychologists who provided emotional support, as well as the Mayan customary practices that took place in their home communities or outside of the Tribunal space, were not overtly represented: all were only present behind the curtain. The interpreter, for example, sat beside the survivor as she gave testimony, speaking her pain alongside her, translating her narrative into the language of the hegemon, and drawing on their particular ethnolinguistic knowledge system that is situated within a more universal Mayan philosophy of life or cosmovision. The judges left the stage now and then to go behind the curtain. One of the organizers witnessed an encounter between a survivor who had just testified and one of the international judges: "They cried together, and they hugged; I still remember that moment, because, without speaking the same language, being from such different places, even with all this, they hugged one another." This scene exemplifies the dialogical nature of the protagonists' truth-telling, which was mostly occluded by the performance of the Tribunal of Conscience. Because such experiences were hidden from most of the audience members, they were prevented from personally experiencing and witnessing the relational process of truth-building and left to interpret this moment from the multifaceted and veiled positioning of outsider observer of another's pain.

Despite its obscuring the dialogical nature of the truth-telling processes, the Tribunal was an important truth-telling event undertaken within an adversarial political context amid ongoing impunity. Its organizers created a public space for women to tell their stories and to be heard. We cannot underestimate the significance of such a moment for the protagonists, as well as for those who organized and participated in the process and for audience members, including ourselves. Participation in this historic accomplishment generated questions about the relational aspects of truth-telling, including the ways in which the stories were presented and heard and taken up—or not—by the audience. One question concerns the ever-present absence of so many husbands, children, and members of the communities of origin of the Mayan women who testified. A second concerns the delicate balance between the Tribunal's potential contribution to the agency of its protagonists and its, albeit unintentional, contribution to reinforcing the salient selfhood of the audience member through her empathetic listening to the pain of others.

Engagements with Community

As discussed in detail in chapter 1, the Mayan protagonists live within families and local geographically based communities. Indeed, following Mohanty (2003) among many others, their identities as women come into being within the lived experience of these social relations, including the experience of sexual violence, which is deeply structural and relational, rather than only an individuated experience of bodily harm. Moreover, indigenous communities in Guatemala have been structured through and have resisted centuries of colonial violence, including the gendered racialized genocide perpetrated during the armed conflict. As Velásquez Nimatuj (2012) pointed out during her expert witness report to the Tribunal, the sexual violence perpetrated against Mayan women was systematic and collective in nature, rather than sporadic and individual, and was thus aimed at the removal of indigeneity from the Guatemalan social and physical landscape (see also Smith, 2005, for an analysis of these issues within the U.S. settler colonial context). The state's counterinsurgency plan, with its PAC system, implicated "the community" as a perpetrator of atrocity, and this and other seeds of destruction continue to bear fruit today, delimiting Mayan women protagonists' capacity to speak aspects of their truths in relation to others in their communities. The lines between victim and perpetrator were not impenetrable; many people were both, including the young Mayan boys abducted into the army and the rural Mayan men forced into the PAC system, thereby creating the enemy within (Nelson, 2009).

Systematic rape produced what Velásquez Nimatuj (2012) refers to as a kind of "cultural terror" for indigenous women, through which they were dehumanized and delegitimized by those around them, including community members: "After the rapes they were located in the lowest strata of their community. They were not seen as survivors of genocide, as human beings who had lived the brutality of the state's scorched earth policy, but rather as women who, because they were raped, had broken internal community structures, ordering, and power" (p. 122).

As discussed earlier, the Chuj protagonist testified during the Tribunal that her community blamed her for her rape. The stigmatization and ostracism of women survivors, as well as ongoing threats of violence, are reasons offered by many protagonists, whose trauma was formally or publicly "known" in the Tribunal and by some intermediaries, for them not having told their families and/or neighbors about their experiences of sexual violence. One woman described the pain she felt at the cruelty of neighbors and family members: "I feel like I am reliving what happened during the war" (Fulchiron et al., 2009, p. 428). An elderly woman in a Tribunal follow-up group interview told us, in great distress, that her children do not believe what she has told them happened to her: they think she is lying. Speaking her truth is often not enough. Two of the 21 protagonists from Huehuetenango told their partners about the rape and reported in workshops with ECAP that, rather than providing support, the partners responded with "abuse and violent aggression that ended in the rupture of the relationship" (ECAP, 2009, p. 17).

While acknowledging the particular historical and social contexts of sexual harm and the complex community dynamics that frame all memory and truth-telling processes designed to document massive violations of human rights (Falla, 2011; Jelin, 2003, among others), it is also important to signal the tensions that can exist among protagonists themselves. Mayan women are not all the same, and their experiences of community and of sexual violence during the war also differ. Some women were kept for months at a time in military camps and were raped on an ongoing basis. Others were raped by PAC members from their own communities. Some were raped in public, in front of their whole community; others were violated in their homes in front of their children. Some women were raped by members of the guerrillas, a major source of tension among the women, given that some members of the group themselves supported the guerrillas, sometimes contributing to their silencing each other within mutual support groups (Fulchiron et al., 2009; for a discussion of this issue in the Peruvian context, see Bueno-Hansen, 2015; Theidon, 2012).

It is thus important to locate indigenous women's experiences and identity formation within their particular cultural, sociohistorical, and political contexts and, further, to question the perceived inherent safety and healing potential of a "women's community" or "women-only spaces," as well as the stability or homogeneity of the category "woman" (Cornwall, 2003; Mohanty, 2003). Moreover, the contested relationships among as well as within indigenous communities, the military, and the counterinsurgency state influenced how violence was experienced and the meanings made of it (McAllister, 2013). As Merry (2009) observes, "In practice, what constitutes gender violence depends on how these actions [of violence] are made meaningful. Cultural interpretation makes everyday events meaningful" (p. 22).

The differences in protagonists' stories and their responses to these differences are often difficult to hear within an overarching essentialized narrative of sexual harm, which either implicitly assumes a hierarchy of harm or a generalizable or static condition of violence against women. Thus, the tendency is to examine the impact of violence on Mayan women as victims as if these experiences and identities are not mutually constitutive (Mohanty, 2003; Ross, 2003). Within such an essentialist framing, we miss an opportunity to understand and deconstruct the continuities and discontinuities of interlocking gendered and racialized structures that stem from histories of colonial violence, war, and militarization in Guatemala. Importantly, as intermediaries we may homogenize individual experiences, failing to critically interrogate the underlying structural and collective dynamics that constrain each woman's or each community's possibilities for protagonism and healing.

A central dilemma in the organization of the Tribunal is that it took place outside of local Mayan communities, in part because of the ongoing conflictual nature of social relations within some of them, as discussed earlier, and in part because of the central location of the capital, Guatemala City, as the site of performance of judicial powers. At that time, the space of the geographic or local community of origin was adverse to relational processes of truth-telling in the wake of the armed conflict, while at the same time being the social space in which protagonists live their lives. The absence of these communities in the Tribunal also called into question the identity of the multiple listeners who were there and their relationship to the pain of others, as well as the continued dominance of Western liberal normative assumptions that frame transitional justice mechanisms and decenter indigenous agency and experience.

The Pain of Others

As discussed earlier, several Tribunal participants commented that the Mayan protagonists who testified did not seem to be embodying the narratives being constructed. Instead, they seemed to be providing the narrative fodder for broader agendas. Yet it is risky to presume that these women were not agents of their own testimonies or to underestimate the intentionality of their testimonies or the relationships some had with intermediaries who helped them create these testimonies (Nolin & Shankar, 2000). And, as discussed earlier, there are diverse ways in which their testimonies were received. Here we ask whether the Tribunal became a space in which some within the transnational audience from diverse communities, constituencies, and countries could, through their spectatorship, "steal the pain of others" (Razack, 2007). Such theft through the consumption of another's pain is, according to Razack (2007), "the antithesis to genuine outrage" in the face of another's violation (p. 376). The desire for "good victims" who provide particular stories of pain with which we as spectators can empathize—and who show their faces to us—may say more about the audience than about those giving testimony. Listening empathically to stories of pain and victimhood of the racialized feminized other becomes, as Razack (2007) puts it, "the source of moral authority and pleasure, obscuring in the process our own participation in the violence that is done to them" (p. 376). Empathy is a slippery concept and can involve the recentering of the white/imperial subject, rather than the colonized other, at least in part because "the nearer you bring the pain, the more the pain and the subject who experiences it disappears, leaving the witness in its place" (Razack, 2007, p. 377; see also Hartman, 1997; Hesford, 2011).

Was participation as an honorary witness or audience member in the Tribunal of Conscience another opportunity "to become without becoming," to use Ahmed's phrase (as cited in Razack, 2007, p. 379); was it another opportunity to reinforce our sense of moral superiority, our subjectivity within colonial and imperial relations of power? Are we in a position really to hear these stories of pain and suffering? Should we even be allowed to? Razack (2007) reminds us how "remembering and revisiting evil changes us, not always for the best" (p. 389), in particular because of the pleasure associated with the voyeurism of hearing another's pain, what Sontag refers to as "the pleasure of flinching" (as cited in Razack, 2007, p. 387). There is certainly an argument to be made that "some things are better left unsaid," and we share this dilemma. Ross (2003), among others, discusses the relational and structural contexts that shaped such testimonies in South Africa and the ways in which they were received, while Tuck (2009) notes the power of damage-centered research to pathologize indigenous communities. But, as Razack (2007) puts it, "How else to change the world and stop the horrors if not by first bringing them to light?" (p. 389). This was certainly the admirable motivation of the Tribunal's organizers, not to mention of the protagonists themselves. As Razack (2007) points out, however, a shift must occur in the relationship between sufferer and nonsufferer that centers the sufferer's claims to subjectivity, as well as the complexity of her life not only as survivor but also as agent and protagonist. But what stories are we willing to hear? How are we able to listen? Why is it that stories of pain, particularly stories of sexual harm, are the stories we most want to hear from (racialized) women survivors? How does this desire preclude or constrain the many other stories protagonists may want to tell?

These critical reflections are developed within continued omnipresent neocolonial relations of power in contexts such as Guatemala. As Tribunal participants and researchers we cannot resort to binaries to explain and make meaning of relationships of protagonists to those with whom they engage; indeed, as we argue throughout this volume, our conception of protagonism is intensely dialogical and constrained by sociohistorical, political, and psychosocial circulations of power. Just as we cannot assume the homogeneity of protagonists' experiences of violence, we cannot assume a homogeneous standpoint on the part of those who listen to and perhaps also try to engage with these stories of pain and social suffering. There were many ways in which such stories were heard during the Tribunal. Indeed, the organizers told us that they were approached during and after the Tribunal by audience members who were themselves survivors and who had heard for the first time a refraction of their experiences in public space. For them, this was the beginning of a process of finding themselves as survivors of violence in relation to others. Yet thousands if not hundreds of thousands of women who were victimized during the armed conflict have yet to hear these stories and to speak, to be heard, and to be acknowledged.

CONCLUDING REFLECTIONS

We have argued in this chapter that truth-telling about sexual harm is an intensely relational and dialogically fractured process. The Mayan and ladina protagonists who testified before the Tribunal are complexly situated in local, national, and transnational processes, wherein they shuttle between speech-acts and silences accompanied by an ever-widening constituency from civil society, including local, regional, national, and international psychologists, feminist activists, human rights workers, and researchers.

As previously discussed in this volume, in undertaking the informed consent process for our research project, Mayan protagonists made clear to us that a condition of their participation was that they did not want to retell their stories of sexual harm, as they had told them to the Consortium as part of the oral history project (Fulchiron et al., 2009). Despite this, during the eight years of this PAR project, they told these stories again, to the National Reparations Program and, some yet again to the Tribunal of Conscience, and in preparation for, as well as, of course, throughout the Sepur Zarco legal case that we discuss in the next chapter. For some, it is simply a story that is too painful to retell and brings the open and raw wound to the surface. This pain is compounded by the strong resistance to hearing these stories, including from protagonists' own families and communities. Revictimization is an ever-present possibility. We suggest that protagonists' resistance to telling stories of sexual harm over and over again also occurs because those stories do not reflect the whole of their lives. Narratives of sexualized harm can overwhelm and subvert stories of resistance and struggle, of endurance or "survivance"[5] (Vizenor, 1994) within the violence and hardship of everyday life. The process of performing protagonism requires the creation of the possibility of telling more complex and messy stories, including those of resistance, and holding certain silences, rather than replicating the gendered and racialized binaries of a genocidal war and its aftermath. Moreover, the approaches that have been embraced by transnationalists like us may rely too much on Western feminist and individual rights-based mechanisms and fail sufficiently to incorporate indigenous customary practices and/or the Mayan cosmovision or to engage with protagonists at the community level.

As discussed in this chapter, engaging an antiracist feminist lens to engender truth-telling is challenging. It brings up questions of how to make visible but not reify or essentialize indigenous women's experiences of racialized violence; how to hear and respond to the pain of others with a politics of accountability, not consumption; how to listen to women's multiplicity of voices and to the silences they choose to keep; how not to "give voice," despite unequal relations of power; and how to center Mayan ways of knowing and being, recognizing ethnolinguistic particularities rather than imposing feminist or human rights discourse, all the while acknowledging that these are mobile processes that are sometimes contradictory and never fully resolved. The truth-telling processes envisioned herein also entail an understanding of the racialized gendered relations of war. Issues of militarized masculinity and "how to work with men" were implicit throughout the Tribunal process and are critical as the work discussed throughout this book moves forward. In chapters 3 and 4, we explore other performances of Mayan women's protagonism within their multiple social worlds and through their engagement in justice and reparation(s)-seeking processes. The following chapter documents and analyzes 15 Q'eqchi' protagonists' experiences of seeking justice through the Western legal system. In collaboration with the Alliance, they presented a collective case of sexual violence as a weapon of war to the Guatemalan courts, based on their experiences of racialized gendered harm at the Sepur Zarco military outpost in the 1980s.

3 · JUDICIALIZING PROTAGONISM

"What Will the Law Say?"

> What will the law say about what happened to us? Will there be justice or
> are things going to stay as they are after all of these years that we've suffered?
> —Q'eqchi' woman testifying in the Sepur Zarco case,
> February 2, 2016

> In the life of a community, justice is neither everything nor nothing...the
> very setting-into-process of public acknowledgment of hurt can allow new
> opportunities to be created for resumption of everyday life.
> —Arthur Kleinman and Veena Das (1997, p. 218)

A strong motivation for Mayan women protagonists' participation in a public truth-telling exercise such as the 2010 Tribunal of Conscience discussed in chapter 2 was to break the silence about sexual violence against women during the armed conflict and to demand justice for harm suffered, including the identification and punishment of the perpetrators. The judicial landscape had shifted in postgenocide Guatemala, with several landmark prosecutions beginning to erode the deep-seated impunity for some crimes related to the war. These include the successful prosecutions in June 2001 and October 2002, respectively, of the perpetrators of the assassination of the architect of the REMHI report, Bishop Juan José Gerardi, in 1998 and of some of the members of the military responsible for the 1990 murder of the anthropologist Myrna Mack, who was researching the situation of internally displaced peoples. The trial in 2013 of former de facto Guatemalan head of state and army general Efraín Ríos Montt and his then-head of intelligence Mauricio Rodríguez Sánchez for genocide and crimes against humanity received international attention: it was the first case of a head of state being prosecuted for these crimes within his own country (Oglesby & Nelson, 2016; OSJI, 2014). Despite the Constitutional Court's vacation of that verdict and the retrial's termination in April 2018 with the death of Ríos Montt (Rodríguez

Sánchez was subsequently retried and acquitted in September 2018), the 2013 trial itself was significant on a number of levels. It was the result of a decade-long struggle by Ixil survivors, who worked with the *Centro para la Acción Legal en Derechos Humanos* [Center for Legal Action in Human Rights] (CALDH) to give their testimonies and build their case, and, together with survivors from other communities and regions targeted during the genocidal violence, formed a victims' group, the *Asociación Justicia y Reconciliación* [Association for Justice and Reconciliation] (AJR). It also mobilized a cross section of the previously fragmented Guatemalan civil society in support of the Ixil community, building important alliances and relationships of mutual support and common cause in the struggle for justice following the atrocities committed during the war. Despite a concerted campaign waged by the powerful sectors in Guatemala—the wealthy elites and the military—to claim that there was no genocide, elements of urban organized civil society were able to come together with rural indigenous communities to collectively assert that genocide had indeed occurred.[1] Moreover the international press attention to these processes was accompanied by increased media coverage within Guatemala, educating a new generation about the armed conflict.

In handing down the verdict in the Ríos Montt trial on May 10, 2013, Judge Yassmín Barrios highlighted the perpetration of sexual violence against women as an integral component of the attempt to destroy the Ixil as an ethnic group and thus as evidence of genocide. The court had heard extensive testimony from women survivors of sexual violence,[2] and the prosecution also drew on the international jurisprudence on sexual violence as a weapon of war to make its case.[3] The sentence highlighted "the pain and suffering that is still experienced by many of the women" (OSJI, 2014, p. 14). In its reparations ruling a few days later, the court stipulated that the Guatemalan state should issue a separate apology to Ixil women. As already mentioned, there was significant civil society mobilization in support of the case, including from members of the Alliance working with the 54 Mayan women protagonists participating in our research. The emphasis on sexual violence within the Ríos Montt trial came about partly as a result of these intersectoral forms of engagement and the involvement of international organizations such as *Consejería en Proyectos* [Project Counseling Service] (PCS) that provided concerted support and accompaniment to the struggle for gender justice in Guatemala, as well as regionally in Latin America (Cabrera Pérez-Armiñan & Lykes, 2007; Crosby, 2009). The work of former attorney general Claudia Paz y Paz Bailey was also instrumental in bringing the Ríos Montt case to trial and in preparing for the Sepur Zarco case.

The Sepur Zarco case was the direct result of the work of the Alliance with the 54 Mayan women protagonists, which began in 2009 with the decision to organize the Tribunal of Conscience. As previously discussed, the Tribunal was created to lay the groundwork for a legal case by identifying potential plaintiffs for a collective case of sexual violence as a weapon of war, preparing them to give testimony, and mobilizing the general public and members of state and civil society organizations to lend their support by increasing their awareness and inviting their solidarity. The Alliance worked closely with the 54 Mayan protagonists in preparatory workshops in Chimaltenango, Huehuetenango, and Alta Verapaz/Izabal in the year leading up to the Tribunal and in months of follow-up workshops after it: these processes contributed to 15 Q'eqchi' women from the community of Sepur Zarco in the Polochic Valley deciding to seek justice through legal means. The other 39 Q'eqchi', Mam, Chuj, Poptí, and Kaqchikel protagonists were less willing to participate in a legal case and in the end decided not to do so. As importantly, the Alliance determined that the experiences of these 15 Q'eqchi' women were more similar and therefore more conducive to a potentially successful court case, in that they had all been confined at the Sepur Zarco military outpost for months at a time over a six-year period following the torture, disappearances, and murders of their husbands. The experiences of the other protagonists were more varied, both in terms of where and when the violations occurred and who the perpetrators were. A case of sexual slavery linked to the Sepur Zarco outpost seemed to be the most winnable, which was important considering it was the first of its kind to be prosecuted in the Guatemalan courts. The decision to move forward with this particular case was made through a series of engagements between intermediaries and protagonists, within the context of the shifting judicial landscape in Guatemala, evolving international law, and limited international funding available for ongoing work in Guatemala on these issues.

This chapter examines the significance of the Sepur Zarco case as part of Mayan women's struggles for redress. We draw out the implications of what Engle (2015) identifies as an increasing "turn to criminal law" within human rights regimes and, for our purposes, within feminist struggles for gender justice, which Jaleel (2013) also refers to as a "carceral feminist paradigm" (p. 117). Retributive justice is a fundamental (but not exclusive) component of struggles for redress through which perpetrators can be held responsible for their crimes, as protagonists themselves have emphasized and demanded. Without achieving justice through legal prosecutions, state-sponsored reparations are often perceived as an attempt to buy victims off. The space of the courtroom also allows for public acknowledgment and validation of harm suffered, and in some cases, giving testimony can be therapeutic (Henry, 2009). However, the reification of sexual harm within the Western legal regime—through the constant retelling of individuated event-based stories of victimization, the definition of the narratological approach itself, and the reliance on spectacles of suffering (Clarke, 2009; Hesford, 2011)—can erode protagonists' capacity to define and shape their own narratives and consequently their own futures. The identity of "the raped woman" presents a very narrow set of possibilities and may also lead to increased stigmatization, ostracism, and exclusion. The experience of giving testimony can also be retraumatizing, both because the need to repeat horrors necessitates reliving them and an adversarial context allows for hostile cross-examination (Henry, 2009; Mertus, 2004).

The turn to the law—and to the Western legal system—is also problematic when the state itself is the main perpetrator of harm suffered and this harm and its perpetration are historical, colonial, and structural in nature. Many of the protagonists in our research located their experience of gendered harm within centuries of colonial racialized dispossession, and their demands were for structural transformation. However, some Q'eqchi' communities have resisted Western law, turning instead toward Mayan spiritualism and customary legal processes as alternatives (Viaene, 2010a); as such, the experience of the Sepur Zarco case is a specific, not universal, experience of Q'eqchi' protagonism. Moreover, holding one or two individual perpetrators to account would seem to be a very meager response to injustice within such a context, even when, as in the case of Ríos Montt, they held architectural responsibilities for these crimes. This approach to holding individual perpetrators to account for mass violations of human rights is, as Clarke (2009) has argued, a key component of the current "global rule of law movement" (p. 4) and can in fact have the effect of "sublimating root causes of violence" (p. 3; see also Clarke & Goodale, 2010). The Ríos Montt and Sepur Zarco cases are very much part of, and have been shaped and informed by, this global rule of law movement, as well as by international feminist legal activism on rape as a weapon of war and genocide (Copelon, 2003; Halley, 2005; MacKinnon, 2006); as such we unpack this turn to the law as a phenomenon through which transnational relations of power, mediated by intermediaries, circulate and influence the content of justice itself.

We begin the chapter by tracing some of the factors that have shaped Mayan women's engagement with justice paradigms in Guatemala, from the formal legal system with its Western underpinnings of individualism and assumptions of "modernity" that were shaped by Liberal rule in the late nineteenth century, to Mayan customary law, fragmented and transformed by colonization, dispossession, and armed conflict. We draw on Carey's (2013) work to foreground the historical participation of indigenous women in the criminal justice system in Guatemala, which serves as an important reminder that Mayan women have always been protagonists, as well as victims, in their relationships to the Guatemalan state and their fellow citizens. Their participation allows us to erase the victim–protagonist binary and to extract the everydayness of justice seeking from its more spectacularized dimensions by seeing the courtroom as a public space through which the multidimensionality of social relations of power is enacted on an ongoing basis, even during periods of repression and violence. We then discuss the Sepur Zarco case in detail. We examine three themes that emerged from our analysis of the trial: (1) how spectacles of suffering were manifested but also contested throughout the trial; (2) protagonists' engagements with justice as mediated and the liminality of justice "in-translation"; and (3) Q'eqchi' men's embodied testimonies of racialized gendered harm that decenter polarized constructions of gender in relation to experiences of harm and of the victim–perpetrator binary. We examine the aftermath of the trial, particularly the reparations ruling and its implementation, which were key state responses to protagonists' insistence that the transitional justice paradigm address structural harm. We conclude with reflections on the impact of the trial on the 14 living Q'eqchi' protagonists who have repositioned themselves within the community of Sepur Zarco itself, as well as the preeminence and significance of a discourse of "violence against women," rooted in international conceptions of gender justice, that emerged from the trial.

MAYAN WOMEN'S ENGAGEMENTS WITH JUSTICE ACROSS TIME AND CONTEXT

Despite its exclusionary nature, Mayan women have engaged with the formal judicial system in Guatemala. Through his extensive analysis of court transcripts and legal archives, as well as interviews with Mayan elders, Carey (2013) situates the particularities of Mayan women's relationship to the Guatemalan judicial system and their assertion of protagonism within historical context. His analysis focuses on the experiences of Kaqchikel women in Patzicía and San Martín Jilotepeque, two municipalities in Chimaltenango, during the first half of the 20th century, which was dominated by the repressive dictatorial regimes of Manuel Estrada Cabrera (1898–1920) and General Jorge Ubico (1931–1944). In those years, although the judicial system was discriminatory toward Mayan women due to their racialized, classed, and gendered positionings, it was not universally exclusionary. As Carey (2013) states, "Because it was one of the few institutions that held ladinos, elites and men accountable, indigenous women used a legal system that often restricted their rights as a mechanism for gaining leverage against their opponents and advancing their positions within their families, communities and nation. Their litigation demonstrates how constraints could be used for opportunities" (p. 4).

In using an intersectional analysis to examine the racialized, classed, and gendered landscape of the judicial system in early 20th-century Guatemala, Carey (2013) highlights the influence of the Liberal period in the latter part of the 19th century, during which attempts to develop Guatemala as "modern" included espousing "the rule of law and statebuilding as the keys to social order and material progress" (p. 5). Patriarchal gender norms were instilled through the redevelopment of criminal and civil codes: "As evidenced by civil codes addressing marriage, children, and parenthood and criminal codes concerning child abandonment, abortion, and infanticide, family preservation was paramount for Liberal national builders. In contrast to their Conservative predecessors who leaned on the Catholic Church to help preserve social order, Liberals envisioned individual families controlled by powerful patriarchs as the cornerstone of their new societies. In short, the male-headed household was foundational to state building" (p. 5). At the same time, the Maya were denied access to citizenship altogether: "Dependent on their labor for the agricultural economy, Liberals were in no hurry to turn *indios* into citizens, particularly after 1877, when, along with forced-labor laws, the Liberal assault began prejudicing indigenous livelihoods" (p. 5). However, this period of liberalism and the establishment of the primacy of the rule of law as key to state governance also presented opportunities for indigenous peoples, who used this discourse of individual rights to present "new demands for citizenship and genuine legal equality that reverberated into the twentieth century, as *indígenas* who contested exclusionary definitions of citizenship and claimed the nation as their own demonstrate" (p. 5).

Using a Gramscian approach to thinking about power, Carey (2013) demonstrates how the Guatemalan state, even during periods of extreme repression such as the period of the first half of the 20th century, continued to draw on the 19th-century liberal assumptions of modernity and progress and sought legitimacy with its citizens through participatory mechanisms such as the judicial system. While this was part of the process of establishing the state's hegemony, its power was not totalizing. Mayan women used their participation in the system to advocate on their own behalf and further their own interests. As Carey (2013, p. 28) argues in his analysis of Mayan women bootleggers,

> Although poor *indígenas* and *ladinos* who used the legal system provide one example of the state's ability to peacefully reproduce its legitimacy, their litigation was seldom an unqualified endorsement of the state. Even under its gaze, indigenous litigants pointed to the need to consider poverty and other social injustices when defining crimes. In their court testimonies, poor, indigenous bootleggers pointed out that they had little choice but to produce and sell moonshine to survive. While intellectuals and state agents asserted that *indígenas'* backwardness and culture explained their failures, indigenous litigants emphasized their diligence and adaptability to highlight capitalist modernization's shortcomings.

Carey shows how Mayan women were able to use the court system to bypass the patriarchal restrictions of Mayan customary law practices, which despite their emphasis on consensus building and community harmony often excluded them. His analysis is not, however, an idealistic portrayal of Mayan women's participation in the legal system, the dangers of which Sieder and Macleod (2009) have highlighted as reproducing colonial binaries of power that emphasize the liberated modernity of the colonial system in contrast to the essential patriarchy of the colonized. Indeed, ladinas were restricted by ladino patriarchal norms from participating in the public space, with men often representing them instead. Yet Carey (2013) points to the kinds of pragmatic decisions some Mayan women made to put forth their demands within an existing legal system to which they had some access. He shows the limitations of the courtroom space in terms of what Mayan women could bring forward: "Much criminal behavior remained beyond the view of the legal system; rapes went unreported, thefts were hidden, domestic violence was obscured" (p. 17). And Mayan women's protagonism was always circumscribed by mostly ladino intermediaries who managed the courtroom space and system: "When women spoke for themselves as litigants or petitioners, their voices were mediated through male notaries, scribes, and often translators" (p. 17). However, such mediation and translation—which became the archival record of "what happened"—did not preclude the intentionality of Mayan women's actions in bringing their complaints to the legal system: "Even though scribes and court officers were the final arbiters of what survived in the record, we should not underestimate the ability of subordinates to inject their opinions or perspectives" (p. 18).

Carey's (2013) work provides us with a historical understanding of how some Mayan women used the criminal justice system in Guatemala as part of their everyday engagements with the Guatemalan state. Although such historical excavations contextualize some Mayan women's current recourse to Western law, we cannot assume any kind of linear causality between past and present judicial participation. Regional specificities of each Mayan group's approaches to justice, as well as within-group differences and the particularities of their experiences of the armed conflict, must be taken into consideration. We must also be mindful of the differences in the kinds of crimes being prosecuted; Carey himself points to how indigenous women could not bring forward their experiences of gender violence to the courts. Judicial accountability for the atrocities of the war against the Mayan people is of a significantly different scope and scale given the history of racist dispossession and violence against indigenous peoples in Guatemala. There is also a question about how protagonists' demands for justice are articulated, particularly in the Western legal realm, and the role that intermediaries play in formulating this demand today. We must also pay attention to how Mayan communities engage with conceptions of indigenous law that are located within Mayan systems of meaning.

Historically, local Mayan judicial practices were destroyed, reshaped, and/or reformed by colonial dispossession, violence, and contestation. The Agreement on Identity and Rights of Indigenous Peoples, signed in 1995 as part of the Peace Accords, did include proposals to replace "the monist state judicial system . . . [with] a pluralist national justice system" (Hessbruegge & Ochoa, 2004, p. 7) that would take indigenous law into account. However, such reforms have been partial and incomplete at best and have only been implemented in certain local contexts due in large part to the organizing efforts of local Mayan community authorities and activists (see Sieder, 2011; Sieder & Flores, 2011; Sieder & Macleod, 2009, for some examples, including in Santa Cruz del Quiché). It is important to emphasize that there is no one hegemonic or singular system of "Mayan law" or approach to

"Mayan justice," nor is there a singular strategy embraced by Mayan women in their mobilization of these systems. As Hessbruegge and Ochoa (2004) state in their analysis of the emergence of Mayan legal practices following the finalization of the Peace Accords in 1996, "There exists no Mayan system of law that applies to all 21 linguistic communities and the thousands of local communities. Mayan law is as heterogeneous as Mayan culture. Due to its inherent pragmatism and flexibility, its concrete local manifestations are incredibly diverse and shaped by local needs, preferences and history" (p. 9).

Despite this heterogeneity, the pan-Mayan movement that emerged in the post–Peace Accord era was geared toward the revitalization of Mayan cultural practices and the construction of a pan-Mayan identity that would bring together all the ethnolinguistic groups; it included attempts to recuperate indigenous law as a set of principles and practices (Bastos, 2008; Bastos et al., 2007; Hessbruegge & Ochoa, 2004; Sieder, 2011; Sieder & Flores, 2011; Sieder & Macleod, 2009; Warren, 1998). This movement engaged in discussions with the Guatemalan state around the implementation of the Agreement on Identity and Rights of Indigenous People, as well as with the international rights regime on the adoption of the International Labor Organization's Convention 169, which was ratified by most Latin American countries, including Guatemala, in the 1990s, and which represented "the first international treaty to recognize the collective rights of indigenous peoples to implement their own laws" (Sieder & Macleod, 2009, p. 51).

Mayan justice narratives are shaped by the Mayan cosmovision, wherein "the universe, nature and the human community are all part of an integrated order" (Hessbruegge & Ochoa, 2004, p. 10). As such, Mayan law "becomes an expression of that order. Its primary purpose is therefore to maintain communal harmony and equilibrium and not to guarantee the engagement of individual rights and entitlements" (p. 10). Conflict threatens this equilibrium and "eat(s) away the communal fabric if . . . left unresolved" (p. 10). While Mayan criminal processes are underpinned by principles of compensation, conciliation, and learning, local indigenous authorities do not address perpetrators who are from outside the community or are no longer members therein (Hessbruegge & Ochoa, 2004). Thus there are often no judicial practices to which Mayan communities have recourse, generating further insecurity in a postwar period characterized by the continued open wounds of the violence and the unfulfilled promises of the Peace Accords.

Sieder and Macleod (2009) identify three factors that have motivated efforts by Mayan activists and intellectuals to revitalize indigenous law. First, there was a need to rethread the fabric of indigenous communities torn apart by atrocities committed during the war and the resulting community tensions and divisions, particularly in relation to the PACs. Second, most indigenous communities did not have access to the state judicial system, and high levels of insecurity and violence had particular implications for the most impoverished, including women. Finally, Mayan activists were intent on building "ethical codes for coexistence based in their own history and cosmovision" (p. 64). A leading Mayan *defensoría* [popular legal defense organization], the *Defensoría Indígena Wajxaqib' No'j* [Wajxaqib' No'j Indigenous Legal Defense Organization] (DIWN), argues that Mayan juridical practices have endured throughout the centuries of colonization and are situated within the everyday: "One of the main principles of [the Mayan] juridical system is that it was built, woven and developed by our Mayan ancestors in the context of everyday life, [it was] continued and preserved; it has survived across time and space until the present through the oral transmission of historical memory" (cited in Sieder, 2011, p. 48).

In the postwar period, defensorías such as DIWN have played a key role in mediating between Mayan customary law and the formal Western judicial system. Sieder (2011) describes them as an "indigenous social movement," which are "effectively networks of community activists coordinating justice auxiliaries in cantons" (p. 52) throughout the country. Often funded by international organizations as part of their support for the peace process, the defensorías also vernacularize human rights norms and practices (Sieder, 2011). As such, local and transnational circulations of power inform and constrain local Mayan juridical practices.

Sieder and Macleod (2009) discuss the role of Mayan women activists in the revitalization of this pan-Mayan movement. As discussed earlier, they problematize the tendency by ladinx and Western outsiders to dismiss indigenous law as essentially patriarchal and excluding women from participation. As antiracist and indigenous feminist scholars have noted, the reification of non-Western cultures as patriarchal can have the colonial effect of producing Western systems of power as relatively enlightened and progressive in approaches to gender and sexuality and enforcing those systems, including those legal practices, as normative (Arvin et al., 2013; Philipose, 2008; Puar, 2008). Patriarchal practices do structure Mayan communities, as they do most communities in Guatemala and throughout the Global North and South. However, gendered relations of power are shaped and indeed come into being in intersection with other relations of power and are dynamic and ever changing (Crenshaw, 1991; Hill Collins & Bilge, 2016). These communities and the social relations that play out in them both facilitate and constrain women's shaping of their identities (Mohanty, 2003). As such, Sieder and Macleod (2009) critique the liberal universalist approach to gender oppression, in which human rights are individuated, as abstracting culture "from its historical, political and economic production" (p. 55). It is also important to situate such analyses of Mayan culture within colonial relations of power, including within the formal legal system itself, through which indigenous women and men are continuously reproduced as gendered racialized others. However, as Otzoy (2008) has argued, it is also critical not to ignore the marginalization of Mayan women's subjectivities and needs within customary legal practices that prioritize communal harmony and order within the family.

Velásquez Nimatuj (2012) highlights the courage of indigenous women protagonists who are seeking justice within a deeply racist Guatemalan legal system "that does not recognize their maternal languages, that racializes them as culturally inferior, and as beings who do not feel, do not suffer, do not dream" (p. 119). She discusses the systematic and pervasive forms of gendered racist exclusion and othering that indigenous women experience in their everyday lives at the hands of the state institutions that are responsible for defending and protecting their interests. As she argues, "Not taking into consideration the culture of the women who lived these crimes means generalizing the causes and impacts of sexual violence within a cultural vacuum and thus reproducing the structural racism that has characterized the Guatemalan state" (p. 120).

The historical and continuing racism of the Guatemalan state and its judicial system is one main reason why many Mayan communities choose not to turn to Western law as a means to seek justice for harm suffered during the armed conflict. Instead, Mayan communities often choose the diverse practices of the Mayan cosmovision to resolve the ongoing injustices of genocidal violence and to engage perpetrators living in their communities. As noted earlier, Viaene's (2010a) ethnographic work in the postwar period with some Q'eqchi' communities in Alta Verapaz between July 2006 and May 2009 (in Nimlasachal, Nimlaha'kok, and Salacüim in the municipality of Cobán) describes "an absence of a demand for justice for those responsible for atrocities" during the war (p. 289). She speculates on the myriad and intersecting reasons for this absence: ongoing conflicts over land; the continuing presence and influence of perpetrators, including the ex-PAC members; and the lack of external actors or intermediaries, including international and national NGOs and state institutions who have played an active role in formulating demands for prosecutions in other areas of the country. She also identifies the emphasis of the Mayan "normative system" on maintaining a balance between "the sacred, harmony, respect and shame" (p. 293) as a possible explanatory factor, noting that "people know that those responsible bear the guilt of having exceeded their position and of elevating themselves to a place of supreme being by deciding between life and death, and are paying for their faults in this life" (p. 297). In communities where victims and perpetrators live side by side, she argues that "impunity . . . is not the end of accountability, nor truth recovery or reparation. Apparently, the internal logic of the cosmos through an invisible force creates a space in which the perpetrator can reintegrate into communal life and through which victims' pain and suffering are acknowledged" (p. 290). As such, there are many ways in which justice may be realized in the life of the community. Viaene's (2010a) findings contrast with the decision of the 15 Q'eqchi' women to seek justice against individual perpetrators through the courts and with the role that intermediaries, in particular members of the Alliance, played in this decision. Her research also reminds us that despite the focus on these 15, 6 other Q'eqchi' protagonists in the original group of 54 decided not to seek justice through the Guatemalan courts; again, intermediaries played an active role in this decision. To explain the reasons for these diverse responses, we turn to the dialogical protagonist–intermediary relationships, as well as to the intersection of (and sometimes conflict between) local and transnational belief systems about what justice entails (Clarke, 2009). The increasing attention to prosecuting rape as a weapon of war within international jurisprudence, which has been strongly advocated by high-profile feminists and taken up by local feminist ladina intermediaries, including lawyers prosecuting cases such as Sepur Zarco, undoubtedly has been vernacularized and informed local understandings of gender justice.[4] The fact that a good deal of the feminist and rights-based work in support of Mayan women's healing and truth-telling took place outside of protagonists' local communities in dialogic relationality with ladina intermediaries may also have influenced the decision to participate—or not—in a legal case.

In seeking to understand Mayan women's current struggles for justice and what weight to give to the Western legal domain, we are mindful of the multidimensionality of power that circulates within public space, including the courtroom. We cannot position power and its effects in any unitary or binary way, nor underestimate the intentionality with which Mayan women have chosen to participate or not in the Western legal system, nor know in advance what the consequences of participation might be in furthering their future citizenship demands vis-à-vis the Guatemalan state. In addition, participation in such systems can provide possibilities for often unintended and unforeseen forms of protagonism and citizenship formation, rather than simply cooptation and collusion, because these experiences often all exist simultaneously. As Kleinman and Das (1997) remind us, justice is an integral but not exclusive component of broader struggles for redress, and the public acknowledgment of harm suffered can open up spaces to begin to put in place the mechanisms to live "ordinary" everyday lives free from violence. In the following section, we analyze the Sepur Zarco case for evidence of Mayan women's protagonism and its contributions to enhancing alternative possibilities for everyday living.

Q'EQCHI' WOMEN'S STRUGGLE FOR JUSTICE: THE SEPUR ZARCO CASE

> The animals knew what was happening, would warn us, so the birds would sing over the house, but although we saw them and heard them we didn't believe them, but when all the killings were over, we never again heard the birds singing, they also left.
> —Q'eqchi' protagonist, as cited in Velásquez Nimatuj (2016, p. 34)

At the heart of Q'eqchi' women's demands for justice is the question of land. In the early 1980s, at the height of the armed conflict, the military built a series of army bases and outposts to protect and expand the large landholdings of national and transnational elites in what is referred to as the Northern Transversal Strip, a resource-intensive area in the northeastern part of Guatemala rich in minerals, oil extraction, and the production of agrofuels (Méndez, 2012; for further analysis of the war and its impact in this particular region of the country, see Grandia, 2009; Grandin, 2004; Hurtado Paz y Paz, 2008; Sanford, 2009; Solano, 2013). As Méndez (2012) states, during this time "the area was the scene of huge waves of land grabs against the peasant farmer population" (p. 2). In the Sepur Zarco trial, Juan Carlos Peláez, a lawyer and expert witness on the history of the region, traced the conflict over land to the establishment of the estate system in the late 19th century during the Liberal era, when the majority of the land was privatized in less than two decades. The Q'eqchi' practice of working communal lands collectively was transformed into their forced labor on the new estates. This privatization was rooted in the practice of colonial dispossession that saw the Q'eqchi' lose their lands to the Spanish at the time of the conquest. Peláez described how these estates were created in the Liberal period not according to any form of constitutional, civil, or agrarian law and therefore could not be subject to a legal challenge. Peláez confirmed that the names of all the plaintiffs' husbands as well as other disappeared men appeared in the *Instituto Nacional de Transformación Agraria* [National Institute for Agrarian Transformation] (INTA) registry as people who had started land claims processes, which would have required the government to inspect land titles in the region; these inspections then would have contributed to the discovery of the inconsistencies and contradictions regarding land ownership. He also talked about how estate owners assumed they had ownership of Q'eqchi' men and women, as well as the land they occupied, and referenced how the series of evictions and displacements of Q'eqchi' people since the late 19th century were accompanied by sexual violence and slavery or servitude "as a symbol of control or power over the land" (research team field notes, Sepur Zarco trial, February 2016).

In August 1982, several of the peasant farmers who were leaders in the Sepur Zarco community and who were seeking legal title to the lands that they had inhabited for generations were captured by the army and local landowners; they were tortured, assassinated, or disappeared (Méndez, 2012). On the same day of their husbands' capture, women were raped in their homes, often in front of their children. Many were condemned to six-month periods of forcible confinement at the Sepur Zarco military outpost over the following six years. Forced labor there included cooking, cleaning, and laundry; they also were regularly sexually assaulted. Women were often expected to provide their own soap for cleaning and corn for making the tortillas for the soldiers, further undermining their capacity to meet their own and their families' subsistence needs. These abuses that Q'eqchi' women suffered were directly tied to the loss of their husbands; indeed, one plaintiff in the Sepur Zarco trial talked about how widows' "service" at the military outpost was seen as a form of "patrolling"; that is, as a replacement for their (now disappeared) husbands' forced labor in the PACs.

In September 2011, almost 30 years after the abuses occurred, 15 Q'eqchi' women and 4 Q'eqchi' men who had been tortured at the Sepur Zarco outpost and who witnessed sexual violence against women at the camp filed a criminal complaint in the local courts in Puerto Barrios (Méndez & Carrera, 2014). The complaint specified genocide and crimes against humanity based on the women's sexual and domestic enslavement in the Sepur Zarco outpost between 1982 and 1986.[5] Interviews were then conducted with the plaintiffs to establish the facts of the case and identify the perpetrators. Key witnesses were also interviewed, and the Ministry of the Interior ratified the victims' testimonies. The Alliance provided accompaniment to the group of women throughout this process, both in terms of legal and psychosocial support, and continued to build relationships of mutual trust and common cause. As stated by the authors of the one of the first books on the case, *Nuestra mirada está en la justicia: Caso Sepur Zarco* [We are looking toward justice: The Sepur Zarco case] (Alvarado, Navarro, Morán, & Barrios, 2013), "a collective case means a dialogue amongst all, and in moving forward, taking into account each person's interests" (p. 22).

As part of the evidentiary process for the criminal complaint, a series of exhumations were requested in the areas where the military outposts had been located to search for the men who had disappeared. As of 2015, two exhumations had been conducted, with 56 sets of remains found, of which 2 had been formally identified. The exhumations were coordinated by the Alliance, the Ministry of the Interior, the *Asociación de Víctimas, Viudas, Huérfanos y Desarraigados del Conflicto Armado Interno de la Sierra de las Minas* [Association of Victims, Widows, Orphans, and People Displaced by the Internal Armed Conflict in the Sierra de las Minas] (AVIHDESMI), and the *Fundación de Antropología Forense de Guatemala* [Foundation of Forensic Anthropology of Guatemala] (FAFG), which conducted the exhumations.

As a next step in the case, in September 2012 the plaintiffs gave testimony in preliminary hearings, which were held in the national courts in Guatemala City due to security concerns, given that the perpetrators, who lived in the same region as the plaintiffs, had not yet been arrested. Méndez (2012) describes the testimonies and their impact: "The women walked up to the judge with confidence. Their old-woman voices expressed sincerity, certainty, and at the same time deep pain, for the atrocities they related. They spoke in their language Q'eqchi' and their words were translated to Spanish by other women from their ethnic group. A profound silence, an atmosphere full of consternation and rage, invaded the public, made up mostly of women who filled the hearing room throughout the week" (p. 3). Because of security concerns, the women's identities were not released, and they wore shawls to hide their faces from the view of the courtroom audience, although the judge himself, seated directly in front of the plaintiffs, could see their faces (Méndez & Carrera, 2014). As Alvarado et. al. (2013) stated, "These shawls have become emblematic of women's courage, decision making, and dignity to not forget, not be silent, and not give up, despite the threats" (p. 38), an issue we come back to in the context of the trial itself. These testimonies were videotaped and used as evidence in the 2016 trial, so that the plaintiffs did not have to testify again. One of the plaintiffs, Doña Magdalena Pop, died of cancer four months after giving evidence, but her testimony was deemed admissible as part of the case.

In June 2012, arrest warrants were issued for two perpetrators, Esteelmer Reyes Girón, the former commander of the Sepur Zarco military outpost, and Heriberto Valdéz Asij, the former military commissioner in the region. Finally, on October 14, 2014, the Juzgado de Mayor Riesgo "B" [Court of First Instance for High Risk Crimes "B"] in Guatemala City ruled that there was sufficient evidence to begin criminal proceedings against Reyes Girón and Valdéz Asij, and both were charged with crimes against humanity (Méndez, 2014). Reyes Girón was charged with sexual violence and sexual slavery, domestic slavery, and the assassination of Dominga Coc and her two daughters; Valdéz Asij was charged with sexual violence and the forced disappearances of the husbands of seven of the plaintiffs.

Méndez (2012) describes the particular salience of the case of Dominga Coc for the 54 protagonists, many of whom knew her. She details Coc's horrific ordeal:

> Dominga, a twenty year-old woman went to the military camp with her two little daughters, Anita and Hermelinda, in search of her husband who had been captured by members of the army in 1982. After arriving at the base, she was captured and raped repeatedly by soldiers in front of her husband and her daughters. After several weeks of being brutally raped, she and her daughters were forcibly disappeared.... The story of Dominga Coc resonated for years among the women enslaved in Sepur Zarco and became a permanent warning of what could happen to any one of them at any time. (p. 2)

Dominga Coc's body was found at the edge of the river as part of the exhumations that were conducted in 2012. Her husband survived and was a witness in the trial, as was her mother. As Méndez (2012) recalled, a dominant refrain by plaintiffs throughout these initial stages of the legal process was, "I don't want to die without seeing justice done" (para. 26). For many of these women, while seeing justice carried out for their perpetrators was important, this priority was integrally tied to the source of the armed conflict and the harm they experienced; that is, their legal title to their land. For example, one protagonist felt "great sadness that she has come to the end of her life without land; she lives with her children but although they have land, they don't have the papers" (Velásquez Nimatuj, 2016, p. 23).

Several expert witness reports were prepared as supporting evidence for various aspects of the case, including a cultural study by K'iche' anthropologist Irma

Alicia Velásquez Nimatuj. Her study was based on interviews she conducted with the plaintiffs in the case in February 2013 and presented to the court in April 2013 during the preliminary hearings and then again during the trial itself (Velásquez Nimatuj, 2016). The study aimed to show the sociocultural impact of the violence experienced by Q'eqchi' women. As in the MTM interviews with protagonists and our own workshops and interviews analyzed in this volume, the issue of structural impoverishment and the loss of land and livelihoods emerged in Velásquez Nimatuj's interviews. As one Q'eqchi' woman put it, "Our crime was to live close to the large landowners" (p. 31). In talking about her fear of giving testimony, which was manifested in constant headaches and fevers, another woman said, "Justice was never on our side, never helped us. Because of this, the landowners called the army so they could take our land, and because of this the men were killed. They killed the men because they were defending their land. The assault we lived through was to take over our land" (p. 33).

As discussed in chapter 1 and as Velásquez Nimatuj (2016) notes, Q'eqchi' women's "culture and identity revolve around agricultural production and survival, which is linked to production to guarantee family food sovereignty, preserve the right to life, and the right to the ownership of their land" (p. 6). She argues that the destruction of women's lives and the community systems around them was part of the ongoing system of colonial repression: "The rapes of Q'eqchi' women are an extension of the colonial relations of dependency and exploitation that have prevailed in Guatemala throughout its history" (p. 5). Recognizing the structural dimensions of racialized gendered violence is therefore paramount if justice is to be "on the side" of protagonists: it prompts the question of whether retributive justice—in the form of the prosecution of individual perpetrators without holding the state responsible for what is both a collective and a structural crime— responds adequately to protagonists' claims for accountability and redress, including the return or recovery of land. The next section analyzes aspects of the trial itself, incorporating quotes from the field notes taken by a member of our research team to demonstrate how racialized gendered harm was taken up within the courtroom space.[6]

SCENES FROM THE COURTROOM

As the Sepur Zarco trial began on February 1, 2016, in the *Sala de Vista* [Vista Room] courtroom of the Guatemalan Supreme Court, on the right side of the courtroom, behind the prosecution table, were three rows of chairs where the 14 Q'eqchi' women and their interpreter were sitting. They had shawls wrapped over and around their heads and shoulders, with only their hands and legs visible underneath. The interpreter, with her *huipil* [blouse] and head and face uncovered, seemed quite conspicuous in the middle of this group. At the crowded prosecution table (actually two tables pushed together) sat the two public prosecutors and the lawyers and representatives from the *querellantes* [co-plaintiffs] in the case, MTM, the plaintiffs' own organization *Jalok U* ["transformation" or "change" in Q'eqchi'], and at the other end of the table, nearest to the public gallery, UNAMG.

On the left side of the courtroom at the defense table sat the two defendants. At the table with them sat their lawyers, Moisés Galindo, who was representing Reyes Girón, and Elvia Ernestina Santizo, the public defender representing Valdéz Asij. There were a couple of chairs placed behind them, one of them empty, the other occupied by Galindo's hat. The trial was taking place in the same courtroom as the genocide trial of former dictator Efraín Ríos Montt and his intelligence chief Mauricio Rodríguez Sánchez in 2013, with some of the same players, including Galindo, who was one of Ríos Montt's lawyers, and two of the three judges, Yassmín Barrios (presiding) and Patricia Bustamente. This was the first time that perpetrators were being prosecuted in their own country for sexual violence and sexual and domestic slavery as crimes against humanity, and the packed courtroom was tense with anticipation.

After repeated attempts by the defense to have the case thrown out (mimicking strategies from the Ríos Montt trial), the proceedings finally got underway. The charges were presented, and the plaintiffs' names and the names of their disappeared loved ones were read out loud in court. When the accused were invited to present themselves to the court, Reyes Girón refused, arguing that the judges had "no basis on which to judge me." Valdéz Asij was somewhat more cooperative, but didn't seem to understand what was going on. He first said he didn't want to present himself, then did so anyway. He told the court he was an innocent man, that his entire family was *guatemalteco* [Guatemalan], that he didn't know where Sepur Zarco was and had never been there. He went on to say that he was uneducated, knew nothing about the law, did not work as a military commissioner but rather was a municipal policeman in Panzós, that he was old, and knew nothing about any of this as he was an agricultural worker. At some point during Valdéz Asij's statement Reyes Girón looked to someone in the audience (later confirmed to be Ricardo Méndez Ruíz, president of the Foundation against Terrorism) and saluted him, with his hand across his forehead, military style. After the charges were read and the pleas entered, the press, who had been huddled around the various speakers in the room, holding up their microphones, started packing up and leaving. . . .

Over the first two days of the trial, the first nine witnesses to testify were eight Q'eqchi' men and one woman who stated that they had been forced to provide their labor at the military outpost, had themselves been tortured and abused (and in the case of the woman, raped), and had witnessed the abuses suffered by the plaintiffs. They also testified to the role of the defendants in the abuses. On day three, projector screens had been set up around the front of the courtroom. And after much vigorous protest from the defense lawyers that their clients' right to a proper defense were being violated (citing the American Convention on Human Rights), the video testimonies of the plaintiffs . . . began to be screened, a process that would unfold over the following two weeks, interspersed with other in-person witness testimony and expert witness reports. . . . The defense objected throughout the trial to the fact that the women were not testifying "live." In the video testimonies, the women recounted their lived experiences of violence, in response to insistent questioning. In one, with the plaintiff in obvious distress, the lawyers asked her question after question about tiny details she either did not remember or did not want to recount. Watching this testimony, a young man in the audience, sitting with some of the civil society organizations, covered his mouth and nose with a sweatshirt he was carrying and put his head in his hands, leaning down on his knees. . . .

On February 9, 2016, day seven of the trial, trial participants and audience members arrived to find 38 large cardboard boxes laid out in front of the courtroom, between the defense and prosecution tables, and separating the witness stand from the judges' bench. A feeling of heaviness permeated the room. All the boxes had the FAFG codes written in black marker on their sides; 33 were marked "Finca Tinajas" and five "Sepur Zarco." After testimony from the forensic anthropologists who had conducted the exhumations of the mass graves found at the Finca Tinajas and Sepur Zarco military outposts, court officials, assisted by one of the forensic anthropologists, started opening the boxes to display the contents for the defense and public to see, part of the procedure to enter them into evidence. This process for the Finca Tinajas boxes alone took four hours, during which the court officials and anthropologist, wearing plastic gloves and face masks, would open each box, take the various plastic and paper bags in which the clothes and bones were held to the front of the court and lay the contents out on the kraft paper spread out on the floor of the stage in front of the judges' bench. After the first box, Judge Barrios recommended that only one sample of the bones be taken out of its bag/ envelope in order to expedite the process and to preserve the evidence. There was a media circus at the front of the room at this point, with over 30 cameras (still and video) lining the front of the courtroom, pressing up against the retractable barrier that had been set up to divide the public gallery from the front of the courtroom. It was hard to know where they had all come from; there had been barely any press the previous day, and there they all were, all of a sudden, running down to the front as soon as the boxes were opened and the contents exhibited. The physical lightness of the boxes that were carried by court officials seemed shocking, given what they contained. The lawyers and co-plaintiff representatives at the prosecution table could hear the women plaintiffs crying behind them, beneath their shawls, as the clothes and remains of their husbands were being taken out of the boxes; they could do nothing. . . .

Throughout the trial, family and community members of the plaintiffs were present in the courtroom, along with other groups of survivors from different regions of the country, and representatives of civil society organizations who continue to search for disappeared loved ones and seek justice. . . . One day a group of high school students were present, holding red carnations and signs that read *#YoSoySepurZarco* [#IamSepurZarco]. And at different moments in the trial, audience members included Nobel Laureates, Jody Williams and Rigoberta Menchú Tum; the U.S. ambassador to Guatemala, Todd Robinson; the UN Special Rapporteur on the Rights of Indigenous Peoples, Victoria Tauli Corpuz; and Executive Secretary of the IACHR, Emilio Álvarez Icaza. As they stood in the security line up to get into the Supreme Court every day, trial attendees could see banners that read "We support the courageous women who are demanding justice; No more sexual abuse and slavery: We are with you"; and "We are looking towards justice for Sepur Zarco," as well as ceremonial circles of candles and flowers. They were also addressed by a man in dark glasses, wearing a camouflage baseball cap and a T-shirt proclaiming *"Los Guatemaltecos no somos genocidas"* [We Guatemalans are not perpetrators of genocide]. From his position across from the courthouse, "Megaphone man" as he came to be called by some regular trial attendees, kept up a steady stream of abuse, referring to the plaintiffs as "delinquents" and "prostitutes," citing their names, as well as those of some of the witnesses, and the amount of money plaintiffs supposedly received in "reparations" for testifying at the trial.

On the afternoon of February 26, 2016, after four weeks of proceedings, including video testimonies by the 15 women plaintiffs, 28 witness testimonies (including testimony from a protected witness who was a former soldier at the Sepur Zarco base via a live video link), and 18 expert witness reports (historical, medical, psychiatric, psychosocial, forensic, cultural, linguistic, among others), and with 8 witnesses for the defense (out of an original 48 who were supposed to be called to testify), Judge Barrios delivered the Tribunal's verdict on behalf of the three judges in the case. The Tribunal found Reyes Girón and Valdéz Asij guilty of crimes against humanity in the form of sexual violence and domestic and sexual slavery. Reyes Girón was also found guilty of the murder of Dominga Coc and her two daughters, and Valdéz Asij was convicted of the forced disappearances of the husbands of seven of the women plaintiffs. They were sentenced to 120 and 240 years in prison, respectively. In reading the ruling, Judge Barrios drew extensively on the testimonies from witnesses and experts to clarify the violence suffered by the women, explaining which evidence confirmed that the accused had command responsibility for the violence perpetrated and emphasizing the women's innocence. She noted, "The judges of this tribunal firmly believe the testimonies of the women who were sexually violated in Sepur Zarco" (Tribunal Primero de Sentencia Penal, C-01076-2012-00021, 2016, p. 493). At a reparations hearing the following week, Reyes Girón was ordered to pay Q5.5 million (US$732,700) to the 11 women plaintiffs,[7] and Valdéz Asij was ordered to pay Q1.7 million (US$226,500) to the families of the seven men who had been disappeared. In the following sections we explore three specific dimensions that emerged from our analysis of courtroom dynamics during the trial: (1) the spectacles of suffering that the courtroom brought into being, (2) the liminality of justice as perpetually "in translation," and (3) the embodiment of racialized gendered harm by Q'eqchi' men during the trial.

Spectacles of Suffering

As evidenced by the scenes from the Sepur Zarco trial drawn from field note observations, the courtroom is a stylized space in which the experience of harm must be performed in adherence to a particular set of normative legal frameworks. As Henry (2009) points out, the law, not the victim, shapes the testimony, which is all too often fragmented to suit the demands of the legal process. As such, it is not her story, but rather the court's. Several scholars have analyzed the reliance of human rights discourse, particularly in the legal domain, on spectacles of suffering through which harm is represented (Clarke, 2009; Hesford, 2011). In her analysis of the role of the ICC in sub-Saharan Africa, and drawing on Derrida, Clarke (2009) describes "the spectacularization of justice through the specter of the victim" (p. 23) within the international rights regime. She refers to Derrida's notion of the "specter" as "the past, returning contingently and repeatedly in new guises and incarnations, which we must in some way learn to recognize and live with" (p. 22). She argues that the "global rule of law movement" deploys "human rights discourses through a spectacularity that involves the abjection of the 'victim' and the rescue of humanity from abhorrent violence" (p. 12), particularly through spectacles of suffering in which the victim is an absent-presence. As such, the "fiction of justice" is "made real through the figure of the victim—a victim to be saved by the rule of law, a victim around whom collective guilt is made visible and reassigned to those seen to be bearing most responsibility" (p. 17). The victim is required to bring the spectacle of suffering into being to legitimate this particular "path to justice" and as such "is both central yet marginal to the justice project itself" (p. 13).

In the Sepur Zarco trial, the absent-presence of the victims was manifested in complex ways. Audience members were struck by the fact that the first two days of the trial were taken up with the witness testimony of seven men who had also been forced to "serve" at the base; a research team member wrote at the time that "it felt like we need to hear men talk about this in order to believe the women." Later in the proceedings, Judge Barrios clarified that the court gives priority to "live" witnesses over documentary evidence, and therefore those witnesses preceded the women plaintiffs' testimonies that were shown as video declarations, having been recorded in the pretrial evidentiary hearings. This meant that throughout the trial, the women plaintiffs did not directly engage with their interlocutors: they sat behind the prosecution table, their heads concealed under shawls similar to those they wore in the video testimonials, obscuring their identities and thus subverting or mediating the spectacle required by the audience, provoking discomfort.[8] As Hesford (2011) argues, "Spectacles are intercorporeal; they cannot be conceived of outside a web of interrelations and discourses of which they are a living part" (p. 11). The absence of the protagonists' live testimonies and their veiling disrupted this intercorporeality, and through this process of disruption, "the visual absence of her body reminds the viewer of the vulnerability of victims in speaking out" (p. 102). What does this disruption do to the possibility for protagonists to assert their subjectivity beyond the identity of "the raped woman," as well as for the audience to cede their own authorial privilege and power of recognition? Hesford describes this dilemma when she asks, "Does the visual absence of the rape victim . . . provide an opportunity for our rhetorical presence and for the construction of a scene of self-recognition? Or does the suspension of the visual spectacle of victimization prompt a politics that moves beyond recognition? Does this particular representation exemplify testimony without intimacy?" (p. 102).

The answer to these questions is not straightforward and holds within it the potential for audience self-recognition and protagonists' resistance to and subversion of such recognition. While plaintiffs were not asked to testify again during the trial and were therefore spared this dangerous intimacy, they were asked on many occasions to tell their stories throughout the legal process and after it—before the courts in the pretrial preliminary hearings, by multiple expert witnesses in the preparation of their reports, and by the lawyers and other intermediaries preparing the case—despite their repeated attempts to resist such interrogations. As Mónica Pinzón, one of the expert witnesses, reported during the trial, one protagonist "doesn't understand why there is a need to give her testimony so many times in the path to justice, but has done so anyways so that her story is not forgotten."

The videos themselves that were shown during the trial were a visceral reminder of the painful demands of legal testimony. Each testimony was between an hour and a half and two and a half hours long. Viewing the videos during the trial, the audience heard protagonists recount their experiences of rape, the disappearance of their husbands, the burning of their homes, and their time at the Sepur Zarco military outpost, where they were forced to cook and clean and were repeatedly raped. A few who were not held at the camp had fled to the mountains after they were raped by soldiers in their homes, spending up to six years there and losing many of their children, who died of starvation, and to whom they could not give a proper burial. They returned with nothing, not even the clothes on their backs. One plaintiff explained how she confronted Reyes Girón about her experience and was told, "Maybe you wanted it; you're used to it like that." At that point, she said, "I knew that somehow they knew which ones of us were alone [as their husbands had been disappeared] and that's why they abused us." It is important to highlight the fact that this woman went to confront Reyes Girón at the camp about what had happened to her—and interviews conducted by MTM with Q'eqchi' protagonists in preparing for the case confirmed that several other women had done the same—emphasizing women's protagonism at the time of these horrific experiences of victimization. What women do and how they choose to act after experiences of violation is not to be taken for granted (Buss, 2009; see González, 2002, for an examination of K'iche' women's everyday protagonism in the wake of surviving sexual violence perpetrated by the military during the war in the town of San Bartolomé Jocotenango, El Quiché).

In this adversarial judicial landscape, protagonists made a claim on truth and a demand for acknowledgment of their pain and suffering: "I am here telling the truth, this is not a lie. It is very painful and it is great sadness, everything I have lived through." In the videos from the preliminary hearings, the lawyers' questioning was insistent, and some protagonists were asked to reveal more and more information as the testimony proceeded, including details about the rapes that they either did not remember or did not want to recount. Further, what might it have meant for the women to sit in the courtroom as plaintiffs, concealed under shawls and hearing their testimony played to the courtroom? The procedural decision to have them present but concealed further disrupted the spectacle of suffering, challenging the interpretation of this particular court performance and its multiple meanings for the protagonists and those in attendance. Protagonists were present as testifiers and as witnesses once again to the gross violations that rendered them embodied representations of Guatemala's genocidal violence; yet they were also an embodied presence of resistance and resilience. Moreover, the concealment of both plaintiffs and some audience members, who also chose to wear shawls covering their heads (some of whom were participants in other legal processes and members of the same group as the plaintiffs), was a strategy that both visibilized and invisibilized themselves to the hungry press as a racialized gendered signifier of pain, suffering, and resistance.

Plaintiffs listened to the mediation and verification of their testimony by the expert witnesses who participated in the trial, many of whom had interviewed them in preparing their reports. Some of these experts were intermediaries with whom they had long-standing relationships; they included the psychologist Mónica Pinzón who had worked for ECAP for many years and the K'iche' anthropologist Irma Alicia Velásquez Nimatuj who had been involved in the work of the Alliance for several years, including participating in the 2010 Tribunal of Conscience. As such, their expert witness reports were framed within relationships built over time with protagonists. The plaintiffs had more distant relationships with other experts with whom they had not interacted as extensively; nevertheless, those experts were also charged with translating protagonists' pain and suffering into the language of the court; that is, a language that defended and supported their claims of having been harmed by the state and its representatives. The expert witnesses themselves were also subjected to aggressive scrutiny from the defense lawyers, who questioned their expertise and affiliations, often implying that their expertise had been bought and as such was compromised. Court proceedings such as these typically challenge the underlying qualifications of expert witnesses, seeking to cast doubt on that which has been designed to document the veracity of protagonists' stories.

One of the most striking expert witness reports was presented by forensic psychiatrist and physician Dr. Karen Peña Juárez, who was then working at the *Instituto Nacional de Ciencias Forenses* [National Institute of Forensic Sciences] (INACIF) and had interviewed all the women plaintiffs and three of the male witnesses. Juárez described how "her patients" had presented with symptoms consistent with having endured torture, violence, and persecution and how these experiences had overwhelmed their ability to cope, causing a psychological burden that altered their bodily and psychic functions, in addition to leaving them with physical injuries and pain from the sexual assaults. She detailed the particular, but often shared, ways in which these experiences manifested, including chronic sadness, depression, sleep problems, fear, gastritis, back pain, headaches, and gynecological issues. She explained that, in her opinion, the victims did not have the capacity or the technical knowledge to invent a story with such complexity and internal consistency or to maintain it over time. She expanded on this point during questioning, explaining how parts of the story would emerge differently, with protagonists at times resisting telling their stories and then spontaneously narrating events with a lot of detail and how the women would pause and sometimes correct and add details to something they had just said, which, she argued, is a sign of telling the truth. When she was asked about how they could remember things so clearly after such a long time, she talked about how traumatic and extraordinary events have the capacity to inscribe themselves much more deeply in our memories than ordinary activities. She discussed the potential revictimization that this court case would bring for the women, as they had to relive the crimes and face their assailants, and explained the face covering as an attempt to protect themselves from this harm. In terms of prognosis, she explained that the impact/harm in most women was permanent because of their age, the extended period over which they suffered the abuses, and the continued stigma and shame that they faced in their communities, which affected their self-esteem and have been integrated into their identity. She added that accompaniment could help improve their quality of life.

Juárez also talked about collective versus individual sensations and perceptions: how the women, when they were narrating things that happened to them individually at the Sepur Zarco military outpost would sometimes speak in the plural, relating a shared experience, but that they related other experiences as only affecting them, such as one woman who talked about having been called "the community witch." When asked about the similarities in the women's narratives she explained that she attributed them to a systematic practice of abuse: all the women had suffered very similar experiences. During questioning, the defense lawyers asked about the stigma and rejection of the women by their own communities, asking if it was normal for "these types of communities" to make such decisions or take such actions of rejection. Juárez responded that, in contexts of fear and repression, people rarely want to be on the bad side of authorities, that these women had been "marked" by authorities, and that in general it is more common for groups to exclude victims than perpetrators.

Our research team member's field notes commented on how heartbreaking and depressing it was to listen to this report, which was in sharp contrast to the nature of our team's ongoing engagement over many years with the protagonists themselves and their stories. An expert report designed to document the women's victim status, as required by the judicial processes in which the women had elected to participate, contributes to pathologizing them through displaying an expertise that reduces suffering, including social suffering, to embodied symptoms of those who have been violated. Intimate details of women's experiences of violence that most had not shared with one another in their mutual groups or in the workshops we facilitated as part of our research were exposed not only in open court but also included in the permanent record of these proceedings. This expert witness report reopened the gulf between protagonists and their interlocutors in the courtroom, inviting the courtroom audience to consume their pain (Razack, 2007) as reconstructed through medical and psychiatric discourses.

Expert witness reports are situated within the courtroom hierarchy; they are designed to mediate the process and validate women's experiences to the court according to previously agreed-on evidentiary procedures. They play a role of interpretation and validation—but to the court, rather than to the protagonists themselves or to those whose worldviews are discordant with those that underlie Western judicial processes. As such, those experts who can successfully defend their worldview and claims have the power to pronounce whether the protagonists' testimonies are in fact true. As we examine in this volume, intermediaries risk prioritizing professionalized discourse to the exclusion of protagonists' lived experiences and their own narratives. Our research team field notes included commentary on the fact that the evidence being presented was very much designed for the court: it was a story shaped by and for that space. This led us to wonder what effect this performance of expertise had on the plaintiffs themselves, who had to be present as other people asserted themselves as experts on their pain, suffering, and the veracity of their testimonies about their experiences, and who had to hear their stories refracted in this way, again reinforcing the spectral quality of victims and their absent-presence within the legal domain.

The protagonists' absent-presence was made even more visceral with the display of the still unidentified remains of their husbands and the family members of so many other community members—there were 50 sets of remains, of which 48 were still unidentified given their deterioration. As one of the forensic anthropologists, Juan Carlos Gatica, testified during the trial, many of the bones were eroded, which he attributed to the sandy soil and to the fact that the area had been sown with sugar cane: a crop that requires the extensive use of chemical pesticides that could have contributed to damaging the remains. Along with the remains, the anthropologists found pieces of cloth that were tied around some of the skulls in the style of a blindfold, as well as synthetic ropes that were tied around the feet, hands, and necks of several of the bodies; in addition, the burial pattern (directly in the ground with no protection, with some facing up and others down) was consistent with a mass or clandestine grave. The conviction of Valdéz Asij for the forced disappearance of the husbands of seven of the plaintiffs seemed to rely on this spectacle, the tremendous personal cost of which to the women and other family members of the disappeared in the courtroom remains unknown (see Rojas-Perez, 2017, for a compelling ethnography of the relationship between the disappeared and their mourning loved ones, particularly Quechua mothers, as mediated by state politics and transitional justice mechanisms in the aftermath of atrocities in Peru). The prosecution lawyers sitting at the table and the audience members beyond them could hear and see their grief, but could do nothing to assuage it. The bones of the dead were picked on by the ravenous press "who had suddenly appeared out of nowhere."[9]

The interviews that Velásquez Nimatuj (2016) conducted for her expert witness report for the trial provide us with some insights into Q'eqchi' plaintiffs' relationships to their husbands since their disappearance. She found that most of the women continued to dream about their lost husbands. As one woman recounted, "I dreamed about my husband, as if he were alive. He asked me: 'Why are you participating in this?' I explained that I am seeking help for me and for my children, but he says: 'Why are you provoking things?' He tells me that I am hurting him. He doesn't like that I am participating, but in real life, he wasn't like that, he didn't hit me, he wasn't problematic" (p. 31). In another woman's dreams, her husband urged her to "come with me, I have a good home. Why are you putting up with things here, why are you here suffering alone?" Her interpretation of the dream was that her husband is the one who is suffering, "because we never found out where his body is" (p. 37). When another woman who was still searching for her disappeared husband saw him in her dreams, she asked him why he left: "And every time I dream about him he comes to leave me with sickness in the back, the head, and he brings me fever. But the sickness is just for me, not the children" (p. 41). One of the few women who did not dream about her husband raised this as an issue to be concerned about: "This is not good, because I can't get out everything inside and so everything stays in my body, and because of this, I am afraid of everything I hear" (p. 41).

A fuller discussion of the significance of dreams within Mayan cosmology is beyond the scope of this chapter. However it is important to note that both the conception of time as circular rather than linear and the strongly held beliefs that the dead are ever present—manifesting through dreams and "appearances" among the living through which they communicate their desires, offer their condolences and advice, and perform their presence in the midst of ongoing painful loss—are deeply felt in many Mayan communities, particularly among those of the generation of the protagonists (see Médicos Descalzos, 2012, and multiple publications of Kaqla, among many others). Significantly, Velásquez Nimatuj's expert witness report contrasted with the discursive medicalization of Juárez, but within the courtroom, despite each expert's knowledge and personal credentials being interrogated, the legal system does not permit a debate about the substance of their testimonies. Their words remained uncontested vis-à-vis each other—awaiting a post-trial interrogation and representing one of the multiple challenges of a pluriethnic, multicultural, wounded community in search of justice for genocidal violence.

The spectacles of suffering that are necessary to the prosecution of harm are produced and made real by the various actors within the legal domain; for example, expert witnesses translated and validated women's suffering through their performance of expertise. The experience of harm within the judicial realm and the truths produced therein are thus always mediated. As such, we argue that justice is always in translation between plaintiffs and their various interlocutors: the judges, prosecution and defense lawyers, expert witnesses, defendants, and courtroom interpreters. We argue further that those mediations have an impact well beyond the particularities of the case or the individuals present and the absent-presence; that is, on Mayan communities as a whole as well as our meaning-making of justice qua justice. In the following section, we examine this notion of justice-in-translation in more depth.

Justice-in-Translation

The courtroom is a mediated space, in which pain and suffering are translated into the language of liberal Western law and are subject to verification: Are protagonists telling the truth as the court sees it? Translation was literally present throughout, given the fact that the trial took place not in the Q'eqchi' language of the plaintiffs, but in Spanish, contributing to the liminality of the courtroom space.

Interpreters translated Q'eqchi'-speaking witnesses' testimonies into Spanish as they sat with the plaintiffs and defense, respectively. In her field notes, a research team member wondered whether the grammatical separations that make sense in Spanish and were used as pauses for interpreting into Q'eqchi' may have rendered the reading of the witnesses' pledge to tell the truth incomprehensible to them.

The defense questioned whether the Q'eqchi' witnesses could in fact have testified in Spanish, despite repeated warnings from the judge that the defense and prosecution had all previously verified the language in which their witnesses would testify. This exchange confirmed both the understanding that translation is not for the benefit of the individuals participating in the trial, but for the Tribunal, and the legal system's resistance to adapting to the multilingual realities of Guatemala affirmed in the Peace Accords. The questioning of witnesses in this way led us to wonder whether some of them would be forced to hide or deny that they were able to understand and speak some Spanish in order to be allowed to declare in Q'eqchi', their mother tongue and the language in which they were more at ease. The defense also repeatedly asked witnesses throughout the trial how they were able to understand the soldiers' orders if they did not speak Spanish. The witnesses responded that there were Q'eqchi'-speaking soldiers at the camp, an assertion that was also confirmed by the testimony of the protected witness, a former Q'eqchi' soldier stationed at the Sepur Zarco camp during the period in question.

One of the expert witnesses addressed the critical set of translation issues related to protagonists' renderings of the types of violations they experienced. This expert, Mayra Nineth Barrios Torres, a linguistic anthropologist from Cobán who was fluent in Q'eqchi', had extensive research experience in Alta Verapaz and with Q'eqchi' communities, including as a fieldworker with the CEH. Her report was based on group interviews with all the plaintiffs, as well as on individual interviews with two of the male witnesses who had been held at the Sepur Zarco camp at the same time. Barrios focused on the Q'eqchi' interviewees' linguistic interpretation of the acts of sexual violence. She concluded that they used a number of different ways to talk about sexual violence in Q'eqchi', with the most common being *muxuk*.[10] Barrios reported that muxuk is translated into Spanish several ways: as *profanar*, meaning to desecrate or defile; as *traspasar*, meaning to transgress or dispose of; and as *ensuciar*, meaning to dirty or defile. In the first person, *xine'xmux'* signifies "I was defiled" or "they ruined my life." Barrios explained how muxuk, which originally meant *pasar encima*, "to pass up, through, or by," underwent a resignification in meaning during the armed conflict so that it was now at the root of idiomatic expressions that refer to violations suffered during that period: *muxuk chaq'rab* can refer to forced disappearances, the burning of crops, the loss of belongings, and many other experiences of violation. Barrios noted that muxuk has deep significance in the Q'eqchi' cosmology and that when women use this word to refer to sexual violence, they are also attaching meaning to having being robbed of their self-respect, as well as the respect of their community. In this sense they also use *maak'a' chik inloq'al*, which means, "I was left without respect," "I was left without dignity," or "I was dishonored." As discussed in chapter 1, community respect is gendered, and for women it is tied to virginity, marriage, and widowhood. Protagonists talked about having lost this respect when they were held at the military outpost.

Apoyo sombra [shadow support] was also available to witnesses. The person who provided such support, from the Ministry of the Interior's Support to Victims' Office (and with prior psychosocial training from ECAP), sat silently beside the witnesses as they testified, available to help them and in some ways act as a mediator or even a buffer between the witnesses who were giving testimony about their pain and suffering, often for the first time, and their courtroom interlocutors. Were they there to, in some sense, absorb some of this pain?

More broadly, lawyers, judges, state officials, and interpreters—as well as the globalized jurisprudence on sexual harm and genocidal violence—mediated women's testimonies and defined the contours of the testimonies they were expected to tell the court. These testimonies were, of course, partial fragments of the broader stories that protagonists had to share about their experiences of and responses to genocidal violence. As highlighted in the quote from Das (2007) that we cite at the beginning of the introduction to this volume, representations of violence are texts "overlaid with commentary" (p. 80)—and this commentary includes the courts' and the various intermediaries' accompanying protagonists (lawyers, psychologists, feminist activists), as well as our commentary as analysts and scholars. Ross reminds us how testimonies are shaped by the particular contexts in which they are told, arguing that "testimonies and telling are fragments, parts of people's narration of their lives. They are particular instances, synopses of experiences, told at particular times for particular audiences and located in specific contexts" (as cited in Henry, 2009, p. 124; for an examination of the role of interpretation in war crimes tribunals, see Doughty, 2017; Elias-Bursac, 2015; Koomen, 2014; and on interpreting justice, see Inghilleri, 2012). As such, they are never the whole truth, but rather fractured fragments of representations of particular moments in time.

Tribunals emphasize narratives of harm because that is the crime that is being prosecuted: it needs to be proven as truth. As in other truth-telling processes such as truth commissions, this emphasis can lead to the reification of harm as the gendered experience of violence. However, with this important caveat in mind, testimonies and courtroom proceedings are also indicators of women's resiliency, agency, and protagonism. As previously mentioned, one of the plaintiffs described how she went to the camp to complain to the perpetrators about her abuse. Interviews conducted with other Q'eqchi' women confirm that this was not a unique occurrence; many women expressed their outrage at their treatment. One of the witnesses who testified in person during the trial was not a plaintiff in the case, but had been forced to serve at the Sepur Zarco camp for a short period and been raped at the Finca Tinajas military outpost; she spoke proudly of teaching her two young sons how to work the fields after she left Sepur Zarco, and of managing to sustain them into adulthood despite all the hardships she had suffered. Women's capacity to continue, to endure, their survivance, is an extraordinary yet every-day instance of protagonism. "I am a miracle because I survived," one plaintiff told the psychologist Mónica Pinzón in an interview she conducted in preparation for her expert witness report. And despite the roles others may play in shaping testi-mony and the content of what can be said, the very act of testifying to the court is an assertion of protagonism, as is the tremendous resilience required to stick with the case through the many years it took to bring it to trial. As Henry (2009) states in her analysis of women's experiences of testifying to international war crimes tribunals, "while valorizing the 'healing powers' of international criminal trials is problematic, dismissing the possibility that victims can derive positive ben-efits from testifying . . . is also problematic, serving to deny both victim agency and resiliency" (p. 118).

Q'eqchi' men also testified during the trial about their experiences of racial-ized gendered harm, expanding the category of gendered harm beyond women's experiences and thus loosening the ties between constructions of woman and victimhood. Their testimonies allow us to examine racialized masculinity in rela-tion to violence and the complexity of the intersections of victim and perpetrator identities, further disrupting the reified binaries of the gendered categorizations of war. We unpack Q'eqchi' men's testimonies of racialized gendered harm in the next section.

Protagonists' testimonies further confirm that despite their individuated form, testimony is a refraction of the collectivity: many protagonists emphasized that they were compelled to speak on behalf of so many who could not. As Henry (2009) argues, "To speak for the dead is memorialization of loved ones who were killed in war; it represents a form of recognition and acknowledgment" (p. 128). The courtroom becomes a space of translation between the living and the dead, yet it simultaneously perverts the Mayan philosophy of the dead's ever presence among the living by constraining the performances through which the dead are brought into this space through particular liberal Western rituals (e.g., as embod-ied through the bones of the dead) and as represented through stories of violence and disappearance.

We concur with those scholars who acknowledge the impossibility of repre-senting or translating another's pain (Das, 2007; Felman & Laub, 1992; Hartman, 1997; Hesford, 2011; Scarry, 1985). As Das (2007) argues, we "cannot claim to know the pain of the other" (p. 39). Felman claims that "translation, as opposed to con-fession . . . becomes a metaphor for the historical necessity of bearing witness" (as cited in Hesford, 2011, p. 54). At the same time, as Hesford (2011) points out in her analysis of Felman and Laub's book *Testimony* (1992), Felman also signals "the impossibility of translation in such contexts, arguing that it is in fact a metaphor for the failure to see—the impossibility of witnessing the original" (p. 54). As such, the courtroom is liminal space, with the boundary between sufferer and nonsufferer being repeatedly drawn and redrawn and the fissures widening as the court repeatedly performs the impossibility of translation. However, this im/possibility also opens up the potentiality for survivor protagonism: the inability of the court—or anyone else—to own the other's pain protects the self and its "poisonous knowledge" (Das, 2007, p. 55) from consumption. The refusal by plaintiffs to be seen—through the veiling—as Hesford (2011) argues in a different context, "signals her refusal to become a visual text" (p. 103). It also shifts the ground, enabling the possibility of witnessing that is not merely consumptive, and moves away from the dangerous intimacy that Hesford (2011) warns of, toward the potential for pragmatic solidarity with protagonists, which we have termed accompaniment.[11] Without diminishing the multiple effects of suffering and resistance for individual protagonists afforded or rendered by judicial processes, our documentation and interpretation of these processes suggest that the spectacle itself has broader structural implications for indigenous people of Guatemala—and beyond.

Embodying Racialized Gendered Harm: Q'eqchi' Men's Testimonies

As mentioned earlier, the first seven witnesses to testify in person during the trial were Q'eqchi' men who had been held at the Sepur Zarco outpost at the same time as the women and who could corroborate the women's stories. A total of 15 Q'eqchi' men testified during the trial, including a protected witness who was a former soldier at the base; for many this was the first time they were testifying in public space about their experiences. Q'eqchi' men's testimonies give us important insights into how racialized gendered harm was embodied by men.

The first witness to testify in the trial explained how soldiers had ordered him and other members of his community who were PAC members to dismantle their homes and carry the building materials to Sepur Zarco. There, they were forced to build the Sepur Zarco camp using these same materials. When asked by one of the prosecutors what would happen if they did not follow these orders, he responded, "They got mad and responded in a bad way," and that he had learned that lesson when his son was killed. He confirmed that Valdez Asij was present at this outpost and that he was military commissioner for the region at the time. He also explained that the Q'eqchi'-speaking soldiers were the ones who organized the PAC members, knew which women had lost their husbands, and went to get those widows to cook for them. He ended his testimony by asking the government for support for the loss of his son—who was disappeared—since he himself is now old and cannot work and has no one to support him. When one of the co-plaintiff's lawyers asked him to tell the court why he was testifying, he responded, "I am here because I am a victim. I lost my wife and I lost my son and I can't do anything apart from ask for justice." We cannot know the impact of giving testimony and whether he would end up feeling cheated if he did not receive reparations for the loss of his son or hear the names of his loved ones in the verdict. Would it be enough if two of the perpetrators were in prison for related crimes? It was clear that this first witness was not familiar with the logic of the trial. When the prosecutor asked him the first question about violence in his community, he began telling his life story, *testimonio* [testimony] style (Gelles, 1998; Hesford, 2011; McAllister, 2013; Nolin & Shankar, 2000; Marín, 1991; Yaeger, 2006).[12] However, he could have responded in this way because he was resisting reducing his testimony to what the court wanted to hear or he read his entire life as threaded with violence and, as such, needed to represent it in its entirety: perhaps his community's experience of violence was his experience of violence, his life story. Here again the issue of testimony and all life story performances by the Maya being a refraction of the collectivity rather than primarily or exclusively an individuated experience come to the fore.

Another male witness testified to being taken to the Sepur Zarco outpost when he was 12 years old and beaten, which left him with broken ribs and a broken hip; there, he witnessed women cooking large quantities of food for the soldiers. In his testimony, he said he recognized one of the accused, Reyes Girón, from the camp and that he knew both of the accused, pointing them out at the defense table. He told of knowing Valdez Asij from when he captured his father and from his own subsequent visits to Panzós to search for his father, whom he never saw again. He insisted, "All these things that I am telling you about didn't only happen to my father, but happened to many people. He [Valdez Asij] was someone with a lot of power there in Panzós."[13] A member of our research team commented in her trial field notes that this witness was by far the most intense and emotional among the Q'eqchi' who testified: the audience could hear the rage in his voice, and tension filled the room. In contrast to the other witnesses, who spoke in low voices, this man spoke loudly, almost yelling for the entire time he testified, which lasted for more than an hour. She wrote,

It almost seemed like he was about to burst. His body mimicked his rising and falling voice, his hands moving up and coming into a half-standing, crouching position over his chair before sitting back down. At one point, while he was talking about being taken to the military camp, he stood up and lifted his shirt almost over his head, energetically pointing to different places on his chest, showing the scars of where he had been beaten and had his bones broken, not pausing to let the interpreter translate. When asked if he could identify "Don Canche" (Valdez Asij), he stared him down; he seemed to be telling him off.

Another of the male witnesses was an auxiliary mayor in his community at the time, and it seemed particularly painful to him that he was treated so horribly despite his position of authority, which he alluded to several times during his testimony: "I said to them, 'I am an authority,' and they did not respect me, they did not listen to me." When he was describing the torture he had been subjected to, he shook his head at several points, wiping his face, eyes, and nose. He explained how his community was trying to legalize their land possession at the time and that the repression from the military forced many to flee to the mountains. They were, in his words, "common folk, like us. They fled out of fear, to save their lives." When asked what they were afraid of, he answered simply, "The soldiers." At one point he also told the court about how the soldiers took him back to his community and tried to force him to indicate where people participating in the land legalization efforts lived. However, he said he "could not do it, because we're all humans with the same God ... [the men] are very grateful to me because they are still alive."

The Q'eqchi' men's testimonies in the trial offer additional insights into the varied dimensions of racialized gendered harm. They talked about how they were forced to give their labor as part of the PACs and were expected to betray and inflict harm on their own community members, a reminder of the intersection of victim and perpetrator identities for indigenous men during the war and its implications for rethreading community. Others were forcibly recruited into the army itself, as a former Q'eqchi' soldier at the Sepur Zarco outpost who testified as a protected witness during the trial reminded us. When one witness was asked why the men had to patrol, he responded that he did not know: "They only told us to see [if we] would inform." Some of these men had to patrol the outpost gates, and some were forced to dig mass graves for members of their communities who were killed. Many were tortured and beaten, and some were forced to witness the rapes of their wives and other women. They told of losing their masculine and indigenous authority as community leaders. They talked about those who did not survive, including their own wives and children, and the disappearance of the plaintiffs' husbands because of their fight to have their lands legalized and whose remains had been displayed for the court to see. Some of them were children themselves when they were abused. The men did not testify to any experiences of sexual harm, although we do know that men were the targets of sexual violence during the war (most often subsumed under the category of torture, if shared at all). Their testimonies not only further validated the women's experiences but also served as a reminder not to reify gendered harm as only occurring to women, while at the same time recognizing that women were disproportionately affected by the particular gendered forms of violence reported herein, including sexual harm.

The Q'eqchi' men's testimonies were emotionally and physically embodied, as they pointed to their scars and expressed their anger at what they had experienced. For many of them, in contrast to the plaintiffs and the other women who testified during the trial, this was the first time they had testified about their experiences in public space, and it was clear that it was an overwhelming and intimidating experience. The women knew how to speak into the microphone and engage with their interlocutors when they testified in pretrial hearings, because of many years of training and participation in workshops such as the ones run by the Alliance. In contrast, Q'eqchi' men's protagonism was less dialogically constructed and performed in the years leading up to the trial. As such, they had not had the same sustained relationships to intermediaries over time.[14] Despite this, their embodied performances during their testimonies—uncovering their heads, displaying their scars—reflected the masculine authority and presence through which they occupied this public space. Hesford (2011) reminds us that "the judicial does not heal the wounds or atrocity or loosen attachments to identity" (p. 120), but it can be a point of beginning. As discussed earlier, for at least some of the men who spoke, this was an opportunity to narrate their testimonio rather than the linear, truncated narrative asked for by the court, and as such they asserted their protagonism and defined their experience as collective rather than only individuated: their lives were a refraction of the community as a whole.

AFTERMATH: THE DEMAND FOR REPARATION(S)

> When the conflict started, it was for the land.... There were some representatives who led a group who gathered like this to fight for the land, and so we can't forget that this struggle is for the land...that they occupied this land and killed much of this community...completely disappeared this group...this is what we live with here. But all of us here now, not only 14...there have been many, many women who have been made widows, but they went to other villages, other communities far away, because here they are afraid. This is what happened to us. What we want now is for the government to buy us the property where we are now, the land. We won't live longer but our grandchildren and children will be here...we don't want this to happen in the future.
>
> —Q'eqchi' protagonist, participant in August 2017 workshop

In August 2017, we traveled for the first time to the community of Sepur Zarco to facilitate a workshop with the 14 living plaintiffs in the Sepur Zarco case focused on their understandings of truth, justice, and reparation(s) after the trial. As this quote from one of the protagonists in the workshop illustrates, land remained a central preoccupation, as it was throughout the trial, where individual Q'eqchi' women and men, as well as the prosecution and co-plaintiff legal teams, sought to make connections between the individual sexual violence suffered by these women and its roots in the state's responses to indigenous peasant leaders' struggles to establish title to their lands at that time. And as one witness in the trial asked, "What will the law say?" Does the law have the capacity to respond to the claim for acknowledgment and provide justice or "are things going to stay as they are after all of these years that we've suffered?" This fear remained months after the trial, as the quote from our workshop emphasized. During sentencing, Judge Barrios did emphasize that "the harm done to victims transcended their bodies and their minds because after returning home, after having fled to the mountains to seek refuge, they were completely dispossessed, their community had changed irrevocably; their homes had been destroyed, their animals killed" (cited in Burt, 2016, para. 18). As discussed earlier, a reparations hearing was held a few days after the end of the trial, on March 2, 2016. As asserted in the hearing ruling, "the reparations to which the victims are entitled involve restoring the rights affected by the crimes, which begins by acknowledging the victim as a person with all of their circumstances as a subject of rights against whom the crime befell" (cited in Impunity Watch & Alliance, 2017, p. 44).

As already mentioned, the reparations hearing stipulated that the two perpetrators had to pay individual reparations to the plaintiffs and their families. The hearing also included 16 reparations measures directed to the Guatemalan state, focusing on health care, education, land, historical memory, and training for security forces. For example, the women's homes should be provided with basic services, the Ministry of Health should build a health center in the community, and the Ministry of Education should improve the local schools. The Ministry of the Interior was charged with searching for the women's disappeared husbands and children. The hearing directed that the sentence should be translated into the 22 Mayan languages, that information about the case be included in school curricula, and that monuments should be built to honor women who suffered sexual violence at the hands of the army. The Ministry of Defense was also ordered to provide training on human rights and violence against women to members of the military. In regard to land, the court stipulated that the requests for land legalization that the women's husbands submitted to the INTA when they were disappeared in 1982 should become the responsibility of the *Fondo de Tierras* [Land Fund], which was set up after the finalization of the Peace Accords to adjudicate land claims from the period of the armed conflict.

At the time of our workshop in August 2017, more than a year after the trial ended, the question remained as to what parts of the reparations ruling would be implemented. It seemed unlikely that Reyes Girón and Valdez Asij would fulfill their responsibility to provide individual reparations, given that one had already filed for bankruptcy and the other was likely to follow suit. The Jalok U Collective, formed by the women protagonists participating in the case and a co-plaintiff in the trial, along with MTM and UNAMG, was arguing for "transformative reparations" that would address the conditions of vulnerability that led to the violations and in which women still find themselves, particularly in regard to access to land and housing. Given how the conflict over land was at the root of what happened to these women, having their lands legalized is fundamental to their search for repair. Jalok U has a membership of 70 women and men from Sepur Zarco and surrounding communities, including the 20 women from the Alliance Group (14 of whom participated in the case). After the reparations hearing, with support from the Alliance, they set up four working groups on land, education, health, and victims (the last group also addresses research, security, and historical memory). They are working with the Alliance to ensure that the nine different state institutions implicated by the reparations sentence fulfill their commitments. Some progress has been made: a mobile health clinic now serves the community and surrounding area, and plans are in the works for a memory museum. The case has also been incorporated into middle school curricula (UNAMG, 2017). As one of the plaintiffs commented during our workshop, "We are very grateful because schools are now telling our story, unlike before when they didn't say anything about it, so there has been a change. Even though it's a small change, it's a good thing that our children and grandchildren learn from us." And as peasant farmers, the women continue to work the lands they are living on, tending to their animals, and, through the Jalok U Collective, have a source of income, making and selling products beyond the community.

During the workshop in August 2017, we asked the women to draw their conceptions of justice, reparation(s), and memory; these drawings were then collectively analyzed and subsequently performed through dramatizations (we used a similar methodology and format to the other creative workshops in this research, as described in chapter 1). What was striking about the justice drawing (Figure 7), was the ever presence of harm suffered; the women's dead husbands were represented by the figure at the top left; also represented was the destruction of their homes, animals, and of nature itself, which was also their refuge. As one participant commented on her group's drawing, with tears in her eyes, "We hid in the mountains from the planes. The tree is large because I lived for six years in the mountains to hide from the airplanes . . . for this reason I survived." The conviction of two perpetrators held responsible for specific crimes against individual victims fails as a response to these structural crimes; the harm remains.

Not surprisingly, given the inability of carceral justice to respond to structural harm, the reparation(s) drawings (Figure 8) focused very concretely on protagonists' demands for land, housing, and infrastructure. As one woman commented, "We put the land here because it's for the fight for land that our husbands died." In looking toward the future, beyond themselves, given their age and precarious health, another said, "We put a table here for writing, for eating . . . we are going to put money there for the children."

CONCLUDING REFLECTIONS

As previously mentioned, Jalok U means "transformation" or "change" in Q'eqchi'. The transformative impact of the Sepur Zarco trial cannot be minimized in a country where the state has historically dispossessed and excluded Mayan peoples

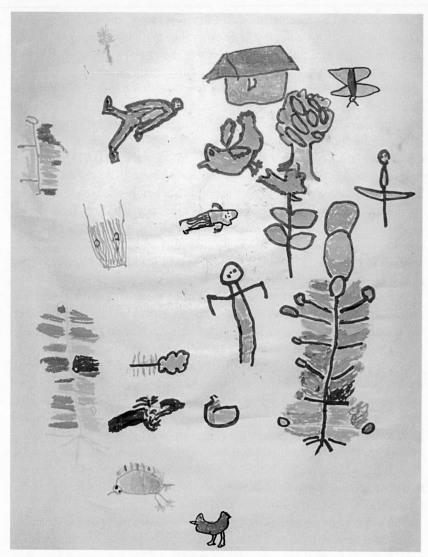

FIGURE 7. Q'eqchi' women's conceptions of justice.

and systematically perpetrated violence against them. The trial had transnational resonance, receiving widespread coverage in the national and international press. In addition the *Asociación Pro Derechos Humanos de España* [Spanish Human Rights Association] (APDHE) awarded Jalok U the 2017 International Human Rights Prize in recognition of the plaintiffs' protagonism. The trial was a tremendous undertaking by a great number of people; the plaintiffs; their fellow protagonists, both in the Polochic Valley as well in Huehuetenango and Chimaltenango, and the Mayan activists; feminist activists; lawyers; psychologists; and Mayan

FIGURE 8. Q'eqchi' women's conceptions of reparation(s).

promoters and interpreters, who had accompanied them over so many years. Despite the gendered community fissures and the dueling yet mutually constituting masculine identities of victim and perpetrator created within the Sepur Zarco community during the war and in its ongoing aftermath, the Sepur Zarco case is an example of Mayan community protagonism—of Q'eqchi' women and men deciding, over time, to participate in a space mediated by intermediaries and to seek justice for racialized gendered harm. There had been concern that the trial could lead to further ostracism and stigmatization and even violence for Q'eqchi' women protagonists within their community. Given the fragility of the community fabric torn apart from the war, and the continuing presence of perpetrators who wielded considerable power, often in positions of community authority (Valdez Asij and Reyes Girón included), for so many years Q'eqchi' women believed that they had to leave their community to speak about what had happened to them. As discussed in this volume, their protagonism was forged within a community of women outside of their own local, geographically based communities. The gendered silences about what had happened to them remained omnipresent in community relations, although many community members knew what had happened without formally being told (silence not being the same as not knowing).

The experiences in the wake of the Sepur Zarco trial suggest that it has contributed to the rethreading of community relations. Family members of the plaintiffs formed a primary network of support throughout the trial, which was also joined by a group of the town's young people, who now educate the community on the legacies of racialized gendered violence through improvisational and puppet theater. Community authorities were also mobilized in support of the trial (Impunity Watch & Alliance, 2017). The plaintiffs, accompanied by the Alliance and representatives from the Ministry of the Interior, were welcomed back to Sepur Zarco by the community during a festival organized the day after the verdict was handed down, February 26, 2016. In what one intermediary described as "a transcendental public moment," they took to the stage, their heads uncovered, to say, "We are the ones who sought justice." And as Demecia Yat, one of the plaintiffs and a Jalok U spokesperson, noted, "People from Panzós, from the plantation, came too, because they found out about the verdict. When the massacre in Panzós happened, it was the same man. So they came up to us and said, 'How great that you all organized, how great that you have the strength to go and ask for justice, how great that these men are in jail now'" (cited in Impunity Watch & Alliance, 2017, p. 29).

For Q'eqchi' men, their participation in the trial marked a new point of coming to terms with their experiences of violence. It was an expression of their protagonism alongside—and in relation to—Q'eqchi' women and to the diverse set of intermediaries who have accompanied them. It also marked a repositioning of Mayan men as perpetrators (albeit through coercion, within the PACs) and victims. Again, we return to our conception of protagonism as inherently dialogical, forged interactively to confront pain and suffering and foster new social relations. This is of course not to say that community tensions do not continue to exist in Sepur Zarco: some protagonists are still subject to threats and hostility from some community women and men, and there are continuing incidences of gender violence. As we discovered during our visit to Sepur Zarco in August 2017, divisions remain and may be further exacerbated by the implementation of the reparations ruling and by the possibility of future prosecutions. These tensions are often fomented by military and paramilitary groups in the region, including ex-PAC members, and by the presence of transnational corporations engaged in resource extraction and exogenous crop cultivation such as the African palm plantations: the land, its ownership and usage, remains a fundamental issue (AVANCSO, 2016).

Members of the Alliance continued to accompany protagonists in Sepur Zarco after the trial. In addition to working to ensure that the Guatemalan state fulfilled the reparations sentence, intermediaries also addressed "the continuum" of gendered violence that Mayan women confront in their everyday lives by implementing various rights-based violence prevention training programs and a census to document the impoverishment of Mayan women (MTM, 2017). The emphasis in the trainings has been on facilitating local Mayan communities' incorporation of the language of rights into their worldview and protagonists' use of the discourse of gender rights as they discuss violence within their communities. This reflected the vernacularization of international rights frameworks and discourses of "women's rights as human rights" and "rape as a weapon of war" that underpinned the legal strategy of the Sepur Zarco case and the broader work of the Alliance. Transnational responses to the trial have also been firmly rooted within this international rights paradigm. For example, in the aftermath of the trial, Nobel Peace Prize laureate Jody Williams, a member of the Nobel Women's Initiative, commented, "These 15 women bravely told their stories to ensure that future generations of Guatemalans will have access to justice . . . around the world, women are watching because wars are still being fought on women's bodies. This case is an important step in ending the nearly complete impunity for such horrific crimes" (as cited in Impunity Watch & Alliance, 2017, p. 50). Violence against women was also identified by members of the Alliance as a unifying force in Guatemala, given that most women in Guatemala have experienced violence in some shape or form: it has brought women and men in Guatemala together in support of the plaintiffs and the trial (Impunity Watch & Alliance, 2017). Although it is an important component in creating transnational and national networks of solidarity and support, indigeneity is again erased—including the structural and colonial nature of the harm suffered by Mayan people—when commonalities of gender are centered or conceptions of "woman" are homogenized within constructions of "violence against women." It is striking how few responses to the trial by non-indigenous commentators, in Guatemala and transnationally, highlighted indigenous dispossession, the racialized and racist dimensions of gendered violence, and the importance of centering Mayan agency in resolving community conflicts, let alone the privileges and power accrued by those of us who are non-indigenous. Hashtags such as #IAmSepurZarco and #WeAreAllSepurZarco, which proliferated transnationally during the trial, hold the potential to erase indigeneity and colonial difference, and center the protagonism of non-indigenous people, making it all about us (see Crosby, Lykes, & Doiron, 2018, for a discussion of affective contestations within the Sepur Zarco trial).

Mayan women's protagonism in the Sepur Zarco trial was shaped through their engagement with mostly (but not exclusively) ladina and international intermediaries oriented toward Western feminist (primarily second wave; see Jaleel, 2013) understandings of gender and of Western notions of justice. However, as we have noted before, Mayan protagonists were not acted on in their engagements with intermediaries; instead, relationality was intentional, multifaceted, and imbued with power. We return to the complexities of these protagonist–intermediary relationships, shaped as they are by structures of racism and colonization, in chapter 5. In chapter 4, we examine in more detail how Mayan protagonists situated the relationship between structural harm and violence against women in their conceptions of reparation(s).

4 · REPAIRING PROTAGONISM
"Carrying a Heavy Load"

They have to pay for everything they did to us, and the damage to our lives when they raped us.

> —Q'eqchi' protagonist interviewed by MTM in 2009

My engagement with the survivors of riots also showed me that life was recovered not through some grand gesture in the realm of the transcendent but through a descent into the ordinary. There was, I argue, a mutual absorption of the violent and the ordinary . . . as if there were tentacles that reach out from the everyday and anchor the event to it in some specific ways.

> —Veena Das (2007, p. 7)

"Who can repair this harm in my heart?" asked the K'iche' protagonist rhetorically when she testified to the Tribunal of Conscience. Beginning with this acknowledgment of the irreparability of harm suffered, this chapter examines how Mayan protagonists make meaning of reparation(s) and what Das (2007) describes as the "everyday work of repair" (p. 62). As discussed in this volume, protagonists' experiences of sexual violence were multifaceted and context specific, and many continue to live in the same communities alongside those who perpetrated violence against them. For many years (2003–2013), a large part of their recovery process and search for—and beyond—repair was carried out in and through relationships with one another and with groups of intermediaries who have been accompanying them, primarily outside of their local communities. Through these gatherings they formed a community of women outside their local geographically based communities, and this pan-communality has had its own reparatory effects, given the often fractious and fraught nature of relationships within local communities torn apart by the devastation of war. Within those local communities there are daily challenges "to live in this very place of devastation" (Das, 2007, p. 6), the site of extreme violations and individual and social suffering.

In the chapter, we draw on data generated from a series of workshops on reparation(s) that we facilitated using creative techniques, including drawing, collage, dramatization, and body sculptures, to elicit protagonists' experiences with, narratives about, and meaning-making of reparation(s). As discussed in chapter 1, creative resources were engaged to generate more embodied, complex, collective, and/or contestational representations of harm suffered and meanings made about these experiences than those that typically emerge from a linear, words-based, and individuated narrative approach characteristic of many transitional justice and interview processes. We also draw on the more descriptive data generated through 48 interviews of the 54 protagonists conducted by the feminist lawyers' organization MTM in 2009 in preparation for a collective demand for reparations from the Guatemalan state that was presented to the IACHR; the complaint had to be rewritten in the wake of the Sepur Zarco verdict to exclude the plaintiffs from that case because the outcome of that trial included reparations. Similar to previous chapters, the processes described in this chapter emphasize Mayan women's protagonism as enacted through dialogical relationships with each other, as well as with the intermediaries who accompany them, ourselves as researchers included.

The chapter begins with an examination of discourses of repair within the transitional justice literature and in the Guatemalan context. We provide an overview of the state-sponsored PNR and then highlight protagonists' conceptions of reparation(s) that emerged from our analysis of the interviews conducted with them by MTM. In these interviews, the protagonists were asked to make a connection between reparation(s) and justice and to specify their past losses. Most spoke of reparation(s) in relation to both the material and symbolic dimensions of loss and named their innocence, as well as the state's culpability. We then move to an analysis of the demand for integral reparation(s) that emerged from the creative workshops we conducted with protagonists, which revealed how they have woven together three main threads as representing their understanding of reparation(s): (1) their experiences of loss and harm, (2) their recognition of the Guatemalan state's duplicity, and (3) their own protagonism in justice-seeking processes. As we discuss in the chapter's conclusion, our analysis of the workshop data revealed how Mayan women locate their struggles for repair within their understanding and articulation of the deep-seated impoverishment that they experience as "violence against women" in their everyday lives and thus this impoverishment is a key focus for their ongoing protagonism. These workshops enabled us to better understand their conception of harm as a set of structural factors manifested in the everyday, rather than as an individuated, spectacularized, singular, sexualized event. This meaning-making frames their current demands for integral reparation(s) that we document and analyze through the workshops discussed in this chapter.

BEYOND REPAIR? "REPAIRING THE IRREPARABLE"

Within the transitional justice literature, reparations, particularly in the form of large-scale reparations programs implemented following truth-telling processes, are perceived to be more victim centered than forms of retributive justice such as prosecutions, although the two, of course, are integrally linked (de Greiff, 2006; Hamber, 2009; Rubio-Marín, 2006, 2009). As previously discussed, drawing on Hamber (2009), we use the concept of reparation(s) in this volume to refer to both *reparation*, "the psychological state in which victims feel that adequate amends have been made for a wrong committed" (p. 97), and *reparations*, "the acts or objects associated with attempts to make amends" (p. 97). Reparations are thus the means through which reparation is sought. As Hamber states, drawing on Klein's psychoanalytic object relations theory, "from an individual psychological perspective, it is helpful to think about the aim of reparations . . . as being able to make reparation" (p. 97; see also Chambers-Letson, 2006; Eng, 2011). Under international law, reparations aim to restore victims to the status quo ante by compensating them for harm suffered. As Minow (1998) puts it, "The core idea of reparations stems from the compensatory theory of justice. Injuries can and must be compensated. Wrongdoers should pay victims for losses. Afterward, the slate can be wiped clean. Or at least some kind of justice has been done" (p. 104). De Greiff (2006) refers to the range of measures to redress harm identified in the UN Basic Principles and Guidelines,[1] including restitution, compensation, rehabilitation, and satisfaction and guarantee of nonrepetition. This set of measures comprises what he terms the broader understanding of reparations and can include truth commissions, prosecutions, and institutional reforms. What he identifies as the "narrower definition" of reparations are large-scale state-sponsored reparations programs that include "measures that provide benefits to victims directly" (p. 453). This narrower understanding of reparations "contrasts with measures which may have reparative effects, and which may be very important (such as punishment of perpetrators, or institutional reforms), but which do not distribute a direct benefit to victims themselves" (p. 453).

Many transitional justice scholars agree that, in situations of massive violations of human rights such as the genocidal armed conflict in Guatemala, it is not possible to adequately compensate for what has been lost; that is, we cannot "repair the irreparable" (Hamber, 2006, p. 567; see also De Greiff, 2006; Lykes & Mersky, 2006; Minow, 1998). As Minow (1998) reminds us, "No market measure exists for the value of living an ordinary life, without nightmares or survivor guilt. Valuing the losses from torture and murder strains the moral imagination" (p. 104). Thus it has been argued that reparation in such contexts is largely symbolic, even when material compensation is provided (Hamber, 2006; Lykes & Mersky, 2006). Minow (1998) references the "small" and "humble" requests made by victims and survivors for reparations: "dignified assertions made by individuals who have no illusions about the possibility of external repair for their losses" (p. 106). However, Miller (2008) makes the important point that this framing of the irreparability of harm can set survivors up for frustration and disappointment, a sense of being deceived, because the acknowledgment that it is not possible to "repair the irreparable" leads to the sense "simultaneously that reparation is necessary as a progressive gesture and that its objectives are inherently unreachable if they include the fantasy of actual repair" (p. 280). Reparation is thus always inherently qualified or indeed phantasmical, bringing cruel hope to survivors of the possibility of something better.

The transitional justice literature also recognizes that it is not possible—or desirable—to return to the status quo ante, particularly given that many armed conflicts are set within histories of colonial violence and dispossession that created the deep-seated structural inequities that led to the violence. This is certainly the case in Guatemala. How to provide redress to indigenous and racialized communities for colonization and slavery—forms of historical violence that continue to structure the present—is an issue of increasing transnational debate (see for example Coates, 2014; Miller & Kumar, 2007; Smith, 2004; Thomas, 2011). De Greiff (2006) argues that the ultimate goal of reparations programs is to "do justice to victims" beyond the juridical realm: to create the conditions for a rethreading of the political community through three core principles: "recognition, civic trust, and social solidarity" (p. 254). These principles emphasize the importance of reparations as relational, dialogical, and future oriented. As Minow (1998) states, reparations "can meet burning needs for acknowledgment, closure, vindication and connection. Reparations provide a specific, narrow invitation for victims and survivors to walk between vengeance and forgiveness. The ultimate quality of that invitation depends on its ability to transform the relationships among victims, bystanders and perpetrators" (p. 106). As such, reparations programs are assessed by their ability to deliver a transformation in social relations between victim-survivors, their fellow citizens, and the state. This is a tall order indeed. De Grieff provides what he refers to as a taxonomy by which to assess the effectiveness of reparations programs: "scope, completeness, comprehensiveness, internal and external integrity or coherence, finality and munificence" (as cited in Rubio-Marín, 2009, p. 11).

Research confirms that recent reparations programs, including those in South Africa and Peru, as well as Guatemala, have failed this taxonomy on all counts, engendering bitterness and disappointment on the part of victim-survivors (de Waardt, 2013; Impunity Watch, 2013; Ross, 2003).[2] Recognition, civic trust, and social solidarity seem further away than ever. Is it then a question of drawing "lessons learned" from previous experiences and striving to do better, as has been the organizational practice of the transitional justice paradigm? Or do we need to rethink the paradigm itself? Like other transitional justice frameworks, the discourse of reparation(s) relies heavily on the language of rights and is underpinned by Western liberal assumptions about progress, participation, and inclusion, despite growing attention to the continued effects of structural inequities that suggest a politics of transformation rather than mechanisms of transition (Gready & Robins, 2014). Moon (2012) emphasizes the political and regulatory aspects of state reparations programs and how they "can work to administer and control social suffering and can sometimes intensify rather than ameliorate it" (p. 2). She urges attention be paid to the multiple instances in which victims refuse reparations from the state. Drawing on examples from South Africa, Northern Ireland, and Argentina, she argues, "Victim refusals of reparation are not a refusal of the gesture of repair per se, but are often a rejection of the range of political and historical meanings, and their coercive potential, to which state reparation is attached in transitional politics" (p. 3).

Miller (2008) has critiqued the "constructed invisibility of economic questions" (p. 266) within the transitional justice paradigm; for a more recent "turn to the economic" within the transitional justice literature, see Bunschuh (2015) and Sankey (2014). Structures of violence and histories of colonization and dispossession are relegated to the background as context, rather than being foregrounded as violations in and of themselves. What is occluded is the question of the redistribution of resources, and in particular of land. While Miller (2008) does not attend to the gendered dimensions of these issues, her critique has resonance with our research.

What does it mean to make meaning of reparation(s) in relation to racialized gendered harm and to build recognition, civic trust, and social solidarity? As much of the literature on gender and reparation(s) has noted, and as is discussed later in this chapter in relation to the Guatemalan context, survivors of racialized gendered harm face stigmatization, ostracism, and exclusion from their families, communities, fellow citizens, and the state. Some of the literature on gender and reparation(s) has focused on how reparations program can be more inclusive of women survivors' needs and demands (Couillard, 2007; Rubio-Marín, 2006, 2009). Others have questioned the hyperfocus on sexual harm within the reparations debate, as within much of the broader transitional justice discourse (Laplante & Theidon, 2007; Ross, 2003; Theidon, 2012). Thus, the challenge in gendering reparation(s) is also to pay attention to the more complex, intersectional, collective, and performative ways in which protagonists make meaning of reparation(s).[3]

As discussed in detail in chapter 2, an antiracist anticolonial feminist lens draws our attention to the intersectional circulations of power within transnational narratives of sexual harm, as well as the desire of Western audiences, feminists included, to hear stories of abjection from racialized gendered subjects (Kapur, 2002; Miller, 2004). Some have argued that this act of witnessing by those in the West is at least partly about deeply imbued colonial fantasies of rescue and the continuous remaking of white selfhood (Ahmed, 2000; Hartman, 1997; Razack,

2007). As such, testimonies of pain and loss involve a dialogic engagement between speaker and listener that is fractured, fraught by historical ongoing relations of power, and tenuous at best. As Sontag (2003) once said, "No 'we' should be taken for granted when the subject is looking at other people's pain" (p. 115). As white North Americans, we are deeply implicated within such dynamics, which require a constant interrogation of our positioning as researchers; that positioning itself can reshape the stories that protagonists want to tell (see the introduction and chapter 5). Thus, it was critical for us to formulate a research methodology that facilitated the displacement of our authorial narrative privilege and would enable other stories to be told and heard. We designed participatory processes through which Mayan protagonists shared their conceptions of reparation(s), thereby enabling multiple levels of collaborative reflection and action among ourselves as researchers, Mayan protagonists, and local intermediaries and coresearchers—and we avoided asking Mayan protagonists to retell their stories of suffering.

Equally challenging in situating this analysis and deepening our understanding of reparation(s) are its linguistic renderings in Guatemala. There are two Spanish terms used to refer to reparation(s), which reflect De Grieff's (2006) distinction between its narrower and broader understandings. *Resarcimiento* is used to refer to economic indemnification in particular and is associated with the state-sponsored PNR that began its work in 2003; in our research, it became shorthand used by participants to talk about the PNR and its efforts. In contrast, as Viaene (2010b) points out, the term *reparación* refers more broadly to "the conjunction of the search for justice, truth-seeking efforts (such as the exhumation of clandestine graves of forcibly disappeared people) and initiatives to recover historical memory" (p. 8). In our research, protagonists also referred to this as *reparación integral*: integral or holistic reparation(s) (see also Consejería en Proyectos, 2010). As discussed later in this chapter, the distinction between resarcimiento and reparación integral reflects protagonists' ambivalence and indeed often bitterness toward the state (they usually referred to resarcimiento in negative terms) and their insistence on something more. They demanded that reparation(s) not be limited to the symbolic, but rather must also address the ravages of genocidal violence—returning the dead and disappeared, bringing those responsible to justice, and acknowledging the truth of harm suffered—and provide redress for dispossession: the loss of land and livelihood that continues to mark the experience of indigeneity in neocolonial and postgenocide Guatemala.

Adding to this complexity is the absence of a direct translation for reparación or resarcimiento in the various Mayan languages spoken by participants in this project. In a group interview we conducted in 2010 with the Mayan women interpreters who worked with us in this research, they indicated that in Q'eqchi', many people use *xii'ti'n*, which means "to repair what is broken."[4] In Kaqchikel, they use *q'ojoj*, which means "to sew something that is ripped or to patch something back together," while emphasizing that it cannot be fully repaired: "it's not the same [as before]." In another workshop where the issue of interpretation was discussed, one Mayan woman protagonist told us that resarcimiento is translated in Kaqchikel as "a little bit of help" because "it is not the price of a loved one nor the cost of being raped." The Q'eqchi'-speaking interpreters emphasized the importance of context in all translation and interpretation: "We tried to find translations through dictionaries but translations aren't always exact; they aren't the same as interpretation. We haven't ever made a literal translation, it's always situated in their lived experience." This resonates with the expert witness testimony of linguistic anthropologist Barrios in the Sepur Zarco trial discussed in chapter 3, where she described the intimate connections of language to the Q'eqchi' cosmovision (see also García Ixmatá et al., 1993/2017). Although we use the Spanish-language terms to situate this work within the broader literature, our inquiry focused on identifying and locating these situated, lived experiences and listening attentively to what the women with whom we were working were representing in their search for truth, justice, and reparation(s). We positioned ourselves alongside them, as we sought, despite our linguistic limitations, to ensure that their knowledge(s) and linguistic framings within their philosophy of life enter into human rights and academic discourse to develop processes that more fully emerge from and resonate with local communities. As discussed previously in this volume, these interpretations and representations constitute a third voice as they are iteratively reconstructed while they journey up through processes scaffolded by us as we seek to decolonize our praxis. Before proceeding to an examination of protagonists' conceptions of reparation(s), we describe in detail the context in Guatemala in which protagonists' reparation(s) struggles unfolded.

The National Reparations Program (PNR)

As previously discussed in this volume, during the 36-year armed conflict in Guatemala, the CEH report (1999) estimated that more than 200,000 people were killed or disappeared, 626 massacres were perpetrated, and 1.5 million people were displaced. The issue of reparations for the victims of the armed conflict first appeared in the Comprehensive Agreement on Human Rights signed by the Guatemalan government and the URNG in Mexico City in 1994 (Viaene, 2010b). The war came to a formal end with the signing of the final set of Peace Accords in 1996, which included the accord governing the creation of the UN-sponsored CEH and its accompanying amnesty bill for perpetrators. The report released by the CEH in 1999 found that Guatemala's indigenous Mayan majority were the particular targets of state-sponsored violence, concluding that the state's actions during the scorched-earth campaign against certain Mayan groups in the 1980s amounted to acts of genocide (which are exempt from amnesty under international law). The CEH issued a series of recommendations to the Guatemalan state to redress the wrongs of the past, including reparations to the victims of the massive violations of human rights committed during the war. The Guatemalan government did not approve a National Reparations Program (PNR) with an initial 13-year mandate until 2003.

The creation of the PNR, after much foot-dragging on the part of successive postwar administrations, was partly due to the fact that in 1999, under the Portillo administration, former members of the PACs received partial compensation for "services to the nation"; this prompted an outraged response from victims' groups and human rights activists, given that PAC members were responsible for committing 18% of atrocities during the armed conflict (CEH,1999, vol. 2, p. 227; see also Amnesty International, 2002; Gamazo & García, 2012; Viaene, 2010b). Nearly two million quetzals [US$269,700] were paid out to some 517,000 former PAC members between 2003 and 2011 under the payment plan that was agreed to by the Portillo government after nearly 20,000 ex-PAC members mobilized in mid-2002, blocking highways and occupying town plazas throughout the country, to demand compensation for the services they rendered to the state during the internal armed conflict (Amnesty International, 2002; Gamazo & García, 2012).

In its definition of beneficiaries, the PNR excludes those registered with or having received payments from the ex-PAC compensation program from also receiving reparations through the PNR (PNR, n.d., Art. 33). In reality, however, the line between victim and victimizer is very hard to draw, given that thousands of mostly indigenous men were forced to patrol and to participate in the atrocities, which were often committed against their own communities, neighbors, and families: the CEH estimates that, in 1982, half of all adult men in Guatemala were enrolled in the PACs (1999, vol. 2, pp. 226–227). As Viaene (2010b) notes, "In Guatemala, the harsh reality of 'victim-perpetrator' identity is seriously underestimated and even neglected, not only by the state but also by civil society and specific organizations that work with victims" (p. 17). Given the extreme poverty in which rural Mayan victims and survivors were left in the aftermath of the armed conflict, many widows readily accepted the ex-PAC payments, which albeit representing a smaller sum per individual, were disbursed much more efficiently and through a better funded program than the PNR; in late 2012 the PNR had only disbursed about half of the amount received by the ex-PACs, benefiting a mere 16,000 families of the many who qualified (Gamazo & García, 2012).

The PNR's Reparations Commission that was responsible for overseeing the program's implementation initially included civil society representatives. However, after deep divisions and acrimony emerged among the participating civil society organizations, and charges of racism were directed against the then-PNR director, exclusive oversight shifted to the government in 2005 (Arriaza & Roht-Arriaza, 2008). Constant restructuring and changes have been enduring characteristics of the PNR (for analyses of these and other changes in the PNR, see

Arriaza & Roht-Arriaza, 2008; Consejería en Proyectos, 2010; Impunity Watch, 2013; Paz y Paz Bailey, 2006; Viaene, 2010b).

In its original policy document, the *Libro Azul [Blue Book]*, the PNR (2003) defined the parameters of its work as including "all the policies, programs and actions that are carried out with the aim to repair, compensate, redress, indemnify, assist, rehabilitate and dignify victims of the armed conflict" (p. 12). It defined victims as "those who have suffered, directly or indirectly, individually or collectively, the human rights violations which are included in this Program" (p. 12). Sexual violence was included in a list of the crimes meriting reparation(s) accepted by the PNR, as well as forced disappearances, extrajudicial executions, torture, forced displacement, and the forced recruitment of minors. The reparations measures to beneficiaries that were contemplated included material restitution (individual and collective), economic indemnification (individual), psychosocial reparation and rehabilitation (individual and collective), dignification of victims (individual and collective), and cultural reparations (collective). In later documents, the PNR (2007) also emphasized the importance of holistic or integral reparations by developing the concept of *maya kem*, which it refers to as a "new holistic paradigm" and defines as "the simultaneous application of reparations measures that are both tangible (quantifiable) and intangible (unquantifiable, such as, for example, dignification and cultural reparation) within the same geographic space and temporal period" (p. 78). According to the PNR, in practice maya kem includes "the active participation of the victims themselves and families of victims who are beneficiaries, in the design, planning and implementation of reparations measures, this being the only way in which to achieve individual repair, reparation of the social fabric, recovery of cultural identity, the exercise of full citizenship and support to the demands for justice" (p. 107). Despite this commitment, one of the main complaints against the PNR has been the lack of consultation with victims and their families, let alone their being able to actively participate in the reparations process. Moreover, there is no mention of rethreading relationships among victims, perpetrators, and bystanders, processes that Minow (1998) identifies as integral to making the transition from "vengeance to forgiveness" (p. 106) and that is a requirement for the achievement of the core principles of "recognition, civil trust, and social solidarity" identified by De Grieff (2006, p. 254) as the primary goal of reparations programs.

The measures implemented by the PNR since 2003 include economic indemnification, with the handing out of checks to some victims after a verification process, and material restitution through a partial housing program (Caxaj, 2014; Consejería en Proyectos, 2010; ODHAG, 2014; Viaene, 2010b). Cultural reparations have been implemented through the (often contested) installation of monuments, plaques, and memorials in some communities and regions of the country most affected during the war, as well as in Guatemala City (Memorial

Para la Concordia, n.d). The *Blue Book* (PNR, 2003) had stipulated that victims could receive compensation for more than one crime: "Victims can access the different benefits or components of the program any time they qualify for the damages suffered" (p. 27). This issue has proven contentious, with many of the 54 Mayan protagonists reporting not having been able to access more than one reparations benefit, despite being victims of multiple violations. In discussing this question with PNR staff in an interview we conducted in June 2013, they explained the *Blue Book* statement as meaning that victims had to declare all violations in their initial statement: they could not add to that statement at a later date. Confusion about the PNR's policy on this issue and the contentious nature of the documentation and verification process more generally have contributed to the deep mistrust felt by many victims toward the PNR and their sense that they are not believed.

As mentioned earlier, sexual violence was included as one of the crimes meriting reparation, and in the *Blue Book* particular emphasis was placed on victims of sexual violence, although the request for support had to come from the victims themselves: "The PNR will give special attention to victims of sexual violence *who ask for it*, and in accordance with their particular needs. Moreover, coordination will take place with other governmental and civil society bodies to promote public policies oriented towards providing permanent support to victims of sexual violence" (PNR, 2003, p. 22; emphasis added). Our research project began as the PNR was finally beginning its implementation phase after having been restructured several times and having had constant changes in staff. We sought to understand how women survivors of sexual violence engaged with this process, including what it meant to them to receive—or be denied—monetary and/or material compensation for sexual harm. Beneficiaries have received Q20,000 (US$2,600) for sexual violence, although some have received as much as Q34,000 (US$4,460) for sexual violence and the loss of a loved one. As discussed earlier, many were denied claims for more than one violation (Caxaj, 2014). Victims of torture have also received Q20,000, while those who lost family members have received Q24,000 (US$3,148). The majority of PNR beneficiaries have been elderly women. For example, in 2012, 65% of the 868 beneficiaries were women. Between 2012 and 2013, of the 2,193 cases receiving reparations, 35% were for extrajudicial executions, 28% for forced disappearance, and 6% for sexual violence (Weber, García, & Montenegro, as cited in Caxaj, 2014, p. 13). All of the 54 Mayan protagonists have asked for compensation, and most have received something from the PNR; however, some are still waiting for reparations, and others have had their applications partially or fully denied. Despite this, none perceive the state to have provided the "permanent support" to them as victims of sexual violence that was stipulated in the *Blue Book* (PNR, 2003, p. 22).

Whatever the intention on the part of the state, for victims, receiving money from the state for sexual harm is extremely fraught. On the one hand, the awarding of compensation is a concrete acknowledgment by the state of harm suffered and therefore is part of the dignification process (Fulchiron et al., 2009). However, some protagonists described feeling like they were "bought off" or "treated like prostitutes."[5] Many were routinely mistreated by PNR staff who often disbelieved their testimony of sexual harm (Fulchiron et al., 2009). In the interview we conducted with PNR staff in 2013, they implied that community members manipulated women to invent stories of sexual harm in order to receive reparations.[6] Receiving reparations for sexual harm also generated conflict with family and community members. A majority of the women with whom we worked had not formally told their family members they were survivors of sexual violence at the time they applied for reparations from the PNR, and receiving a check for this crime outed them as such, often leading to stigmatization and ostracism within their families and communities (Paz y Paz Bailey, 2006). As revealed in the MTM interviews, one woman was accused by community members of "receiving money for the bones: you are eating bones." Some family members appropriated the funds received from the PNR, or the women gave the money to their children. Other women used the money to pay for health care for the long-term illnesses and bodily harm resulting from the original experiences of sexual violence. Our research with protagonists confirmed that health care for survivors of sexual violence, one of the PNR's commitments, has not been provided for the most part (see also Caxaj, 2014).

Protagonists' Conceptions of Reparation(s)

As noted earlier, we were given access to the transcripts of interviews that the feminist lawyers' organization, MTM, conducted in 2009 with 48 individuals (i.e. the majority of participants in this project) in all three regions of the country (Huehuetenango, Chimaltenango, and Alta Verapaz/Izabal) to generate data for a collective *denuncia* [complaint] against the Guatemalan state for its failure to provide integral reparation(s). This complaint was presented initially to the IACHR in 2013, but was redrafted in light of the Sepur Zarco reparations ruling. Despite the linear structure of these interviews, because we had promised the 54 Mayan protagonists that we would respect their desire and not ask them to retell their stories, we drew on their descriptions of harm suffered in their geographically based communities to inform the creative resources used in our workshops, through which we explored their understandings of reparation(s).

The interviews followed a structured protocol, designed by MTM, with some deviations. Each interview was conducted by one of the MTM lawyers, accompanied by one of the Mayan women interpreters who had been working in close collaboration with the Alliance and the Mayan protagonists since 2003. While the interviewers spoke in Spanish, most of the women responded in their own language, through the interpreter.[7] To document the parameters of each woman's demand for reparation(s), the protocol began with detailed background questions about their lives before the war, which were followed by questions about the violence itself. Some of the interviewers asked whether the woman's husband knew about the rape, what would happen if he did, if children witnessed it, what that was like, and how the rape affected their past and current relationships. The interviews went on to examine the effects of the violence, including the women's perceptions of its impact on their health and well-being and whether they could imagine their lives if there had been no war. They were then asked a series of questions related to the demand for reparation(s) and justice, including "If the president were here, what would you say [*que diría*] to him?" or alternatively, "If a representative of the government were here, what would you ask [*que pediría*] them for given everything that happened during the war?" As a member of our research team reflected in her coding notes, the questions, "*que diría* [what would you say] and *que pediría* [what would you ask for] were pretty evenly split (among the interviewees). Mainly *pedir* is to the government while *decir* is to the president." Interviewees were also asked these questions: "What does justice mean to you?"; "What do you need to live well, to be happy, to be at peace?"; and "What would you ask for as reparation for everything that happened during the war?" The interviewers used either reparación or resarcimiento in this question; it varied between interviewers. The coding notes include this comment on how the interviews were conducted: "Sometimes the interviewers try to describe *reparación* or *resarcimiento* without using the words. In this case sometimes the interviewees get a bit confused, and the interviewer has to explain some more, talking about payment and debt, while other times interviewees respond by spontaneously using the terms *justicia, reparación* or *resarcimiento*." In some of the interviews, the women were asked whether they had received reparations from the PNR, with follow-up questions about whether the interviewee had applied for it for themselves, or "just" for the loss of family members. These commentaries in the coding process reflect the multiple understandings—or lack of understanding—of the Spanish-language terms by the Mayan protagonists, their efforts to engage the interviewers on their terms, as well as the importance of alternative non-oral strategies through which the women might share their understandings (a major impetus for the creative workshops we discuss in the following section).

It is also important to highlight here that the format constructed by MTM to prepare for the IACHR case shaped protagonists' understandings of reparation(s) and justice: the terms used had to fit within the language of an international rights-based framework required to demand reparation(s). The distinction made during the interviews between a protagonist's applying for reparations for her own experience of harm versus "just" for family members may tell us more about what the MTM lawyers (who were educated, urban, middle-class, professional ladina women) and the IACHR understood by reparation(s) and justice than about how the Mayan women themselves understood these concepts. As discussed in this volume, Mayan conceptions of justice are more communal in approach, although the individual is also interwoven therein. Chirix García (2003), Hernández Castillo (2016), and Otzoy (2008), among others, describe Mayan sociality, in which individuality and collectivity are dialectically situated. Chirix García (2003) and Grupo de Mujeres Mayas Kaqla (2009, 2011) situate this understanding of Maya subjectivities vis-à-vis the cosmovision as well as the chronos, confirming the critical importance of spirituality and time for any rendering of loss and repair. Thus, one should not underestimate the ongoing and integral relationship of the living to the dead, as discussed in the previous chapter in relation to the Sepur Zarco courtroom scene where the as-yet unidentified remains of the protagonists'—and other community members'—family members were displayed for all to see.

The demands of the IACHR case thus shaped the understandings of reparation(s) and justice sought by MTM in the interviews they conducted—another example of the dialogic co-constructed nature of all knowledge(s)—and framed the data that we inductively coded. The interview transcripts of protagonists' understanding of what reparation(s) meant to them within this context, as well as their conceptions or meaning-making of justice, added a dimension to those performed in the creative workshops discussed in the next section. The themes that we identified revealed some of the women's understandings and/or assessments of resarcimiento (i.e., the reparations being administered by the Guatemalan state through the PNR), of a demand for more integral reparation(s) and for justice, and of the multiple effects of the violation of their rights and the sexual violence they survived. The analysis elucidated some of the ways in which a particular interviewer's questions, constrained by the broader framework of MTM's IACHR case, may have influenced the responses, giving additional evidence of the dialogic nature of the co-construction of meanings in these processes. Despite the linear question–answer method, the interviews did elicit the Mayan protagonists' naming of their losses and demands for repair and redress.

Reparation(s) for Material and Symbolic Losses: Content and Framing. Economic support emerged as the most commonly requested form of reparations (88% of participants mentioned it), even for participants who had already received reparations payments from the PNR. Other frequently requested forms of reparations were for houses (52%), health care (50%), and land (48%) and, less often, animals (15%). Women also demanded repair for the loss of their husbands (43%): 23% of women referred to the impact of the loss of their husbands' labor (and access to land), which deepened their impoverishment, and 21% also mentioned the affective loss of their partners, noting how things with subsequent partners/ husbands were not the same or how being alone is "so hard."

The coding process revealed a linguistic distinction between how women talked about reparation(s) and how they referred to justice. References to reparation(s) were framed in the language of need, through terms such as asking, requesting, deserving, and needing when talking about redistributive/material components, while more retributive/symbolic notions of justice were framed in terms of resistance, through use of words that reflected declarations, talking back, telling off, and refusing silence. Participants asked for *un poco* or *un poquito*—that is, "a little"—when talking about reparation(s); for example: "a little food"; "that they help us a little"; "a little money"; "recover a little"; "so that we can be a little more at ease." It is possible that these constructions were due to translation choices, but they were quite common and noticeable across more than one ethnolinguistic group/translator. This construct suggests two possible meanings: it might be a gesture of humility or supplication (which matches the language of need that is also used) and/or a recognition that, to the government, women's requests are peanuts and so are the reparations payments. It is notable that no one asked for a "little bit of justice." The justice discourse was much more direct and holistic.

In line with the transitional justice literature more generally, the interviews revealed consensus that resarcimiento/reparations do not pay for losses, erase the past, or end pain; they are not enough, and in fact, nothing is enough. Injury or harm (including but not only the experience of sexual violence) was articulated as something permanent and unfixable, unhealable. This was articulated explicitly and repeatedly, with never-ending pain: "I am never going to heal, this heart is injured, this heart will never heal." Protagonists' responses evidenced their recognition that there is no compensation for this pain and for everything that had been lost, for which the state is responsible: "It's not because of this payment that the pain will go away"; "although I received a payment, I don't forget, they [the state] don't think we are worth anything." All meanings converged to confirm the irreparableness of the harm and suffering these women have survived.

Relationship between Reparation(s) and Justice. The transitional justice literature widely acknowledges the importance of a constitutive relationship between justice and reparation(s) (De Grieff, 2006; Hamber, 2009; Minow, 1998) while also recognizing the irreparability of harm and suffering in the wake of gross violations of human rights (see Hamber, 2009; Lykes & Mersky, 2006, among others). As Hamber (2009) states, "Without justice, generally through the courts, survivors tend to see reparations and compensation as attempts to buy their silence or to force them into colluding with a state's lack of will to prosecute those responsible for violence against them" (p. 109). Our coding of the MTM interviews revealed the various ways in which protagonists juxtaposed justice and reparation(s). A number of women stated that they wanted both justice and resarcimiento/material repayment; for example, one woman said, "What I would like the most is justice because even though I have the money everything that happened to me has not left me." Another protagonist stated, "The government owes us a lot, for example, to recover the crops, for example the houses they burned . . . but I am also very happy because we are now going to maybe have justice pay," which she went on to describe as distinct from economic forms of reparation(s). In only 11 interviews did the interviewer mention justice explicitly in their questions (most likely because the framework of the IACHR case was the demand for reparation(s)), but respondents often used the term spontaneously.

The president-themed question was the most commonly posed question by interviewers (in 44 interviews). We noted that some women were asked, "What would you say to the president/government?" while others were asked, "What would you ask the president/government?" In the coding process, we started to notice that women responded more frequently with an explicit and implicit use of justice language when they were asked about what they would say rather than what they would request. To some extent the language of the question was mirrored in the response, an indication of the co-construction of knowledge through the interview process. We had generally expected the terms "justice" and "reparation" to mirror each other, but the use of the verbs to ask and to say turned out to significantly influence participants' responses. This distinction seems to have functioned as a prompt toward either retributive/symbolic notions of justice (to say) or the redistributive/material aspects of repair (to ask): the idea of declaring, talking back, telling off, or refusing silence versus that of asking, requesting, being humble, deserving, or needing. Even when people who were asked the diría question were more focused on asking for reparations/money than on a trial, some told the president he owed them money (rather than saying, "I would ask him for it"). This could speak to women's own construction of themselves as subjects, even if contradictory and limited by circumstance. And while reparation(s) were framed in the language of want or need and often qualified by the use of "a little"—for example, "a little bit of help"—the references to justice were much more direct, framed as a demand against the Guatemalan state.

Despite the aforementioned constraints underlying the MTM interviews, our coding of the transcripts revealed specificities in protagonists' conceptions of and demands for justice, as distinct from reparation(s). These included multifaceted understandings of justice as punishment and accountability; as enabling public recognition of harm suffered; as resolving questions of innocence, guilt, and responsibility; as payment and debt for harm suffered; as a means to find out why this happened to them and to ensure it never happened again; and as an assertion of their rights as indigenous women and as citizens. The interviews complemented the testifiers' demands in the Tribunal of Conscience for the punishment of the perpetrators, who should be imprisoned and, according to one woman, even killed. A few women were particularly worried that they knew the identity of the perpetrators, some of whom continued to occupy positions of power in their communities. Others who did not know the identity of the perpetrators (or did not want to say they knew) were concerned that their lack of knowledge would negatively influence the possibility for justice. The need for the government's and general public's recognition of the harm suffered was more clearly articulated in relation to justice than to reparation(s). Many of the women interviewed envisioned themselves talking back to the government, declaring that their rapes were not their fault and that instead the government (whether articulated as the local mayor, the military commissioner, or the president himself) was responsible. The demand for accountability was also often expressed as a desire to have broader public recognition of the harm suffered and a need to speak out: "People should know that we suffered"; "I have to say something, for example about the harm they did to us, about the rape, that is a harm they did to us."

The issue of payment as a form of justice also came up, sometimes explicitly in terms of monetary compensation. There were many references to payment for what had been done to the women: "They have to pay for everything they did to us and the damage to our lives when they raped us." The irreparability of suffering was concretized through mention of the inadequacy of the reparations payments. It was also described as a failure of justice in terms of paying the government's debt to women survivors: "You cannot pay for harm." The women also articulated ideas about debt as not being completely monetary; for example, the importance of the state helping, supporting, or caring for the women: "It's the government's obligation to help us." There were many references to the need for health care because of the many illnesses suffered as a result of the violations. In the wake of the Sepur Zarco ruling, both the absence and presence of state payment for harm suffered continued to preoccupy protagonists (see Figure 8, p. 125).

Justice was also described as a means of giving protagonists an answer for why harm was done to them: "I want to know what reason he [the president] could give as to why he gave the orders for all they did to our communities." Some stressed that justice was important to ensure nonrepetition and an end to the fear of further violence: "I want to testify so that this does not happen again . . . now we have our children and we don't want what we suffered to happen to them." Justice was also framed in the language of rights, of speaking out and claiming rights: "Justice means achieving our rights." This use of the language of rights also signaled protagonists' understanding of what was required in the preparation of the IACHR case; "I am in this group to prepare a demand for justice." This statement is interesting in that it framed the IACHR case as pursuing justice, not reparation(s), perhaps signaling that these concepts are sometimes interchangeable within their understanding of rights discourse. As discussed in the previous chapter, there was an expectation of reparations on the part of plaintiffs participating in judicial cases, and the converse was perhaps also true, in line with the transitional justice literature: reparation(s) seeking must include justice for harm suffered. Compensation—in particular monetary compensation—is not enough (and justice without compensation is also insufficient).

Specifying Losses from the Past. In the interviews, as in their testimonies in the Sepur Zarco case discussed in the previous chapter, Q'eqchi' women described how their husbands were abducted (and later killed or disappeared) by the military over a land dispute and how they were subsequently raped by soldiers in their homes. The military then took advantage of their widowhood to force them to serve at the army camp for several months at a time over a period of six years. In discussing justice, several Q'eqchi' women made the (gendered) distinction between seeking recognition for the harm suffered due to the loss of their husbands and the harm suffered due to the sexual violence: "that they [the state/army] ask for forgiveness for the harm they did to us as women separately, first when they killed our husbands, and secondly when they took advantage of us as women." There was also the sense of a community of women established through suffering. As one woman said, "It was not just I who suffered, so many women, so many women," referring to the many women who had not yet had a chance to tell their stories and to all those who had died.

Naming One's Innocence and the State's Culpability. Women's assertion of their own innocence was often paired with articulations of the government's and/or military's responsibility or guilt; these are the aspects of acknowledgment and validation that Minow (1998) identifies as central to conceptions of reparation(s). "It's not my fault; it's the government's fault," said one woman. Several women laid the blame squarely on the president himself: "I know that he is the one who ordered that we be harmed," asserted one, while another added, "He should ask for forgiveness." One woman sought to publicly shame the state: "The whole country should know that it is the government that was to blame." Ongoing feelings of fear and shame were implicitly linked to the lack of justice. There was also a quite widely shared understanding of the need to name and punish those who ordered the violations, as well as those who carried them out, as a way to exculpate the women's alleged guilt: "It was not fair because we are honorable, we are peasants, we know how to work, we are not delinquents."

The thematic coding shed additional light on protagonists' understandings of reparation(s) in terms of whom they held responsible for their losses, the specific demands they made, and how they framed those demands. As discussed earlier, Mayan interpreters facilitated these Spanish-language interviews conducted by ladina MTM lawyers who had designed the format in preparation for the Tribunal of Conscience and for submission of a complaint to the IACHR. Thus the data presented were informed by multiple dialogic co-constructions: those between the interviewer and the interviewee, as mediated by the interpreter, and those between us as researchers coding their words and the text. Mayan women interpreters acted as intermediaries between the lawyers and protagonists, as they did in the workshops and interviews we designed and implemented throughout our research, as well as within the broader Alliance project. Intermediaries, ourselves included, played a role in shaping interpretations of the meanings made and the ways through which this particular group of Mayan women's stories of justice and repair would be told to wider publics who would listen to their mediated speech-acts. Thus we were involved in the co-construction of the multiple meanings they produced. The specific and multiple roles of the intermediaries, as well as our analysis of these co-constructions. are discussed in detail in chapter 5.

PERFORMING INTEGRAL REPARATION(S)

As discussed earlier, in July 2012 and June 2013 we facilitated a series of participatory workshops with Mayan protagonists who had survived sexual violence to further explore their understandings of reparation(s), this time within a collective, more dialogical, creative, and open-ended setting (in contrast to the testimonies and interviews for the Tribunal, Sepur Zarco, and IACHR processes discussed in the last three chapters). These workshops used creative techniques, including dramatization, collage, drawing, and image theater, to engage protagonists' storytelling, their emotional and embodied responses, and their demands for justice and repair. Rather than relying exclusively on linear, individuated narratives characteristic of much interview-based research and transitional justice processes, the creative resources we deployed were designed to facilitate women's embodied and collective engagement with the harms they experienced and their aftermath, enabling them to interact across linguistic and literacy barriers while sharing experiences of how they envisioned redress and repair through the arts and their creativity. The interpreters and protagonists began these processes by inviting all the women to participate in a set of rituals that invoked their Mayan beliefs and practices through representations of the four cardinal points of the universe, lighting candles, and calling to mind the day's nawal (Chirix, 2003; Grupo de Mujeres Mayas Kaqla, 2009).

Even with these participatory resources, the dialogical processes described here were still constrained by the inequities of power and linguistic challenges that had limited protagonists' previous narratives, as well as their direct engagement with one another, let alone with us and us with them. As outlined in the introduction to this volume and as discussed in detail in chapters 1 and 5, the epistemology that informs our research recognizes that there is no unmediated voice in any of these processes. At the same time, we seek to avoid the conclusion that processes such as these are always overdetermined. Mayan women protagonists have something to say that they wish others to hear and on the basis of which they are taking action: this was a primary motivation for our initiating this collaborative feminist PAR process. And in turn, such a speech-act demands a response (Theidon, 2007).

In this section, we briefly outline the specific activities through which protagonists performed their understandings and meaning-making of integral reparation(s) and their and our coding of the data generated through these participatory processes. In July 2012, participants were invited to work within their particular ethnolinguistic groups—Kaqchikel, Chuj, Mam, and Q'eqchi'—to create a collage from newspaper clippings that conveyed their shared understanding(s) of reparation(s) (see Figure 4 in chapter 1, a photograph of the Mam collage, included as part of our discussion of protagonists' meaning-making of creative resources). This activity was preceded by a brainstorming session with the whole group in which they generated a set of free associations to the Spanish-language terms deployed in Guatemala for reparation(s): resarcimiento and the term used by the women themselves to capture a more inclusive reparation(s), reparación integral. The women drew from this list and from ideas generated in their ethnolinguistic group conversations to develop collages in their groups, which were then presented to the whole group and collectively analyzed: first by the group as a whole, excluding the collage's creators, in terms of what they saw in the collages, and then by the collage creators in terms of what they hoped to represent.

In the workshop held in June 2013 with many of these same women, the first set of participatory activities focused on a review and assessment of the collages produced in 2012 and of a set of collages created by intermediaries in a 2010 workshop, including members of the Alliance, Mayan women interpreters, and ourselves as researchers. A second set of activities used adaptations from image theater and Boal's Theater of the Oppressed[8] (Boal, 1985), in which each of the four Mayan groups as well as UNAMG staff designed and then performed a series of body sculptures that re-presented an image of reparation(s) based on the cohort-based group's interpretations of the collages. The entire group then collectively analyzed these performances, with the audience first recounting what they had seen and then the performers providing their explanation.

The creative production, as well as the protagonists' discussion and analysis of their creative outputs, constituted the data for generating protagonists' collective understandings of reparation(s), as a counterpoint to those understandings generated through the more linear, individuated, and structured interviews by MTM described previously. As mentioned, we used a multilevel approach to analyze material generated throughout the creative processes. Participants themselves generated a first level of analysis through comments on their peers' and then their own creative output: their collages and dramatizations. These processes were documented through notes on newsprint, photographs, audio recordings, and detailed field notes taken by the research team. Thus each collage, dramatization, and image theater performance was accompanied by interpretive discourse that was recorded verbatim. We then engaged in a collaborative analysis of all textual data generated in the creative workshops, following the first two thematic coding levels of constructivist grounded theory (Charmaz, 2014).Through this process we identified three main thematic areas related to protagonists' conceptions of reparation(s): (1) as an articulation of loss and harm, (2) as a relationship to the state, and (3) as the embodiment of their emerging sense of protagonism.

"A Lump in the Throat": Articulations of Loss and Harm

In performing, visualizing, and then discussing reparation(s), participants reported experiences of loss and harm in both material and symbolic dimensions, similar to the codes that we identified in the individual interviews conducted by MTM. Continuities of violence from the past to the present emerged as a new dimension through the collective and participatory creative exercises. Thus the irreparable nature of the harm suffered continued to be front and center: what was lost cannot be replaced. The material dimensions of loss and harm emphasized the all-encompassing destruction of lives and livelihoods: "The armed conflict destroyed all that we had." Homes were burned to the ground, crops were destroyed, animals were killed, and land and all belongings and possessions were lost: "We became refugees and left everything, we left naked," and on their return, "we found we had no land."[9]

Given the overwhelming nature of loss and harm, what material compensation that was provided by the PNR was rejected as being inherently inadequate: "By paying money, they didn't make up for it." As one woman said, "It can never be recovered, they killed my father, they never gave me anything; even if they gave me Q20,000 [US$2,600], it wouldn't make up for his life." The transformative nature of loss was also represented in images and highlighted in their words depicting a culture and a way of life: "We left our lives but also our culture; we no longer live as we did before."

The creative processes generated a more explicit set of references to the embodied nature of the violence experienced by the women. Sexual violence left a permanent embodied mark that continued to be ever present, 30 years later: "Soldiers raped us and it affected our health." The long-term effects on health were a repeated refrain in analyzing an image theater performance: "Women remain ill over a long period of time, but no one gives them any attention." The affective dimensions of loss and harm were a constant motif. Protagonists referred to their fear and sadness, their sense of isolation and rejection, their shame and their shyness, particularly before they started working together: "This is how we were found. We did not look at each other, we did not understand what was happening," and "we couldn't talk . . . nobody listened to us." But some also emphasized their desire for change: "We wanted to talk, we wanted to relieve our suffering; it was the lump in our throat."

Central to participants' collective performance and analysis of reparation(s) of loss and harm was their emphasis on continuities between the past and present experiences of violence and impoverishment: "Today is similar; we are shut in, closed in on estates, cornered into the worst land"; "they left us in poverty, we live in poverty." Many participants were facing violent evictions over land disputes with transnational corporations, particularly in the Polochic Valley (Alta Verapaz/ Izabal), which they connected to their experience of violence during the war and the loss of their husbands due to disputes over land. Additionally, they described the psychosocial effects of the armed conflict as ongoing: "What happened during the war was present in our heads; what happened in the 80s is present now." They also emphasized the gendered nature of their continuous experience of loss and harm: "Women continue to be mistreated and discriminated against." This ever-present emphasis on the continuities of war and violence is absent from our coding of the individual interviews conducted by MTM or in the individual testimonies of Mayan protagonists at the Tribunal of Conscience discussed in chapter 2 and the Sepur Zarco trial discussed in chapter 3.

One striking image in the reparation(s) collages was the photograph of a woman carrying a heavy load as representing women's daily labor. The creators of this collage described the image as "violence against women." This representation of the weight or burden women bear was but one example of protagonists' ongoing insistence on locating violence within its structural and economic dimensions, on emphasizing the impoverishment the war caused in addition to the experience of bodily harm, and on drawing attention to the continuing presence of violence in contemporary daily life. Protagonists' resignification of the meaning of gendered violence resonates with Miller's (2008) critique of the invisibilization of the economic within the transitional justice paradigm and the tendency when addressing violence to "background structural factors in favor of more obvious concerns about physical violence" (p. 267).

"We Were Duped": Relationship to the Guatemalan State

There was clarity among all the protagonists that the Guatemalan state was responsible for the atrocities committed against them and for their continued structural impoverishment. It was thus the state's responsibility to provide reparation(s). They articulated their relationship to the state in a number of ways: the responsibility of the state for both past and present violence; their demand of the state for reparation(s); and repeated representations of how the state had deceived them, cheated them, lied to them, and discriminated against them as indigenous women. "Nos engañaron"—they duped or deceived us—was a constant refrain throughout multiple workshop discussions.

The responsibility of the state for the violence perpetrated during the armed conflict was in part centered around the former army general and de facto head of state during the worst of the genocidal violence in the early 1980s, Ríos Montt, a recurring figure in the reparation(s) collages and interpretations of their meanings: "It was Ríos Montt's fault that we suffered; yes, there was genocide." *Si hubo genocidio* [yes there was genocide] was a recurrent refrain throughout the Rios Montt genocide trial in 2013, in response to the country's elites' vociferous denials. The 2013 workshop took place not long after the trial. There were also many direct references to the army's role in the violence, although the women's lack of precision in their attribution of responsibility may also have reflected the much smaller number of violations that the CEH (1999) attributed to the guerrillas, who raped a small number of women in this group of 54 protagonists. They made statements such as the following: "Soldiers raped us"; "during the violence they burned everything"; and "they destroyed the coffee and harvested our crops." The women also connected the violence in the past and the violence and impoverishment they continued to suffer to the continued power of economic elites and the military: "Ríos Montt has economic power, that is why he was freed." The role of oligarchic power in the current violence was a constant theme, in particular in reference to the violent land evictions in the Polochic Valley where the Q'eqchi' women were living: "Campesinos occupy the land and the rich send guards or soldiers to defend themselves; they use violence not dialogue."

As in the individual interviews, the women's demands of the state to provide reparation(s) had material and symbolic dimensions. Protagonists emphasized that state-sponsored reparations should include land, as well as capital, including seed money for projects such as coffee plants, and access to jobs. They also highlighted the need for houses and furniture, crops and animals, health care, and education, particularly scholarships for their children. It is interesting to note the distinction the women seemed to be making between the negative consequences of receiving a check as reparation for sexual harm (their references to being "treated like prostitutes," being seen by their neighbors as having been "bought off"), and the demand for capital and material forms of restitution. There is something particularly transactional (and marketized) about direct financial payment for embodied harm as opposed to investing in material infrastructure through which they would be able to work to support themselves and their children and in their children's education, also perceived as obligations of the state that have never been adequately provided to Mayan communities. The dignification of victims by the state was also important; that the state should recognize and promote broader societal awareness of the suffering of women survivors during the armed conflict and destigmatize survivors by acknowledging that this violence was not their fault. Some scholars refer to the latter demand for destigmatization as the "redistribution of shame" from victims to perpetrators (Askin, 2001; K. Engle & Lottman, 2010; Franke, 2006; Theidon, 2007).

The most visceral aspect of protagonists' discussion of their relationship to the Guatemalan state was the sense that the state had failed them when it came to fulfilling the initial promise of the PNR to provide integral reparation(s) in a holistic way, not just in terms of monetary compensation. We perceived a palpable feeling of bitterness toward the PNR. One women verbalized it: "When it [the

PNR] started, it was to recognize/acknowledge victims; now the government considers it past, they no longer want to talk about it, it's no longer in fashion." Another said, "It's just to distract; treating you like a child so you don't complain." A third woman noted, "It's to shut you up, cover your mouth," and a fourth stated, "It's not right, not valid." The overly bureaucratic PNR demanded "requirements [documents] we don't have," and lands were not returned. There were several references to the PNR's inadequate housing program, with half-constructed homes and the expectation that victims provide their own building materials. One woman critiqued the failure to provide education to children or survivors, stating that one of the collages "reflects children studying but it makes us sad because peasant communities don't have this chance to learn how to read and write, which the PNR has in its scholarship programs but this is not given to the victims. We think it is only the rich who have this possibility."

All of the inadequacies and unfulfilled promises of the PNR process have led to survivors' sense of having been deceived and lied to by the government: "This government lies"; "while the government lives happily, we live in poverty." Several women affirmed their experiences of discrimination as due to their being indigenous women: "As indigenous women they continue to use us through deception." This deep-seated mistrust toward the Guatemalan state and the PNR is echoed in other research on this issue. Nos engañaron was the prevailing sentiment among Q'eqchi' women toward the PNR in research conducted by the *Oficina de Derechos Humanos del Arzobispado de Guatemala* [Human Rights Office of the Archbishopric of Guatemala] (ODHAG) in 2014 in six communities in Alta Verapaz in 2013 and 2014. According to the committee of women victims of the armed conflict from the community of Cambayal, "the PNR only makes promises and almost always benefits people who are members of the political party [in power] and many times these people are trying to divide the communities ... to date there has been little progress in our [reparation(s)] processes" (ODHAG, 2014, back cover). And testimonies collected by CAFCA in 2010 with women in the same region reflected a similar perspective: "Despite having told our story and fulfilled the requirements, the state is not concerned with our situation; they just make promises that in the end they don't keep; we women we are tired of all the hoops we have to jump through and we don't get a positive result" (as cited in ODHAG, 2014, p. 79). Here we see confirmation of Miller's (2008) concerns, discussed earlier, about how the consensus within the transitional justice paradigm that, despite all the promises and commitments contained in reparations programs, reparations can only be symbolic (i.e., that they cannot repair the irreparable and they can lead to deep-seated feelings of deception on the part of survivors).

An Emerging Sense of Protagonism

The reparation(s) collages and image theater performances exemplified an explicit expression of protagonism within and across their ethnolinguistic groups and as a community of women, a protagonism engendered by participants' engagement in collective struggles for truth, justice, and reparation(s). Protagonists performed dramatic re-presentations of their experiences of organizing, including participating in demonstrations and commemorative activities to demand that their rights be respected, and of their active engagement in community decision-making processes. These embodied performances echoed and transformed previous tellings of their stories that had been documented and passed down to their children and grandchildren (Fulchiron et al., 2009). The intersection of justice- and reparation(s)-seeking efforts was reflected in the decision of some to testify before the Guatemalan courts in the Sepur Zarco case discussed in the previous chapter. The convergence of these struggles was dramatized and defended through their workshop performances: "We are organizing to demand that they listen, and analyzing our histories during the armed conflict"; "we are mobilizing to get the government to comply [with our demands]." They also located their activism within their own communities, extending their engagement to work with other women: "We are demonstrating and creating women's committees in our community."

In these collective and creative processes, they described the relationships of trust that they had built among themselves as women in their own communities, working with others beyond the group of 54 protagonists: "It is necessary to give support to other women; I am not going to stay with my arms crossed if I see another woman's suffering." Again, they experienced this relationship as dialogical and affective: "When other women help, it makes us happy." They were conscious of how many women still had no access to any kind of redress and of the need to extend the work to others; as one woman noted, "How are we going to accomplish reparations for women who have not received them?" An important affective component of protagonism was evidenced both in their embodied performances and in their talk about feelings of happiness in participating in this process: "Now we feel happy. Before we were ashamed to give opinions and talk but not now." Nature was often used in the collages to represent affect; for example, the drawings of flowers around the newspaper cutouts in the collages were described as reflecting who they were: "because we are beautiful women like the flowers and we want to pass on a good story to our children and grandchildren." Protagonists noted that a major driving force for them was to ensure that the violations they experienced would never happen to their daughters and granddaughters.

The audience for the image theater performances was comprised of intermediaries from the organizations (including UNAMG, ECAP, and MTM) who have accompanied protagonists over many years; as such, the performances themselves were perhaps at least in part shaped by intermediaries' perceived expectations. Additionally, the intermediaries, including ourselves, structured the exercises in ways that elicited and facilitated less linear, more participatory, re-creations. As discussed in this volume, the dialogical nature of women's protagonism includes their relationships with the organizations that have accompanied them over a decade. They represented the organizations and us as participatory action researchers in their drawings. They talked about how these organizations "helped us overcome our fear," stating that "now with the organizations we can participate— which was also medicine for us." The role of intermediaries in these processes is complex, oscillating among and engaging with webs of power and inequities that surround and inform the participatory research (Merry, 2006; Merry & Levitt, 2017).

CONCLUDING REFLECTIONS

Protagonists' use of a photograph of a woman carrying a heavy load to illustrate their understanding of "violence against women" is emblematic of a constant thread running through the eight years of our research: the burden of extreme impoverishment that Mayan women carry is rooted not only within the 36 years of armed conflict but also within centuries of colonial dispossession of Guatemala's indigenous peoples, and it takes shape in their everyday efforts to feed and educate their children and take care of themselves. As such, what women want repaired is not only the harm to their individual bodies but also the structural harm and loss experienced by the collective body; that is, Mayan women and the indigenous communities in which they live. Their understandings of harm and the demand for integral reparation(s) do not negate their experiences of individuated harm, but rather urge those who accompany and represent them within national and transnational domains to recognize this demand within its legacies of structural violence or, in the words of anthropologists and social psychologists, as social suffering (Kleinman et al., 1997) and psychosocial trauma (Martín-Baró, 1994).

As we have argued throughout this volume, sexual harm is sometimes exceptionalized or spectacularized within transitional justice processes. Through the participatory workshops, we sought to generate alternative spaces for storytelling and embodied performances that elicited and illuminated these women survivors' protagonism and facilitated their performances of and engagement with their multifaceted and integral demands for repair. Many of the experiences they represented through embodied images and performances and then reflected on were of everyday structural violence, of "women carrying a heavy load." As such, they were demanding from the Guatemalan state access to land, housing, capital, and health care, as well as a guarantee of the nonrepetition of the violence, so that their daughters and granddaughters, sons and grandsons would both have access to the education that they were denied and would never experience similar violations.

Over the past three chapters, we have followed Mayan protagonists' struggles for truth, justice, and reparation(s) in relation to the intermediaries who have accompanied them. Despite our use of participatory processes in our research to facilitate and reveal the co-constructed, dialogic nature of all knowledge(s), the complexity of the protagonist–intermediary relationship, mediated by structural racism and colonial power, and how it shapes narratives and struggles for redress and the content of protagonism itself, need to be further analyzed. The next chapter explores the intermediary role more explicitly. Through participatory workshops and in-depth interviews with the intermediaries, we analyze their positionalities as they articulated the multiple meanings they made of the Mayan protagonists' journeys, as well as their self-understandings as Mayan and ladina activists, feminists, lawyers, healers, and interpreters accompanying these women. We revisit our own positionality as feminist PARers and conclude by further interrogating the possibilities and limitations of generating liberatory research processes in the context of ongoing impunity, white supremacy, and 21st-century neocolonial power.

5 · ACCOMPANYING PROTAGONISM

"Facing Two Directions"

[Are] we telling them what [reparation(s)] means for us and not [listening to] what they think it is?

—Kaqchikel intermediary, participant
in a July 2011 workshop

Psychosocial accompaniment as a practice is rooted in an interdependent understanding of psychological and community well-being, not in an individualistic paradigm of psychological suffering. The one who accompanies holds the individual's suffering and well-being in the light of the sociocultural and historical context.... Insofar as psychological and community symptoms memorialize violations that have occurred, the one who accompanies is also a witness. This witnessing is a particularly crucial antidote when the events or conditions suffered have been repressed or denied by the wider culture. The creation of opportunities for testimony enables those who have suffered violence and social exclusion to exercise their agency and to bring their experience into the public arena to be acknowledged and witnessed.

—Mary Watkins (2015, p. 327)

We have argued throughout this volume that Mayan women's protagonism, as reflected in their struggles for redress for harm suffered during Guatemala's genocidal violence, is intensely dialogical: it is constructed through engagement with others, who include both fellow survivors and community members, as well as the multiple intermediaries who are accompanying them during their lengthy journey. Mayan protagonists are situated at the interstices of their local geographically based communities and the community of women through which they have chosen to speak openly about their experiences of violence, specifically sexual violence. In this chapter we focus on the intermediaries, including ourselves, and analyze the roles we have played in mediating, translating, and facilitating protagonists' narratives, creative representations, and organized actions in truth-telling, justice-seeking, and reparation(s) processes. We frame our analysis using the k'ot, a symbol that has a long tradition among the Maya and is often woven by Ixil women into their blouses. The k'ot—a double-headed eagle that looks both ways, in two directions—has multiple significations that have evolved over time. Scholars have traced the image to the coat of arms of the 16th-century Holy Roman Emperor, Charles V; it is seen in coins minted in this period, with the double-headed eagle described as representing the empire (Chandler & Cordón, 2015; de Jonch, 1965). Both Mayan and Christian symbols incorporate dialectics or dialogical images often represented as dualisms, including, for example, good and evil, heaven and earth. Our accompaniment—similar to the Mayan protagonists' lives—looked forward and backward or, in the words of a Mayan intermediary, drawing on the image of the k'ot, we were focused "in two directions." As feminist and antiracist participatory action researchers we brought a critical lens to this dual or bi-focality (Weis & Fine, 2012). One direction was grounded in and framed by our efforts to decolonize our North American intellectual training as informed by multiple decades of human rights and feminist activism within and beyond Guatemala, while the other is reflected in our position of pragmatic solidarity as accompaniers, seeking to listen carefully to Mayan women's multiple interpretations of their lived experiences in conversation with the narratives and theoretical frameworks generated by those who accompany them. This volume thus affirms the accomplishments of Mayan protagonists and their Mayan, ladina, and North American accompaniers, including ourselves. Simultaneously, it critically interrogates how transnational transitional justice mechanisms shaped and were refracted in intermediaries' ways of knowing and acting, which all too often occlude histories and structures of racialized gendered violence while also marginalizing indigenous knowledge, practices, and strategies of resistance.

Those of us who accompanied these Mayan women positioned ourselves as lawyers, psychologists, feminists, Mayan healers, interpreters, and participatory researchers and as ladinas, Maya, white, Guatemalans, Canadians, and United-statesians, with varying levels of education and employment. We worked with Mayan protagonists for different lengths of time, and represent here, through words and images, how despite our rhetoric of accompanying their journeys, we are implicated in these processes in multiple ways given our diverse positionings that both facilitated and constrained certain types of storytelling, knowledge construction, and actions. As authors who engaged in feminist PAR processes with intermediaries and protagonists over the eight years of the project, we framed our engagement through the discourse of accompaniment, drawing on scholarship that emphasizes the ideological and political positionalities of those who walk in pragmatic solidarity, accompanying local protagonists toward co-constructing knowledge and actions from the bottom up. Drawing on earlier work in human rights and feminist advocacy and activism by Merry (2006; see also Levitt & Merry, 2009; Merry & Levitt, 2017), we situate all accompaniers as intermediaries. As we discuss in this volume, intermediaries—"the people in the middle" (Merry, 2006)—negotiate systems of meanings among local, regional, national, and international systems, "translat[ing] the discourses and practices from the arena of international law and legal institutions to specific situations of suffering and violation" (p. 39). We build on these ideas, extending them through our interdisciplinary positionalities and through the knowledge construction journeys from below, alongside the Mayan protagonists, into national and international domains. Listening versus telling is a critical frame through which we explore the multiple performances and interpretations gathered through workshops with intermediaries and in our interviews with them.

The chapter contributes to clarifying the knowledge(s) constructed through the dialogic relationships between protagonists and diverse intermediaries over eight years, in a context of interlocking social relations of gender, racialization, and class within situations of ongoing oppression, exclusion, and impoverishment, while recognizing that neither these relations nor the meanings made through them are static or universal. We examine the significance, challenges, and implications of positioning oneself or being positioned "facing in two directions." In the words of one Mayan interpreter-intermediary, "It's very complicated because we have to concentrate on what the person is saying, but we also know that there is another person who wants to know what is being said." Multilingual Mayan translators who work as intermediaries interpret indigenous women's experiences for other protagonists and for intermediaries, in preparation for and in performance of their testimonies in public contexts, in judicial processes, and in our creative workshops. They perform multilevel linguistic and positional interpretations, whereas all other intermediaries interpret primarily through their professional and activist positionalities. As discussed previously in this volume, all too frequently as lawyers, psychologists, researchers, or interpreters we risk mediating or translating in ways that objectify or essentialize protagonists, forcing them to repeat painful stories of atrocity, loss, and survival; sometimes we talk or write over their knowledge, favoring a disciplinary, feminist, or transitional justice discourse. Top-down vernacularization of international human rights norms that frame many of the truth-telling, justice-seeking, and reparatory processes threaten to speak over Mayan protagonists' voices, rather than generating audiences to listen to, engage with, and act on the protagonists' knowledge(s). Although it is only Mayan protagonists who can speak their stories, the story available to outsiders is itself reframed and re-storied by the mechanisms of transitional justice and activist scholarship to which those who accompany them have direct access and through which they and we have been socialized. Despite this, as argued previously, this does not negate that the 54 Mayan protagonists are speaking their truth through these processes.

We begin the chapter by situating our conception of accompaniment within feminist PAR and some of the relevant literature. We revisit our own positionality within this multiyear feminist PAR process, seeking to further problematize our roles as intermediaries. We analyze data from semi-structured interviews with 12 of the intermediaries—6 Mayan and 6 ladina; of these 9 are from the three organizations of the Alliance and 3 are Mayan consultants who worked with the Mayan protagonists within this project and in a related project in Chajul (Lykes & Crosby, 2015a). One or both of us conducted interviews with 11 of these intermediaries in Spanish (some were interviewed more than once), and another member of the research team interviewed the 12th intermediary. All interviews were completed by 2015, before the Sepur Zarco trial described in chapter 3. We deployed a grounded theory analysis (Charmaz, 2014) of intermediaries' descriptions and meaning-makings of their performative work accompanying Mayan protagonists. We triangulated analyses of data from the workshops and in-depth interviews to construct a mosaic that reflects the intermediaries' praxis. These analyses also illuminated similarities and diversities across the 12 intermediaries, including some of the complex performances of positionalities at the intersections of racialized and classed dynamics rooted in ongoing structural racism that constrain Maya–ladina relationships. The analyses showed multiple ways in which the Mayan and ladina intermediaries constructed and represented the Mayan protagonists, as well as how the Mayan intermediaries whose personal characteristics and experiences intersected or overlapped with the Mayan protagonists negotiated those positionalities. Finally, we revisited the image theater techniques used in the workshop conducted in June 2013 with both protagonists and intermediaries to explore the knowledge(s) constructed over time through this feminist PAR process including the gaps, fissures, and ongoing silences and points of contestation.

FRAMING ACCOMPANIMENT WITHIN FEMINIST PAR

The psychosocial accompaniment of survivors of gross violations of human rights has roots in liberation theology and psychology and in Latin American human rights activism (Gates, 1998). This relational and ethical stance involves walking and working with those "on the margins . . . who desire . . . a space to develop critical inquiry and joint imagination and action to address desired and needed change" (Watkins, 2015, p. 1). In Guatemala, Mayan and ladina feminist activists have sought to generate spaces of accompaniment in which Mayan women survivors could tell their truths about sexual violations perpetrated during the armed conflict through relational processes that promoted women survivors' agency and protagonism (Fulchiron et al., 2009). The physician and anthropologist Farmer (2013) has reclaimed the classic North-South 20th-century term "solidarity," coupling it with pragmatism to represent a praxis of transnational interdisciplinary accompaniment that partners with those materially marginalized from power and decision making (see also Griffin & Block, 2013). Seeking to avoid the ideological abstractions of postmodernity, Farmer (2013) argues that all knowledge constructed from the bottom up must be mobilized through practice that redresses structural inequalities and directly benefits the knowledge makers. He writes, "To accompany someone is to go somewhere with him or her, to break bread together, to be present on a journey with a beginning and an end. There's an element of mystery, of openness, of trust, in accompaniment. The companion, the accompagnateur, says: 'I'll go with you and support you on your journey wherever it leads. I'll share your fate for a while—and by 'a while,' I don't mean a little while.' Accompaniment is about sticking with a task until it's deemed completed—not by the accompagnateur, but by the person being accompanied" (p. 234).

Watkins (2015) writes about the particular challenges facing psychologists who seek to accompany survivors of gross violations of human rights and those who have survived humanitarian disasters and forced displacement. She draws on earlier work by Fanon (1967a, b; 1963/2004) who gave up his practice as a psychiatrist to accompany Algerians engaged in a liberation struggle against colonial France, as well as the liberation psychology of Martín-Baró (1994) articulated most clearly in his work with peasants during the Salvadoran civil war. Martín-Baró (1994) theorized trauma as psychosocial, arguing that the socioemotional effects of violence in El Salvador's armed conflict that marked survivors is grounded in an individual-community dialectic that is iteratively constructed in and made meaningful through sociocultural-historical processes. We deployed feminist PAR to accompany Mayan protagonists in ways that responded to their social suffering through pragmatic solidarity while standing alongside them to facilitate participatory processes through which they and other intermediaries could document and critically reflect on their struggles for redress.

The colonial project and the political-military incursions of the United States that frame Guatemala's development as a nation-state, as well as ongoing institutional racism and neocolonial global capitalism, constrain the ongoing struggles for redress reported in this book. Accompaniment from those who continue to benefit disproportionately from the legacies of these ongoing power structures—in this case the ladina and North American intermediaries—all too frequently slides into action or knowledge construction processes that reinstate settler selfhood and positions situated within ongoing histories of colonization and gendered racialized power (Hartman, 1997). Mohanty (2003) has critically interrogated Western feminist researchers' self-positioning vis-à-vis women of the Global South, who are depicted as a victimized homogeneous other in opposition to the liberated Western female self, as well as the positioning of elite or more formally educated women within countries of the Global South who seek to speak for others across class, racialized, and other divides. As such, our discursive reproductions, as well as those inherent in transitional justice processes and those produced by ladina-dominated NGOs, often draw on exogenous analytical categories that risk positioning women such as the 54 Mayan protagonists as the racialized gendered other. Arvin et al. (2013) urge researchers and other outsiders to critique this tendency in settler colonial contexts whose structures are persistently linked with heteropatriarchy. These neocolonial heteropatriarchal dynamics have powerful effects that are all too often reproduced in collaborative work between indigenous survivors and settler intermediaries, accompaniers, or researchers. Ongoing global capitalism and white supremacy, as well as the particular assumptions underlying transitional justice mechanisms as discussed in this volume, constrain knowledge(s) that are constructed, as well as the engagements and actions that are facilitated.

Recognizing these constraints and our own positionalities we sought to situate our accompaniment of the 54 Mayan protagonists in dialogue with the Mayan healing beliefs and practices articulated by several Mayan-led organizations. Several of the women who were interviewed in this project were founding members of Kaqla, a Mayan women's organization formed in 1996, and so we drew heavily on their work. As discussed in chapter 1, Kaqla (Grupo de Mujeres Mayas Kaqla, 2014) critically analyzes historic exclusions of the Maya due to colonization, patriarchy, and structural impoverishment, each of which continues to constrain and facilitate present-day Maya–ladinx and Maya–Maya relationships. Their analysis of the continuum of violence since the colonial period facilitates a critical consciousness by recognizing and critiquing the historical and structural roots of oppression and embracing Mayan histories of resistance (Grupo de Mujeres Mayas Kaqla, 2014). Kaqla also critiques academic knowledge production and mass media, whose discriminatory imaginaries about the Maya normalize poverty and violence (Grupo de Mujeres Mayas Kaqla, 2011), denying historical contributions that constitute these oppressive conditions while constraining Mayan women to caring for others (Grupo de Mujeres Mayas Kaqla, 2014).

Kaqla members' healing processes include the documentation and critical interrogation of Mayan women's internalization of feelings of inferiority and silencing of their own oppression. Mayan women's internalization of the culture of the oppressor and embodiment of racialized and gendered oppression are positioned and performed within their embodied and historical memories across generations (Grupo de Mujeres Mayas Kaqla, 2010, 2014). Mayan self-healing engages family and community and is realized through energetic interconnections of human experience, the earth, and the universe: the "network of life" (Grupo de Mujeres Mayas Kaqla, 2004). Healing requires that women analyze their communities, the country, and the planet and how each affects Mayan women's politics of transformation through which they create new subjectivities (Grupo de Mujeres Mayas Kaqla, 2010).

The work of Médicos Descalzos also informs our understanding of the Mayan intermediaries' descriptions of their work. Drawing on traditional therapies from the El Quiché department of Guatemala, Médicos Descalzos identified and ana-lyzed common Mayan illnesses, some of which are associated with a distancing from Mayan values and traditions and an embrace of Western cultural practices. They argued that people affected by these illnesses have lost connections to their Mayan roots, culture, identity, and self-esteem. Similarly, other illnesses occur when the individual transgresses social norms—with or without noticing it—and behaves in ways that are contrary to Mayan traditional values. Healing is actual-ized through entrusting oneself to the spirits of the ancestors, which represents a return to Mayan traditions and values (Asociación Médicos Descalzos, 2012). Médicos Descalzos critically engages Western psychiatric and psychological knowledge and practices while emphasizing the centrality of Mayan knowledge for psychosocial accompaniment and pressing for the legitimacy of the Mayan medical paradigm (Asociación Médicos Descalzos, 2012).

Kaqla's and Médicos Descalzos's healing praxis is deeply informed by the Mayan cosmovision. Other Guatemalan NGOs also draw on Mayan practices and beliefs to address mental health problems in the wake of the armed conflict. These organizations rely primarily on verbal techniques more commonly found in West-ern mental health knowledge systems. They include diocesan programs that worked with teachers and parish leaders from local communities (e.g., Ford, Cabrera, & Searing, 2000) and university-NGO partnership programs that trained community-based promoters from different parts of the country (e.g., Duque, 2009; ECAP, n.d., "Publicaciones"). The goals of these programs were to enhance participants' understandings of the social and political conditions that gave rise to the genocidal violence, to bring about personal healing, and to develop their capacities to promote transformative changes in their communities, despite ongo-ing poverty and injustice. The ECAP program was the one in which all Alliance interpreters were trained as mental health promoters.

CRITICALLY INTERROGATING OUR POSITIONALITIES AND FORGING A SHARED AGENDA

As participatory and feminist researchers we have written extensively about the critical importance of locating ourselves and reflexively interrogating our praxis within feminist PAR as we undertake collaborative work beyond the borders of our own communities (Lykes & Crosby, 2014b, 2015a, 2015b). We situate ourselves and are defined by that location as we perform our subjectivities through networks of relationality (St. Louis & Barton, 2002) in which circulations of power due to "race," class, gender, and other socially significant identities are engaged—or structurally constrain these performances. Within this framing of positionality, similarities and differences along these socially ascribed dimensions facilitate our access to and accompaniment of local participants in a context of persistent power differences (Chereni, 2014). Additionally, we are challenged to rethread life in the wake of genocidal violence in Guatemala, during which much of the trust that undergirds people's performances of familial and community relationality was ruptured. Relationality is impossible or, at least, inaccessible without what Maguire (1987) suggests is just enough trust, a praxis and value that allowed her and the indigenous survivors of sexual violence whom she accompanied to walk alongside each other through experiences similar to some of those described in the first four chapters of this book.

UNAMG, ECAP, and MTM formed the Alliance in 2009 to continue their work with the 54 Mayan protagonists. We partnered with UNAMG in this eight-year feminist PAR process and through that partnership accompanied the Alliance in its work with these protagonists. As white North Americans (Canadian and Unitedstatesian), we are situated in matrices of intertwining social interactions that both constrain and facilitate the relationships we have developed, as well as the action and research processes we have generated. Our onto-epistemologies challenge linear and static notions of "insider" and "outsider," or "researcher" and "participant," that dominate positivist social science research methodologies and emphasize the mediated and processual nature of relationships developed through iterative and co-constructed action-reflection processes. Although our positionality at the interstices of racialized, economic, national, and educational privilege lies outside of Mayan and ladina communities of women, we have chosen to situate ourselves—and engage actively—within circulations of power with long and complex trajectories in protagonists' communities of origin from whence they have collectively developed a community of women that we have accompanied. The Indian action researcher Rahman (2004) suggested that the "desired relation between external activists and people [with whom they seek to collaborate] is best expressed by the [Bantu] term *uglolana,* meaning 'sharpening each other'" and by a "companion concept . . . *uakana,* meaning 'to build each other'" (p. 17). These ideas complement and inform processes of psychosocial accompaniment and pragmatic solidarity. We sought to accompany the Mayan protagonists and local intermediaries by articulating ourselves within these ongoing and iterative sets of relationships and refashioning an intersectional antiracist feminist, participatory, and activist discursive praxis.

Having both worked for many years in Guatemala, we first came together in 2007 to collaborate on a transnational process of action-reflection to support women survivors of wartime sexual violence in Guatemala, Peru, and Colombia, as well as the lawyers, psychologists, community advocates, and feminist activists who work with them (Cabrera Pérez-Armiñan & Lykes, 2007; Crosby, 2009).

We began the most recent iteration of work in Guatemala accompanying the 54 women protagonists in coordination with the UNAMG in 2009. As institutional collaborators we were challenged to identify a shared action research focus. We entered this relationship with a set of questions already in mind, a strategy all too typical of outsider researchers seeking to build partnerships with activist or community-based organizations. We based our research interests on a careful reading of previous work on gendered and racialized violence and of Guatemala, our previous experiences in Guatemala, and knowledge we both had about UNAMG and its ongoing work with these 54 women protagonists. Having entered an ongoing set of actions when we partnered with UNAMG, we offered to engage with them in collaborative reflection on these actions and to engage in a negotiated set of questions about the complex journey of seeking reparation(s) for the irreparable. Through our institutional negotiations with UNAMG before we developed the specific focus of the collaborative processes, they introduced us to their own research priorities and their hopes to strengthen research as an organizational praxis and enhance staff expertise in the area. Thus we agreed on the general parameters of a collaboration between ourselves as university-based researchers and staff within UNAMG (see, e.g., Institute for Community Research, n.d., for similar examples).

Despite these overlapping interests, feminist PAR emphasizes the importance of the research focus or question being something that is renegotiated among all coresearchers and participants once the partnership has been articulated (Lykes & Crosby, 2014b). Levin and Greenwood (2008), for example, suggest pragmatism within the problem identification processes, noting that such collaborations are typically characterized by working *with* people, not *for* them. Despite this careful attention to negotiating the feminist PAR process with the NGOs accompanying the 54 Mayan protagonists, we relied on UNAMG to be our interlocutor with them, a decision that reflected our respect for the large and diverse number of outsiders who were accompanying the women in 2009 and the recognition that our access to them, given their dispersed living conditions, would have to have been through a local intermediary. Yet these decisions and self-positioning meant that at no point did we negotiate our proposed project or research focus directly with the protagonists themselves. Despite this limitation, our collaboration with the Alliance afforded multiple opportunities for better understanding their performance of intermediarity, to which we now turn.

UNDERSTANDING INTERMEDIARIES IN THEIR OWN WORDS AND CREATIVE REPRESENTATIONS

Although members of the Alliance have facilitated actions for redress alongside the 54 Mayan protagonists for more than a decade, relatively little attention has been paid to documenting their work as activists and advocates. To the contrary, much of the work has unfolded within the domain of transitional justice, wherein documentation and advocacy strategies are, at least implicitly, grounded in assumptions of critical realism. Thus NGOs represent themselves as facilitating the speech-acts of survivors, situating themselves as facilitators of their voices, or sometimes, within feminist circles, arguing that they have empowered women whose voices are typically not heard or intentionally marginalized. This discourse has been performed in many feminist efforts to break the silence enshrouding sexual violence, including the use of women as *botín de guerra* [spoils of war]. Many, ourselves included, have written about the invisibilization and then hyper-visibilization of rape as an instrument of armed conflict. In this volume we seek to critically interrogate the idea that protagonists' stories are unmediated, arguing that all speech-acts are constructed. More specifically, we deconstruct the particularities of differently positioned women who have accompanied a relatively small number of women survivors of racialized gendered violence during Guatemala's internal armed conflict.

Through constructivist grounded theory analyses of in-depth semi-structured interviews that we conducted with 12 intermediaries, we documented their understanding of their work in their own words. Of the six Maya, two work as interpreters in local NGOs that are part of the Alliance.[1] The other four have facilitated workshops that used the Mayan cosmovision and creative techniques to facilitate Mayan protagonists' voicing of their understandings of truth, justice, and reparation(s). One of them also served as an expert witness in the Tribunal of Conscience and the Sepur Zarco case. All Mayan intermediaries speak or at least understand their indigenous language (Kaqchikel, Ixil, or K'iche') as well as Spanish; one also speaks English. Their educational levels range from sixth grade to a doctorate, with several having completed university educations and one was enrolled in an MA degree in psychology at the time of the interview. Of the six ladinas, all are professionals working in local NGOs of the Alliance, all speak Spanish, and at least one is fluent in English—although none speak any of the 22 Mayan languages. They have a range of higher education degrees and leadership roles within these NGOs. As previously discussed, these ladina intermediaries have accompanied the 54 Mayan protagonists at multiple phases of the decade-long transitional justice work. Some among the ladinas had survived clandestine lives in and beyond Guatemala's borders for many years in the wake of the disappearances and/or deaths of family members, close friends, or political allies during the armed conflict. Thus, although the stories they reported in these interviews and that are analyzed in this chapter focused almost exclusively on their accompaniment of the 54 Mayan protagonists, they too were directly and/or indirectly affected by the same internal armed conflict. In terms of our own intermediary positionings, we have each completed our PhDs in social sciences within the Global North and are fluent in Spanish, English, and French, but do not speak any of the Mayan languages.

As discussed earlier, given that many of the 54 women whom we accompanied only speak a Mayan language, although most understand Spanish, we relied heavily on the Mayan women interpreters and the in-between role they play in the vernacularization of human rights and feminist discourse. These interpreters, as well as other Mayan intermediaries, noted what is frequently recognized in therapeutic work: even when a survivor of gross violations of human rights has some understanding and speaking capacity in a second language, she usually prefers to use her language of origin (Tijerina, 2009). As discussed in the expert witness testimony of Barrios in the Sepur Zarco trial described in chapter 3 and by García Ixmatá et al. (1993/2017) and Viaene (2015), the Mayan languages and the Mayan cosmovision are intricately interwoven. The several linguistic groups among the Mayan protagonists made this work even more challenging, as interpreter intermediaries had to translate among diverse ethnolinguistic Mayan groups, as well as between those groups and the Spanish-speaking ladina and North American researchers, and vice versa. Of the six Mayan intermediaries interviewed, all but one experienced the disappearances, rapes, or murders of immediate family members during the internal armed conflict, and some were displaced in the *Comunidades de Poblaciones en Resistencia* [Communities of Populations in Resistance] (CPR) or in Mexico for many years.

Another challenge that several interpreters reported was the nonexistence of words in one or another of the multiple Mayan languages. For example, as discussed in previous chapters, several words related to Spanish words for reparation(s) and sexual violence do not exist or differ from each other within and between Mayan languages. Interpreters reported finding ways to explain terms from transitional justice and Western mental health paradigms to the survivors: for example, describing local practices and literal, more material indigenous actions, such as sewing a cloth, as repairing, from the Kaqchikel, for the Spanish term "reparación." Thus, the interpreters multiply positioned themselves as accompaniers. Despite having received training in community-based mental health work through ECAP, none had received any training in interpretation.

Relational accompaniment across diverse communities such as those engaged in this work requires layers of interpretation, including translation across multiple languages. Linguistic and interpretive resources and limitations facilitate and constrain healing, justice-seeking, and knowledge-production processes. Despite the reliance on the creative arts, many exchanges relied on oral communication—that is, the use of codes imposed on the speaker's ideas and feelings—and often necessitating more than one interpreter. The Mayan interpreters were challenged to decode and then encode between and sometimes among multiple languages.

In addressing the aftermath of violence, local promoters and activists often serve as informal interpreters for non-indigenous language speakers. In these cases, promoters often speak on behalf of or make decisions for those they accompany. Tijerina (2009) stresses that interpretation differs from advocacy, arguing that the goal of the former is to communicate another's message impartially and with transparency. Berman and Tyyskä (2011), in contrast, suggest that interpreters' knowledge about the local context, including cultural understandings and diverse perspectives performed by those who live there, often contribute to their engagement in advocacy, thus challenging Tijerina's (2009) suggestion that interpreters can be neutral.

Interviews with Mayan intermediaries confirm the complexities suggested by these authors, as well as the multiple and diverse demands on their interpretive skills. Our work with them suggests that, in addition to shuttling between performances as interpreters and advocates, they are challenged to negotiate their own well-being. As discussed later, many witnessed a broad range of gross violations of human rights within their families and communities. We argue that these personal experiences differently positioned the Mayan interpreters as intermediaries.

As mentioned earlier, we organized annual coresearcher team meetings with UNAMG staff as well as workshops using creative techniques with staff from all three NGOs in the Alliance in 2010, 2011, and 2013; nine of the interviewees were involved in these workshops. Brainstorming and small group discussions were complemented by activities that engaged participants in generating embodied and creatively imagined drawings, collages, and dramatizations. Given the professional training of most of the intermediaries and their reliance on the spoken word for most of their human rights advocacy and activism, the creative techniques sought to tap into their implicit understandings of gender and racial hierarchies, as well as their underlying assumptions about transitional justice processes and how they interfaced not only with genocidal practices within the armed conflict but also the psychosocial accompaniment, advocacy, and activism in which they were engaged alongside Mayan protagonists. For the Mayan intermediaries, the workshops were also an opportunity to explore the interface of creative techniques with the Mayan cosmovision, practices, and rituals. The workshops' creative and embodied performances also facilitated the nonformally educated and non-Spanish-speaking Mayan protagonists' access to the intermediaries' meaning-making and understandings of transitional justice processes. The playful nature of these activities leveled the playing field across professional and educational training while also tapping into frequently unarticulated onto-epistemologies held by staff collaborators.

As part of the iterative and participatory research process, coresearchers as well as other Alliance staff presented preliminary findings from the project at professional meetings over the course of the 8-year project. UNAMG also hosted a Dialogue in Guatemala City in June 2013 to which all Alliance staff as well as additional key informants who had participated in the 8-year project were invited. All the participants were sent documents based on the research findings that had been analyzed to date, and graduate students took notes on the discussion, which was also audio recorded. The analyses presented in this chapter draw on the minutes and field notes from these gatherings.

Exploring Underlying Assumptions

In June 2010 we gathered with 17 intermediaries from UNAMG, ECAP, and MTM and two international graduate students in a conference room in Zone 1 of Guatemala City. Participants were invited to explore their understandings of integral reparation(s), justice, and gender and to analyze shared or contrasting understandings of the transitional justice work in which they were currently engaged with the 54 Mayan protagonists. The workshop's goals had emerged from a series of interviews that we had conducted after the Tribunal of Conscience concluded, in which we identified differing interpretations of what had transpired, perspectives that we sought to better understand. A second objective was to engage the intermediaries in a training of the trainers workshop through which they might hone their expertise in using creative resources to enhance their engagement in future work with protagonists as they prepared for their next actions, including the Sepur Zarco case.

We began with a brainstorming session in which Mayan and ladina intermediaries, including psychologists, lawyers, feminist activists, and interpreters, identified post-Tribunal preoccupations and concerns. The pending completion and presentation of a demand for integral reparation(s) to the IACHR emerged as a shared anxiety and led to an activity in which the group broke up into four small groups, which were each invited to develop a collage representing integral reparation(s). The groups were (1) staff from MTM and ECAP, (2) interpreters/promoters, (3) staff from UNAMG, and (4) the international PARers, ourselves included. The interpretive process was similar to that described in chapter 1: the collage's creators asked others in the room to interpret their collage, after which they added anything that had not been mentioned that they had sought to represent through the collage. In contrast to the process with Mayan protagonists, the training of the trainer workshop with intermediaries included two additional elements. The first asked participants to reflect on their feelings during the exercise: what they liked, what they found difficult, and why. At the end of the exercise they were invited to reflect on how similar resources might contribute to their work with the Mayan protagonists, including any possible challenges and limitations.

The collages developed by the professional ladina and North American intermediaries in Groups 1, 3, and 4—in contrast to the collages created by the 54 Mayan protagonists in their workshops and by the Mayan promoters/interpreters in Group 2—used the entire page, often including overlapping images or exceeding the boundaries of the paper. The vast majority of the images, again in contrast to the collages of the Maya, were of women and children, and the ladina and North American intermediaries made use of idealized images of the

Maya from *Instituto Guatemalteco de Turismo* [Guatemalan Tourism Institute] (INGUAT) brochures. The Maya typically eschewed such images that most, even those who used them in their collages, criticized as objectifying and othering the Maya.

The interpretation of the collages—including the creators' contributions—were similarly clustered, with the promoters/interpreters focusing on reparation(s) as linked to economic and material resources including food, a home, work, health care, education, money for planting crops; there was little effort to either represent the violations that had preceded the demand for reparation(s) or the more abstract claims for women's participation, well-being, or justice vis-à-vis those responsible for human rights violations and violence against women. Two of the three collages of the intermediaries had images of judges: the collage by MTM and ECAP staff replaced the male judge's head with that of a woman (see Figure 9), and the collage completed by UNAMG included handcuffs (see Figure 10) that the staff noted represented their search for justice not only for those responsible for the massacres but for those currently destroying the environment. This group also noted the importance of historical memory as a dimension of integral reparation(s).

Of note are the combined material and abstract demands reflected in the collages' representations of integral reparation(s) and being sought by the intermediaries. The exercise facilitated the representation of an interweaving of justice, truth, and reparation(s), rather than the more segmented strategies—and processes for actualizing one's demands—found within conventional transitional justice mechanisms, including those that these intermediaries were undertaking with the 54 Mayan protagonists as described in the three previous chapters. The imaginaries that they represented in their collages extended those mechanisms into aspirational demands in which women's protagonism was front and center, despite the more stereotypical images of the Maya in the materials they had at their disposition for creating the collages. Several participants indeed noted the limited materials available for their collages, particularly the absence of images of the Maya in the mainstream press and the idealized and romanticized objectification of them in the INGUAT publicity.

The Alliance has defined itself as a feminist initiative, and the work of its three component organizations is focused on achieving justice for women. A second activity invited participants to complete an individual drawing that represented barriers to achieving gender equity in Guatemala. Several of the 19 individual drawings contrasted men and women and represented lived experiences of each, often contrasting women's relegation to the private domain of the home to men's public responsibilities as peasants and/or government functionaries (Figure 11). Interestingly this image also included women's hypothesized or desired access to judicial processes.

FIGURE 9. ECAP and MTM collage: integral reparation(s).

Other more symbolic images represented destruction, for example, through an animal not known through direct experience by the local population—that is, an elephant—but easily recognized as exceptionally heavy whose movements crush all within its path (see Figure 12). A third drawing captures one of the underlying but rarely openly discussed dimensions of this work: how it is financed. The male figure in the center of the page is surrounded by a set of scales suspended over the head of a woman who seems to be in pain or suffering (see Figure 13).

FIGURE 10. UNAMG collage: integral reparation(s).

Other images in this drawing represent institutions that serve local communities, the church and a school, and those that are needed if justice for the 54 Mayan protagonists is to be realized: the law and the judicial system. The representation of the institutions and funds represented by coins with U.S. dollar signs suggest that without the financial resources needed to reduce gender inequity and achieve justice the institutions cannot realize their goals.

Once each individual drawing was completed, it was used as an elicitation image, with participants noting words that came to mind in examining the drawings, when they were interpreting the images drawn by their peers. The 10 to 15 words and phrases evoked by each drawing reflected factors at the micro-, meso-, and macro-levels (Bronfenbrenner, 1992) that constitute levels of engagement of individuals-in-communities in which circulations of gendered oppressions are organized and deployed. They included concrete experiences of everyday discrimination and more structural realities; for example, patriarchy and authoritarianism. Of interest is that some drawings elicited words reflecting the causes of gender inequality, whereas others pointed to women's pain and suffering or the abuse of women's bodies; that is, an effect of gender inequity and oppressions. Others focused more on women's search for liberty, their self-determination, happiness, freedom, and capacity to fly: factors contributing to their overcoming these barriers and achieving personal well-being in the wake of those struggles.

FIGURE 11. Individual drawing of barriers to gender equity.

The subsequent discussion revealed considerable consensus about the systemic roots of the oppression of women and that any reparative measure, particularly integral reparation(s), required "the transformation of [underlying] conditions of exclusion and oppression": this process would avoid a conflict in which women became the battleground on which the struggle for reparation(s) was waged. As significantly, the discussion pointed to what a growing number of scholars have recognized as some of the limits of transitional justice in which "any attempts to deal with the past are brought, in a global frame, into the realm of international trade and humanitarian aid" (Stanley, 2002, p. 13) or all too frequently focus on a country's transition to neoliberal capitalism rather than facilitating systemic or structural change (Miller, 2008; Muvingi, 2009). Many grassroots groups, including families of the disappeared in multiple Latin American countries, among others, demand that transitional justice mechanisms not only repair damages from past injustice, including racialized gendered violence, but also transform institutional structures with an aim of preventing future violations. Indigenous groups also call for a transformation in transitional justice as currently construed toward incorporating more indigenous justice strategies (Balint, Evansy, & McMillan, 2014; Million, 2013; Nagy, 2013).

Despite their emphasis on structural inequalities, neither the intermediaries' images nor their discussion problematized racism. Some noted that the drawings

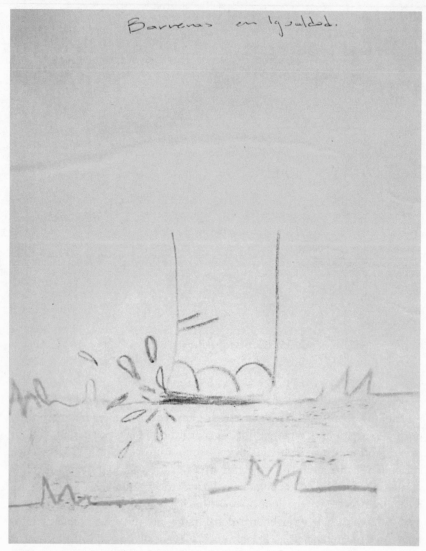

FIGURE 12. Individual drawing of barriers to gender equity.

of barriers to achieving their feminist goals in their work with the 54 protagonists offered an opportunity to visualize limitations that some dared not verbalize. Systems of gendered oppression, control, and domination, rather than men qua men, were identified as the source of women's oppression. Yet some words evoked by the images referred to women's timidity and self-silencing as causes of inequity. Of note was an unspoken underlying assumption—or onto-epistemology— of an essential woman: one whose inequity did not vary due to "race," social class, language, ethnicity, education, and so on. Despite the critique of the objec-

FIGURE 13. Individual drawing of barriers to gender equity.

tification of Mayan women evident in their analyses of the INGUAT materials, there was neither discussion of racialized gendered violence nor of the intersecting ways in which power circulations in Guatemala contribute to the differential treatment of ladina and Mayan women in diverse urban and rural locations and class positionings.

Finally, the intermediaries revalued their own experiences with creative resources, strategies that many had used in work with nonformally educated women, children, and youth but that they now recognized as also contributing to their identification of and more critical engagement with their own underlying assumptions and as a resource in interprofessional dialogue, particularly across varying educational levels. Others acknowledged not having considered how one process might build on another; for example, the importance of warm-up exercises before attempting a dramatization or a Boalian image theater exercise.

We pursued these issues further in a July 2011 workshop with Mayan and ladinx intermediaries from the Alliance, where participants were invited to break into two working groups and design a creative mini-workshop-based activity or experience. One group was instructed that they could use words as a creative technique while the second group was asked to design an experience without using words as the primary resource. Each small group was asked to imagine their peers as group participants and to focus the activity on integral reparation(s). That is, each was asked to design an experience through which participant Mayan peers or other intermediaries could share their own and their peers' understanding(s) of integral reparation(s). After designing and facilitating these experiences the two small groups joined together to discuss the strengths and weaknesses of each technique as resources for clarifying meaning-making processes and for communicating those meanings beyond their professional circles with rural Mayan protagonists. Then each small group developed a group definition of integral reparation(s) in words, drawing on the previous activities and the subsequent discussion. Group 1, which was allowed to use words, defined integral reparation(s) as "a process for repairing the damage caused to survivors of sexual violence due to violations of their human rights through justice, acknowledgment of them as victims, integral health, rightful *patrimonio* [inheritance], and a guarantee of NON-repetition, toward the improvement of individual and social life conditions" (capitalization in the original). Group 2 defined integral reparation(s) as "a process including multiple actions (justice, health, education, work, and a dignified home) that also encompasses guarantee of nonrepetition and societal consciousness raising that denaturalizes sexual violence as a sexual act and categorizes it as a crime."

As did the drawings and collages developed during the previous year, these definitions pointed to the underlying causes of sexual violence; the need for specific redress for violations, including health, education, and housing; and the importance of shifting public perception toward recognizing sexual violence as a crime, as something not "natural." As in the earlier workshop, again there was the absence of any discussion of racism or the colonial history of Guatemala as relevant to their understandings of integral reparation(s), either as causal agents or in terms of expected redress. This was confirmed in the discussion about the definitions that circulated around the idea of denaturalizing sexual violence, during which one of the ladina participants noted, "I don't think that there is a difference [in experiences of sexual violence]. All women are 'spoils of war,' whether ladina or indigenous." She added that the context may shape the particular articulation of sexual violence, with that in the countryside being genocide and extermination and in the city being torture. Silence followed this statement, a silence that may have reflected agreement, or exhaustion from the process, or anxiety about entering into a conversation that some assumed would have been contentious. As facilitators, we allowed the moment to pass, but revisited this issue later in the afternoon.

The afternoon discussion focused on how the two groups might communicate the definitions of integral reparation(s) they had developed in the morning to the multilingual and multicultural group of 54 Mayan protagonists—and, more importantly, how they could generate participatory processes through which we as facilitators or intermediaries could listen to and understand the multiple meanings that Mayan protagonists make of integral reparation(s). Thus, rather than assume that our primary or exclusive task was to vernacularize international legal and human rights discourse on integral reparation(s), the participatory workshops prioritized listening to or developing additional resources for facilitating listening to Mayan experiences and their indigenous or locally grounded meaning-making.

Group 1, comprised of one Q'eqchi' Maya and four ladinas, used verbal discussion to represent their definition, which reflected divergent understandings among the participants and between ladinx and Mayan intermediaries in the other group. Bilingual Mayan interpreters/promoters noted, for example, that many of the indigenous languages did not have specific terms to capture the abstract ideas in the definitions of integral reparation(s) and required a series of more materially grounded words to approximate what in Spanish is a single term. Another question was raised about how to translate abstract legal ideas such as nonrepetition. A ladina intermediary minimized differences between ladina and Mayan definitions. She suggested that instead of talking about their rights to their inheritance, Mayan protagonists spoke with greater specificity or concreteness about the homes and animals that they had lost. And instead of talking about nonrepetition, they demanded "that what happened to them would never happen to their daughters or to other women, that it does not ever happen again to them." However, she did note that the Maya spoke more about the collectivity than the ladinas.

Extending this idea, another ladina suggested that the Maya had a different conception of the world and that they, as ladinas, needed to take that into consideration. A debate ensued around ideas of collectivism and the Mayan understanding of continuities between the natural world, the living, and the dead; this veered into a discussion of relationships that had been ruptured by the armed conflict. A ladina suggested that the Mayan protagonists idealized the past and that women did not suffer that collective or intergenerational destruction as they had already been expelled or marginalized from that community when they had been sexually violated. Others disagreed; several of the Mayan interpreters clarified that part of the challenge of integral reparation(s) rested in the Mayan understanding that what they expected was not *reparar* [to repair] but *remendar* [to patch]: "it will never be the same; one would have to raise our ancestors from the dead" for the former to be realizable. It was also noted that the multiply worded Spanish translation sometimes differs in connotation and denotation from the Mayan term; for example, mending a garment (in which the tear is always visible) versus the Spanish term "resarcimiento," which suggests a return to the status prior to the violation and thus to an untorn garment. The irreparability of these violations is thus built into and reflective of the Mayan words. One Mayan intermediary offered an alternative understanding of the criticism that Mayan protagonists were idealizing the past in talk about reparation(s), instead suggesting that they actually "had never before lived through the extermination process of the armed conflict . . . nor the nightmares that followed"—and that was the past that they juxtaposed to their present situations. Others added that there was no way to repair this damage that was now "installed in the bodies of women." This exercise and reflexive discussion were designed to create a space in which ladina and Mayan intermediaries could reflect on accomplishments and challenges to date as they shed light on their overall struggle for justice and redress alongside the Mayan protagonists and planned next steps in these ongoing processes. As summarized earlier, the discussion laid bare a diversity of unexplored assumptions underlying the collaborative work of the Alliance.

Group 2, comprised of two Kaqchikel women, one ladino (the only man in this group of intermediaries) and three ladinas, performed their understanding of integral reparation(s) using a combination of two creative techniques: a drawing and a performance. Their drawing (see Figure 14) was ripped into pieces by the ladino group participant, after which two women, one Kaqchikel and one ladina, sought to put the picture back together with masking tape. In the ensuing discussion with the larger group, they acknowledged challenges they had experienced in trying to design an activity through which to vernacularize integral reparation(s) for Mayan women peasants living in rural communities. A Q'eqchi' intermediary from the larger group suggested that the masking tape represented one legacy of sexual violence, its "scars." A Kaqchikel intermediary from the small group described the tape as representing "sewing that which is broken," putting a patch on it and putting it back together, "but it will not be the same." She noted further that it is not only the individual who was ruptured but also the social, the collective, and that "both must be mended." The second Kaqchikel small group member summarized the group's envisioning and representing integral reparation(s) as an aspiration to "live life a bit better, to have a place which one can call one's own," without so many economic deprivations.

The small group process—and larger group discussions—brought to the surface an underlying tension between ladinas who resisted Mayan claims to a particular understanding of their world and their lived experiences and tended toward essentializing women particularly vis-à-vis sexual violence, and those ladinas or mestizas who were open to considering or even to embracing intersectional positioning, in which the circulations of power differently located ladinas and Mayan women. As such, these mestizas acknowledged that Mayan women have particular beliefs and practices that have sustained them across 500 years of colonial oppression, including the most recent 36-year armed conflict. One Kaqchikel participant articulated an important challenge facing all intermediaries in this work: Are "we telling them [the Mayan protagonists] what this means for us and not [listening to] what they think it is?" This question frames the analyses from the

FIGURE 14. Group 2 explains integral reparation(s).

interviews with 12 of the intermediaries reported in the next sections. We sought to better understand the meanings they made of their work accompanying Mayan protagonists, how they positioned themselves, and how, from these positionings, they understood the Mayan protagonists' lived experiences and demands for truth, justice, and reparation(s). This exploration of their self-understandings and mosaic of meanings foregrounds the various mediations that facilitate and constrain Mayan protagonists' knowledge(s) and actions.

Intermediaries Position Themselves and Mayan Protagonists

The analyses in the previous section suggest that these participatory creative processes and subsequent dialogues helped bring to the surface ladinas' implicit assumptions. The in-depth interviews with six ladina and six Mayan intermediaries offer an additional lens for making meaning of some of these processes and of the co-constructed knowledge(s) and actions documented through this feminist PAR process. Merry's (2006) framing of, and research about, intermediaries (Merry & Levitt, 2017; Levitt & Merry, 2009) as knowledge brokers assumes that those who move in the circles of power represented by the UN and the multiple other transitional justice mechanisms institutionalized in the wake of World War II (e.g., international tribunals and the ICC, among others) can interpret what are argued to be universal principles and that through deploying the institutional human rights mechanisms, local grievances will be heard and justice realized. Their empirical assessment of how such processes are engaged in by women in different countries suggests that local cultural and linguistic practices constrain these universal mechanisms and those that are more pronounced or heeded as more important transform universal principles in particular ways (Levitt & Merry, 2009; Merry & Levitt, 2017).

The intermediaries in Guatemala vary in their performance of international human rights mechanisms and feminist discourses, as well as in their professional training (e.g., as psychologists, feminists, social science researchers, and Mayan healers). Some are associated closely and seem compatible with international Western norms, whereas others are more typically seen as local and indigenous and often as extraneous to the justice-seeking work or, as suggested by Merry and Levitt's (2017) research, as shaping it in more local ways. In contrast, the indigenous intermediaries play a critical role (beyond that of linguistic interpreters) when the work of vernacularization travels in both directions: when local, particular realities are valued and seen as equally relevant to justice-seeking processes as international, more universal, norms and as capable of traveling up. The interviews sought to better understand—in the intermediaries' own words—how they understand themselves and their work in terms of answering the question posed by the Kaqchikel intermediary in the previous section: Whose stories are being told in the various transitional justice arenas described in this volume and how do the 54 Mayan protagonists understand or make meaning of the repair that they are seeking?

Of the six ladinas, three worked for UNAMG, one for ECAP, one for MTM, and one for the Actors for Change Collective; of these, five were working in leadership positions in the three organizations that made up the Alliance at the time of the interviews and had collaborated in the earlier Consortium. Of the six Maya, two were interpreters/promoters, one of whom worked for UNAMG and the other for ECAP; two were founders or early members of Kaqla, one of whom had collaborated in the Consortium; one was an anthropologist who served as an expert witness in the Tribunal and Sepur Zarco trial, and one was a community leader and interpreter/promoter working in Chajul and the surrounding villages in the Quiché (see Lykes, 2001; Lykes et al., 1999; Women of PhotoVoice/ADMI & Lykes, 2000). All six Maya had accompanied survivors of gross violations of human rights and sexual violence, and all were themselves direct victims of violence during the armed conflict.

The constructivist grounded theory analyses of the in-depth semi-structured interviews with these intermediaries elucidate the dynamic relationships through which Mayan protagonists and intermediaries engage and construct Mayan healing praxis. These dynamic processes through which intermediaries performed their accompaniment are represented in particular ways that are reflective of the expertise of intermediaries and their personal journeys, as well as of the demands of the immediate context and our own positionalities as intermediaries and authors. Despite multiple diversities, our analysis confirms that the six Mayan intermediaries centered their accompaniment of Mayan protagonists in *sanación* [healing] processes, which they located within a dialogic relationality that is grounded in the intergenerational Mayan community—and connected to the earth and nature—as well as in critical interrogation of and engagement with patriarchal, racialized, and impoverishing social structures that took particularly brutal form through the genocidal violence of the Guatemalan armed conflict. They positioned themselves vis-à-vis their shared identities—that is, as members of a single indigenous *pueblo* [people]—and acknowledged that they themselves survived that violence and needed healing; in that sense, too, they positioned themselves as similar to the 54 protagonists (see Távara, Lykes, & Crosby, 2018, for a more detailed discussion of Mayan intermediary positionings).

In contrast, the ladina intermediaries put much more emphasis on their individual actions, strategies, and decisions vis-à-vis transitional justice processes and players—for example, the IACHR and the local justice system—noting that the challenges the 54 Mayan protagonists face in the wake of the armed conflict include securing truth, justice, and reparation(s), as well as gender equity. They noted the multiple barriers and threats that they must face as advocates and activists, as well as the multiple harms suffered by the 54 Mayan protagonists.

Through coding these in-depth interviews, we identified four distinctive positions and/or performances: (1) intermediary positionality through accompaniment; (2) performances of accompaniment through psychosocial and healing processes; (3) interpretation and communication processes; and (4) intermediaries' representations of Mayan protagonists' constructions of truth, justice, and reparation(s).

Positioning through Accompaniment. Despite the diversities among the Mayan and ladina intermediaries in terms of lived experiences and professional or paraprofessional training, each situated her work within the local context of

Guatemala and the historical context of the armed conflict. They spoke about their families and communities, the organizations in which they worked, their coworkers and peers, and their stances vis-à-vis the state. The ladina intermediaries, when locating their work, were more focused on state and international actors who violated or defended universal human rights, whereas the Maya were more likely to talk about their ancestors and the continuities of Mayan community, grounding their discourse in the particularities of the Mayan cosmovision, as seen through the positioning of their particular ethnolinguistic group. Both Mayan and ladina intermediaries mentioned a wide range of other NGOs with whom they were or had collaborated, as well as different educational and training experiences through which they had developed their professional skills (e.g., in critical psychology) and honed their understandings of transitional justice, feminism, and popular education. Others spoke about learning more about alternative radio and the arts as resources in healing and in organizing work alongside the Mayan protagonists. Most of the ladinas—many of whom were administrative staff or directors of their organizations—described the economic challenges of supporting the training and the organizational work. Some spoke of other institutional challenges presented by the decision to accompany the 54 Mayan protagonists. For example, ECAP shifted its focus to make sexual violence and gender violence a priority of the organization after taking up this work. The collaborations were built on previous regional work of each organization, something that strengthened their capacities to develop just enough trust with the Mayan protagonists but also sometimes contributed to organization-based territoriality in which certain protagonists were described as more aligned with or as "belonging to" the organization with whom they had previously worked.

Both Mayan and ladina intermediaries described their personal histories and the various contexts that had prepared them—or not—for this work. Mayan women spoke nearly twice as frequently as ladinas about the socioemotional dimensions of earlier personal experiences, including education and training, as having prepared them for this work. One of the Mayan intermediaries said that she spoke little to no Spanish when she began this work, and another had never before worked for an organization. In contrast, one of the Mayan intermediaries had postgraduate training. Thus the range of previous educational experiences or related work among the Maya was much greater than that among the ladina intermediaries.

Although we learned through supplementary information published about them that each of the ladina intermediaries had survived direct or indirect human rights violations during the armed conflict, they did not note these experiences in their interviews. In contrast, most of the six Maya acknowledged that they and the 54 protagonists were "both victims" and that this both "complicated" their work while also making it "easier to understand their [the Mayan protagonists'] situation." At different points in the interviews, the Mayan women shared some details of their experiences as survivors of trauma and violence, aligning themselves in solidarity with protagonists, a solidarity they noted emerged from shared histories, community, and experiences during the armed conflict. The Mayan intermediaries also spoke more than the ladinas about their own socioemotional experiences in this work, describing the multiple lessons that they had learned from this work. They noted that despite the pain in listening to and interpreting and/or defending the Mayan protagonists' stories of social suffering in which they too partook as "wounded healers" (Nouwen, 1979), this shared suffering enhanced their work by better positioning them to collaborate in the protagonists' healing processes.

When describing their work with the 54 Mayan protagonists, several intermediaries talked about it as "accompaniment," but they were more likely to use terms such as "helping," "supporting," "consulting with," "conscienticizing" (Freire, 1970/2000), or "motivating" protagonists. The language of consulting, conscienticizing, and motivating included intermediaries' mention of interpreting human rights universal norms and psychological theories, thereby referencing their positions as knowledge brokers. This language was used more by the ladinas, reflecting a self-positioning as other—as a member of a different professional and racialized community from that of the 54 Mayan protagonists. Another indicator of this distancing was reflected in the ladinas' sense of responsibility for what they were accomplishing—or not—in the struggle for truth, justice, and reparation(s). They spoke regularly and repeatedly about the lack of support from the broader civil society for the work that they had undertaken, the threats to them and other human rights workers, and their deep worries about the ongoing stigmatization that the women faced in their communities. They expressed fatigue, sometimes exhaustion, in the face of these diverse challenges and a deep worry about whether they were succeeding in taking care of the Mayan protagonists.

The ladinas' self-positioning oscillated between descriptions of horizontal relationality as peers versus more hierarchical relationships with the Mayan protagonists; the latter suggested a performance of maternal caretaking. This was noted in interactions that they described in terms of "telling the women," "making it possible that something [a court appearance] happened," or "giving them something." They self-identified most explicitly as intermediaries when talking about the court cases and their roles in bringing the case for integral reparation(s) to the IACHR, functions that the Mayan protagonists clearly could not have handled "on their own." Thus they felt that the apparatus of the human rights and transitional justice regimes remained inaccessible to many of those most directly affected by gross violations of human rights without the intercession and translation of multiple professionals and paraprofessionals skilled in the language and performative requirements of these regimes.

The ladina intermediaries spoke of the challenges they faced in convincing the Mayan protagonists that they "deserved reparation(s)" and how they supported them to "speak for themselves" and "name what they needed," steering away from a discourse of victimhood toward strengthening their sense of empowerment. The language of empowerment is complex, as it emphasizes the importance of the Mayan protagonists acting from their own desires and capacities while also implicitly assuming that power is being transferred from the ladina intermediary to the Mayan protagonists. Archibald and Wilson (2011) and Ellsworth (1989), among others, critique empowerment as failing to critically situate and interrogate circulations of power and as rooted in individual psychological processes. Adding to that complexity are a number of statements by some of the ladina intermediaries describing the challenges of strengthening a sense of alliance between themselves and the protagonists, one in which they were building something together. One ladina noted, "Not only in our organization but as feminists. . . . We are trying to serve as interlocutors in dialogue with Mayan women." Yet, she expressed concern that the Mayan cosmovision not become a "new oppression," concluding that despite her experience as a mestiza who lacked an experiential understanding of the Mayan cosmovision, she feared that it was something other than "an experience of liberation with the potential to emancipate women." These concerns echoed those debated in the 2011 workshop with intermediaries described in the previous section, but were expressed in this setting more as doubts than assertions by someone seeking communication, exchange, and relationality.

Mayan intermediaries expressed awareness of these and similar oscillations, as reflected in comments about their being resigned to the paternalism they experienced from ladina organizations and their decisions to keep these perceptions to themselves, because, in one Mayan intermediary's words, it was "a waste of time" to focus on them. Another Mayan intermediary mentioned that the "paternalism of ladina-led women's organizations doesn't help to create synergy" in the work with the Mayan protagonists.

Although both groups of women described their professional, educational, and feminist training and preparation for the work they had undertaken with the Mayan protagonists, there were notable differences in the emphasis placed by each subgroup of intermediaries on their identification as Maya or ladina. The former always self-identified as Maya, also acknowledging their hybrid or mestiza origins; that is, the racialization of all contemporary Guatemalan identities. One Mayan intermediary noted this as another of the many ruptures she as a Maya has suffered—and added that naming this rupture contributed to her being "judged and criticized by others in the indigenous world who asked why we are questioning ourselves like this." In addition to these ruptures, generated at least in part by Mayan reflexivity and resulting in a distancing by some within the Mayan community, this Mayan intermediary and others spoke about the critical importance of their indigenous worlds and of the need to recover their ancestral values from their positions at the intersection of their self-understandings as Maya and as women. Several Mayan intermediaries self-identified as feminist and spoke of this work as an opportunity to perform an integral sense of self, "neither negating [their] Mayan spirituality nor [their] feminism." Some reported the challenges of this integration, recognizing the contributions of feminism toward deconstructing their subordinated positions within Mayan communities; yet they also noted that their urban situatedness and their middle-class status distanced them from their Mayan roots, even eliciting fear among some family and friends that they were "no longer loyal to our ancestors" or not "pure Maya," an additional sign of the diversities of performances of being Maya. Another described their work as an opportunity to "combine women's leadership with what the Mayan ancestors" had taught them. Others described this positioning as enabling them to break with oppressive paradigms and structures within Mayan communities and those of some "women's communities" that failed to appreciate Mayan beliefs and practices or were overtly discriminatory. The three Mayan intermediaries who still lived in their rural communities—at least during the weekends—were less likely to identify explicitly as feminists nor to experience otherness or othering within Mayan communities as described by urban or more highly educated Maya; however, they spoke about the importance of women's community in contributing to their valuing of themselves as Mayan women—and the critical contributions that their beliefs and practices made to the accompaniment work with protagonists. Despite positioning themselves as similar to protagonists in these ways, one Ixil woman acknowledged the diversities of religious practices in Mayan communities today and the need to recognize the Catholic and evangelical Christian performances and beliefs of locally based Mayan women survivors of gross violations of human rights, again reaffirming the diversity of performances as Maya.

An explicit naming and often an analysis of racism, discrimination, and economic marginalization and oppression of the Maya accompanied their intersectional positioning as Mayan women and/or feminists. The urban and more highly educated Maya were more likely than the other Mayan intermediaries to describe contemporary racism in the context of the 500 years of colonial oppression and to situate the armed conflict as the next iteration of this history. All spoke at different points of the centrality of this analysis in their work with the 54 Mayan protagonists and how being of the same pueblo facilitated their ability to empathize with and understand the struggles of protagonists. Several urban and professional Maya noted, however, that there is no single pueblo and that being urbanized and not living in community had allowed them to develop alternative paradigms and embrace diverse performances of being Maya. They were rupturing a notion of an essential Maya. This included recognizing that, despite ongoing discrimination and racism exercised by ladinas, that they too as Maya had internalized racialized inferiority and that our "work together [as Mayan women] has taught us that we too have an ugly part of ourselves, a part that discriminates, that we too have a sun and a shadow and in that sense we are like all women." This complexity and diversity of performance are discussed further in exploring the healing processes that they mobilized through this work.

Of note was the absence of any reference to institutional or structural racism in the interviews with the six ladina intermediaries. Although one ladina intermediary acknowledged ethnic and linguistic diversities among the intermediaries in her organization, she did not acknowledge her own or others' privileged racialized position as ladinas. Even though we did not ask explicitly about their understandings of the causes or effects of the armed conflict or about racism per se, several of of the Mayan intermediaries discussed this material in their responses to questions about their work with Mayan protagonists and in their engagements in transitional justice processes compared to only one of the ladina intermediaries.

In contrast, despite the ladina intermediaries' lack of focus on discrimination, racism, or on their ethnolinguistic privileges in their self-positionings or in their descriptions of their performances as intermediaries, several mentioned the importance of trying to build relations across communities in their collaborative work accompanying the Mayan women—and the challenges to achieving it. One ladina intermediary suggested that it was easier for international accompaniers like ourselves to, for example, raise questions or reservations about the Mayan cosmovision than for Guatemalans, because such questioning was interpreted as a critique or rejection. She concluded, "This made it difficult to have an open dialogue which was necessary to build a movement."

Ladina intermediaries were much more likely than their Mayan peers to emphasize their professional training and their development as feminists, descriptions that seemed to assume the privilege of access to these resources and meaning-making frames without ever explicitly acknowledging it. They also shared multiple details about their personal journeys, information that was emphasized to a much lesser degree by the Mayan intermediaries who situated themselves more readily in terms of intergenerational family and community. These differences in self-positioning and in the frames that these different groups of intermediaries brought to their work may have contributed to one Mayan intermediary's comment, noted earlier, of it not being worth their time to focus on the ways in which ladina-run organizations marginalize them. They also further contextualize some of the debates that emerged in the workshops with intermediaries in which the Maya and ladinas positioned themselves differently in relation to articulated differences in worldviews and access to power within Guatemala today and the implications of these realities for their understanding of sexual violence and for their work with protagonists.

One final but important area of self-positioning and performance centered on the intermediaries' reflections on their own growth and change through their work with protagonists. The ladina intermediaries were more likely to situate their talk about these developments within their organizations, rather than as individual shifts (e.g., ECAP as developing a gendered focus for its long-standing psychosocial accompaniment work; MTM as enhancing its interdisciplinary legal work through collaborations with psychologists who were increasingly important in accompanying protagonists). Interestingly one ladina emphasized her work as a member of a women's human rights organization, noting, "As women working in women's human rights organizations in Guatemala we have a life, a life story, of being victims who resist." Despite differences, their work as human rights activists and feminists united them across racialized and linguistic borders. She added that their shared status as victims brought Mayan protagonists and intermediaries together, whereas "factors such as ethnicity, class, education, etc. mark their roles as intermediaries" as distinct from those of the Mayan protagonists.

In contrast, most of the Mayan intermediaries—perhaps partly because only two of them were staff members of the three NGOs facilitating this work and/or none was in the leadership of the organizations—focused more on individual-level growth and change. Ironically these differences may be partly due to the fact that they developed these skills outside of their communities of origin, and for the ladinas the NGO constituted a community. Yet those Mayan intermediaries who functioned primarily as interpreters and promoters valued their training with ECAP in which they learned about Western mental health practices and about how to care for themselves as also having survived gross violations of human rights in their families and communities. Others acknowledged their performances of "healing" as opportunities to integrate resources from training experiences with Kaqla and the struggle for redress. Of note were the Mayan intermediaries who acknowledged their own need to heal from their experiences in the wake of the internal armed conflict. They noted their coming to renewed or new awareness of their own internalized oppression and that their struggles in self-healing from these processes contributed to a deeper appreciation of the challenges facing the 54 Mayan protagonists. Others said that their developing a range of skills from the training and performances of creative and embodied resources contributed to their own healing. Thus the Mayan intermediaries reported acquiring both new technical skills and embodied knowledge from the accompaniment processes with members of their own community, "women like us" or "we are like them." They noted that they had been previously performing some of these things, such as facilitating meetings or creative techniques, but had not known that that was what they were doing nor that they were defending their own human rights when they spoke up for themselves in local meetings. Thus the work as interpreters and promoters enabled them to appropriate words through which to name a range of lived experiences and to position themselves as intermediaries.

Performing Accompaniment. Mayan and ladina intermediaries differently positioned themselves as intermediaries relative to their personal and professional trajectories and their racialized and gendered intersectional identities. Interestingly, although the work was deeply interdisciplinary there was a division of labor that centered at least partly along the lines of expertise of the three organizations, but also in terms of those identified positionings. The interview analyses confirm that Mayan intermediaries talked twice as often as ladina intermediaries about the effects of the armed conflict and the work of healing and psychosocial accompaniment; the reverse was true for talk related to truth-telling, justice seeking, and reparation(s). The talk of the lawyers and feminist activists was heavily weighted in terms of the transitional justice work, whereas the healers and promoters were more likely to focus on the wake of the armed conflict and the critical importance of psychosocial accompaniment. The ladinas who were professional psychologists sat at the intersection of this work, equally emphasizing both sets of performances. These findings confirm the diverse positions and co-constructions of knowledge discussed earlier, suggesting that despite the interdisciplinarity of the work, many described themselves and their performed actions as related to the educational and experiential resources that they brought to the process. Another possible interpretation is that they were constrained by those skills, with the demands of the transitional justice regime dominating the performances in which each subgroup of intermediaries engaged. Equally suggestive is the finding that the contributions of the Mayan intermediaries did not seem to affect the discursive performances of transitional justice reflected in the ladina intermediaries' descriptions of themselves and their work. Thus, despite the multiple-year Maya–ladina collaboration and the incorporation of Western psychological and legal knowledge(s) in the discursive performances of the Maya, the analysis of these interviews suggests limited to no bidirectionality in these processes.

Interpretation and Communication. When analyzing the role of intermediaries in the transitional justice processes discussed in this volume, the work of rights translation and interpretation is key. Merry and Levitt (2017; see also Levitt & Merry, 2009; Merry, 2006) document diverse ways in which transnational human rights discourse travels to local contexts in which it is spread and adopted, in part depending on its being embedded in or responsive to local cultures, and Engle (2012) confirms varying degrees of such travel. As our research has also found, translation of rights discourses and claims is not a simple process, particularly within and across distinctive languages, and in some occasions, translation results in transformation. Tijerina (2009) argues that, rather than being neutral, the interpreter makes choices about how to decode and encode and that these processes are neither linear nor always straightforward. In a study conducted in rural China and cited in chapter 2, Woodman (2011) found that translation sometimes obscures the voices of the survivors: the activists' interpretations and the technical language they used often reframed what was said and/or had a disempowering effect on the people from the villages, preventing them from participating in justice processes that were about their rights. As discussed throughout this volume, none of the ladina or international intermediaries spoke a Mayan language. Moreover, Doughty's (2017) study of translation and interpretation within transitional justice processes in Rwanda documents multiple complexities associated with these judicial processes. These studies, although small in number, show how mediators or intermediaries are not mere conduits; they transform, translate, distort, and modify the meaning of the elements they seek to carry into new sites (Doughty, 2017; Woodman, 2011).

The theme of translation and interpretation was perhaps the most starkly divergent thread within these interviews. Among the ladinas, the psychologists of ECAP, who coordinated and facilitated the mental health training of the Mayan interpreters and promoters, talked most about interpretation in that context. Others who did so were staff members of UNAMG who relied on interpreters not only for this work but also for other feminist organizing and educational work with women's groups in rural Mayan communities. In contrast, the six Mayan intermediaries spoke nearly twice as frequently about interpretation, and much of that conversation came from the interviews with the three community-based interpreters and promoters.

It is perhaps not surprising that those interpreting for the Mayan protagonists in their work across ethnolinguistic groups, for the ladina intermediaries and the North American researchers in our participatory workshops, and for the wider public in multiple transitional justice spaces were more attentive than others to the work of interpretation and translation. Read from another perspective, this significant difference might also reflect the unrecognized assumption that Spanish is the lingua franca in Latin American transitional justice contexts, despite the implicit if not verbalized acknowledgment of all participants in these processes that Guatemala is a pluriethnic and multilingual country. Mayan intermediaries' reflections about their work as interpreters, both in these interviews and in a group conversation that we conducted several months after the March 2010 Tribunal of Conscience with four of the Mayan intermediaries who worked as interpreters with ECAP and UNAMG and in the Tribunal, provide additional insight into how these Mayan intermediaries understand the work of interpretation and translation alongside the Mayan protagonists.

Mayan interpreters emphasized the challenges of having to suspend a focus on themselves or on what they thought or felt about what was being said and to focus instead on the speaker and what she meant, which they then had to interpret; that is, understand and then translate into Spanish and/or a Mayan language. Several noted the lack of parallelism between Spanish and the Mayan languages they were interpreting, emphasizing that one word in Spanish, such as reparation(s), might require a phrase in Q'eqchi' or in Kaqchikel. Those who worked as interpreters in the Tribunal of Conscience spoke about the difficulties of translating the expert witness reports, particularly those by specialists whose fields were not familiar to them and/or who might shift their presentation from the written text that the interpreters had been given before the Tribunal. Most reported that they received minimal training prior to the Tribunal, with those who were to oversee them telling them "not to worry" and that the "equipment was easy to use." Although the Q'eqchi' interpreter managed to secure a Spanish-Q'eqchi' dictionary for review before the Tribunal, interpreters for the other ethnolinguistic groups were not so fortunate.

Their descriptions of translating for the Mayan protagonists who testified at the Tribunal of Conscience were steeped in emotion, with examples of how challenging it was when the woman who testified broke down in tears. Since they were behind a screen, the interpreter mentioned not being sure how to communicate these emotions to the public in attendance. Also challenging was translating the woman's description of her violation from Q'eqchi' into Spanish because of the multiple dimensions of Mayan representations of sexual violence. She interpreted the words as saying, "They ended my life, ripped my life in two by causing me harm," leaving me "damaged and very sad." The interpreter described her anxiety and concern that she had not captured in Spanish the specificity of the testimony or adequately represented the meaning of the violence against her. Similar challenges of interpretation were discussed by Barrios in her expert witness testimony in the Sepur Zarco trial discussed in chapter 3 (Tribunal Primero de Sentencia Penal, C-01076-2012-0021, 2016, pp. 109–112). She also noted the integral connections between language and the Q'eqchi' cosmovision, confirming the multiple ways in which the Q'eqchi' word for sexual violence, muxuk, captures the physical, emotional, moral, and cultural experiences of the violation of Q'eqchi' women—complexities absent from the Spanish translation. On exiting from behind the screen at the Tribunal of Conscience, the interpreter encountered another interpreter and a bilingual Q'eqchi' woman who affirmed that her translation was very good. She imagined that, because they spoke both Q'eqchi' and Spanish, she had "transmitted the meanings as best as I could."

Several others of those who translated for the Tribunal of Conscience reiterated the challenges, but also celebrated their accomplishments. They noted that they had been accompanying the Q'eqchi' protagonists for several years, were trained as promoters and working as interpreters in multiple contexts, and that the Tribunal was for them "like a graduation ceremony." Despite the emotional challenges and the extraordinary work required to prepare for it, they experienced carrying it out as their own and the Mayan protagonists' accomplishment. This achievement was explained as due to their shared identity as Maya and to their skills as bilingual promoters.

As previously discussed, in describing the challenges of interpreting and translating, several Mayan intermediaries confirmed that they had never been trained as interpreters but rather only as mental health promoters. They noted that the mental health promoter training provided by ECAP offered both techniques for processing the emotional weight of listening and then interpreting Mayan protagonists' stories and resources for their community visits to protagonists as they prepared for the various actions that they took together. They also valued the *compañerismo* [companionship] and the peer supervision that they offered each other. Finally, some reported that ECAP's supervision helped them sustain and support what they sometimes experienced as the impossible task of adequately interpreting for the Mayan protagonists, performing among different Mayan languages and back and forth between Spanish and several of these languages.

Those who interpreted for the Mayan protagonists for multiple years and in preparation for the Tribunal of Conscience noted the particular challenges of interpreting for physicians and others who sought information about sexuality or sexual violence. They noted that most of the protagonists were older than they were and had been raised with strict rules not to speak about these topics or about their sexual organs. Thus the specific focus of this work challenged traditional cultural values and the respect that they felt was due to the women as their elders. They sometimes refused to translate or searched for "more respectful" ways to ask questions.

This parallels another noteworthy finding in our analyses of all 12 intermediaries' interviews. Very few interviewees focused on the theme of sexual violence in describing their work with the 54 protagonists, despite this being a major focus of the more than decade-long accompaniment provided by intermediaries. Surprised by this finding, we did a word count of terms that included sexual violence and/or violation, sexual abuse, to violate, and violation; we found these concepts were mentioned nearly twice as frequently by the ladina than the Mayan intermediaries in reporting on and making meaning of their work. For the Maya, two of the professionally trained Mayan intermediaries were responsible for the vast majority of these terms' usage. Thus, despite the focus on breaking the silence about sexual violence in the wake of Guatemala's armed conflict and in the previous truth commissions, there was surprisingly little explicit conversation about sexual violence. This may be at least in part because the intermediaries were socialized in the same and/or similar contexts as were the Mayan protagonists: one that suppressed or silenced "talk about one's body" and/or sexuality more broadly and sexual violence more specifically. It also may be that sexual violence was an assumption underlying the raison d'être of the work and therefore did not need to be spoken. Or it might be that neither the intermediaries nor we as researchers felt it necessary to explicitly engage those silences due to our recognition of and respect for the Mayan protagonists or to our concerns about not contributing to its hypervisibilization. Despite these silences we often noted that the 54 Mayan protagonists expressed their emotions and their affection much more openly than many of the Mayan women with whom we have worked over many years in Guatemala. Thus emotional expressivity and embodiment had increased over time through these iterative processes of action and reflection.

Constructions and Representations of Mayan Protagonists. Intermediaries spoke about the Mayan protagonists in diverse ways when reporting on their shared actions and in talking about the overall work in which they were engaged within their NGOs and their local communities. In the interviews the Mayan intermediaries exhibited greater diversity and frequency in talk about the protagonists than did the ladina intermediaries, but the differences between the two groups were not as stark as those reported in other areas. The similarities and differences across groups mirrored the positionalities described earlier in this chapter. Although ladina intermediaries eschewed the language of victimhood, they were most likely to talk about the Mayan protagonists in terms of the transitional justice processes in which they were involved. Specifically, they focused on the effects of how the Mayan protagonists as a group presented themselves in the public processes in the Tribunal of Conscience or in the Sepur Zarco case (e.g., covered by a shawl to conceal their faces or uncovered). Most of their talk about the Mayan protagonists was focused on the women as survivors of sexual violence and in search of truth, justice, and reparation(s). In contrast, the Mayan intermediaries focused on their accompaniment of the Mayan protagonists in the transitional justice processes, as well as in their activities within their families and their home communities. Specifically, they described protagonists' performances of Mayan healing actions as well as community-based activities, including visiting the dead and participating in local women's groups. Thus the Mayan intermediaries described multiple performances of Mayan protagonism, experiences to which they had access not only as members of a shared pueblo but also in their work as promoters and interpreters that was both locally and nationally based. The Mayan intermediary who served as an expert witness in the Sepur Zarco case visited and interviewed the plaintiffs in their local communities and therefore had a more integral vision of their positionalities. In June 2013, additional understandings of how the Mayan protagonists viewed the intermediaries were discussed in the Dialogue and performed in a final creative workshop with the intermediaries and Mayan protagonists, which we discuss in the following section.

CRITICALLY ENGAGING WITH NGOS AND WITH OURSELVES AS INTERMEDIARIES

In June 2013, together with UNAMG, we organized a Dialogue that brought together those Mayan and ladinx intermediaries who had accompanied the 54 Mayan protagonists and with whom we had engaged throughout our research, most of whom we had also interviewed for their perspectives on their roles as intermediaries. Additional participants included a Unitedstatesian and a Spaniard who had accompanied this research at different moments in the eight-year process and who had both lived and worked in Guatemala for more than 25 years.

Before the Dialogue, UNAMG had circulated a paper written by several of their staff (Caxaj et al., 2013), as well as two of our initial publications (Crosby & Lykes, 2011; Lykes & Crosby, 2015a) that we had had translated into Spanish and in which we presented preliminary findings from our first four years of feminist PAR. UNAMG convened and chaired the Dialogue and invited us to provide some opening remarks, in which we summarized key themes that we had identified as next steps or pending issues. With participants' informed consent, the conversation was recorded, and two research assistants took notes. The Dialogue was structured to allow us to step back from our more typical role as facilitators of the workshops and listen to the reflections of all present.

As we reviewed and reflected on the field notes and tape recordings of the Dialogue, we observed that much of the conversation moved away from a focus on our feminist PAR as presented in our articles and toward a discussion of broader issues related to transitional justice, feminist organizing, and sexual violence. The conversation took the form of a cross-organization reflection process through which participants repositioned their own or their organization's particular contributions to Mayan women's struggles for justice and reparation(s) in the wake of sexual violence. That shift in focus—and the multiple-year journey of the work we were discussing—confirmed the multiple ways through which, in Das's (2007) words, time "is an agent that 'works' on relationships" (p. 87), through which narratives and the experiences they recount are continuously and dialogically re-storied.

For example, as discussed in this volume, lawyers, psychologists, feminist activists, interpreters, Mayan healers, and expert witnesses had worked together for more than a decade in a variety of iterations of accompaniment processes through which the 54 Mayan women protagonists sought redress. In our Dialogue, as in some of the individual interviews with ladina intermediaries described in this chapter, many performed their professional, political, and ethnolinguistic and/or national identities. For instance, a psychologist spoke repeatedly of the diverse emotions emerging throughout these processes, particularly from the women's creative workshops and in the Ríos Montt trial, while the lawyers resisted what they perceived to be a "reduction" of complex legal issues to socioemotional experiences. The latter challenged our tendency to eschew a language of victimhood, arguing that victims' rights were achieved through considerable legal and judicial struggle and should be celebrated rather than submerged in a discourse of hypervisibilization of harm. One lawyer asserted several times that Mayan protagonists' telling of their stories or their testimonies within the context of this work had been healing for them, whereas others, including ourselves, recognized the necessity of such speaking out while also questioning the purported healing power of such testimonies (Hamber, 2009) and defending protagonists' stated desire to not be asked to tell their stories yet again. Those who self-identified as feminist activists focused repeatedly on the importance of the women's stories or testimonies as a necessary part of the transitional justice process, but also emphasized the importance of protagonists' leadership development and activism for future organizing efforts. Despite these professional and/or disciplinary "pushes" reflected in particular performances that tended to separate those gathered, and despite our multiple critiques of the limitations of transitional justice processes in this context and across these many years of work, our analyses of the field notes suggested that these processes performed what we might call a more salutary function than what we had identified previously: they served as a "pull," engaging a diverse group of Mayan and ladina women in a set of shared or collective processes in search of redress for racialized gendered violence (something similar happened in the Ríos Montt case across a diverse range of civil society). Thus despite differences embedded in professional training and/or self-identifications or positionalities as evidenced through the accompaniment processes and in the interviews, this diverse group of women (and one man) from an equally diverse group of organizations had come together under the umbrella of transitional justice to speak truth to power. And the relationships that were formed and persisted, as well as about what and how all spoke, shifted in multiple ways over time.

There were shifts in the discursive constructions of transitional justice that dominated the Guatemalan context over the eight years of this process: from reparation(s) to the judicialization of justice. Each of the participants and their organizations underwent changes in leadership, staffing, funding, and the nature of their work with the 54 Mayan women protagonists. Some of these changes reflected the changing terrain of transitional justice and the diverse expertise required from each organization, while others resulted from the ongoing transitions in relationships among the organizations, as well as the multiple challenges of keeping each organization and the Alliance financially solvent during the many years over which the work had been extended. We documented the ongoing accompaniment of the 54 women despite these changes, acknowledging the continuities of accompaniment despite some organizations' fractures and reconfigurations. Although an in-depth discussion of those changes is beyond the scope of this book, they reflected the dynamic nature of individual and institutional relationships that are all too often read as static or as unchanging contexts. Those transitions and reconfigurations then reshaped some of the accompaniment processes that were, of course, reconfigured over time within and across the dynamics generated in preparation for and in the unfolding of the Tribunal of Conscience and the Sepur Zarco trial. The intermediaries and we as researchers are also protagonists whose positionalities and repositionings over time contributed to the strengthening or straining of the Alliance during some moments over these eight years, and its reconfiguration at other times. Some of these changes reflected the natural ebb and flow of membership and employment, while others were the result of fractures emerging from different professional, ideological, political, and racialized emphases about what was needed from whom and how to provide it at particular historical moments in particular contexts. Despite these challenges, all involved sought to remain faithful to their accompaniment of the 54 Mayan protagonists. We now examine some of these diversities within the continuities of accompaniment as they emerged during the Dialogue

Some of the ladina intermediaries and international participants commented on the critical remarks we had made in one of our articles (Crosby & Lykes, 2011) about the hypervisibility of sexual harm, arguing that while those accompanying the group of 54 and the group itself had been engaged in speaking out about sexual violence for at least a decade, much of Guatemalan society was only now slowly beginning to acknowledge what had happened to Mayan women. Thus they suggested that such a critique of a tendency in feminism in some contexts was not relevant to or important in Guatemala. For some Mayan intermediaries, our critique had more resonance, and some of their comments added thickness to our subsequent descriptions and analyses of our research, including in this volume. One Mayan intermediary connected her reflections on the hypervisibility of sexual violence to an earlier point in the discussion about Mayan indigenous women as victims or protagonists, noting, "In the life of indigenous women there is a before and after. When they are being sexually violated, yes, they are victims. If we don't analyze this moment and all that they lived through as victims, we can't situate sexual violence as part of genocide. There has always been sexual violence; now is the first time it has been taken to the courts."

Another Mayan accompanier questioned how we could ensure that "sexual violence is an event that has occurred in our lives, but that it does not define who we are." She emphasized the need to persist in the struggle against racialized gendered violence—and to be aware of its consequences—while not expecting women protagonists themselves to remain positioned in and through these particular stories of harm. She asked, "How have we who have accompanied these processes, but are not victims, been marked by them? How can we ensure that this topic continues to be a focus of struggle without the women themselves having to tell their stories again?" Thus the conversation of hypervisibilization and invisibility was nuanced and contextualized within and across discourses of time—as a before and an after but not a forever—despite the forever and ever-present nature of the multiple effects of racialized gendered violence noted by some of the 54 women and their families. As reported in the individual interviews with Mayan intermediaries, those in the Dialogue located themselves alongside the women they accompanied while noting that they too had been affected by these processes.

In contrast to the interviews with intermediaries that reported little to no mention of sexuality in talking about the work with the 54 Mayan protagonists, there was some discussion of Mayan women's sexuality during the Dialogue. Several ladina and international participants noted that the feminist PAR processes provided Mayan women with an opportunity to move away or distance themselves from a primary or exclusive focus on damage or harm that permeated so much of the work with them as they repeatedly gave their testimonies. They noted that the creative resources of the workshops facilitated Mayan women's positive engagement with their bodies and their sexuality through the arts. Some drew themselves or dramatized their relationships into an imagined future, one that they had created together, even if only within the workshops, in which they played with the unthinkable harm that they experienced and the repositioning of themselves in solidarity with others similarly harmed. Thus, as discussed in chapter 1 these workshops facilitated protagonists' recognition and acknowledgment of each other, a critical move away from the isolation and silence that had characterized many of their lives for so long.

We noticed a similar turn toward a recognition of similarities in a discussion of the still mostly pending work to be done with Mayan and ladino men. Some Dialogue participants located the challenge of working with men as one that is deeply situated within Mayan communities, noting that Mayan men were neither exclusively perpetrators nor victims. One ladina said, "Working with men needs to focus on a recognition that men have lived the same fears and the same impunity [as women]. We need to work with them not as aggressors but as men who have lived within the same social structures" as women.

Other Mayan participants spoke about the pending challenges of working "in community," in contrast to much of the work of the Consortium and the Alliance that took place outside of the Mayan protagonists' local communities. One Mayan intermediary noted, "It is very complicated to work in [Mayan] communities, as the context is very different and many of these situations provoke stigmatization" of women. Of note are the multiple ways in which the transitional justice processes discussed in this volume were played out in urban and transnational centers of power, rather than within the rural communities that were decimated during the genocide and in which the women suffered such brutal violations. Thus the circulations of power and dispossession played out in urban and rural contexts over centuries are repeated not only in the genocidal violence of the war but also in ongoing settler colonialism in which these efforts to redress the harms of racialized gendered violence are being carried out.

Finally, all Mayan intermediaries present in the Dialogue spoke repeatedly of the structural racism underlying and threaded through the sexual violence against Mayan women, noting its historical and contemporary roots and practices, while commenting, as discussed earlier, on how the absence of a clear analysis of racism both informed and constrained the relationships between Mayan and non-Mayan intermediaries in this work. In the words of one Mayan intermediary, "If we don't use a theoretical framing of racism [for analyzing sexual violence] then we cannot understand why indigenous women have lived with this violence since colonization." Although not directly engaged in the debate or discussion of racism, several ladina intermediaries acknowledged the need to have better resources for thinking through and analyzing racism. These issues are taken up in different forms in the following section, which explores discussions and performances of integral reparation(s) within and across intermediaries and Mayan protagonists.

MULTIPLE CONSTRUCTIONS OF INTEGRAL REPARATION(S) WITHIN AND ACROSS COMMUNITIES

In June 2013 Mayan protagonists revisited the multiple understandings of integral reparation(s) that we had generated together over the previous four years. This was an opportunity to look back at the contributions of the ladina and Mayan intermediaries in relation to their understanding of the ongoing transitional justice processes, with a focus on the struggle for reparation(s) (some aspects of this workshop were also discussed in chapter 4 in terms of the Mayan protagonists' understandings of reparation(s)). Fourteen of the 54 Mayan women protagonists participated: seven Q'eqchi', two Chuj, three Kaqchikel, and two women living in a returnee community of Chaculá in Huehuetenango. Three interpreters/promoters (Chuj, Q'eqchi, Kaqchikel), five UNAMG staff (three of whom were among the Mayan and ladina intermediaries whom we had interviewed and two were additional interpreters/promoters), and two PhD students (members of our research team) joined us for the day.

This workshop was focused on "looking back" with the aim of better understanding not only the co-constructed nature of our work but also the diversities in understanding and perspective, with a particular focus on the Mayan protagonists' meaning-making, including their interpretations of the representations of the intermediaries. We revisited previous representations of integral reparation(s) created through three collages produced by some of the Mayan protagonists from each region (discussed in chapters 1 and 4), as well as the four collages generated by staff from each organization and by the international researchers analyzed earlier in this chapter and engaged in image theater. As discussed in chapter 1, Boal's image theater was designed to facilitate an embodied encounter with and performance of both external and internalized experiences of oppression and/or circulations of power around a particular issue, in this case, integral reparation(s). One of its goals was to generate additional understandings about the phenomena, particularly those that might be more out of one's immediate awareness.

Therefore, the first moment in this reflective exercise drew on participants' interpretations of the collages: the representations of integral reparation(s) generated first by other Mayan protagonists and then by the ladina intermediaries and participatory researchers between 2010 and 2013. The Mayan protagonists in the workshop were divided into two groups, each with an interpreter/promoter who could facilitate their shared dialogue. They were invited to do a walk about the room, examine the collages that had been clustered on opposite walls, and then gather in the small group to discuss what they had noticed about them. Each group described and interpreted its own collages—that is, those created by some of them and by other Mayan protagonists—as confirming (1) that the armed conflict and violence against women had destroyed everything while also violating their rights; (2) that the PNR had failed to provide reparations as promised; (3) that their eviction from their lands had not been resolved and, moreover, that other lands were being confiscated by big businesses; (4) that their health continued to be poor; (5) that they needed corn and beans as well as homes; (6) that this genocide did happen and was the fault of Ríos Montt; and, finally, (7) that they as indigenous women continued to be taken advantage of through manipulation.

The insights generated through the Mayan protagonists' analyses of the intermediaries' collages shared some items with those of their own collages listed earlier, but there were more of them and they were more varied in content, perhaps reflecting the larger number of images on those collages. Of the 15 issues listed it was of note that when the images reflected what might be interpreted as a loss that had been repaired—for example, children studying or having adequate food—the Mayan protagonists were quick to add that although this was what the image depicted, it was not true in their communities: children were not in school because the PNR had not met its obligations and families are still impoverished. They also noted that the images suggested that they needed to speak more openly about their demand for integral reparation(s) and justice in the face of the genocide that resulted from the orders of Ríos Montt, issues that were not represented in their own collages.

Joining together, the two groups then engaged in further discussion of these observations. Many of the Mayan protagonists discussed the intermediaries' representations in the collages of what might be imagined to be the benefits that they should be reaping from reparations, but that some women had not received most, if any, of these resources. These comparisons elicited a series of denunciations about the government and the PNR and the latter's failure to deliver what they had been demanding. Although their critique seemed to implicitly implicate the intermediaries as imagining a better life for them but having failed to deliver it, several of the protagonists countered this unspoken implication by thanking UNAMG and others who came from afar to listen to their concerns. Thus, although some of the protagonists risked a critique of the ladina-run organizations and, by association, of us as researchers, others assumed a more typical position of gratitude for our accompanying their struggles, focusing their frustration, anger, and criticisms instead on the Ríos Montt dictatorship and the current PNR.

Building on this analysis, and cognizant that the financial resources that had been leveraged to facilitate this community of women for more than a decade were rapidly being depleted and that there were many more women in their communities of origin in need of the resources and accompaniment that these 54 women had been receiving, we organized an activity that invited the Mayan protagonists and the UNAMG-based intermediaries to reflect on their ongoing and potential locally based efforts to secure justice and reparation(s). The participants were divided into four groups for this activity: three groups of Mayan protagonists with interpreters/promoters and a fourth group that included UNAMG's Mayan and ladina staff. The groups were asked to think about where they were now in their search for reparation(s) within their local communities, at the national level, and internationally, as well as to describe processes in which they were engaged in daily life.

The report-back of the UNAMG group was organized at the three levels of engagement (local, national, and international). They reported on multiple ongoing work, in addition to that with the 54 Mayan protagonists, including a series of actions designed to increase societal awareness of sexual violence and to highlight the importance of engaging in ongoing research, organizing, and transitional justice demands for justice and reparation(s). In their group, Q'eqchi' and Huehuetenango participants, including two Chuj women and two returnee women, spoke about their local community-based actions, including work as midwives and in facilitating meetings with other women. They noted that working at the local level where men are present has helped them overcome fear and shame of speaking in mixed groups. Others asserted their knowledge of their rights and how that knowledge has facilitated their skills and desires to talk about the armed conflict and how it has affected them with those with whom they live in community. Of interest was the absence of any reports of resistance to change, repression, or discrimination. In contrast, the Kaqchikel women from Chimaltenango and its villages described communities wherein people "don't want to talk, only want money for projects." Some described husbands who were very supportive of their ongoing participation in the group of 54, while others talked about husbands who refused to let their wives or partners go to meetings. These women also focused on themselves as victims and in need of ongoing work with UNAMG.

In contrast to these differences in local protagonism, all four groups spoke about participation in national marches and protests in regional cities and in Guatemala City. These demonstrations were organized to demand truth and justice, including demands made to international bodies for reparation(s). Most also described their ongoing collaborations with international activists and researchers, both their participation in economic projects and their sharing their stories with those who were interested. Thus it seems that in Alta Verapaz/Izabal and Huehuetenango, two of the three regions of Guatemala, the Mayan protagonists have transferred the confidence and skills gained through these years to local initiatives and are reaching out to other women and men in their communities. Importantly, they described combining these resources with those that they have acquired through their local Mayan traditions (e.g., as midwives). Their reports wove a seamless story of themselves at the intersection of these multiple subjectivities. In contrast, although the UNAMG report discussed the importance of recognizing and respecting cultural diversity in their local initiatives, there was no mention of particular linguistic or cultural resources infused in their work. Finally, the Kaqchikel women of Chimaltenango continued to struggle with some of the losses experienced nearly 40 years ago and to position themselves and their communities as requiring outside financial resources in order to be able to take any actions. The diversities of responses challenge a homogenized positioning of Mayan women exclusively in terms of their ethnolinguistic subjectivities, suggesting the importance of understanding their actions at the intersections of various circulations of power reflected in the wider sociopolitical and economic dynamics of the country and how they shaped local protagonisms during the armed conflict and continue to do so today vis-à-vis extractive industries and global capital.

We then divided participants into five small groups, which differed from the previous ones. Due to their larger number, and so they could talk to each other without interpretation, the Q'eqchi' women formed two small groups, while three other groups were mixed (as they were able to use Spanish to communicate with each other), and UNAMG formed their own group. Each Mayan group had one interpreter/promoter who helped facilitate the development of an embodied image: a dramatization without words that reflected their understandings of how integral reparation(s) was being engaged by or thwarted in their local communities. Participants were encouraged to draw on what they had learned over the four years and in particular to review the work produced during this workshop as they developed their presentation. Each group was then invited to perform its embodied image before the group as a whole, who served as their audience and interlocutors in the subsequent discussion that began with audience feedback and was followed by each group's explanation of what it had hoped to represent.

Group 1, which included the two Kaqchikel women and two returnee women, dramatized a demonstration in which they demanded justice from the Guatemalan government. Government officials were performed as "busy talking on the phone" and "uninterested" in their demands. They noted in the discussion that followed that they had wanted to represent the government's disinterest in them as Maya and also its wealth and well-being, as well as the need to keep struggling even if there is no hope to realize their demands in their lifetimes. They explained that the struggle was not only for "our generation but for our children and the generations to come."

The three Q'eqchi' women in Group 2 dramatized a small group of women in which one was motivating another woman in her local community who had been mistreated to seek help. In describing their performance, they noted the sadness that women experience when they suffer from violence and the importance of having other women accompany them and help them seek relief. They noted that their performance sought to represent women who help each other in their local communities.

Two Chuj women and one Kaqchikel woman in Group 3 represented a doctor's office at which a woman was seeking help. In describing their performance, a Chuj woman noted that they had decided on this focus because so many women received no medical attention in the wake of the war and that even when help was provided, it was only to give a prescription for medication for which they could not pay. She also noted that the illnesses were not only physical, concluding that the organizations that accompanied them invited their participation and that this participation was "a medicine for us."

Group 4 included four Q'eqchi' women, and their embodied image was more symbolic than the three previous representations. One woman was alone, with her head covered, and the others approached her, taking her by the hand. Another woman then uncovered her head and slowly opened her mouth and eyes. All three women faced forward, and each had one foot in front of the other. The audience noted the solitary figure whom they described as "abandoned" and interpreted the closed eyes and mouth as representing the lack of insight and understanding about the armed conflict that characterized so many of them when they began this work. Others noted the shame, shyness, and fear in the woman whose head was covered and the role of the other women in accompanying her in her journey toward self-confidence through solidarity. In their commentary the Q'eqchi' women affirmed the interpretation of themselves before and after the work with the organization, noting that UNAMG was not the only organization with whom they had worked and thanking all of them for their help. They noted that they too analyzed the solitary woman's situation and wanted to help her, moving to stand in union with her.

The fifth and final performance was done by ladina and Mayan intermediaries in UNAMG and was both symbolic and representational—but, unlike the others, it included words. One woman stood on a chair, holding up a flower, while the other women surrounded her with scarves that had been knotted together, moving themselves to standing side by side with the woman on the chair and shouting, "Neither forgetting, nor silence" (one of the Alliance's key refrains). The audience's interpretation referred to the importance of standing together and of inviting those beyond one's group to join them. Others noted the force of being united. The UNAMG participants added that they had hoped to represent that "sexual violence is not an identity" and that the Mayan woman on the chair represented all indigenous women who have ruptured silence and who serve as an example for all of us. Another noted that they had hoped to combine two of their actions, representing the Tribunal of Conscience and the then upcoming Sepur Zarco trial, both of which reflected the women's successes in demanding justice.

Taken together, the five performances represented the integration of the diversity of ways in which Mayan protagonists and the intermediaries who accompanied them position themselves; it reflected some of the particularities of protagonists' experiences in their ethnolinguistic or geographically based communities that informed their engagement with this broader community of women. Some Chuj and Kaqchikel protagonists continued to mourn openly, recognizing and naming their need for help as represented by doctor's prescriptions while also acknowledging that the work in a community of women has provided some solace. Q'eqchi' women emphasized the critical importance of solidarity among women and positioned themselves within their local communities more so than beyond them. Equally important were the continued demands for justice and accountability as well as reparations from the state. Finally, the intermediaries, despite an absence of talk about the possible contributions and/or conflicts in ways that are inclusive of the Mayan cosmovision, concepts of justice, linguistic diversities, and so on, or about sexual violence in most of their interviews and in other workshops, centered their embodied image around a Mayan protagonist who had survived and broken silence about sexual violence. She was lifted above them, held up by a chair and holding a flower. One interpretation is that they were embodying their accompaniment of the 54 Mayan protagonists through this repositioning of a victim. Yet as outsider researchers conscious of our own white privilege and our power to mediate knowledge through our and their accompaniment of the Mayan protagonists, we also question in what ways elevating her above themselves may represent yet another moment of "othering" (see Hale, 2006, for a discussion of ladinx perspectives on the Maya).

CONCLUDING REFLECTIONS

This chapter has focused on the intermediaries, those who translated human rights and feminist discourses and transitional justice policies and praxis grounded in international circuits of power to facilitate local processes through which Mayan women from diverse linguistic-ethnic groups who survived racialized gendered violence could perform their experiences of violation, resilience, and resistance, demanding truth, justice and reparation(s). We drew on multiple participatory processes and in-depth interviews through which they performed and reflected on this praxis and attended to the knowledge(s) they brought to and generated through their multiple encounters with some of the 54 Mayan protagonists. We noted not only the particularities of their ethnolinguistic diversities but also of their professional and experiential training. The major comparisons generated in these analyses centered on differences between the Mayan and ladina intermediaries, but we also noted similarities and diversities within each of these groups and some that were clustered around professional training. The Mayan intermediaries' experiences at the intersection of patriarchal, racialized, and class power circulations deeply informed their knowledge(s) generated in part through their identifications with the Mayan protagonists from the base of a shared cosmovision and related experiences of healing. In contrast, despite their own experiences during the armed conflict and in postgenocide organizing, the ladina intermediaries minimized differences between themselves and Mayan protagonists, emphasizing shared gendered experiences constrained by patriarchal power and violence. As significant, there was relatively little ladina performance or discussion of institutional or cultural racism, its colonial roots, and its persistence in the current struggles for truth, justice, and reparation(s). The creative workshop performances and subsequent discussions and exchanges complemented rather than contradicted the silences illuminated through the analysis of the in-depth interviews with intermediaries.

In the conclusion to this volume we revisit the overall goals of this research and interrogate the multiple performances of accompaniment, intermediarity, and pragmatic solidarity represented over the 8 years. As white North Americans we have been humbled by the multiple ways in which we have been challenged to interrogate our own positionalities and privileges at the intersections of racism, patriarchy, and impoverishment through these years. The multiple and ongoing encounters with these 54 protagonists and the Mayan and ladina intermediaries have challenged us to deepen our efforts to decolonize our academic training as we listen deeply to their positionalities and performances that are permeated by what one Q'eqchi' Maya referred to as "the violence from before which is in front of us" (AVANCSO, 2017). We have characterized our encounters with the 54 Mayan protagonists as mobilized by our commitments to accompany them through pragmatic solidarity. We return to the query of the Kaqchikel intermediary cited at the beginning of the chapter that we embrace as a cautionary tale, reminding ourselves of the risks of walking alongside the ladina intermediaries with whom we share multiple identities despite our differences, and of reproducing a research project that is more attentive to international norms as resources for achieving justice and reparation(s) and less engaged by what the Mayan women protagonists themselves understand by and desire from integral reparation(s). In the conclusion we identify some ontological-epistemological and methodological implications of feminist PAR for our co-constructions of multiple knowledge(s) in this project and for other feminist antiracist activists committed to working with communities in the wake of genocidal violence.

CONCLUSION

Feminism has allowed us to identify many gaps, to walk many roads. The Mayan cosmovision is a life project, a political project. I don't call myself a feminist. I am a Mayan woman. I embrace feminism as a system of analysis but not as my identity. All of us here are working with Mayan women. It's therefore very important to examine how we work with/from the Mayan cosmovision.

—K'iche' intermediary, authors' interview, June 2013

We do not realize that certain practical tools and desires from which we work, carry, or maintain legacies [that] oftentimes reproduce the systems of domination that we aim to contradict.... we are urged to question our own tools and actions of inquiry as well as our theoretical and political approaches that have sought and still seek stability.

—Edgar Esquit (2017, p. xvii)

Our feminist participatory action research over the past 8 years with the 54 Mayan protagonists and the local and transnational interpreters, feminists, activists, psychologists, lawyers, and researchers who have accompanied them was framed by a persistent and seemingly rhetorical question that drives most transitional justice processes today: Is it possible to repair the psychosocial, embodied, material, individual, and collective harm left by the experience of racialized, gendered, genocidal violence through actions administered by the very state that was primarily responsible for perpetrating this social suffering? Knowing that these processes are particular and context specific, while transitional justice processes presume a level of universality and are underpinned by Western normative assumptions, we documented the multiple ways in which Mayan protagonists have performed the embodiment and naming of their ever-present pasts and their search for a better future. With them, we asked what it has meant for them to speak their truth, achieve some justice, and receive what reparation(s) the state has awarded for what they and many scholars deem to be irreparable harm. In this conclusion, we read across the volume and identify threads that constitute the woof through which Mayan women are weaving 21st-century praxis to transform the warp of colonial power that constrains their protagonism. First, we critically reengage the knowledge(s) constructed about the 54 protagonists from several ethnolinguistic groups and the methodologies we used to learn about their everyday realities through accompaniment and pragmatic solidarity. The knowledge(s) produced through this critique are not intended to dissuade others from pursuing these methodologies, but rather to press for multiply informed strategies for engaging them. Second, we discuss diverse ways in which intermediaries accompanied these 54 protagonists through the multiple performances described in this volume, and the contributions and limits of this work as it was primarily carried out within the community of women constructed by protagonists and intermediaries. We reflect on how protagonists' lived experiences, struggles, and dialogic engagements within local, geographically based communities were somewhat obscured by the nearly exclusive focus on a community of women. We caution that many, including ourselves, remain hesitant to cede our racialized privilege to Mayan protagonists or indigenous scholars or activists, confirming through the performances documented herein that, despite our critique of Western liberal rights regimes and our commitment to decolonize our praxis, the universal human rights discourse and transitional justice praxis inform our tendency to vernacularize from these positions of discursive power. Third, we return to our discussion of the judicialization of transitional justice. Despite the critical contributions of this turn to the law—for Mayan protagonists, intermediaries, and Guatemalan society more broadly—we suggest that it risks reinstating rather than decentering Western liberalism and universal human rights by failing to adequately listen to and act on not only Mayan beliefs and customary practices but also the protagonism of the 54 women. We conclude with a brief review of the knowledge(s) that we as North American white activist scholars take away from these more than 8 years of accompaniment of Mayan, ladina, and mestiza protagonists and intermediaries and reaffirm our pragmatic solidarity—despite the many contradictions discussed in this volume—with them.

THE SIGNIFICANCE OF FEMINIST PAR AND CREATIVE RESOURCES

We turn to the protagonists for their insights into the contributions of feminist PAR and creative resources as strategies for engagement in activist scholarship within and across gendered, racialized, and classed ethnolinguistic differences. As a final component of a 2011 workshop, we asked protagonists to identify the creative resources they knew from their work with us and other intermediaries, and to explain and analyze how they had been used. They listed collective drawing, dramatization, and painting—both body painting and murals—as well as plasticine and newspapers used to make collages. Of note were the large number of embodied exercises and techniques that they described, including body movement, dance, group dynamics, and massage. When next asked to identify an issue or problem affecting their lives and then pick the creative resource that had helped them most to address this issue and move forward from the experiences of the past toward the present or future, all three subgroups chose dramatizations (each subgroup included Chuj, Mam, and Kaqchikel participants, as well as an UNAMG staff person). They designed, facilitated, and enacted participatory workshops and other embodied experiences, with two of the three incorporating massage into their dramatizations. Also noteworthy was that two of the three subgroups incorporated a ritual into their dramatization: both used ceremonial candles, although one group's ritual was clearly Mayan and the other's was clearly Christian. After the ritual, one of the subgroup's dramatizations included massage and a reflective exercise in which the facilitator asked participants how they were feeling. The women began to talk about their experiences of sexual violence and the fact that the army was responsible for these violations.. They then performed massages on one another, in pairs. At the end of the dramatization, women brushed themselves with basil on different parts of their bodies. The participants in all three subgroups displayed their capacities to identify an issue or concern, choose a methodological resource, and engage their peers in a participatory creative process through each of the dramatizations. These performances confirm that these protagonists had embraced the creative techniques and participatory processes and knew how to engage them as resources for their own well-being in both this community of women and in their local geographically based communities.

After the dramatizations, we asked participants to talk about why they thought these techniques were used. They generated extensive descriptions, not unlike those offered by other Mayan women with whom we have collaborated in similar creative workshops (Lykes & Crosby, 2015a). Some protagonists reported that group dynamics and warm-up exercises "helped [us] share feelings and emotions—sadness, negative memories, suffering that we have lived through"; can "explain new ideas and/or help us to understand what is being said—especially if we don't speak Spanish"; are "energizers that get rid of our pain"; and help "[us] stop being shy"; and "when we play our body relaxes and goes soft . . . we are more flexible when we play." One protagonist suggested, "When we don't understand the language in a workshop, they [facilitators] don't take us into consideration and then we don't pay attention and we don't learn things." Another talked about engagement with her body as a process of becoming aware of changes in herself. Participatory theater exercises and role playing were described by one protagonist as "practicing something before you actually have to do it"; they were means through which she and others could prepare themselves for the "real activity." Dramatic play and dramatizations were described as resources to develop new ideas about how to move forward: "to share our lives with each other and generate alternative ways of doing things"; to feel "relieved and calmer and more able to face the reality of the everyday"; and "through dramatizations we were better able to understand what we as women do to take care of the basic necessities of our lives." These group processes helped women "discover that we are not alone and that we all have the same problems." Protagonists situated the creative exercises, embodied performances, and Mayan practices as resources at the interface of physical and psychoemotional experiences. Specifically, some described massage as a resource to "rid ourselves of sorrows, fears, pain, and shame" resulting from sexual violations, adding that "medicinal plants rid us of negative energy." One woman noted that these "techniques not only help to rid myself of negative emotion but also to express positive emotion and happiness."

The creative methodologies within the PAR processes were described as contributing to the group's formation and sustenance as a community of women. It was clear that protagonists valued the opportunity to work together within and across ethnolinguistic groups. This was in stark contrast to their multiple representations and descriptions of themselves in drawings discussed in chapter 1, in which they pictured themselves before their engagements with each other and with intermediaries as alone, lonely, and unable to leave their homes, gather together, or speak about what was on their minds. In their assessments, protagonists referred to the importance of speaking "within the group" and "organizing ourselves" and how the group experiences "help us become less isolated."

These protagonists embraced creative methodologies while also integrating Mayan ceremonies and other practices, including, for example, using herbs as healing resources. The creative methodologies and feminist PAR processes—introduced by local Mayan and ladina intermediaries and international activist scholars—resonated with local experiences and cultural practices and proved accessible to women with nonformal educational experiences. Through these processes, protagonists performed past suffering and embodied imagined future transformative praxis that often reflected a more just life for themselves and their families and communities.

We demonstrated through our data analysis how this participatory and embodied praxis facilitated the performances of nonlinearity in workshops that took place as these protagonists and intermediaries participated in the judicialized practices discussed in chapters 2 and 3 and the PNR-driven constructions of reparation(s) described in chapter 4. This praxis enabled intermediaries, including ourselves, to document how protagonists understood and made meaning of the personal changes that they experienced in their lives, but could not easily verbalize. They performed protagonism through creative dramatizations and reflexivity, cooperatively or collectively naming harm suffered and challenging the government's past and ongoing abuses of them. As such, this protagonism both complemented and contested the more formal transitional justice actions discussed in this volume.

Similarly, our analyses of in-depth interviews with intermediaries and our critical reflexivity statements in chapter 5 disrupted assumptions underlying much social science research about how knowledge(s) are constructed and underlined the dialogic understanding of the co-construction of all knowing. Ladina and Mayan intermediaries constructed different ways of knowing, both of their accompaniment processes and of Mayan protagonists' meaning-making. Mayan intermediaries drew on a diverse range of experiences as members of the same but diverse pueblo as protagonists, addressing the multiple psychosocial and everyday material and structural challenges facing protagonists, and recognizing and critically analyzing experiences of racism and related complexities in working with ladina intermediaries. Ladinas and mestizas were less attentive to or focused on the geographically based experiences of protagonists and more embedded in facilitating their search for redress for sexual harm, albeit within the context of ongoing structural impoverishment. The multiple encounters within and across different groups of intermediaries and protagonists afforded diversities of meaning-making and knowledge constructions, enhancing what could be known and pointing toward some of the multiple silences, differences, and divisions sustained within and across communities in contexts of ongoing neocolonial circulations of power.

As coresearchers, we and other intermediaries were able to name and document the 54 Mayan participants' protagonisms and to listen more deeply to Mayan meaning-making despite our limited linguistic resources. Feminist PAR facilitated processes through which protagonists, intermediaries, and coresearchers analyzed racialized gendered violence within and beyond women's geographically based communities, while refusing to hypervisibilize sexual harm despite its ubiquity in the transitional justice actions recounted in this volume. Feminist PAR also captured the processual dimensions of protagonists' lives, resisting both linear constructions of their survivance or static notions of self, memory, and remembering. The iterative and participatory data analytic processes facilitated representations of the dialogic nature of all knowledge construction and meaning-making, as well as the articulation of a third voice generated through these processes. The action-reflection processes shifted the primacy of knowledge construction from the academy to the field, with university-trained researchers positioned alongside local participants, facilitating their protagonism and documenting their knowledge(s). Traditional hierarchies were challenged and direct experience performed and foregrounded through such iterative in situ interpretive processes. Similar feminist PAR processes have been facilitated in multiple other contexts of humanitarian disasters (Lykes, 2013) and in a wide variety of other educational, health, and community contexts within and across national borders (Bradbury, 2015; Reason & Bradbury, 2008).

Despite these many strengths, feminist PAR processes have their challenges, contradictions, and limitations (see, for example, AVANCSO, 2016, 2017; Cooke & Kothari, 2001; Hickey & Mohan, 2004). As is evident throughout this volume, despite the prioritizing of embodied performances, language is a critical mediator of knowledge construction and thus these practices are also highly dependent on interpreters when working across multiple ethnolinguistic groups. Rather than creative resources and PAR processes reducing the need for interpretation, they foregrounded its significance, suggesting that we should have paid greater attention to the need for additional multilingual peer coresearchers in this project. Second, the feminist PAR processes and the in-depth interviews with intermediaries discussed in detail in chapter 5 facilitated critical engagement with differences within and across groups of intermediaries relating to the naming, analysis, and redress of institutional racism. Yet, despite the multiple actions we engaged in with intermediaries and the 54 protagonists across the eight years, at no point did we explicitly seek to "undo racism" (People's Institute for Survival and Beyond, n.d.) among our groups of intermediaries or through the participatory research processes. The actions undertaken by the Consortium and then the Alliance alongside the 54 protagonists challenged sexual violence and sought redress for its effects while remaining mostly silent on racism or the particularities of racialized gendered violence. That said, there was a growing recognition of the deep and long-standing realities and effects of impoverishment on protagonists. Thus the transitional justice processes illuminated some intersectional aspects of gendered violence, while the PAR processes and creative resources contributed to the performances of others; for example, the structural racism that constrains Maya–ladinx relationships. Despite this, these processes did not contribute directly to redressing racism's long-standing effects nor did we directly challenge these silences, which some Mayan intermediaries engaged through their interviews with us, as well as through drawings, dramatizations, or interpretive processes, as discussed in chapter 5 (see also Távara et al., 2018). We suggest here that feminist PAR and activist scholarship emphasize the ways in which people self-present and how they perform their positionalities within the group. However, by positioning our PAR processes alongside transitional justice mechanisms, we may have accommodated the essentializing tendencies of universal human rights and feminist discourses and paradigms that decenter or even occlude racism and ongoing colonial power and privilege. This accommodation, coupled with the emphasis in this project on partnering with the community of women, may have obscured some locally embedded indigenous knowledge systems while constructing alternative gendered ways of knowing.

UNPACKING INTERMEDIARITY AND COMMUNITY

We facilitated the feminist PAR processes described in this volume alongside multiple actions for redress that were developed and carried out by protagonists and the ladina and Mayan intermediaries who accompanied them. We negotiated the partnership and the research focus with UNAMG, not directly with the 54 protagonists. One important consequence of this decision to work with and through UNAMG was that we implicitly agreed to work with the Mayan protagonists as a community of women and, other than the workshop we facilitated in Sepur Zarco in 2017, only visited their geographically based communities within the context of processes developed by UNAMG and the other participating NGOs for gathering data for the transitional justice processes.

As discussed throughout the book, the work of these 54 Mayan women protagonists was carried out beyond the geographically based communities they left in order to form women's spaces wherein the intermediaries determined that they would feel safer to describe the horrific violations that they had survived, given that their perpetrators often still lived within or in close proximity to their local communities. Protagonists and intermediaries described "women's spaces" as sites in which embodied performances were more easily engaged. For protagonists, being in those spaces seemed to have led to a greater ease with their bodies, more possibilities of naming the shame and humiliation associated with having experienced sexual violence, and increased physical embrace of each other in the workshops. It is also important to note that most if not all protagonists associated these spaces and processes with the presence of intermediaries who provided funding that enabled them to leave their geographically based communities and participate in the workshops and who introduced many of these techniques.

As we conclude this process, we neither challenge our decision-making process to work with the 54 Mayan protagonists and the ladina and Mayan intermediaries in these spaces nor the important accomplishments that ensued. Rather we ask ourselves how we, as white North American activist scholars, might have reframed our praxis had we taken a more critical posture when we undertook this collaborative process. This reflexive and critical self-interrogation suggests to us that our decision making at the outset of this process reinscribed rather than contested protagonists' organization as a community of women rather than within their geographically based communities; it also reinforced the power of the ladina NGO leadership, as well as our own as white northern researchers documenting these processes. The research design, modeled on the existing NGO relationships with protagonists and embedded in our respect for their processes and in recognition of our limitations as outsider researchers who had ongoing university commitments in the Global North, may also have contributed to our missing an opportunity to accompany the alternative knowledge(s) emerging from the feminist PAR processes; this knowledge might have contributed to a more gender-responsive embodiment of Mayan customary legal praxis, had we been able to more effectively listen to it and facilitate its travel from the bottom up. For example, the description of the image of the Mayan woman carrying a heavy burden in the collage discussed in chapter 4 as representing violence against women suggested to us not only that the Mayan creators of this collage experienced the embodied materiality and impoverishment of racialized gendered violence but also represented these as a single entity, not as cause and effect or as violence and repair. The context situating the image was the countryside, not the courtroom, suggesting that redress might best be actualized through reconfiguring relationships through local praxis. Yet the female embodiment calls the viewer's attention to the need to center women's protagonism. This knowledge from the bottom up resonates with but is not identical to those within transitional justice circles who call for transformative justice that seeks redress and change in relation to structural impoverishment (Gready & Robins, 2014) and those within feminist circles who challenge us to listen more deeply to women's multiple experiences of violence and resistance (Ross, 2003; Theidon, 2012). The image and its local interpretations are deeply Mayan, situating materiality and spirituality, past and present within a single representation (Chirix García, 2003; Grupo de Mujeres Mayas Kaqla, 2009): they challenge the Western dualisms and linear causal representations of violations and their wake, suggesting that feminist, human rights, and transitional justice paradigms, as embraced in the collaborations described here, may be a "Trojan horse of recolonization" (Esteva & Prakash, 1998/2014).

PAR emphasizes educational processes as central to research, as mobilized frequently through conscientization processes of action-reflection toward mobilizing personal and structural change. Although the extensive literature discussing these processes is beyond the scope of this book—and despite Freire's (1970/2000) commitment to respecting the knowledge "of the people"—a critical examination of the various methods that university-based researchers like ourselves deploy within feminist PAR processes, whose epistemology and methodology seek to disrupt "intellectual colonialism" (Fals-Borda & Mora-Osejo, 2003, p. 35), suggests possible contradictions. We embrace Fals-Borda's and Rahman's (1991) understanding of "knowledge existing as local or indigenous science and wisdom [that is] to be advanced by the people's self-inquiry" (p. 31) while recognizing the limits of our capacities to access that local or indigenous science and wisdom. Some of our own earlier PAR work with Maya Ixil and K'iche' women (Lykes, 2010), as well as the theorization of these collaborative processes as developments of third voices, stands in tension with Fals-Borda's and Rahman's goals or those of some of our Latin American colleagues who demonstrate their valuing of indigenous or local knowledge(s) through an *encuentro de saberes* [meeting of knowledge(s)] (see, e.g., AVANCSO, 2016, 2017; Hernández Castillo, 2016). Such an encuentro is particularly challenging—if not impossible—within the framework of transitional justice processes in which one is positioned as an intermediary who vernacularizes the so-called universal human rights discourse.

As we conclude this research we take up this additional challenge to those like ourselves, who seek to decolonize our thinking and encounter rather than talk over the multiple ways of knowing and being represented through the performances of the 54 Mayan protagonists in this study as well as their families and communities. We eschew a much too familiar performance of northern privilege: that the wider Guatemalan and transnational communities only recognize and acknowledge Mayan performances of resistance when they/we can define and constrain their parameters. Relatedly we ask whether or not positionality as an intermediary privileges the intellectual and discursive communities in which we were educated and are employed, as well as the human rights regime in which the local intermediaries had invited protagonists to participate or through which they have volunteered to accompany them. Thus by vernacularizing human rights discourse "from above" we implicitly reinscribe its value. The feminist PAR onto-epistemology that values, as discussed earlier, local knowledge(s) stands in tension with the posture of vernacularization. Merry and Levitt (2017) document how local cultures influence, even dilute, universal human rights, while we seek to lift up those local knowledge(s) and beliefs and position them at least on par with our onto-epistemologies as northern educated researchers. Yet where do we position universal human rights? Are we vernacularizing indigenous people's collective rights and ways of knowing and being? In what ways, if at all, do the local knowledge(s) developed through these processes travel into transnational systems of knowing? Can we accompany these processes both as intermediaries who vernacularize universal human rights and as feminist PARers who disrupt positivism as well as colonialism?

This challenge is exemplified through the discussions in chapters 4 and 5 concerning the Kaqchikel word for reparation(s). Several Mayan interpreters helped clarify at different points in our process that the Kaqchikel word used for repair referenced a torn cloth that could be sewn back together or patched, but that could never be returned to its original state. Thus we see that the irreparable nature of reparation(s) for racialized gendered harm is built into the ways in which these Kaqchikel interpreters moved between Spanish-language transitional justice terminology and their language. In contrast, Western truth-telling and justice-seeking processes and reparations programs generate the expectation that repair is not only possible but is also to be expected, while at the same time multiple transitional justice scholars increasingly document the irreparability of these losses (see Hamber, 2009, among many others). The point here is to emphasize the important contribution of knowledge from the bottom up—and to suggest that intermediaries need to, as noted by some of the Mayan interpreters, be positioned to listen and interpret from and in two directions.

We sought to explore some of these and other related issues through our commitment to engage in critical reflexivity throughout these PAR processes. This posture was not always successful nor was it embraced by or threaded through the participation of all intermediaries. Thus, as Lal (1996) writes, "Unreflexive attempts to get beyond the binarisms of Self and Other can end up reconstituting them" (p. 205). In an effort not to hypervisibilize protagonists exclusively as survivors of sexual violence, we drew on some of the contributions of Anzaldúa (1987/2012), who positioned herself and other *latinas* in the United States in borderlands. These hybrid spaces affirmed the multiplicities of their self-identifications and position-alities through which "from ... racial, ideological, cultural and biological cross-pollinization, an 'alien' consciousness is presently in the making—a new mestiza consciousness, *una conciencia de mujer*" (p. 102). As discussed repeatedly in this volume, we situate our work with the 54 Mayan women protagonists in dialogic relationality, arguing that it is central to how Mayan women's protagonism is shaped both by engagement with each other and with a diverse set of intermediaries who have accompanied them in their search for redress, ourselves as researchers included. We argue that we, as others, perform ourselves alongside them as they iteratively perform themselves, alongside us, through processes of mutual co-recognition and co-construction, or, as Anzaldúa suggests, in the hopes of generating performances as nos-otras (Torre, 2009).[1] The feminist PAR processes were designed to facilitate and/or illuminate Mayan borderland consciousness and multiple subjectivities of 54 protagonists' survivance.

Despite this positioning and co-creation of mutuality, our work raises provocative questions about whether or not and, if so, in what ways we North American researchers and the Guatemalan ladinas who collaborated in these processes are poised to acknowledge this mobile and diverse gendered Mayan consciousness as a center while recognizing that such a positioning resituates us in multiple peripheries, as *otra* [other]. Can we cede power and privilege and follow indigenous leadership to engage the processes of resistance and transformation that they propose? In their engagement in truth-, reparation(s)-, and justice-seeking initiatives discussed in chapters 2–4, Mayan protagonists were required to turn toward their non-Mayan counterparts and accept the primacy of individual rights-based frameworks—in contrast to the customs and practices grounded in and emerging from a geographically based we-in-community—to resolve what is in essence an ongoing colonial dynamic. In many of the processes discussed in this volume, it was the "hegemonic partner in the relationship" (Coulthard, 2014, p. 17) who shaped the terrain—whether it was the state in the form of the PNR that gave out or denied reparations checks, the Public Ministry that decided which cases to prosecute, the psychologists who diagnosed and treated trauma, the lawyers who translated harm suffered to the court, the judges who decided the cases, the feminist activists who provided training in women's rights in Mayan communities, or the researchers who discursively framed and analyzed protagonists' and intermediaries' voice and agency.

In seeking to address this hegemonic dynamic, we generated provisional contexts of dialogic relationality through the feminist PAR processes described and analyzed in this volume. This praxis of activist scholarship sought to name and then reframe subjectivities constrained by individualized rights-based "power-over" while accompanying Mayan protagonists and Mayan and ladina intermediaries in the judicialization processes that they judged to be the best—or only—access to justice and integral reparation(s) in Guatemala today. Although those of us who are non-Mayan intermediaries were not required to turn toward Mayan culture and strategies for redress, we were provisionally invited into these spaces. Thus, although the transitional justice terrain remains a colonial one and the structures of domination stay intact, we sought to create alternative micro-spaces within these terrains—or cracks in the walls—through which we co-created and performed third voices as nos-otras. We recognize that those spaces have not transformed colonialism nor the ongoing circuits of power and privilege through which we perform our work as feminist PARers. Nor have they necessarily or definitively redressed internalized racial superiority (People's Institute for Survival and Beyond, n.d.) within participating NGOs or our research praxis, despite our ongoing efforts to confront these realities. Yet we continue to position ourselves in ways that seek to generate knowledge from the bottom up, pushing it into circles of power through which it disrupts and regenerates activist knowledge, and to critically and reflexively interrogate our white privilege and challenge long-standing dualisms and binaries toward third voices.

SITUATING PROTAGONISM AND DECOLONIAL PRAXIS WITHIN AND BEYOND THE "JUDICIAL SPRING"

Forged in the shadow of the Guatemalan state's National Reparations Program (PNR), the research discussed in this volume began in 2009 and sought to understand what reparation(s) meant from the standpoint of these 54 Q'eqchi', Kaqchikel, Chuj, Mam, and Poptí protagonists who had survived sexual violence during Guatemala's genocidal armed conflict. Reparation(s) was the buzzword of the times, both in Guatemala and in the transnational spaces of international human rights regimes. Our research accompanied and documented Mayan protagonists' understandings and articulations of the impossibility of repair for harm suffered. Drawing on their ethnolinguistic understandings as interpreted for us through multilingual Mayan intermediaries, we heard their affirmations that what has been torn apart can be mended and patched, but will never be what it once was. In other words, there is no return to the status quo ante: "We would have to raise our ancestors from the dead for that to happen," a Mayan interpreter-intermediary told us in one workshop in June 2011. Yet, Mayan protagonists demanded what they referred to as integral or transformative reparation(s): land, housing, capital, health care, education for their children, and a guarantee of nonrepetition. Some of them spoke openly in public about their experiences and demands for justice and repair through the Tribunal of Conscience in Guatemala City in 2010, while others pressed their demands for integral reparation(s) in both the local and national justice systems (through the Sepur Zarco trial) and in the international system (through the demand for reparation(s) presented to the IACHR). This book documented these seemingly contradictory struggles at the interstices of living with irreparable harm as protagonists demand reparation(s)—the material and psychosocial conditions necessary to create a better future—as well as the successes and limitations of this demand as presented within select contexts. As discussed in chapter 4, protagonists were bitterly disappointed by the PNR's failure to adequately respond to their demands for redress and indeed have felt bought off, silenced, lied to, and deceived. Given the Guatemalan state's direct responsibility for the harm suffered through its genocidal counterinsurgency campaigns, the ongoing militarization and oligarchic corruption of state structures that continue to violate their lands through support of and collusion with extractive industries and single-crop export processes, and the continued presence in government of the architects and perpetrators of the violence, the PNR's duplicitous relationship with protagonists is not surprising.

Nelson (2009) identifies this broader "dialectics of deception" (p. xxii) or "two-facedness"—an ironic and tragic reframing of the k'ot, or double-headed eagle, discussed in chapter 5, that looks both ways, in two directions—as integral to the relationship between the Guatemalan state and its citizenry: this is an ongoing relationship that was established during the war (and has deeper roots in the history of colonialism). As Nelson argues, in the postwar period "the state has assumed a democratic mask hiding the ongoing power of military and economic elites" (p. xxiv). The protagonism of the 54 Mayan women and those who have accompanied them have revealed the many ways in which they have identified and resisted that power—naming and then claiming their space within a postgenocide Guatemala, thereby contesting multiple circulations of dispossession (Fine & Ruglis, 2009) operationalized by the state.

Protagonists asked for retributive justice, and as discussed in chapter 3, 15 Q'eqchi' women were plaintiffs in the successful prosecution in February 2016 of the Sepur Zarco outpost's military commander and a regional military commissioner for crimes against humanity in the form of sexual violence and domestic and sexual slavery. We completed this volume in 2018 in the wake of the Sepur Zarco trial and with several others on the horizon. "Justice" (through prosecutions) had become the new buzzword in Guatemalan transitional justice circles (OSJI, 2016; Ramos, 2016; Villatoro, 2016). In our post-Sepur Zarco trial debrief with members of the Alliance in July 2016, one of our interviewees referred to this moment as a "judicial spring," acknowledging that she was not sure how much longer it would last. Her words recall Henry's (2009) reflections on what weight to give prosecutions in the aftermath of atrocity. Henry cautions us both against what Reisman terms "judicial romanticism" and what Osiel calls a "hyperbolic dismissal of the law" (p. 133). As such, the meaning of justice is always caught up within, but must also always move beyond the bounds of its judicialization. It is also important to recognize the plurality of legal mechanisms. Indigenous struggles for justice adopt a multiplicity of legal strategies, from contextually specific forms of customary or indigenous law, often referred to as *derecho propio* [one's own law], to national and international legal systems and universal human rights standards (Hernández Castillo, 2016; Sieder, 2017). Viewed through an intersectional lens, these legal pluralities contain multiple racialized gendered specificities, complexities, and challenges (Hernández Castillo, 2016; Otzoy, 2008; Sieder, 2017. As such, we are challenged to recognize the many ways in which local protagonists anchor their "sense of justice" to the particular historical and contextual ground on which harm occurs and redress is sought, rather than to a liberal Rawlsian "ahistorical and aspatial" (Brunnegger & Faulk, 2016, p. 13) notion of justice as a "moral capacity of good" that must then be translated into practice (p. 2). Thus Brunnegger and Faulk remind us that what we understand and perform as justice "emerges from the spaces of lived experience" (p. 13) of those we accompany (see also Kesselring, 2017; Sieder, 2017).

The preparation for and realization of the Sepur Zarco trial reflected such an understanding of justice as emerging from protagonists' lived experience. Protagonists told us and the trial sentence affirmed that these crimes would not be tolerated and perpetrators would be punished. The ruling recognized Mayan indigenous women as citizens. However, given the multiple limitations of the law in responding to mass atrocity—including, for example, the participation of only a few protagonists when so many thousands more suffered similar experiences and the ability to punish only a few individuals for what were systemic and structural crimes perpetrated by many—we wanted to look beyond the law, to examine what Mayan protagonists and intermediaries call integral or transformative reparations, and which Henry (2009) terms "full justice": "the identification of missing bodies, the return of property, reparations, apologies, economic and social security, safety, stability and community reintegration, as well as the arrest and prosecution of war criminals" (p. 134). The Sepur Zarco trial and the forms of protagonism that led up to it and that it engendered were noteworthy for their agency in moving this agenda forward. Henry (2009) notes both the partiality and the necessity of legal justice as one aspect of the struggle for redress: "Full justice through criminal courts will always be incomplete. The logic of law cannot erase the physical and emotional scars of warfare. . . . Yet, as history has taught us, to do nothing to redress wartime sexual violence is itself an intolerable form of injustice" (p. 134).

In 21st-century postgenocide Guatemala, for Mayan protagonists and the intermediaries who have accompanied them, "doing something" about wartime sexual violence has signified a turn toward the rule of law and the liberal language of women's rights as human rights for redress, despite protagonists' oft-repeated location of their violation and resulting impoverishment in experiences of persistent colonial dispossession and genocidal violence against them as Mayan women. The seeming dissonance between these two ontological positions is constituted through relational epistemological performances including, for example, the Sepur Zarco trial and the IACHR petition, reflecting a belief in the liberal assumption of personhood built on structures of colonial dispossession, as we saw in the

Liberal period in 19th-century Guatemala (see Carey, 2013; Grandin et al., 2011, among many others). As such, Eng (2011) has argued that conceptions of human rights, reparations, and justice are themselves framed within histories of colonial violence and dispossession and are shaped by "Western subjectivity and conceptions of the human" (p. 580). As he elaborates, "Mediated by the normative institutions of the law, and by political notions of agency and will, reparations and claims for human rights seek justice and apology for violence through the fetishizing of equivalence—through the belief that past harms between victim and victimizer can be quantified and secured" (p. 583).

This "fetishizing of equivalence" is a key feature of transitional justice mechanisms in Guatemala that overlay or perhaps in fact facilitate and make possible the ongoing structural dispossession of indigenous peoples' lands and territory. Indigenous movements around *defensa del territorio* [territorial defense] in Guatemala have sought to contest such an equivalence, as Mayan communities throughout the country confront corporate occupation of their lands for rampant—and violent—resource extraction, which constitutes ongoing economic colonialism (Solano, 2013). Mayan women have been at the forefront of resistance to this corporate and state violence (Macleod, 2017), which has included rapes by private security forces, as well as by the police and military charged with protecting corporate interests (Russell, 2010; Vásquez, 2011). And as discussed throughout this volume, protagonists in our research have continuously made the connections between the past and the present in terms of their interrelated experiences of dispossession of land, violence, impoverishment—the heavy load they carry—and their strategies of resistance and contestation. Tuck and Yang (2012) remind us that, "decolonization is not a metaphor," but rather entails the "repatriation of Indigenous land and life" (p. 1).

As such, despite the momentary spaces of relative successes experienced during this judicial spring and, more particularly, through the Sepur Zarco trial, we recognize the limits of the judicialization of justice and its multiple contradictions, some of which we have described earlier. We welcomed hearing in our post-trial debrief interviews that some follow-up work by intermediaries in the community of Sepur Zarco has focused on how local communities can become less patriarchal and violent and how Guatemalan law can be applied there. We also welcomed some ladina intermediaries' acknowledgment of needing to further their education about racism in Guatemala. But at no point did we hear a corresponding conversation about how Mayan customary law and practices might be engaged to contest the racist patriarchal structures of the Guatemalan state. The state's commitment to recognize Mayan ways of knowing and being that was articulated within the Peace Accords has never been enacted, yet alone changed the terms of engagement between the Guatemalan state, its indigenous peoples, and the rest of the Guatemalan citizenry. When so many of the genocidal systems and structures of colonial power have remained the same, one has to wonder what is "in transition." The evolution and enactment of transitional justice mechanisms purportedly denote efforts to effect a shift from violence and authoritarianism to peace and Western liberal democracy. The actual lived experiences of the aftermath of genocide in Guatemala (and many places elsewhere) has shown that, while the violence may be less overt (although not always), the structures of domination remain the same behind the democratic mask that often slips to reveal what lies beneath (McAllister & Nelson, 2013).

As discussed throughout this volume, in Guatemala, Mayan women activists and theorists have looked away from the language of individual rights toward the Mayan cosmovision and its principles of collectivity, autonomy, and self-determination (Ajxup Pelicó, 2000; Álvarez Medrano, 2006; Chirix García, 2003; Curruchich, 2000; Grupo de Mujeres Mayas Kaqla, 2009, 2010, 2011; Jocón, 2005; Velásquez Nimatuj, 2012) in their struggles for and conceptions of a decolonized language of justice. Indeed, at one point the Mayan women's organization Kaqla, whose work is discussed in chapters 1 and 5 and in which several of the Mayan intermediaries in our research have participated, was criticized by some within Guatemalan civil society for its focus on looking within, rather than outward toward the broader society. It was felt that Kaqla had a responsibility to engage with others beyond themselves to effect change. But the Mayan women whom we interviewed who were members of Kaqla spoke of looking inward as having allowed them to draw on and reposition themselves vis-à-vis their understandings and reinterpretations of a diversity of Mayan practices; it has enabled them to heal from and resist the ongoing racist and patriarchal violence of colonization that many face each day in their professional lives working within Guatemalan civil society, and then better address structural violence in accompaniment of their communities. As discussed in chapter 5, structural racism is an underlying tension in relationships between ladina and Mayan intermediaries accompanying the 54 protagonists, with the former seen as paternalistic in their engagement by their Mayan counterparts. A refusal to engage on the other's terms is a strategy of resistance to and contestation of colonial power. And such contestations can occur within a liberal politics of recognition, as a means to subvert and transform. One such example, discussed in chapters 2 and 3 in relation to the Tribunal of Conscience and the Sepur Zarco trial, was Mayan protagonists' use of shawls to turn away from the hegemonic gaze hungry to consume the spectacle of racialized sexualized suffering.

TURNING TOWARD: IN DIALOGUE WITH MULTIPLE NOS-OTRAS

Indigenous thought and struggles for decolonization are multifaceted, heterogeneous, and context specific, and, of course, as people who are non-indigenous, it is not up to us to define the terrain for such struggles or what they should look like. This has been precisely the problem within, and an ongoing facet of, colonial discourse and practice. But through this 8-year collaborative process we have seen more clearly how we can choose to step back from our authorial privilege, critically interrogate and seek to transform the multiple ways in which we benefit from and perpetuate white supremacy, accept our unknowingness, and be willing to seek to create different kinds of relationships that decenter Western rights-based regimes that have been shaped through the experience of colonial domination and recenter other forms of becoming nos-otras. As discussed in chapter 5, Farmer (2013) identifies a willingness to stay with someone on her journey until she determines that she has reached her goals as a key aspect of pragmatic solidarity. And if we are willing to turn toward and follow others to create a new path as we go, does the ability to choose such a turn again signify hegemonic power? And who invites whom into such aspirations toward mutual relationality? One has to wonder whether the hashtags #IAmSepurZarco and #WeAreAllSepurZarco that rapidly grew throughout the trial, taken on by audience members and those supporting the trial both in Guatemala and beyond, were one more example of "becoming without becoming" (Ahmed as cited in Razack, 2007, p. 379), where yet again the experience becomes more about "us" than "them" and the structures of colonial power remain intact. The occupation of the space of the other through the appropriation of the experience of racialized gendered harm as a gesture of solidarity seems facile at best. What seems more important is to cede the terrain of defining what the terms of engagement should be and what struggles for redress should look like. As cited in chapter 5, in her definition of the terrain of psychosocial accompaniment, Watkins (2015) talks about how the "creation of opportunities for testimony enables those who have suffered violence and social exclusion to exercise their agency" (p. 327). But the question then becomes, Who creates these opportunities and how, and on whose terms? The feminist PAR engaged over these 8 years raises the specter that defining the terms of engagement sets the parameters for agency therein.

The transitional justice mechanisms discussed in this volume, from a truth-telling tribunal to a court case to a reparation(s) program, focus on the experience of harm for which redress is sought, and in our recounting of protagonists' engagement with these mechanisms we too have risked replicating these stories of harm. We began this volume with Tuck's (2009) warning against the perils of damage-centered research on indigenous communities conducted by outsiders, however well intentioned, and her call for a desire-based framework that "accounts for the loss and despair, but also the hope, the visions, the wisdom of lived lives and communities" (p. 417). As we highlighted in detail in chapter 1, in our research, we used creative resources as a means to decenter linear narratives of individuated harm (Bueno-Hansen, 2015) and to listen to how protagonists' narrate and perform their multifaceted and collective experiences of the everyday work of repair (Das, 2007). The repeated iterations of suffering and engagement with resistance in protagonists' stories, actions, and embodied representations are resonant with Weis's and Fine's (2012) praxis of critical bifocality.

The use of creative resources and embodied practices in workshops with intermediaries facilitated their performances of desire, as well as their joy at engaging with others who shared their experiences and with whom they were increasingly organizing. They also revealed the intermediaries' implicit understandings of gender and racial hierarchies and frequently unarticulated onto-epistemological assumptions about transitional justice processes and how they interfaced with not only the violence of the war but also the psychosocial accompaniment, advocacy, and activism in which they were engaged alongside Mayan protagonists. Revealing these assumptions allowed us to denaturalize and denormalize transitional justice processes and understand how they are shaped by multiple positionings and circulations of power. Given intermediaries' reliance on the spoken word in their advocacy work, their creative and embodied performances also facilitated the non-formally educated and non-Spanish-speaking Mayan protagonists' access to the intermediaries' meaning-making and understandings of transitional justice processes, thus constructing a bridge of mutuality that makes possible the co-construction of knowledge, a key goal of our feminist PAR process.

We have argued in this volume that the work of vernacularization must travel both ways: local indigenous contexts and realities must be seen as central and relevant in struggles for redress, not simply the other way around as is the historical and continuing norm. Mayan intermediaries, and interpreter-intermediaries in particular, are those most able to look both ways, or face in two directions, as represented by the k'ot. As discussed in chapter 5, our analysis of workshops and interviews revealed that ladina intermediaries tended to place more emphasis on their own actions, strategies, and decision making in relationship to transitional justice processes. In contrast, despite their class and spatial differences in terms of urban or rural locations, Mayan intermediaries positioned themselves vis-à-vis their shared identities with protagonists as members of an indigenous pueblo and as having survived colonial violence and being in need of healing: they positioned themselves as wounded healers (Nouwen, 1979) in the ongoing journey to secure indigenous rights and well-being. As such, collectivism both was a shared resource on which they could draw and a shared space within which to ground themselves.

Our feminist PAR processes were developed and took shape over many years of dialogic engagement with Mayan protagonists in multiple sites in Guatemala and through more recent collaborations with Mayan women of Kaqla. These processes sought to decenter underlying assumptions of Western conceptions of the self and subjectivity, listening to and then situating our work in contexts informed by Mayan beliefs and practices and their iterative reformulations by Mayan protagonists and intermediaries. These PAR processes were, of course, facilitated—

and constrained—by our lived experiences as white activist academics from the Global North. Additionally, they were structured to both recognize and document the intentionality with which Mayan protagonists chose both to participate in and resist our invitations to engage these processes, as well as their expressions of joy and liberation, in addition to those of pain and suffering: "I am like a bird. I can fly with large wings." To deny their agency in shaping their protagonism—to see them as merely acted on by those with whom they engage—would replicate the colonial discourse and rescue narratives we have sought to contest and subvert in this volume. All of those involved—both protagonists and intermediaries— have been transformed by our engagement in the action and research processes described in this volume. Protagonists are working together and with others to change the conditions in which they live and enact strategies of resistance in their everyday lives: "I am not going to stay with my arms crossed if I see another woman's suffering." In Sepur Zarco, they have formed the organization Jalok U that represented them during the trial and now has a membership of more than 70 women and men who are working to hold the state accountable for the repa- rations ruling that was part of the trial verdict. This remains challenging terrain, given the concerns raised earlier about the dialectics of deception inherent in the relationship between the Guatemalan state and its indigenous peoples. Protago- nists in Sepur Zarco have also had to contend with threats and acts of intimida- tion. As Ross (2003) points out in her summary of her findings from her research with women survivors of apartheid in South Africa, we must be mindful not to assume closure of the multiple experiences of harm suffered—or to assume there is only one way to act or one path to justice. This is a reminder to us to not reify the experiences of both suffering and protagonism of the "group of 54," which have been varied and contextually specific. As such, protagonists in Huehuetenango and Chimaltenango continue to explore the meaning of justice outside the bounds of its judicialization as they struggle toward well-being. And many Mayan women outside of this group of 54 have been influenced by their struggle and strategies of resistance, as they too continue to contest the structural effects of their experi- ences of racialized gendered harm. The challenge as we complete this volume and look ahead is for Mayan women's multiple experiences of suffering and struggle, of voice and silence, to be recognized and addressed on their own terms and in continuous dialogue with multiple nos-otras—adding further complexity and nuance to understandings of everyday forms of resistance to racialized gendered harm and enabling others to "fly with large wings."

ACKNOWLEDGMENTS

This book is the culmination of several very long journeys, beginning most importantly with the one that 54 Maya Q'eqchi', Kaqchikel, Mam, Chuj, and Poptí protagonists began in 2003, when they started working with the Actoras de Cambio Consortium to seek redress for the racialized gendered harm they had suffered during Guatemala's genocidal violence. There are no words that can adequately express our gratitude to them for allowing us to accompany them in a very small way along their path. Their courage and determination are our continued source of inspiration. They taught us to "fly with large wings." We are also immensely grateful to the accomplished women involved with our research partner UNAMG. They include Luz Méndez, who took a leap of faith and started the conversation with us in 2008, and has remained a steadfast and invaluable advisor; Maya Alvarado, a most generous and creative colleague; and then-research team leader Brisna Caxaj, our talented and very patient collaborator without whom none of this would have been possible; we are particularly indebted to Brisna. Much appreciation and thanks also to Jeanette Asencio, Carmelita Chonay, Xiomara Chutan, Elisabeth Desgranges, Paola González, Norma Herrera, Florinda Itzol, Sofía Ramírez, Sandra Sanchez, Libertad Sagüí, Olivia Tox, and Ada Valenzuela. We extend our heartfelt thanks to our past and present colleagues in ECAP and MTM for their continued engagement with our research over the years and their patience with our multiple requests, including among others too numerous to name, in ECAP—Vilma Duque, Judith Erazo, Susanna Navarro, Olga Alicia Paz, Monica Pinzón, Ana Alicia Ramírez Pop, and Amalia Sub—and in MTM: Paula Barrios, Jennifer Bravo, and Lucia Morán. We are especially appreciative of the amazing women from UNAMG and ECAP who worked with us as interpreters in the workshops: their capacity to "look both ways" amplified our research and understanding immeasurably. We value enormously the many collaborations and friendships that emerged from our engagement with those who were part of the Alliance at one time or another.

Several graduate students from York University and Boston College have been invaluable collaborators in this research: Rocío Sánchez Ares, Liliana Mamani Condori, Heather Evans, Rachel Hershberg, Emily Rosser, Erin Sibley, Gabriela Távara, and Caren Weisbart. We are very grateful for and appreciative of all their contributions. It is impossible to adequately convey the role Fabienne Doiron has played in this research and how much we have benefited from her research talents and deep and long-standing commitment to social justice and, most particularly, gender justice in Guatemala. Fabienne has been with us every step of the way, conducting interviews, organizing workshops, taking field notes, coding data, writing with us, and providing invaluable research, edits, and comments on the book manuscript right up to the end. We are immensely grateful.

We are so appreciative of the many friends and colleagues in Guatemala who provided invaluable support to us throughout our research and collaborated in intellectual, personal, and engaged actions too numerous to list: they include Yolanda Aguilar, Sara Álvarez Medrano, Francisca Álvarez Medrano, Ana Caba Mateo, Luisa Cabrera Pérez-Armiñan, José García Noval, Rafael Herrarte, Helen Mack, Rosa Macz, Liduvina Méndez García, Antonia Susana Sanic Caba, María Eugenia Solis, Ruth del Valle, and Irma Alicia Velásquez Nimatuj. Megan Thomas generously hosted us many times in her home in Guatemala City and accompanied us as advisor and friend.

We have benefited from our participation in a number of collaborative projects that have enabled us to put our work into broader contexts and engage in stimulating debate. Thanks in particular to Brandon Hamber for inviting us to think along with other colleagues about psychosocial approaches to trauma, through which our focus on creative methodologies became integral to our research and conception of protagonism; to Diane Nelson and Elizabeth Oglesby for bringing together a group of us to engage "the question of genocide" and the implications of the Ríos Montt trial; to Morna Macleod, Natalia De Marinis, and all participating colleagues for motivating us to think more precisely about the significance of "emotional communities" in relation to multiple struggles to resist violence in Latin America; and to Sharlene Hesse-Biber, Diane Bretheron, and Siew Fang Law for invitations to share our methodological contributions to activist scholarship with wider audiences. Our engagement in these collaborations has affirmed once again the importance of dialogical knowledge co-construction. We are also grateful to the many other colleagues and friends who served as co-panelists and discussants at the numerous conferences and workshops where we presented our work in progress, who accompanied us during fieldwork, or who engaged in lengthy consultations in diverse corners of the world. Among these we thank particularly Malathi de Alwis, Carlos Martín Beristain, Pascha Bueno-Hansen, Urmitapa Dutta, Joseph Gone, Michelle Fine, Jennifer Hyndman, Deborah Levenson, Ramsay Liem, Alison Mountz, Susan Murdock, David Murray, Bradley Olson, Jenny Pearce, Pilar Riaño, Rachel Sieder, Christopher Sonn, and Gabriela Torres. Marcie Mersky introduced us to each other on a hot July day in New York in 2006 and has been a constant source of wisdom and friendship. Our interactions with these friends and colleagues, as well as those in our respective universities, greatly enriched and stimulated our thinking.

We are inspired by Yolanda Aguilar and Amandine Fulchiron, who together initiated the accompaniment work in support of Mayan women survivors of sexual violence in Guatemala, as well as by the work of Guatemalan activist scholars—including Ricardo Falla, Myrna Mack, Joaquín Noval, and Irma Alicia

Velásquez Nimatuj—for their committed and engaged anthropology with rural Mayan communities. We first started working together when we collaborated with our colleagues at PCS, Christina Laur and Samantha Sams, to design and facilitate a workshop with mental health promoters from Guatemala, Peru, and Colombia in Guatemala in 2007. PCS has played a vital role in Latin America in developing and supporting work with women survivors of sexual violence during armed conflicts; it was then led by our very dear and much missed colleague Diana Ávila, whose vision and tireless activism in the promotion of social justice live on. PCS first facilitated Alison's engagement with Actoras de Cambio in 2003. At the time, Alison was working for the Canadian social justice organization Inter Pares, and she is very grateful to all her friends and colleagues there and to the organization as a whole, without whom this research would not have happened. Much appreciation goes especially to the "Latin America cluster"—David Bruer, Brian Murphy, and Jean Symes—and to Peter Gillespie, the ultimate co-conspirator whose legacy is ever present among those of us fortunate enough to have known and worked with him. Peter inspired and motivated Alison and Rita Morbia to facilitate an exchange between Guatemalan and Burmese women in 2002 and 2003 when how to address sexual violence in war surfaced as a pressing concern, providing an important impetus for this research. Brinton's life was transformed by a 1983 meeting with members of the Guatemalan Church in Exile who had recently fled what were only several decades later to be fully acknowledged as acts of genocide. Thanks especially to María Caba Mateo and other Mayan women who first urged her to visit their homeland during the second decade of its armed conflict, welcomed her into their families, and have accompanied her in this journey ever since; to Esteban Costa, Juan Jorge Michel Fariña, Patricia Goudvis, Rosa Maciel, and Luciano Suardi with whom she planned the first creative workshops in Guatemala; to Marco Tulio Gutiérrez and ASECSA for their invitation to facilitate multiyear creative workshops with community-based health promoters and displaced children and their caretakers in the Guatemalan Highlands during the 1980s; and to the remarkable and resilient Maya Ixil and K'iche' women of Chajul and their families with whom she has journeyed for over three decades.

We would like to thank the Faculty of Liberal Arts & Professional Studies, York University, Toronto, Canada, for the financial support it provided to this work. We also acknowledge the financial support provided for this research from the Social Sciences and Humanities Research Council of Canada (SSHRC), the International Development Research Centre (IDRC), and the Center for Human Rights and International Justice (CHRIJ) at Boston College, as well as the sabbatical leaves from our respective universities. The project was jointly housed at the Centre for Research on Latin America and the Caribbean (CERLAC) at York and the CHRIJ at Boston College. At CERLAC, much appreciation and thanks to former directors Eduardo Canel and Carlota McAllister and former and current coordinators Marshall Beck and Camila Bonifaz, as well as the rest of the CER-LAC community, for their input into and support for this project and ongoing commitment to engaged activist research in Latin America, the Caribbean, and their diasporas. At the CHRIJ our thanks go to Timothy Karcz and Bonnie Waldron who scheduled multiple meetings and travel while ensuring balanced budgets and that we were fed; to Daniel Kanstroom for his friendship and ongoing collaboration in multiple teaching-learning processes; and to the CHRIJ's former directors and co-founders, David Hollenbach, S. J. and Donald Hafner, who supported this work from its beginnings. Thanks also to colleagues and staff at the Centre for Feminist Research (CFR) at York, including former director Enakshi Dua, and most particularly to coordinator Julia Pyryeskina for tolerating Alison's distraction during the final stages of preparing the manuscript. Our particular thanks to our editor at Rutgers University Press, Lisa Banning, who has supported the book project since learning about our earlier work and who has been a constant source of advice and support throughout the process of finalizing the manuscript. We also extremely appreciate the in-depth and insightful feedback provided by the anonymous external reviewers, which greatly strengthened the manuscript.

Chapter 1 of this volume is adapted with permission from Springer Nature from a book chapter, "Creative Methodologies as a Resource for Mayan Women's Protagonism," by M. Brinton Lykes and Alison Crosby, *Psychosocial Perspectives on Peacebuilding* (pp. 147–186), edited by Brandon Hamber and Elizabeth Gallagher, © Springer International Publishing, Switzerland 2015. With permission from Oxford University Press, chapter 2 is derived in part from an article, "Mayan Women Survivors Speak: The Gendered Relations of Truth-Telling in Postwar Guatemala," by Alison Crosby and M. Brinton Lykes, *International Journal of Transitional Justice*, 5(3), pp. 456–476, © Oxford University Press 2011, available online at https://doi.org/10.1093/ijtj/ijr017. And with permission from Taylor & Francis, chapter 4 is derived in part from an article, "Carrying a Heavy Load: Mayan Women's Understandings of Reparation in the Aftermath of Genocide," by Alison Crosby, M. Brinton Lykes, and Brisna Caxaj, *Journal of Genocide Research*, 18(2–3), pp. 265–283, © Taylor & Francis 2016, available online at http://dx.doi.org/10.1080/14623528.2016.1186952.

Our loved ones, including partners, friends, and families, have been an infinite source of support and encouragement throughout the many years of research and writing. Alison would like to thank her parents for providing such an inspirational example of how to live in practice a commitment to social justice. Special appreciation goes to Cathy for accompanying Brinton for many years and for so generously tolerating many marathon all-consuming writing sessions in her home, and to Tearney for patiently accompanying us through seemingly endless discussions of the cover design and title, creating fantastic mock-ups, and finding the Colaj painting *Personajes* that provided such an apt cover for this book. We thank the

Colaj family for very generously allowing us to use *Personajes,* as well as Ana Lucía at Galería El Túnel for facilitating communications.

We are grateful for the multiple contributions of those with whom we have journeyed for nearly a decade, apologize to those who remain unnamed, and take full responsibility for any errors of fact or differences of interpretation within these pages.

NOTES

INTRODUCTION

1. All direct quotations in this volume, unless otherwise noted, are drawn from transcripts of interviews, focus groups, and participatory workshops conducted as part of the PAR process. We translated these quotes from Spanish—which sometimes was a translation from a Mayan language. We did not include the names of those who agreed to be interviewed to protect their confidentiality and anonymity.

2. This research project was initially approved by York University's Ethics Review Board (May 6, 2009) and the Boston College Institutional Review Board (May 15, 2009) and renewed every year thereafter through 2018.

3. Spirituals are typically sung in a call-and-response form, with one person improvising a line and then another, often a chorus, providing the refrain. They were sometimes referred to as "sorrow songs," because they often reflected the suffering and struggles of slaves and frequently were used in sending coded messages that facilitated slaves' escape; see, for example, "Go down Moses" through which Harriet Tubman identified herself to slaves wanting to flee to the North (Pershey, 2000).

4. Drawing on Taylor (2003), we use the concept of performance to pay attention to protagonists' embodied practices as dialogical ways of knowing. As Taylor (2003) argues, "Performances can function as vital acts of transfer, transmitting social knowledge, memory, and a sense of identity through reiterated, or what Richard Schechner has called 'twice-behaved behavior'" (p. 3).

5. In this volume, we use the terms *ladina* (feminine), *ladino* (masculine), or *ladinx* (to denote the gender-neutral term, following the recent trend to use the "x" for gender-neutral language): in Guatemala, ladino/a are the most commonly used terms to describe those who are not Mayan. As Grandin, Levenson, and Oglesby (2011) explain, the term "ladino" was "first utilized in Guatemala in the 1500s to refer to Mayas who spoke Spanish, its meanings hav[ing] changed over time. In the 1800s and early 1900s, Ladino sometimes referred to all lower-class people in the city and countryside who did not use Maya clothes or languages but also did not belong to the Creole elite. The concept evolved to mean 'non-Maya,' a claim that disguises the reality that many Ladinos are descendants of Mayas and Europeans and are thus 'mixed' by definition" (p. 129; see also Martínez Peláez, 2011). Some participants in our research explicitly identify as *mestiza*, rather than ladina, to reclaim their history of being "mixed," and thus we use "mestiza" (or *mestizx*) when quoting those who self-identify as such.

6. The Polochic Valley, where the Q'eqchi' women are from, sits at the border of the departments of Alta Verapaz and Izabal. The community of Sepur Zarco has been identified in different times as belonging to either department. It is currently part of the municipality of El Estor, Izabal (see Méndez & Carrera, 2014, pp. 23–24).

7. We use the term "racialized gendered violence" when talking about the forms of gendered violence experienced by the Maya, which include but are not limited to sexual harm. The intersectional framing inherent in our use of the term recognizes how racialization, gender, sexuality, class, and other relations of power are integral to understandings of genocidal violence. As such, the term "gendered racialized violence" could also be used. We also sometimes refer to the armed conflict as *la violencia* [the violence], as this is how many Guatemalans, and in particular rural indigenous communities, describe the war.

8. While the CEH concluded that acts of genocide were perpetrated against certain Mayan communities during the height of the war between 1981 and 1983, we use the terms "genocidal violence" and "genocidal harm" in this volume to refer to the violence committed against indigenous peoples during the armed conflict, in recognition of the targeting of Mayan communities as a whole by the Guatemalan state and paramilitary groups. Under international law, an "intent to destroy" must be demonstrated to prove genocide. In regard to the Guatemalan armed conflict, there is much debate as to whether the state's intent was to destroy the guerrillas through its counterinsurgency strategy or whether it intended to destroy the Maya as an ethnic group. As Oglesby and Nelson (2016) point out, the CEH (1999) report and the 2013 Ríos Montt genocide trial verdict distinguished between intent and motivation, "which made it possible to argue that the Guatemalan Army's ultimate motivation was to defeat the guerrillas, but in order to do so, it *intentionally* targeted entire groups, like the Maya-Ixil, that it considered to be enemies of the state" (p. 139; emphasis in the original). We concur with Oglesby and Nelson's conclusion that "the question is not whether the violence was counterinsurgency or genocide; the point is that it was both counterinsurgent and genocidal" (p. 139). See note 5 in chapter 3 for a discussion of the legal strategy in the Sepur Zarco trial concerning the use of "genocide" and "crimes against humanity" (see also Impunity Watch & Alliance, 2017). Our use of the term "postgenocide," in addition to "postwar," acknowledges the scope, scale, and ongoing effects of the genocidal violence perpetrated against the country's indigenous peoples (McAllister & Nelson, 2013).

9. There are various ways of counting the number of Mayan languages (as well as naming them). When citing other sources, we use their numbers. We ourselves refer to 22 Mayan languages, per the Academy of Mayan Languages, as cited in López López (2017, p. 47 and note 54, p. 54).

10. For example, the Global Summit to End Sexual Violence in Conflict, which took place in June 2014, brought together representatives from 117 countries, as well as UN and aid agencies, NGOs, survivors, and around 2,000 delegates; see Sherwood (2014) and a follow-up piece that critically assessed the summit's achievements (Townsend, 2015).

11. UNAMG was founded in 1980 in Guatemala. In 1985, during a period of intense repression and political violence targeting activists in Guatemala City, the then-president of UNAMG, Silvia Galvéz, was kidnapped and disappeared. Many of the organization's original members left Guatemala during some of the worst repression of the armed conflict. In the wake of the signing of the final Peace Accords on December 29, 1996, some who had participated in UNAMG in Mexico and had since returned to Guatemala made initial contacts with each other and began a slow process of rebuilding the organization. UNAMG describes itself as a women's organization positioned at the intersection of feminist and left political thought that strives to understand and change through transformative praxis the existing social reality that marginalizes women (Alvarado Chavéz, 2015). It builds partnerships with other like-minded organizations, welcoming women from all walks of life and valuing the diversities of women's experiences, on the principle that only through networking with other organizations can transformative change be achieved. Most recently, as a member of the Alliance it has exercised critical leadership in defense of the rights of Mayan survivors of sexual violence during the internal armed conflict.

ECAP traces its roots to the aftermath of the Peace Accords. This association of psychologists describes its mission as responding to the need for psychosocial reparation in communities affected by political violence during and after the internal armed conflict (ECAP, n.d., "Misión y Visión"). Although the association was founded by psychologists, the current team is interdisciplinary and emphasizes the importance of the local community's active participation in identifying and responding to its needs. It began its work by accompanying survivors in the community of Rabinal in Baja Verapaz and defines psychosocial reparation as a "theoretical and methodological response to the effects of terror" (Community Action Group et al., 2005, p. 11). The team grounds its interventions in local Mayan conceptions of community, seeking to facilitate participants' self-organization through mutual support groups. It aims to redress the psychosocial impact of gross violations of human rights, recognizing the particular effects on women and indigenous populations who have been and continue to be structurally and systemically marginalized within Guatemala. One of the many resources that ECAP has developed is the *Diplomado de Salud Mental Comunitaria* [Diploma in Community Mental Health] in which the interpreters and translators working on the transitional justice processes discussed in this volume have participated (Duque, 2009). They have been actively accompanying the 54 Mayan women survivors of racialized sexual violence since the formation of the Consortium and, more recently, as part of the Alliance.

MTM is a legal collective that began its work following the April 2008 trial of the rapist of Juana Méndez Rodríguez, one of the judges in the Tribunal of Conscience discussed in chapter 2 (Gaviola, 2008). An ex-police officer, Antonio Rutilo Matías López, was accused of aggravated rape and abuse of authority for having raped Méndez when she was detained in the Nebaj Police Station in January 2005; he was convicted by the Sentencing Tribunal of El Quiché. The sentencing was a victory for justice and for women, setting precedents for other cases in which women prisoners suffered sexual abuse and rape and for the "breaking the silence" movement more broadly. Staff from the *Instituto de Estudios Comparados en Ciencias Penales de Guatemala* [Institute for Comparative Studies in Criminal Sciences of Guatemala] (ICCPG) who prosecuted the case went on to form MTM, through which they could focus their legal work on gender justice. The interdisciplinary team of lawyers and psychologists who today constitute MTM provide a range of legal, educational, training, and psychosocial services for those seeking justice for human rights and domestic violations. They work with young women in a variety of preventive programs, educating them on how to resist sexual violations and abuse. As happens in many organizations and community groups in wartime and postwar situations, the founders of MTM encountered a number of challenging issues that split the group: some of the founding members chose to leave the organization and form another collective, the *Asociación Sororidad Activa* [Active Sisterhood Association] (ASA) in 2012. Both organizations continue to work in the defense of women's rights.

12. Arvin et al. (2013) discuss Chow's concept of "the ascendancy to whiteness" as "denoting the multiple ways that the condition of being white, and enjoying the often nationalist privileges of that whiteness, is made to seem neutral and inviting or inclusive of racial, sexual and other minorities" (p. 10).

13. The research team included our coresearchers at UNAMG, led by Brisna Caxaj who was the coordinator of UNAMG's research department for most of the period of the research, as well as Jeanette Asencio, Carmelita Chonay, Elisabeth Desgranges, Florinda Itzol, Sofía Ramírez and Olivia Tox; Luisa Cabrera Pérez-Armiñan, who worked with us on the creative methodologies subproject; and graduate students from York University and Boston College, including Rocío Sánchez Ares, Rachel Hershberg, Emily Rosser, Erin Sibley, Gabriela Távara, and Caren Weisbart, and most significantly Fabienne Doiron, who has been with us throughout this journey.

CHAPTER 1   DOCUMENTING PROTAGONISM

1. There is extensive scholarship, including that of Kobrak (2003) and Falla (2011), among others, documenting the guerrillas' presence, particularly that of the EGP, in these and other areas of Huehuetenango at this time.

2. In Mayan spirituality, all natural beings and elements are seen as having a protective spirit or energy, called a nawal. In contrast to the Gregorian calendar brought to Guatemala by the Spaniards, the ancient Maya counted cycles of time, beginning from the creation of the world, represented by diverse calendars that formed a "calendar system" (Asociación Médicos Descalzos, 2014, p. 34). Within that system, a nawal is attributed to each of the 20 days, which combined with 13 numbers, form the 260-day cycle of the sacred Maya calendar (*Cholq'ij* in K'iche'). The nawal of a particular day is seen as influencing the character of people born on that day, permitting them to understand their gift or vocation. See Grupo de Mujeres Mayas Kaqla (2010, pp. 22–24) for further discussion of Mayan spirituality, the Mayan cosmovision, and nawales.

CHAPTER 2   RECOUNTING PROTAGONISM

1. Within the context of the Tribunal, we refer to women survivors as protagonists and sometimes testifiers or survivors, and to those who played an active role as judges, prosecutors, honorary witnesses, and expert witnesses as participants and sometimes intermediaries, to distinguish them from general audience members.

2. Feminists and human rights activists in Guatemala have come to use the term "feminicide" to describe increasing levels and intensity of violence against women in the postwar period—a phenomenon in which more than 9,000 women have been killed since 2000 (GGM, 2015). The concept builds on the work of Russell (Radford & Russell, 1992), translating and adapting the concept of femicide to the Latin American context to name "murders of women and girls founded on a gender power structure . . . . implicating both the state (directly or indirectly) and individual perpetrators (private or state actors); it thus encompasses systematic, widespread, and everyday interpersonal violence . . . . [that is] rooted in social, political, economic, and cultural inequalities" (Fregoso & Bejarano, 2010, p. 4).

3. In Guatemala, similar to other Latin American contexts, embodied pain and suffering are captured in the idea of susto, which is described by cultural anthropologists and psychiatrists as a "loss of the essential life force as a result of fright" and as associated with "depression; weakness; loss of appetite; restlessness; lack of interest in work, duties and personal hygiene; disturbing dreams; fatigue; diarrhea; and vomiting. If left untreated, the victim literally (though often slowly) wastes away" (Green, 1999, pp. 120–121). See also Zur (1998) and Asociación Médicos Descalzos (2012).

4. The *Consejos Comunitarios de Desarrollo* [Community Development Councils] (COCODES) are the first echelon of the *Sistema de Consejos de Desarollo* [Development Council System] whose function is to ensure the "participation and representation of the Maya, Xinca, Garifuna, and non-indigenous population" in planning public policies related to community development (Congreso de la República de Guatemala, 2002). The Urban and Rural Development Council Law was amended in 2002 to include community-level councils in order to comply with provisions in the Peace Accords that called for the decentralization of state power.

5. In the U.S. context, Vizenor has used the concept of survivance to refer to the ways in which indigenous communities have learned to move "beyond our basic survival in the face of overwhelming cultural genocide to create spaces of synthesis and renewal" (as cited in Tuck, 2009, p. 422; see also Brayboy, 2008; Grande, 2004; Vizenor, 2008).

CHAPTER 3   JUDICIALIZING PROTAGONISM

1. During the Ríos Montt trial, a series of inserts titled *La Farsa del Genocidio: Conspiración marxista desde la Igelsia Católica* [The farce of genocide in Guatemala: A Marxist conspiracy by the Catholic Church] appeared in *El Periódico*, one of Guatemala City's main newspapers. The 20-page color inserts were published by the *Fundación Contra el Terrorismo* [Foundation against Terrorism], led by Ricardo Méndez Ruiz and with the involvement of a number of retired high-ranking military as well as Moisés Galindo, a lawyer involved in defending many ex-military charged with crimes committed during the internal armed conflict, including Ríos Montt and Reyes Girón. Under the guise of defending the Guatemalan Army from what they call a "public lynching" (Gamazo, 2013, para. 9), the content of these inserts was dedicated to discrediting human rights organizations and activists, ex-guerrilla groups, judges and public prosecutors, and even Guatemala's then-attorney general, Claudia Paz y Paz Bailey, accusing them all of being "terrorists" and "traitors." Above a footer reading ¡*El mundo merece conocer la verdad!* [The world deserves to know the truth!], tag lines such as *La farsa del genocidio en Guatemala: Un buen negocio* [The farces of genocide in Guatemala: A good business], *El delito del genocidio jamás existió en Guatemala* [The crime of genocide has never existed in Guatemala], and *Un reconocimiento otorgado por hacer daño: Rigoberta Menchú, Nobel 1992* [A prize awarded for doing harm: Rigoberta Menchú, Nobel 1992] dominated the front pages of these inserts, along with photos of injured soldiers. Since the Ríos Montt trial, large vinyl banners carrying these same images with messages denying genocide and accusing complainants and human rights organizations of making money off of reparations have been hung on the outside of the courthouse throughout every major trial related to the internal armed conflict. The Foundation's actions have been compared to the "mechanisms of psychological war used in the past" and likened to threats and "incitements to hate" (Gamazo, 2013, para. 5).

2. Of a total of 97 prosecution witnesses (61 men and 36 women), 12 women focused their testimonies on experiences of sexual violence (most talked about their mother/daughter/other women as well as themselves). At least three men also talked about witnessing sexual violence.

3. For example, expert witness testimony during the trial by Spanish lawyer Paloma Soria drew on Common Article 3 of the Geneva Conventions and Additional Protocol II to the Conventions that refer to sexual violence, as well as the Furundzija case at the International Criminal Tribunal for the former Yugoslavia (ICTY) and Rule 70 of the ICC's Rules of Procedure and Evidence relating to sexual violence. See Roht-Arriaza and Kemp (2013).

4. Members of the Alliance cite a number of international gendered legal norms, frameworks, and jurisprudence that influenced the Sepur Zarco litigation strategy, including the Rome Statute of ICC, the International Tribunals for the Former Yugoslavia and Rwanda, CEDAW, and UN Security Council Resolution 1325 (Impunity Watch & Alliance, 2017).

5. There was significant debate within the Alliance as well as the judiciary on how to prosecute these crimes and whether to include the charge of genocide. Some insisted that the alleged perpetrators should be tried as committing "genocide and crimes against humanity" as per the original complaint filed in 2011, and in the context of the recently completed Ríos Montt genocide trial. Prosecutor Hilda Piñeda argued against including genocide charges. As she reflected post-trial,

> It was not prudent to prosecute it as a genocide case, because the legal definition of that crime includes the mass killing of people and stipulates the scenario for it to be considered a genocide, and in this specific case we only had the 3 deaths of the 3 women—the 2 girls and the adult woman—and in my perspective as prosecutor we could not frame it as genocide, right. It was difficult to qualify it legally and uphold it in that way. So it

was more viable to present the case based on crimes against humanity because the legal concept does entail physical aggression and all kinds of inhumane and degrading treatment against women, which is what I perceive occurred, right, as relates to international humanitarian law and conventions. (Cited in Impunity Watch & Alliance, 2017, p. 16)

In the pretrial hearings, Judge Gálvez had argued that the case should be presented as war crimes, with sexual violence included under the category of torture (Impunity Watch & Alliance, 2017, p. 17). Members of the Alliance argued that "crimes against humanity" would allow for more visibility for the crimes of sexual violence and sexual and domestic slavery. In the end, the perpetrators were prosecuted for crimes against humanity, specified as sexual violence, sexual and domestic slavery, murder, and forced disappearances.

6. Some of the information contained in these "Scenes from the Courtroom" was published during the trial in blog entries authored by Fabienne Doiron, based on field notes taken for this research project ("Sepur Zarco: 33 years for Justice," 2016). In this chapter, unless otherwise indicated, quotes and descriptions from the courtroom are from Doiron's field notes.

7. Of the 15 women who gave evidence in the preliminary hearings that took place in 2012, 12 women (one of whom, Doña Magdalena Pop, died after giving evidence in the preliminary hearings) were victims of sexual violence inside the Sepur Zarco outpost, and another 3 were victims of forced displacement and sexual violence. Judge Gálvez did not allow the latter three women to be part of the case that went to trial, because he considered that they had not been abused by the accused. These women's complaints are still under investigation. However, all 14 women protagonists sat together in the courtroom and the videos that were played during the trial included all of them. Although the court's ruling did not relate to this group of three, these women felt that the guilty decision also vindicated them. The group of 14 had sought justice together, and together they celebrated the outcome. And the references to the 15 Q'eqchi' women seeking justice include Doña Magdalena, whose testimony was used during the trial.

8. The plaintiffs did discuss uncovering their heads for the day of sentencing, but MTM convinced them not to. In interviews with MTM staff in July 2016 they explained that they wanted to avoid the women appearing to put on "a show" or to give the impression that the sentence as such was responsible for them having recovered their dignity. They emphasized that the objective of the trial was not for them to uncover their heads, but to achieve justice. Later, the women did uncover their heads, and there is a photo of them at the courthouse door, waving to people in the Human Rights Plaza [*Plaza de Derechos Humanos*] (see De Leon, 2006; Sarkar, 2016; "Sembramos justicia," 2016).

9. Some members of the Alliance told us that there was some controversy surrounding the inclusion of skeletal evidence at the trial: some involved in the Ríos Montt genocide trial had argued that it would divert attention away from the focus on sexual violence. However, MTM discussed with Public Ministry officials and FAFG how this evidence could be used effectively in conjunction with the expert witness reports. Part of the value they foresaw was that people would see, with their own eyes, the actual bones of people killed, something normally seen only by forensic teams involved in exhumations. At the trial, the judges directed court officials to open the sacks of bones and overruled protests by MTM that these officials were not qualified to handle this type of evidence. In any case, the judges were able to see skulls that showed evidence of violence, usually a bullet hole or a fracture.

10. As Viaene (2015) states, muxuk "signifies *profanar* [to desecrate or defile], *mancillar* [to taint or contaminate], to violate the sacred or the spiritual value of something. Thus this phrase clearly reflects the desecration of the natural, social and spiritual world that the armed conflict caused" (p. 77). The word is spelled in a number of ways in the documentation from the trial to which we had access, most particularly the sentence (Tribunal Primero de Sentencia

Penal, C-01076-2012-0021, 2016, pp. 109–112), an online Q'eqchi'-English dictionary, and Viaene (2015). Spellings include muxuk and muxuc. This diversity is likely attributable to the spoken language and the various pronunciations of c, k, and x.

11. Beyond the momentary effects of the trial on the particular victims who testified or those who were present is the systemic process of the judicialization of indigenous life documented by, among others, Million (2013) in her study of Canadian indigenous struggles. Despite the particularities of each indigenous group and settler colonial context, her meticulous tracing of the transformation of indigenous communal performance of justice and resistance within the trauma regime that has characterized the late 20th and early 21st centuries—a regime that has medicalized, pathologized, and individualized a people's rights—is an important framework for thinking about this case. Indigenous communities that have been violated and ruptured must then be rescued and "healed" from the effects of those violations by the very regime responsible for the processes through which the regime reinstates its neocolonial power.

12. Gelles (1998) defines testimonio as "a form of collective autobiographical witnessing that gives voice to oppressed peoples and has played an important role in developing and supporting international human rights, solidarity movements and liberation struggles . . . such a narrative is always linked to a group or class situation marked by marginalization, oppression and struggle, the loss of which moves the piece from testimonio to autobiography" (as cited in Nolin & Shankar, 2000, p. 3). And as McAllister (2013) emphasizes in the context of truth-telling processes, in addition to providing the facts of a violation, "a *testimonio* must convey the 'signs of harm' (Colvin, 2004) that appeal to the compassionate imagination as well as the forensic judgement of its audience" (p. 93). A well-known Guatemalan example of testimonio is *I Rigoberta Menchú: An Indian Woman in Guatemala*, which begins, "My name is Rigoberta Menchú. I am twenty-three years old. This is my testimony. I didn't learn it from a book and I didn't learn it alone. I'd like to stress that it's not only *my* life, it's also the testimony of my people. . . . The important thing is that what happened to me has happened to many other people too: my story is the story of all poor Guatemalans. My personal experience is the reality of a whole people" (as cited in Nolin & Shankar, 2000, pp. 266–267; emphasis in the original).

13. Valdez Asij was the military commissioner of Panzós. As discussed in chapter 1, the border between the departments of Izabal and Alta Verapaz and thus the location of Sepur Zarco shifted during these years, with Sepur Zarco falling on either side of the border at different times.

14. The male witnesses did participate in the pretrial preparatory work with the women plaintiffs and the other witnesses. These preparations included both practice for their moment in court, as well as discussions of the role their testimonies would play in the search for justice. MTM gave sessions on how the trial would proceed, who would be in the courtroom, and where they would sit. The work took place over a number of weeks, part of it in the community and part in the MTM offices.

CHAPTER 4   REPAIRING PROTAGONISM

1. The UN Basic Principles and Guidelines on the Right to a Remedy and Reparation for Victims of Gross Violations of International Human Rights Law and Serious Violations of International Humanitarian Law were finally approved by the General Assembly in 2005 (UN General Assembly Resolution 60/147).

2. For an analysis of one of the more extensive reparations programs, see Lira and Loveman's (2005) examination of Chile's reparation(s) policies between 1990 and 2004, which were noteworthy for their longevity, open-endedness, and scope. Despite their comprehensiveness, the Mapuche in Chile have criticized these reparations policies and related truth-telling processes for having failed to represent violations of their rights during the Pinochet regime as well as their silencing of Mapuche accounts of violence (Jara, Badilla, Figueiredo, Cornejo, & Riveros, 2018). Additionally, they accused the Chilean state not only of repressive violence against their leaders but of having used anti-terrorism laws to prosecute and incarcerate Mapuche leaders who were involved in legally guaranteed protests demanding their land rights. The Mapuche won a judgment from the Inter-American Court of Human Rights, which found the Chilean government guilty of having violated their rights, ordered leaders released from jail, and mandated reparations (Vargas, 2017). The Mapuche claims illustrate the limitations of the Chilean transitional justice processes, and the importance of collective claims of indigenous groups throughout the Americas. For an analysis of reparations policies and initiatives within the Inter-American Human Rights System, see Beristain (2008).

3. Kim (2006) develops a practice-oriented theory of social reparation, a "holistic, communal project of institutional apology and conciliation" (p. 221) through which to "heal and avenge" (p. 222) the so-called comfort women abused by the Japanese army during World War II.

4. See Viaene (2010b) for a discussion of Q'eqchi' conceptions of reparation(s) in Alta Verapaz and the linguistic complexities inherent in the PNR's efforts to translate the concept.

5. See also 2015 South Korean protests of their government's offer of financial compensation for the more than 304 people, mostly children, who were killed in the Sewol ferry disaster. Refusing to be "paid off," fathers shaved their heads and demanded a full investigation of the causes of the disaster (Glum, 2015).

6. According to a social audit of the PNR conducted by the *Centro de Análisis Forense y Ciencias Aplicadas* [Center for Forensic Analysis and Applied Sciences] (CAFCA) in 2012, reparation payments to victims of sexual violence were suspended in 2009 "when the PNR started to consider that women were lying in their declarations and testimonies" (as cited in ODHAG, 2014, p. 68). According to the former coordinator of the PNR in the Ixcán, El Quiché, Benjamín Pérez Gómez, "in terms of the cases of sexual violence, we had to suspend them while we sought an alternative solution to how we analyze the applications" (p. 68).

7. In the interviews conducted by MTM, 30 interviewees spoke in their native language throughout the interview, 13 spoke in Spanish, and the rest went back and forth.

8. Image theater is a technique through which participants position co-participants to embody a theme either identified by the group or assigned by a facilitator. Roles are rotated, giving each participant the opportunity to "position" and "be positioned." The embodied scenes are then "read" by the audience and subsequently by the co-participants. Emotions emerging from the performers and audience are shared, deepening multiple understandings of and meanings made about the chosen theme.

9. As previously discussed in this volume, the husbands of all the Q'eqchi' women were disappeared by the military over a land dispute with wealthy plantation owners, and many of the Chuj, Mam, and Kaqchikel women were also widowed. The loss of their husbands often led to the loss of land and livelihoods and therefore a deepening impoverishment (see Zur, 1998, for a detailed discussion of the experience of widowhood in El Quiché during the armed conflict).

CHAPTER 5   ACCOMPANYING PROTAGONISM

1. The purposes underlying the creative workshops and other action reflection processes described in this chapter were explained prior to participants giving oral or written consent for each workshop. The 12 intermediaries gave their written informed consent prior to the tape-recorded interviews; each received a transcription of her interview and was invited to

share comments with us prior to our analyses of the data. The interviews lasted between 60 and 90 minutes and the questions focused on the intermediaries' experiences in and the meanings they made of the activities in which they engaged with women survivors, including the Tribunal of Conscience, creative methodologies workshops, the preparation for the Sepur Zarco trial of sexual violence as a crime against humanity, and psychosocial accompaniment processes described in the previous four chapters of this volume. The interview questions were weighted towards the psychosocial and participatory aspects of the work and also included a number of questions about justice, truth-telling, and reparation-seeking processes. Sample questions included: "How do you see your role as an interpreter?"; "How did the women survivors feel when you incorporated Mayan practices in the workshops?"; "What expectations do you perceive women [survivors] have in relation to the trial?" The intermediaries were also asked about their own training and self-care in their work accompanying the Mayan survivors. Our analysis of interview data used constructivist grounded theory (Charmaz, 2014), which allowed us to explore intermediaries' meaning-making of their accompaniment from the bottom up. In its constructivist approach to data collection and interpretation, grounded theory recognizes the researchers' positionality as framing and actively shaping the collection, analysis, and interpretation of the data. Interviewing and coding were done in Spanish and we translated the quotes cited herein.

Some of the intermediaries have written about and/or told their life stories in a variety of published contexts. For example, the stories of two ladina and one Mayan intermediary were published in the 2008 book of testimonies of Guatemalan women, *Tejedoras de paz: Testimonios de mujeres en Guatemala* [Weavers of peace: Testimonies of women in Guatemala] (MOLOJ, CONAVIGUA, & ICCPG, 2008). One of these women also participated in an oral history interview conducted and published by the Joan B. Kroc Institute for Peace and Justice. Although these documents were not systematically coded, the analyses described herein are informed by these secondary sources and by ongoing relationships that we have had with most of the intermediaries over many years of collaborations in Guatemala.

CONCLUSION

1. As Anzaldúa explains in an interview with Karin Ikas (Anzaldúa, as cited by Torre, 2009, pp. 106–107):

> I have a term that is called nos-otras, and I put a dash between the nos and otras. The nos is the subject "we," that is the people who were in power and colonized others. The otras is the "other," the colonized group. Then there is also the dash, the divide between us. However, what is happening, after years of colonization, is that all of the divides disappear a little bit because the colonizer, in his or her interaction with the colonized takes on a lot of their attributes. And, of course, the person who is colonizing leaks into our stuff. So we are neither one nor the other; we are really both. There is not a pure other; there is not a pure subject and not a pure object. We are implicated in each other's lives.

This dialogic co-construction echoes the framing of the relationality in this volume and our hypothesizing of a third voice throughout the text.

REFERENCES

Adams, A. (2001). The transformation of the Tzuultaq'a: Jorge Ubico, protestants and other Verapaz Maya at the crossroads of community, state and transnational interests. *Journal of Latin American Anthropology, 6*(2), 198–233. Retrieved from https://doi.org/10.1525/jlca .2001.6.2.198

Adams, R. N. (2000). *Joaquín Noval como indigenista, antropólogo y revolucionario* [Joaquín Noval as an indigenist, anthropologist, and revolutionary]. Cuadernos de Pensamiento Universitario [Notebooks of University Thought]. Guatemala City, Guatemala: Editorial Universitaria, Universidad de San Carlos de Guatemala.

Agreement on Identity and Rights of Indigenous Peoples (Government of Guatemala-Unidad Revolucionaria Nacional Guatemalteca) (1995, March 31). Retrieved from http://www.usip .org/sites/default/files/file/resources/collections/peace_agreements/guat_950331.pdf

Aguilar, Y., & Fulchiron, A. (2005). El carácter sexual de la cultura de violencia contra las mujeres [The sexual character of violence against women]. In R. Zepeda López (Ed.), *Las violencias en Guatemala: Algunas Perspectivas* [Violence in Guatemala: Selected perspectives] (pp. 149–245). Guatemala City, Guatemala: FLACSO/UNESCO.

Ahmed, S. (2000). *Strange encounters: Embodied others in post-coloniality.* New York, NY: Routledge.

Ajxup Pelicó, V. (2000). Género y etnicidad, cosmovisión y mujer [Gender and ethnicity, cosmovision and woman]. In M. Macleod & M.L. Cabrera Pérez-Armiñan (Eds.), *Identidad: Rostros sin máscara: Reflexiones sobre cosmovisión, género y etnicidad* [Identity: Faces without masks: Reflections on cosmovision, gender and ethnicity] (pp. 57–72). Guatemala City, Guatemala: Oxfam Australia.

Al-Kassim, D. (2008). Archiving resistance: Women's testimony at the threshold of the state. *Cultural Dynamics, 20*(2), 167–192. doi:10.1177/0921374008094287

Alvarado Chavéz, M. V. (2015, December 16). 35 años de UNAMG. Reivindicamos la alegría, la resistencia y la rebeldía de las mujeres [35 years of UNAMG. Reclaiming women's joy, resistance and rebellion]. *Pueblos: Revista de Información y Debate, 67,* 53–55. Retrieved from http://www.revistapueblos.org/?p=20190

Alvarado, M., Navarro, S., Morán, A. L., & Barrios, P. (Eds.). (2013). *Nuestra mirada está en la justicia: Caso Sepur Zarco* [Our eyes are on justice: Sepur Zarco Case]. Guatemala City, Guatemala: Alianza Rompiendo el Silencio y la Impunidad. Retrieved from http://ecapguatemala .org.gt/publicaciones/nuesta-mirada-est%C3%A1-en-la-justicia-caso-sepur-zarco

Álvarez Medrano, C. (2006). Cosmovisión maya y feminismo: Caminos que se unen? [Mayan cosmovision and feminism: Paths that unite?]. In A. E. Cumes y A. S. Monzón (Eds.), *La encrucijada de las identidades: Mujeres, feminismos y mayanismos en diálogo* [The crossroads of identities: Women, feminisms and mayanisms in dialogue] (pp. 19–29). Guatemala City, Guatemala: Intervida World Alliance (INWA).

Álvarez Medrano, S. A. (2016, December). *Experiencia de sanación colectiva y aportes al bienestar de las mujeres mayas Kaqla* [Mayan women of Kaqla's experiences of collective healing and contributions to well-being]. (Unpublished master's thesis). Universidad del Valle de Guatemala, Guatemala City.

Amnesty International. (2002). *Guatemala's lethal legacy: Past impunity and renewed human rights violations.* Retrieved from https://www.amnesty.org/en/documents/AMR34/001/2002/en/

Anzaldúa, G. (2012). *Borderlands/La frontera: The new mestiza.* San Francisco, CA: Aunt Lute Books. (Original work published 1987)

Archibald, L., & Dewar, J. (2010). Creative arts, culture, and healing: Building an evidence base. *Pimatisiwin: A Journal of Aboriginal and Indigenous Community Health, 8*(3), 1–25.

Archibald, T., & Wilson, A. L. (2011). Rethinking empowerment: Theories of power and the potential for emancipatory praxis. *Proceedings of the Adult Education Research Conference, Toronto, ON, Canada.* Retrieved from http://newprairiepress.org/cgi/viewcontent.cgi?article=3127&context=aerc

Arriaza, L., & Roht-Arriaza, N. (2008). Social reconstruction as a local process. *International Journal of Transitional Justice, 2*(2), 152–172. doi:10.1093/ijtj/ijn010

Arvin, M., Tuck, E., & Morrill, A. (2013). Decolonizing feminism: Challenging connections between settler colonialism and heteropatriarchy. *Feminist Formations, 25*(1), 8–34. doi:10.1353/ff.2013.0006

Askin, K. M. (2001). Comfort women—Shifting shame and stigma from victims to victimizers. *International Criminal Law Review, 1*(1), 5–32. doi:10.1163/15718120121002522

Asociación Médicos Descalzos Chinique. (2012).*¿Yab'il xane K'oqil? ¿Enfermedades o Consecuencias? Seis psicopatologías identificadas y tratadas por los terapeutas Maya'ib' K'iche'ib* [Yab'il xane K'oqil. Illnesses or consequences? Six psychopathologies identified and treated by Maya'ib K'iche'ib therapists]. El Quiché, Guatemala: Author.

Asociación Médicos Descalzos Chinique. (2014). *Q'ij Alaxik. La importancia de desarrollar nuestras vocaciones para tener bienestar mental y una convivencia armónica con los demás* [Q'il Alaxij. The importance of developing our vocations for mental wellbeing and harmonious coexistence with others]. El Quiché, Guatemala: Author.

Asociación Médicos Descalzos Chinique. (2016). *Médicos Descalzos Chinique* [Barefoot Doctors Chinic]. Retrieved from https://sites.google.com/site/medicosdescalzoschinique/home

AVANCSO—Asociación para el Avance de las Ciencias Sociales en Guatemala [Association for the Advancement of Social Sciences in Guatemala]. (1990). *Política institucional hacia el desplazado interno en Guatemala* [Institutional policy towards the internally displaced in Guatemala]. Cuaderno de Investigación 6 [Research Notebook 6]. Guatemala City, Guatemala: Author.

AVANCSO. (1992). *¿Dónde esta el futuro? Procesos de reintegración en comunidades de retornados,* [Where is the future? Reintegration processes in returnee communities]. Cuaderno de Investigación 8 [Research Notebook 8]. Guatemala City, Guatemala: Author.

AVANCSO. (2016). *Elq'ak ut kawil ch'oolej: Rilb'al li teep releb'aal iq' b'ar nake' risi xq'emal li xch'ochel Tuzulutlan-Verapaz/Despojos y resistencias: Una mirada a la región extractiva norte desde Tezulutlán-Verapaz,* [Dispossession and resistances: A look at the northern extractive region from Tezulutlan-Verapaz]. Cuaderno de Investigación 28 [Research Notebook 28]. Guatemala City, Guatemala: Author.

AVANCSO. (2017). *"La violencia de antes está adelante . . ." Mujeres indígenas: Su relación con la violencia y "las justicias"* [The violence from before is ahead . . . Indigenous women: Their relation with violence and with "justices"]. Cuaderno de Investigación 29 [Research Notebook 29]. Guatemala City, Guatemala: Author.

Bakhtin, M. (1984). *Problems of Dostoevsky's poetics* (C. Emerson, Ed. and Trans.). Minneapolis: University of Minnesota Press.

Balint, J., Evansy, J., & McMillan, N. (2014). Rethinking transitional justice, redressing indigenous harm: A new conceptual approach. *International Journal of Transitional Justice, 8*(2), 194–216. doi:10.1093/ijtj/iju004

Bannerji, H. (1995). *Thinking through: Essays on feminism, Marxism and anti-racism.* Toronto, Ontario: Women's Press.

Barad, K. (2007). *Meeting the universe halfway: Quantum physics and the entanglement of matter and meaning*. Durham, NC: Duke University Press.

Bartunek, J. M., & Louis, M. R. (1996). *Insider/outsider team research*. London, UK: SAGE.

Bastos, S. (2008). La normalización multicultural en la Guatemala neoliberal postconflicto [Multicultural normalization in neoliberal postconflict Guatemala]. In F. García (Ed.), *Identidades, etnicidad y racismo en América Latina* [Identities, ethnicity, and racism in Latin America] (pp. 27–45). Quito, Ecuador: FLACSO Ecuador/Ministerio De Cultura de Ecuador. Retrieved from http://www.flacsoandes.edu.ec/libros/digital/41402.pdf

Bastos, S., Cumes, A., & Lemus, L. (2007). *Mayanización y vida cotidiana. La ideología multicultural en la sociedad guatemalteca* [Mayanization and everyday life: The multicultural ideology in Guatemalan society]. Guatemala City, Guatemala: FLACSO, CIRMA, CHOLSAMAJ.

Belenky, M. F., Clinchy, B. M., Goldberger, N. R., & Tarule, J. M. (1997). *Women's ways of knowing: The development of self, voice, and mind*. New York, NY: Basic Books.

Bell, C. (2009). Transitional justice, interdisciplinarity and the state of the 'field' or 'non-field'. *International Journal of Transitional Justice, 3*(1), 5–27. doi:10.1093/ijtj/ijn044

Beristain, C. M. (2008). *Diálogos sobre la reparación: Experiencias en el Sistema Interamericano de Derechos Humanos. Tomo 1* [Dialogue about reparation: Experiences in the Inter-American Human Rights System. Vol. 1]. San José, Costa Rica: Instituto Interamericano de Derechos Humanos IIDH.

Beristain, C. M., Paez, D., & González, J. L. (2000). Rituals, social sharing, silence, emotions and collective memory claims in the case of the Guatemalan genocide. *Psicothema, 12* (Suppl.), 117–130.

Berman, R. C., & Tyyskä, V. (2011). A critical reflection on the use of translators/interpreters in a qualitative cross-language research project. *International Journal of Qualitative Methods, 10*(2), 178–190. doi:10.1177/160940691101000206

Blacklock, C., & Crosby, A. (2004). The sounds of silence: Feminist research across time in Guatemala. In W. Giles and J. Hyndman (Eds.), *Sites of violence: Gender and conflict zones* (pp. 45–72). Berkeley: University of California Press.doi:10.1525/california/9780520230729.001.0001

Boal, A. (1985). *Theater of the oppressed*. (C. A. & M.-O. Leal McBride, Trans.). New York, NY: Theatre Communications Group.

Bradbury, H. (Ed.). (2015). *Handbook of action research III*. Thousand Oaks, CA: SAGE.

Brayboy, B. M. J. (2008). "Yakkity yak" and "talking back": An examination of sites of survivance in Indigenous knowledge. In S. R. Neugebauer, K. R. Venegas, & M. Villagas (Eds.), *Indigenous knowledge and education: Sites of struggle, strength, and survivance* (pp. 339–346). Cambridge, MA: Harvard Educational Review.

Bronfenbrenner, U. (1992). Ecological systems theory. In R. Vasta (Ed.), *Six theories of child development: Revised formulations and current issues* (pp. 187–250). London, UK: Jessica Kingsley Publisher, Ltd.

Brunnegger, S., & Faulk, K. (Eds.). (2016). *A sense of justice: Legal knowledge and lived experience in Latin America*. Stanford, CA: Stanford University Press.

Bueno-Hansen, P. (2015). *Feminist and human rights struggles in Peru: Decolonizing transitional justice*. Champaign: University of Illinois Press.

Bueno-Hansen, P. (2016). Ending the colonial/modern occupation of indigenous women's bodies in Guatemala and Perú. *The Feminist Wire*. Retrieved from http://www.thefeministwire.com/2016/05/ending-occupation/

Bunschuh, T. (2015). Enabling transitional justice, restoring capabilities: The imperatives of participation and normative integrity. *International Journal of Transitional Justice, 9*(1), 10–32. doi:10.1093/ijtj/iju030

Burt, J. M. (2016, March 4). *Military officers convicted in landmark Sepur Zarco sexual violence case*. Retrieved from International Justice Monitor website: https://www.ijmonitor.org /2016/03/military-officers-convicted-in-landmark-sepur-zarco-sexual-violence-case/

Buss, D. E. (2009). Rethinking "rape as a weapon of war." *Feminist Legal Studies, 17*(2), 145–163. doi:10.1007/s10691-009-9118-5

Butalia, U. (2000). *The other side of silence: Voices from the partition of India*. Durham, NC: Duke University Press.

Butler-Kisber, L., & Poldma, T. (2010). The power of visual approaches in qualitative inquiry: The use of collage making and concept mapping in experiential research. *Journal of Research Practice, 6*(2), Article M18. Retrieved from http://jrp.icaap.org/index.php/jrp/article/view /197/196

Cabrera Pérez-Armiñan, M. L., & Lykes, M. B. (2007). *Compartir la memoria colectiva: Acompañamiento psicosocial y justicia integral para mujeres víctimas de violencia sexual en conflictos armados* [Sharing our collective memory: Psychosocial accompaniment and integral justice for women, victims of sexual violence in armed conflict]. Guatemala City, Guatemala: PCS-Consejería en Proyectos.

Caja Lúdica (2000). *Lúdica creativa, arte y diversidad cultural* [Playful creativity, art and diversity]. Retrieved from http://www.cajaludica.org/

CALDH—Centro para la Acción Legal en Derechos Humanos [Center for Legal Action in Human Rights]. (2014). *Las voces de las mujeres persisten en la memoria colectiva de sus pueblos: Continuum de violencias y resistencias en la vida, cuerpo y territorio de las mujeres* [Women's voices persist in their peoples' collective memory: Continuities of violence and resistance in women's life, body and territory]. Guatemala City, Guatemala: Author.

Cannella, G. S., & Manuelito, K. D. (2008). Feminisms from unthought locations: Indigenous worldviews, marginalized feminisms, and revisioning an anticolonial social science. In N. K. Denzin, Y. S. Lincoln, & L. Tuhiwai Smith (Eds.), *Handbook of critical and indigenous methodologies* (pp. 45–59). Thousand Oaks, CA: SAGE.

Carey, D. (2013). *I ask for justice: Maya women, dictators, and crime in Guatemala, 1898–1944*. Austin: University of Texas Press.

Carey, D., & Torres, M. G. (2010). Precursors to femicide: Guatemalan women in a vortex of violence. *Latin American Research Review, 45*(3), 142–164. Retrieved from https://muse.jhu .edu/article/406422/summary

Castellano, M. B. (2006). *Final report of the Aboriginal Healing Foundation: Vol. 1. A healing journey: Reclaiming wellness*. Ottawa, Ontario: Aboriginal Healing Foundation.

Caxaj, B. (2014, May). Avances y retos en las luchas y demandas de memoria histórica, justicia y reparaciones de mujeres sobrevivientes de violencia sexual en Guatemala [Progress and challenges in the struggles and claims for historical memory, justice, and reparation for women survivors of sexual violence in Guatemala]. Paper presented at Democracy and Memory, XXXII International Congress of the Latin American Studies Association, Chicago, IL.

Caxaj, B., Chutan, X., & Herrera, N. (2013). *Memoria histórica, justicia y reparaciones a mujeres sobrevivientes de violencia sexual en Guatemala* [Historical memory, justice and reparations for women survivors of sexual violence in Guatemala]. Unpublished manuscript. Guatemala City, Guatemala: UNAMG.

CEH—Comisión para el Esclarecimiento Histórico [Commission for Historical Clarification]. (1999). *Guatemala: Memoria del silencio Tz'inil Na'tab'al* [Guatemala: Memory of silence]. Guatemala City, Guatemala: Oficina de Servicios para Proyectos de las Naciones Unidas (UNOPS). Retrieved from http://www.centrodememoriahistorica.gov.co/descargas /guatemala-memoria-silencio/guatemala-memoria-del-silencio.pdf

Chambers-Letson, J. (2006). Reparative feminisms, repairing feminism—reparation, postcolonial violence and feminism. *Women & Performance, A Journal of Feminist Theory, 16*(2), 169–189. doi:10.1080/07407700600744287

Chandler, D., & Cordón, T. (2015). *Traditional weavers of Guatemala: Their stories, their lives.* Loveland, CO: Thrums Books.

Charmaz, K. (2014). *Constructing grounded theory: A practical guide through qualitative analysis.* (2nd ed.). Thousand Oaks, CA: SAGE.

Chereni, A. (2014). Positionality and collaboration during fieldwork: Insights from research with co-nationals living abroad. *FQS Forum: Qualitative Social Research, 15*(3). Retrieved from http://nbn-resolving.de/urn:nbn:de:0114-fqs1403111

Chirix García, E. D. (2003). *Alas y raíces: Afectividad de las mujeres Mayas = Rik'in ruxik' y ruxe'il: ronojel kajowab'al ri mayab' taq ixoqi'* [Wings and roots: Mayan women's affectivity]. Guatemala City, Guatemala: Grupo de Mujeres Mayas Kaqla.

Clarke, K. M. (2009). *Fictions of justice: The International Criminal Court and the challenge of legal pluralism in sub-Saharan Africa.* Cambridge, UK: Cambridge University Press.

Clarke, K. M., & Goodale, M. (2010). *Mirrors of justice: Law and power in the post-cold war era.* Cambridge, UK: Cambridge University Press.

Coates, T.-N. (2014, June). The case for reparations. *The Atlantic.* Retrieved from https://www.theatlantic.com/magazine/archive/2014/06/the-case-for-reparations/361631/

Colectivo Actoras de Cambio. (2011). *9 historias de vida: Yo soy voz de la memoria y cuerpo de la libertad* [9 life histories: I am memory's voice and liberty's body]. Guatemala City, Guatemala: Author.

Combahee River Collective. (1983). Combahee River Collective: A black feminist statement. In B. Smith (Ed.), *Home girls: A black feminist anthology* (pp. 264–274). New York, NY: Kitchen Table Women of Color Press.

Community Action Group, ECAP, University of Pennsylvania, & PASMI. (2005). *Monitoring of the community and psychosocial impact of exhumation processes of mass graves in Latin America. An international collaborative project based on local NGOs work.* Retrieved from http://www.forcedmigration.org/psychosocial/papers/PWGpapers.htm/Exhumations_paper_no_appendices.pdf

Congreso de la República de Guatemala [Congress of the Republic of Guatemala]. (2002, March 12). *Reforma a la ley de los consejos de desarrollo urbano y rural,* Decreto 11-2002. [Reform to the law of urban and rural development councils, Decree-Law 11-2002]. Retrieved from http://www.unicef.org/guatemala/spanish/LeyConsejosDesarrollo.pdf

Consejería en Proyectos [Project Counselling Service] (2010). *¡Cuento la verdad! Voces sobre reparación en Guatemala* [I'm telling the truth! Voices on reparation in Guatemala]. Guatemala City, Guatemala: Author.

Cooke, B., & Kothari, U. (Eds.). (2001). *Participation: The new tyranny?* London, UK: Zed Books.

Convention on the Elimination of All Forms of Discrimination against Women, Dec. 18, 1979, 1249 U.N.T.S. 13. Retrieved from: http://www.refworld.org/docid/3ae6b3970.html

Copelon, R. (2003). International human rights dimensions of intimate violence: Another strand in the dialectic of feminist lawmaking. *American University Journal of Gender, Social Policy and Law, 11*(3), 865–877. Retrieved from http://www.heinonline.org.proxy.bc.edu/HOL/Page?handle=hein.journals/ajgsp11&start_page=865&collection=journals&id=879

Cornwall, A. (2003). Whose voices? Whose choices? Reflections on gender and participatory development. *World Development, 31*(8), 1325–1342. http://dx.doi.org/10.1016/S0305-750X(03)00086-X

Couillard, V. (2007). The Nairobi Declaration: Redefining reparation for women victims of sexual violence. *International Journal of Transitional Justice, 1*(3), 444–453. doi:10.1093/ijtj/ijm030

Coulthard, G. S. (2014). *Red skin, white masks: Rejecting the colonial politics of recognition.* Minneapolis: University of Minnesota Press.

Crenshaw, K. (1991). Mapping the margins: Intersectionality, identity politics, and violence against women of color. *Stanford Law Review, 43*(6), 1241–1299. doi:10.2307/1229039

Crosby, A. (1999). To whom shall the nation belong? The gender and ethnic dimensions of refugee return and struggles for peace in Guatemala. In A. Simmons and L. North (Eds.), *Journeys of fear: Refugee return and national transformation in Guatemala* (pp. 176–195). Kingston, Ontario: McGill-Queens University Press.

Crosby, A. (2000). Return to the nation: The organizational challenges confronted by Guatemalan refugee women. *Refuge: Canada's Periodical on Refugees, 19*(3), 32–37.

Crosby, A. (2009). Anatomy of a workshop: Women's struggles for transformative participation in Latin America. *Feminism & Psychology, 19*(3), 342–353. doi:10.1177/0959353509105625

Crosby, A., & Lykes, M. B. (2011). Mayan women survivors speak: The gendered relations of truth-telling in postwar Guatemala. *International Journal of Transitional Justice, 5*(3), 456–476. doi: 10.1093/ijtj/ijr017

Crosby, A., Lykes, M. B. & Caxaj, B. (2016). Carrying a heavy load: Mayan women's understandings of reparation in the aftermath of genocide. *Journal of Genocide Research. 18*(2–3), 265–283. doi:10.1080/14623528.2016.1186952

Crosby, A., Lykes, M. B., & Doiron, F. (2018). Affective contestations: Engaging emotion through the Sepur Zarco trial. In M. Macleod & N. De Marinis (Eds.), *Resisting violence: Emotional communities in Latin America* (pp. 163–185). London, UK: Palgrave Macmillan.

Curruchich, M. L. (2000). La cosmovisión maya y la perspectiva de género [Mayan cosmovision and gender perspective]. In M. Macleod & M. L. Cabrera Pérez–Armiñan (Eds.), *Identidad: Rostros sin máscara: Reflexiones sobre cosmovisión, género y etnicidad* (pp. 45–55). Guatemala City, Guatemala: Oxfam Australia.

Dary F, C. (2014, November). Joaquín Noval y su pensamiento en torno al rol del Instituto Indigenista Nacional en el "desarrollo de la comunidad" [Joaquín Noval and his thoughts on the role of the National Indigenous Institute in the "development of the community"]. *Estudios Interétnicos, 20*(25), 17–48.

Das, V. (2007). *Life and words: Violence and the descent into the ordinary.* Berkeley: University of California Press.

Das, V., & Kleinman, A. (Eds.). (2000). *Violence and subjectivity.* Berkeley: University of California Press.

De Grieff, P. (2006). Justice and reparations. In P. De Grieff (Ed.), *The handbook of reparations* (pp. 251–477). New York, NY: Oxford University Press. Retrieved from http://www.oxfordscholarship.com/view/10.1093/0199291926.001.0001/acprof-9780199291922-chapter-13

De Jonch Osborne, L. (1965). *Indian crafts of Guatemala and El Salvador.* Norman: University of Oklahoma Press.

De Leon, E. (2016, February 27). Juicio Sepur Zarco: Defensa de condenados preparan la impugnación [Sepur Zarco Trial: Convicted's defense are preparing appeal]. *Soy 502.* Retrieved from http://www.soy502.com/articulo/juicio-sepur-zarco-defensa-condenados-prepara-impugnacion

De Waardt, M. (2013). Are Peruvian victims being mocked? Politicization of victimhood and victims' motivations for reparations. *Human Rights Quarterly, 35*(4), 830–849. doi:10.1353/hrq.2013.0066

Diez, A., & Herrera, K. (2004). *Violencia contra las mujeres: Tratamiento por parte de la justicia penal de Guatemala* [Violence against women: Treatment by criminal justice in Guatemala]. Guatemala City, Guatemala: Instituto de Estudios Comparados en Ciencias Penales de Guatemala. doi:10.1093/ijtj/ijn044

Doughty, K. C. (2016). *Remediation in Rwanda: Grassroots legal forums.* Philadelphia: University of Pennsylvania Press.

Doughty, K. C. (2017). Language and international criminal justice in Africa: Interpretation at the ICTR. *International Journal of Transitional Justice, 11*(2), 239–256. https://doi.org/10.1093/ijtj/ijx005

Duffy, L. (2018). Viewing gendered violence in Guatemala through photovoice. *Violence against Women, 24*(4), 421–451. doi:10.1177/1077801217708058

Duque, V. (2009). *Buenas prácticas: De víctimas del conflicto armado a promotores de cambio: Trabajo psicosocial y liderazgo maya en Guatemala* [Good practices: From victims of the armed conflict to promoters of change: Psychosocial work and Mayan leadership in Guatemala]. Frankfurt, Germany: PROINDIGENA/German Federal Ministry for Economic Cooperation and Development (GTZ). Retrieved from http://www.bivica.org/upload/buenas-practicas-victima-conflicto.pdf

ECAP—Equipo de Estudios Comunitarias y Acción Psicosocial [Community Studies and Psychosocial Action Team]. (n.d.). *Misión y visón* [Mission and vision]. Retrieved from http://ecapguatemala.org.gt/plan-estrategico/misión-y-visión

ECAP. (n.d.). *Publicaciones* [Publications]. Retrieved from http://ecapguatemala.org.gt/publicaciones

ECAP. (2009). *Mujeres rompiendo el silencio: Intervención psicosocial con sobrevivientes de violaciones sexuales durante el conflicto armado en Guatemala* [Women breaking the silence: Psychosocial intervention with women survivors of sexual violations during the internal conflict in Guatemala]. Guatemala City, Guatemala: Author.

Eichler, M. (2014). Militarized masculinities in international relations. *Brown Journal of World Affairs, 21*(1), 81–93. Retrieved from http://heinonline.org/HOL/LandingPage?handle=hein.journals/brownjwa21&div=9&id=&page=

Elias-Bursac, E. (2015). *Translating evidence and interpreting testimony at a war crimes tribunal: Working in a tug-of-war.* London, UK: Palgrave MacMillan.

Ellsworth, E. (1989). Why doesn't this feel empowering? Working through the repressive myths of critical pedagogy. *Harvard Educational Review, 59*(3): 297–324. doi:10.17763/haer.59.3.058342114k266250

El Taller. (1995, October 5). *Justice through the eyes of women: Introduction.* Retrieved from http://www.hartford-hwp.com/archives/51/002.html

Eng, D. (2011). Reparations and the human. *Columbia Journal and Gender and Law, 21*(2), 561–583.

Engle, D. M. (2012). Vertical and horizontal perspectives of rights consciousness. *Indiana Journal of Legal Studies, 19* (2), 423–455.

Engle, K. (2005). Feminism and its (dis)contents: Criminalizing wartime rape in Bosnia and Herzegovina. *American Journal of International Law, 99*(4), 778–817. doi:10.2307/3396669

Engle, K. (2015). Anti-impunity and the truth to criminal law in human rights. *Cornell Law Review, 100*(5), 1069–1127.

Engle, K., & Lottmann, A. (2010). The force of shame. In C. McGlynn & V. E. Munro (Eds.), *Rethinking rape law: International and comparative perspectives* (pp. 76–91). New York, NY: Routledge. doi:10.4324/9780203852194

Esquit, E. (2017). Forward. In L. López López, *The making of indigeneity, curriculum history, and the limits of diversity* (pp. vii–xx). New York, NY: Routledge.

Esteva, G., & Prakash, M. S. (2014). *Grassroots post-modernism: Remaking the soil of cultures.* London, UK: Zed Books. (Original work published 1998)

Falla, R. (1994). *Massacres in the Jungle. Ixcán, Guatemala, 1975–1982* (J. Howland, Trans.). Boulder, CO: Westview Press. (Original work published 1992)

Falla, R. (2001). *Quiché rebelde: Religious conversion, politics, and ethnic identity in Guatemala.* Austin: University of Texas Press.

Falla, R. (2011). *Negreaba de zopilotes . . . : Masacre y sobrevivencia, Finca San Francisco, Nentón* [Blackened with vultures . . . : Massacre and survival, San Francisco Finca, Nentón]. Guatemala City, Guatemala: AVANCSO.

Fals-Borda, O., & Mora-Osejo, L. E. (2003). Context and diffusion of knowledge: A critique of Eurocentrism. *Action Research, 1*(1), 29–73. doi:10.1177/14767503030011003

Fals-Borda, O., & Rahman, M. A. (1991). *Action and knowledge: Breaking the monopoly with participatory action-research.* New York, NY: APEX Press.

Fanon, F. (1967a). *Black skin, white masks* (C. L. Markmann, Trans.). New York, NY: Grove Press.

Fanon, F. (1967b). *Toward the African revolution* (H. Chevalier, Trans.). New York, NY: Grove Press.

Fanon, F. (2004). *The wretched of the earth* (R. Philcox, Trans.). New York, NY: Grove Press. (Original work published 1963)

Farmer, P. (2003). *Pathologies of power: Health, human rights, and the new war on the poor.* Berkeley: University of California Press.

Farmer, P. (2013). *To repair the world: Paul Farmer speaks to the next generation.* Berkeley: University of California Press.

Felman, S., & Laub, D. (1992). *Testimony: Crises of witnessing in literature, psychoanalysis, and history.* New York, NY: Taylor & Francis.

Fine, M. (1992). Passions, politics and power: Feminist research possibilities. In M. Fine (Ed.), *Disruptive voices: The transgressive possibilities of feminist research* (pp. 205–231). Ann Arbor: University of Michigan Press.

Fine, M., & Ruglis, J. (2009). Circuits and consequences of dispossession: The racialized realignment of the public sphere for U.S. youth. *Transforming Anthropology, 17*(1), 20–33. doi:10.1111/j.1548-7466.2009.01037.x

Ford, B., Cabrera, R., & Searing, V. (2000). *Buscando una buena vida: Tres experiencias de salud mental comunitaria* [Looking for a good life: Three experiences of community mental health]. Guatemala City, Guatemala: Redd Barna.

Franke, K. M. (2006). Gendered subject of transitional justice. *Columbia Journal of Gender & Law, 15*(3), 813–828. Retrieved from http://www2.law.columbia.edu/faculty_franke /Franke%20%28Final%20Version%29.pdf

Fregoso, R.-L., & Bejarano, C. (2010). Introduction: A cartography of feminicide in the Américas. In R.-L. Fregoso & C. Bejarano (Eds.), *Terrorizing women: Feminicide in the Américas* (pp. 1–42). Durham, NC: Duke University Press.

Freire, P. (2000). *Pedagogy of the oppressed* (30th anniversary ed.). New York, NY: Continuum. (Original English-language work published 1970)

Fulchiron, A. (2017). Actoras de Cambio en Guatemala: Poner el cuerpo y la vida de las mujeres en el centro de la justicia [Actors for Change in Guatemala: Putting women's bodies and lives in the center of justice]. In I. Mendia Azkue, G. Guzmán Orellana, & I. Zirion Landaluze (Eds.), *Género y justicia transicional: Movimientos de mujeres contra la impunidad* [Gender and transitional justice: Women's movements against impunity] (pp. 65–112). Bilbao, Spain: Hegoa.

Fulchiron, A., Paz, O. A., & López, A. (2009). *Tejidos que lleva el alma: Memoria de las mujeres mayas sobrevivientes de violación sexual durante el conflicto armado* [Weavings of the soul:

Memories of Mayan women survivors of sexual violence during the armed conflict]. Guatemala City, Guatemala: ECAP, UNAMG, & F&G Editores.

Gamazo, C. (2013, June 25). El club de la balanza y la daga [The club of the scale and the dagger]. *Plaza Publica*. Retrieved from https://www.plazapublica.com.gt/content/el-club-de-la-balanza-y-la-daga

Gamazo, C., & García, J. L. (2012, October 15). Los últimos árboles de los Ex PAC (que costaron Q2 mil millones) [The last trees of the Ex PAC (that cost 2 thousand million quetzals)]. *Plaza Pública*. Retrieved from https://www.plazapublica.com.gt/content/los-ultimos-arboles-de-los-ex-pac

García Ixmatá, P., England, N. C., García Mátzar, P. O., Sis Iboy, M. J., Fodrígues Guaján, J. O., López Ixcoy, C. D., & Benito Pérez, J. G. (2017). *Maya' Chii': Los idiomas mayas de Guatemala* [Maya' Chii': Mayan languages of Guatemala]. Guatemala City, Guatemala: Xtz'aj pa Iximulew, Editorial Maya' Wuj, & OKMA. (Original work published 1993)

Gates, A. (1998, October 20) *Santa Elena project of accompaniment*. Retrieved from http://www.oberlin.edu/external/EOG/SEPA/Gatesletter.html

Gaviola, E. (2008). *Sólo se hizo justicia. Informe de sistematización Caso de Doña Juana Méndez Rodríguez* [Only justice was done: Systematization report on the Doña Juana Méndez Rodríguez]. Guatemala City, Guatemala: Instituto de Estudios Comparados en Ciencias Penales de Guatemala. Retrieved from http://www.bantaba.ehu.es/ext/Libro_Sistematizacion_ICCPG.indd-1.pdf

Gelles, P. H. (1998). Testimonio, ethnography and processes of authorship. *Anthropology News* 39(3), 16–17.

GGM—Grupo Guatemalteco de Mujeres [Guatemalan Women's Group]. (2015). *Cuadro: Muertes violentas de mujeres (MVM), Guatemala, 2000 al 2015* [Table: Violent deaths of women, Guatemala, 2000-2015]. Retrieved from http://ggm.org.gt/wp-content/uploads/2012/08/Hist%C3%B3rico.pdf

Glum, J. (2015, April 2). South Korea ferry disaster: Victims' parents shave heads to protest government compensation, investigation. *International Business Times*. Retrieved from http://www.ibtimes.com/south-korea-ferry-disaster-victims-parents-shave-heads-protest-government-1867738

Gómez, M. (1993). *Donde no hay abogado: Manual* [Where there is no lawyer: Manual]. Guatemala City, Guatemala: ODHAG.

González, M. (2002). *Se cambió el tiempo: Conflicto y poder en territorio K'iche' 1880–1996* [Time changed: Conflict and power in the K'iche' territory 1880–1996]. Guatemala City, Guatemala: AVANCSO.

González, P. B. (2011). Entretejiendo una justicia alternativa desde las mujeres: "Experiencias sobre tribunales de consciencia contra la violencia hacia las mujeres en etapa postconflicto" [Weaving together alternative justice from the perspective of women: "Experiences of tribunals of conscience against violence against women in the postconflict period"]. *Memorias del II Coloquio de Antropología y Sociología de la Universidad del Valle de Guatemala, Comunidades y medio ambiente* [Proceedings of the II Anthropology and Sociology Colloquium of the University del Valle, Guatemala, Community and the environment], 71–79. Guatemala City, Guatemala: Edición AECCSSE. Retrieved from https://aeccsseuvg.files.wordpress.com/2011/02/08-gonzc3a1les_entretejiendo-una-justicia-alternativa-desde-las-mujeres.pdf

Goodale, M., & Merry, S. E. (2007). *The practice of human rights: Tracking law between the global and the local*. Cambridge, UK: Cambridge University Press.

Goudvis, P. (1991). *Trabajando para un futuro mejor: Talleres creativos con niños* [Working for a better future: Creative workshops with children]. Unpublished CD available from M. B. Lykes.

Grande, S. (2004). *Red pedagogy: Native American social and political thought.* Lanham, MD: Rowman & Littlefield.

Grandia, L. (2009). *Tz'aptz'ooqeb' El despojo recurrente al pueblo q'eqchi'.* [Tz'aptz'ooqeb' The ongoing dispossession of the q'eqchi' people]. Guatemala City, Guatemala: AVANCSO.

Grandin G. (2004). *The last colonial massacre: Latin America in the cold war.* Chicago, IL: University of Chicago Press.

Grandin, G., Levenson, D. T., & Oglesby, E. (Eds.). (2011). *The Guatemala reader: History, culture, politics.* Durham, NC: Duke University Press.

Gready, P., & Robins, S. (2014). From transitional to transformative justice: A new agenda for practice. *International Journal of Transitional Justice, 8*(3), 339–361. doi:10.1093/ijtj/iju013

Green, L. (1999). *Fear as a way of life: Mayan widows in rural Guatemala.* New York, NY: Columbia University Press.

Grewal, I. (2005). *Transnational America: Feminisms, diasporas, neoliberalisms.* Durham, NC: Duke University Press.

Grewal, I., & Kaplan, C. (2000). Postcolonial studies and transnational feminist practices. *Jouvert: A Journal of Postcolonial Studies, 5*(1). Retrieved from https://english.chass.ncsu.edu/jouvert/v5i1/grewal.htm

Griffin, M., & Block, J. W. (Eds.). (2013). *In the company of the poor: Conversations with Dr. Paul Farmer and Fr. Gustavo Gutiérrez.* Maryknoll, NY: Orbis Books.

Grupo de Mujeres Mayas Kaqla [Kaqla Mayan Women's Group]. (2004). *La palabra y el sentir de las mujeres Mayas de Kaqla* [The words and feelings of the Mayan women of Kaqla]. Guatemala City, Guatemala: Author.

Grupo de Mujeres Mayas Kaqla. (2006). *La internalización de la opresión. Una propuesta metodológica* [The internalization of oppression: A methodological proposal]. Guatemala City, Guatemala: Author.

Grupo de Mujeres Mayas Kaqla. (2009). *Mujeres Mayas: Universo y vida: Kinojib'al Qati't* [Mayan women: Universe and life: *Kinojib'al Qati't*]. Guatemala City, Guatemala: Iximulew.

Grupo de Mujeres Mayas Kaqla. (2010). *Caminos para la plenitud de las Mujeres Mayas y nuestros pueblos* [Paths for the plenitude of Mayan women and our people]. Guatemala City, Guatemala: Author.

Grupo de Mujeres Mayas Kaqla (2011). *Tramas y transcendencias: Reconstruyendo historias con nuestras abuelas y madres* [Connections and transcendences: Reconstructing our histories with our grandmothers and mothers]. Guatemala City, Guatemala: Author.

Grupo de Mujeres Mayas Kaqla. (2014). *Las voces de las mujeres persisten en la memoria colectiva de sus pueblos* [The voices of the women persist in the collective memory of their people]. Guatemala City, Guatemala: Author.

Hale, C. (2006). *Más que un indio* [More than an Indian]: *Racial ambivalence and neoliberal multiculturalism in Guatemala.* Santa Fe, NM: School of American Research Press.

Hale, C. (Ed.). (2008). *Engaging contradictions: Theory, politics, and methods of activist scholarship.* Berkeley: University of California Press.

Halley, J. (2005). The politics of injury: A review of Robin West's *Caring for Justice. Unbound, 1,* 65–92.

Hamber, B. (2006). Narrowing the micro and macro: A psychological perspective on reparations in societies in transition. In De Grieff (Ed.), *The handbook of reparations* (pp. 560–588). New York, NY: Oxford University Press.

Hamber, B. (2009). *Transforming societies after political violence.* Cham, Switzerland: Springer International.

Hamber, B., & Gallagher, E. (Eds.). (2015). *Psychosocial perspectives on peacebuilding.* Peace Psychology Book Series. Cham, Switzerland: Springer International.

Harding, S. (1991). *Whose science? Whose knowledge? Thinking from women's lives.* Ithaca, NY: Cornell University Press.

Hartman, S. (1997). *Scenes of subjection: Terror, slavery, and self-making in nineteenth-century America.* New York, NY: Oxford University Press.

Hayner, P. B. (2011). *Unspeakable truths: Transitional justice and the challenge of truth commissions* (2nd ed.). New York, NY: Routledge.

Henry, N. (2009). Witness to rape: The limits and potential of international war crimes trials for victims of wartime sexual violence. *International Journal of Transitional Justice, 3*(1), 114–134. doi:10.1093/ijtj/ijn036

Hernández Castillo, R. A. (2016). *Indigenous women, law and political struggle in Latin America: Multiple injustices.* Tucson: University of Arizona Press.

Hernández, O. J. (2012, October 1). Sepur Zarco: El recreo de los soldados [Sepur Zarco: The soldiers' playground]. *Plaza Pública.* Retrieved from https://www.plazapublica.com.gt/content/sepur-zarco-el-recreo-de-los-soldados

Hesford, W. (2011). *Spectacular rhetorics: Human rights visions, recognitions, feminisms.* Durham, NC: Duke University Press.

Hessbruegge, J. A., & Ochoa, C. F. (2004). *Mayan law in post-conflict Guatemala.* Retrieved from http://www.ilo.org/wcmsp5/groups/public/—ed_norm/—normes/documents/event/wcms_084059.pdf

Hickey, S., & Mohan, G. (Eds.). (2004). *Participation: From tyranny to transformation? Exploring new approaches to participation in development.* London, UK: Zed Books.

Hickson, H. (2016). Becoming a critical narrativist: Using critical reflection and narrative inquiry as research methodology. *Qualitative Social Work, 15,* 380–391. doi:10.1177/1473325015617344

Hill Collins, P., & Bilge, S. (2016). *Intersectionality.* Hoboken, NJ: John Wiley & Sons.

Hollander, T., & Gill, B. (2014). Every day the war continues in my body: Examining the marked body in postconflict Northern Uganda. *International Journal of Transitional Justice, 8*(2), 217–234. doi:10.1093/ijtj/iju007

Hooks, M. (1991). *Guatemalan women speak.* London, UK: Catholic Institute for International Relations.

Hope, A. E., & Timmel, S. J. (Eds.). (2014). *Training for transformation in practice.* Rugby, UK: Practical Action Publishing. http://dx.doi.org/10.3362/9781780448312.000

Hurtado Paz y Paz, L. (2008). *Dinámicas agrarias y reproducción campesina en la globalización: El caso de Alta Verapaz 1970–2007* [Agrarian dynamics and peasant reproduction in globalization: The case of Alta Verapaz 1970–2007]. Guatemala City, Guatemala: F&G Editores.

Impunity Watch. (2009). *Recognizing the past: Challenges in the combat of impunity in Guatemala.* Retrieved from http://www.impunitywatch.org/docs/Guatemala_BCR_Summary_English.pdf

Impunity Watch. (2013). *Policy brief: Derecho a la reparación en Guatemala: Por la senda de la negación* [The right to reparation in Guatemala: On the path of denial]. Retrieved from://www.impunitywatch.org/docs/14960

Impunity Watch and Alliance to Break the Silence and Impunity (ECAP, MTM, UNAMG). (2017). *Changing the face of justice: Keys to the strategic litigation of the Sepur Zarco case.* Guatemala City, Guatemala: Authors. Retrieved from https://www.impunitywatch.org/docs/Changing_the_face_of_justice_final.pdf

Inghilleri, M. (2012). *Interpreting justice: Ethics, politics and language.* New York, NY: Routledge.

Institute for Community Research. (n.d.). *About ICR.* Retrieved from https://icrweb.org/about-icr/

Jaleel, R. (2013). Weapons of sex, weapons of war. *Cultural Studies, 27*(1), 115–135. doi:10.1080/09502386.2012.722302

Jara, D., Badilla, M., Figueiredo, A., Cornejo, M., & Riveros, V. (2018). Tracing Mapuche exclusion from post-dictatorial truth commissions in Chile: Official and grassroots initiatives. *International Journal of Transitional Justice, 12*(3), 491–510.

Jelin, E. (2003). *State repression and labors of memory.* Minneapolis: University of Minnesota Press.

Jocón, M. (2005). *Fortalecimiento de la participación política de las mujeres mayas* [Strengthening Mayan women's political participation]. Chimaltenango, Guatemala: Asociación Maya Uk'u'x B'e.

Jonas, S. (2000). *Of centaurs and doves: Guatemala's peace process.* Oxford, UK: Westview Press.

Jonas, S., McCaughan, E., & Sutherland, E. (Eds.). (1984). *Guatemala, tyranny on trial: Permanent Peoples' Tribunal.* San Francisco, CA: Synthesis Publications.

Kapur, R. (2002). The tragedy of victimization rhetoric: Resurrecting the "Native" subject in international-post-colonial feminist legal politics. *Harvard Human Rights Journal, 15*(1), 1–17.

Kesselring, R. (2017). *Bodies of truth: Law, memory, and emancipation in post-apartheid South Africa.* Stanford, CA: Stanford University Press.

Kim, E. T. (2006). Performing social reparation: "Comfort women" and the path to political forgiveness. *Women & Performance: A Journal of Feminist Theory, 16*(2), 221–249. doi: 10.1080/07407700600744535

Kistler, A. (2010). Disappeared but not forgotten: A Guatemalan community achieves a landmark verdict. *NACLA Report on the Americas, 43*(1), 9–13. http://dx.doi.org/10.1080/10714839.2010.11722208

Kleinman, A., Das, V. & Lock, M. M. (Eds.). (1997). *Social suffering.* Berkeley: University of California Press.

Kobrak, P. H. (2003). *Huehuetenango: Historia de una guerra* [Huehuetenango: History of a war]. Huehuetenango, Guatemala: CEDFOG.

Koomen, J. (2014). Language work at International Criminal Courts. *International Feminist Journal of Politics, 16*(4), 581–600. doi.org/10.1080/14616742.2014.947732

Kritz, N. (Ed.). (1995). *Transitional justice: How emerging democracies reckon with former regimes.* Washington, DC: United States Institute of Peace Press.

Lal, J. (1996). Situating locations: The politics of self, identity, and 'other' in living and writing the text. In D. L. Wolf (Ed.), *Feminist dilemmas in fieldwork* (pp. 185–214). Boulder, CO: Westview Press.

Lambourne, W. (2009). Transitional justice and peacebuilding after mass violence. *International Journal of Transitional Justice, 3*(1), 28–48. doi:10.1093/ijtj/ijn037

Laplante, L. J., & Theidon, K. (2007). Truth with consequences: Justice and reparations in post-truth commission Peru. *Human Rights Quarterly, 29*(1), 228–250. doi:10.1353/hrq.2007.0009.

LASA—[Latin American Studies Association]. (2018). *LASA Sections: Otros Saberes* [Other knowledges]. Retrieved from https://lasa.international.pitt.edu/eng/sections/otros-saberes.aspx

Levin, M., & Greenwood, D. J. (2008). The future of universities: Action research and the transformation of higher education. In P. Reason & H. Bradbury (Eds.), *The SAGE handbook of action research: Participative inquiry and practice* (pp. 211–226). Thousand Oaks, CA: SAGE.

Levitt, P., & Merry, S. E. (2009). Vernacularization on the ground: Local uses of global women's rights in Peru, China, India and the United States. *Global Networks, 9*(4), 441–461. doi:10.1111/j.1471-0374.2009.00263.x

Lewin, K. (1946). Action research and minority problems. *Journal of Social Issues, 2*(4), 34–46.

Lewin, K. (1951). *Field theory in social science: Selected theoretical papers.* New York, NY: Harper and Row.

Lira, E., & Loveman, B. (2005). *Políticas de reparación: Chile 1990–2004* [Reparations policies: Chile 1990–2004)]. Santiago, Chile: Lom Ediciones.

López López, L. (2017). *The making of indigeneity, curriculum history, and the limits of diversity.* New York, NY: Routledge.

Lykes, M. B. (1994). Terror, silencing, and children: International multidisciplinary collaboration with Guatemalan Maya communities. *Social Science and Medicine, 38*(4), 543–552. doi:10.1016/0277-9536(94)90250-X

Lykes, M. B. (2001). Creative arts and photography in participatory action research in Guatemala. In P. Reason & H. Bradbury (Eds.), *Handbook of action research* (pp. 363–371). Thousand Oaks, CA: SAGE.

Lykes, M. B. (2010). Silence(ing), memory(ies) and voice(s): Feminist participatory action research and photo-narratives in the wake of gross violations of human rights. *Visual Studies, 25*(3), 238–254. doi:10.1080/1472586X.2010.523276

Lykes, M. B. (2013). Participatory and action research as a transformative praxis: Responding to humanitarian crises from the margins. *American Psychologist, 68*(8), 774–783. doi:10.1037/a0034360

Lykes, M. B., Beristain, C. M., & Cabrera Pérez-Armiñan, M. L. (2007). Political violence, impunity, and emotional climate in Maya communities. *Journal of Social Issues, 63*(2), 369–385. doi:10.1111/j.1540-4560.2007.00514.x

Lykes, M. B., Caba Mateo, A., Chávez, J., Laynez Caba, A., Ruiz, U., & Williams, J. W. (1999). Telling stories—rethreading lives: Community education, women's development, and social change among the Maya Ixil. *International Journal of Leadership in Education: Theory and Practice, 2*(3), 207–227.

Lykes, M. B., & Crosby, A. (2014a). Creativity as an intervention strategy with Mayan women in Guatemala. *Intervention: International Journal of Mental Health, Psychosocial Work and Counselling in Areas of Armed Conflict, 12*(1), 30–42. doi:10.1097/WTF.0000000000000021

Lykes, M. B., & Crosby, A. (2014b). Feminist practice of community and participatory and action research. In S. Hesse-Biber (Ed.), *Feminist research practice: A primer* (2nd ed., pp. 145–181). Thousand Oaks, CA: SAGE.

Lykes, M. B., & Crosby, A. (2015a). Creative methodologies as a resource for Mayan women's protagonism. In B. Hamber & E. Gallagher (Eds.), *Psychosocial perspectives on peacebuilding* (pp. 147–186). Cham, Switzerland: Springer International.

Lykes, M. B., & Crosby, A. (2015b). Participatory action research as a resource for community regeneration in post-conflict contexts. In D. Bretherton & S. F. Law (Eds.), *Methodologies in peace psychology: Peace research by peaceful means* (pp. 237–254). New York, NY: Springer.

Lykes, M. B., & Hershberg, R. (2012). Participatory action research and feminisms: Social inequalities and transformative praxis. In S. Hesse-Biber (Ed.), *Handbook of feminist research II: Theory and praxis* (pp. 331–367). Thousand Oaks, CA: SAGE.

Lykes, M. B., & Mersky, M. (2006). Reparations and mental health: Psychosocial interventions towards healing, human agency, and rethreading social realities. In P. De Greiff (Ed.), *The handbook of reparations* (pp. 589–622). Oxford, UK: Oxford University Press.

Lykes, M. B., Rosales, J., Siguenza, E., et al. (1994). *Trauma psicosocial y adolescentes Latinoamericanos: Formas de acción grupal.* [Psychosocial trauma and Latin American youth: Forms of group action]. D. Becker, G. Morales & M. I. Aguilar (Eds.). Santiago, Chile: ILAS.

Lykes, M. B., TerreBlanche, M., & Hamber, B. (2003). Narrating survival and change in Guatemala and South Africa: The politics of representation and a liberatory community psychology. *American Journal of Community Psychology, 31*(1/2), 79–90. doi:10.1023/A:1023074620506

MacKinnon, C. (2006). Defining rape internationally: A comment on Akayesu. *Columbia Journal of Transnational Law, 44*(3), 940–958.

Macleod, M. (2011). *Nietas del fuego, creadoras del alba: Luchas político-culturales de mujeres Mayas* [Granddaughters of fire, creators of the dawn: The political-cultural struggles of Mayan women]. Guatemala City, Guatemala: FLASCO.

Macleod, M. (2017). Grievances and crevices of resistance: Maya women defy Goldcorp. In R. Sieder (Ed.), *Demanding justice and security: Indigenous women and legal pluralities in Latin America* (pp. 220–241). New Brunswick, NJ: Rutgers University Press.

Maguire, P. (1987). *Doing participatory research: A feminist approach.* Amherst, MA: Center for International Education, University of Massachusetts.

Mama, A. (2013). *Challenging militarized masculinities.* Paper presented at the Nobel Women's Initiative conference, Moving beyond Militarism and War: Women-Driven Solutions for a Nonviolent World, Belfast, Ireland. Retrieved from https://www.opendemocracy.net/5050/amina-mama/challenging-militarized-masculinities

Marín, L. (1991). Speaking out together: Testimonial of Latin American women. *Latin American Perspectives 18*(3), 51–68. Retrieved from https://www.jstor.org/stable/2633739

Martín-Baró, I. (1994). *Toward a liberation psychology. Writings for a liberation psychology.* (A. Aron & S. Corne, Eds. and Trans.). Cambridge, MA: Harvard University Press.

Martínez Peláez, S. (2011). The ladino. In G. Grandin, D. Levenson & E. Oglesby (Eds.), *The Guatemala reader: History, politics, culture* (pp. 129–131). Durham, NC: Duke University Press.

McAllister, C. (2013). Testimonial truths and revolutionary mysteries. In C. McAllister & D. M. Nelson (Eds.), *War by other means: Aftermath in post-genocide Guatemala* (pp. 93–115). Durham, NC: Duke University Press.

McAllister, C., & Nelson, D. M. (2013). Aftermath: Harvests of violence and histories of the future. In C. McAllister & D. M. Nelson (Eds.), *War by other means: Aftermath in post-genocide Guatemala* (pp. 2–43). Durham NC: Duke University Press.

McEvoy, K., & McGregor, L. (Eds.). (2008). *Transitional justice from below: Grassroots activism and the struggle for change.* Oxford, UK: Hart.

Melville, M., & Lykes, M. B. (1992). Guatemalan Indian children and the sociocultural effects of government-sponsored terrorism. *Social Science and Medicine, 34*(5), 533–548. doi:10.1016/0277-9536(92)90209-9

Memorial para la Concordia. (n.d). http://memorialparalaconcordia.org/

Méndez, L. (2012, October 23). No me quiero morir sin alcanzar justicia. Esclavitud sexual durante el conflicto armado en Guatemala [I do not want to die without achieving justice: Sexual slavery during the armed conflict in Guatemala]. *Cimacnoticias.* Retrieved from http://cimacnoticias.com.mx/?q=node/61780

Méndez, L. (2014, October 28). Guatemalan officers face sexual slavery charges in historic trial. *Interpress Services. News agency.* Retrieved from http://www.ipsnews.net/2014/10/guatemalan-officers-face-sexual-slavery-charges-in-historic-trial/

Méndez, L., & Carrera, A. (2014). *Mujeres indígenas. Clamor por la justicia. Violencia sexual, conflicto armado y despojo violento de tierras* [Indigenous women: Demand for justice. Sexual violence, armed conflict, and violent land dispossession]. Guatemala City, Guatemala: F&G Editores.

Mendia Azkue, I., & Guzmán Orellana, G. (Eds.). (2012). *Ni olvido, ni silencio: Tribunal de Conciencia contra la violencia sexual hacia las mujeres durante el conflicto armado en Guatemala* [No forgetting, no silence: Tribunal of Conscience against violence against women during the armed conflict in Guatemala]. Bilbao, Spain: Universidad de Pais Vasco, Hegoa, & UNAMG.

Merry, S. E. (2006). Transnational human rights and local activism: Mapping the middle. *American Anthropologist, 108*(1), 38–51. doi:10.1525/aa.2006.108.1.38

Merry, S. E. (2009). *Gender violence: A cultural perspective*. Oxford, UK: Wiley-Blackwell.

Merry, S. E., & Levitt, P. (2017). The vernacularization of women's human rights. In S. Hopgood, J. Snyder, & L. Vinjamuri (Eds.), *Human rights futures* (pp. 213–236). Cambridge, UK: Cambridge University Press. doi:10.1017/9781108147767.009

Mertus, J. (2004). Shouting from the bottom of the well: The impact of international trials for wartime rape on women's agency. *International Feminist Journal of Politics, 6*(1), 110–128. doi:10.1080/1461674032000165950

Miller, A. (2004). Sexuality, violence against women and human rights: Women make demands, ladies get protection. *Health and Human Rights, 7*(2), 16–47. doi:10.2307/4065347

Miller, J., & Kumar, R. (Eds.). (2007). *Reparations: Interdisciplinary inquiries*. New York, NY: Oxford University Press.

Miller, Z. (2008). Effects of invisibility: In search of the 'economic' in transitional justice. *International Journal of Transitional Justice, 2*(3), 266–291. doi:10.1093/ijtj/ijn022

Million, D. (2013). *Therapeutic nations: Healing in an age of indigenous human rights*. Tucson: University of Arizona Press.

Minow, M. (1998). *Between vengeance and forgiveness: Facing history after genocide and mass violence*. Boston, MA: Beacon Press.

Mohanty, C. T. (2003). *Feminism without borders: Decolonizing theory, practicing solidarity*. Durham, NC: Duke University Press.

MOLOJ—Asociación Política de Mujeres [Political Association of Women], CONAVIGUA— Coordinadora Nacional de Viudas de Guatemala [National Coordination of Widows of Guatemala], & ICCPG—Instituto de Estudios Comparados en Ciencias Penales de Guatemala [Institute for Comparative Studies in Criminal Sciences of Guatemala] (Eds.). (2008). *Tejedoras de paz: Testimonios de mujeres de Guatemala* [Weavers of peace: Testimonies of women in Guatemala]. Guatemala City, Guatemala: Magna Terra.

Moon, C. (2012). 'Who'll pay reparations on my soul?': Compensation, social control, and social suffering. *Social & Legal Studies, 21*(2), 187–199. doi:10.1177/0964663911433670

Muñoz, L. (2010, June 15). Romper el silencio: La lucha por la justicia para las víctimas de violencia sexual durante el genocidio [Breaking the silence: The struggle for justice for victims of sexual violence during the genocide]. *América Latina en Movimiento*. Retrieved from http://www.alainet.org/es/active/38911

MTM—Mujeres Transformando el Mundo [Women Transforming the World]. (2017). *Línea base de Sepur Zarco y comunidades aledañas. Informe final*. [Baseline for Sepur Zarco and surrounding communities. Final report.] Guatemala City, Guatemala: MTM.

Muvingi, I. (2009). Sitting on powder kegs: Socioeconomic rights in transitional societies. *International Journal of Transitional Justice, 3*(2), 163–182. doi:10.1093/ijtj/ijp010

Nagy, R. L. (2013). The scope and bounds of transitional justice and the Canadian Truth and Reconciliation Commission. *International Journal of Transitional Justice 7*(1), 52–73. doi:10.1093/ijtj/ijs034

Nelson, D. M. (2009). *Reckoning: The ends of war in Guatemala*. Durham, NC: Duke University Press.

Ní Aoláin, F., & Rooney, E. (2007). Underenforcement and intersectionality: Gendered aspects of transition for women. *International Journal of Transitional Justice, 1*(3), 338–354, doi:10.1093/ijtj/ijm031

Nolin, C., & Shankar, F. (2000). Gendered spaces of terror and assault: The testimonio of REMHI and the Commission of Historical Clarification of Guatemala. *Gender, Place and Culture, 7*(3), 265–286. doi:10.1080/713668875

Nouwen, H. (1979). *The wounded healer: Ministry in contemporary society.* Colorado Springs, CO: Image Books.

Noval, J. (1960).El principio de la autonomía cultural [The principle of cultural autonomy]. In *Boletín del Instituto Indigenista Nacional*, 3(1–4). Guatemala City, Guatemala: Instituto Indigenista Nacional. Editorial del Ministerio de Educación Pública José de Pineda Ibarra.

Nowrojee, B. (2005). *"Your justice is too slow": Will the ICTR fail Rwanda's rape victims?* Geneva, Switzerland: UN Research Institute for Social Development.

ODHAG—Oficina de Derechos Humanos del Arzobispo de Guatemala [The Human Rights Office of the Archbishopric of Guatemala]. (1998). *Nunca Más: Impactos de la Violencia, Informe del Proyecto Interdiocesano de Recuperación de la Memoria* [Never again: Impact of the violence, Report of the Interdiocesan Recovery of Memory Project]. Guatemala City, Guatemala: Litografía e Imprenta LIL, SA [also referred to as the REMHI Report].

ODHAG. (2014). *Silenciaron nuestra historia . . . ahora queremos justicia: Las violaciones a los derechos humanos cometidos contra las mujeres durante el conflicto armado interno en la región Q'eqchi'* [They silenced our history . . . now we want justice: The human rights violations committed against women during the internal armed conflict in the Q'eqchi' region]. Guatemala City, Guatemala: ODHAG and CAFCA.

Oglesby, E., & Nelson, D. M. (2016). Guatemala's genocide trial and the nexus of racism and counterinsurgency. *Journal of Genocide Research, 18*(2–3), 133–142. doi:10.1080/14623528.2016.1186436.

OSJI—Open Society Justice Initiative. (2014). *Judging a dictator: The trial of Guatemala's Ríos Montt.* New York, NY: Author. Retrieved from https://www.opensocietyfoundations.org /sites/default/files/judging-dicatator-trial-guatemala-rios-montt-11072013.pdf

OSJI. (2016). *Against the odds: CICIG in Guatemala.* New York, NY: Author. Retrieved from https://www.opensocietyfoundations.org/sites/default/files/against-odds-cicig -guatemala-20160321.pdf

Otzoy, I. (2008). Indigenous law and gender dialogues. In P. Pitarch, S. Speek, & X. Leyva Solano (Eds.), *Human rights in the Maya region* (pp. 171–185). Durham, NC: Duke University Press.

Patterson-Markowitz, R., Oglesby, E., & Marston, S. (2012). "Subjects of change": Feminist geopolitics and gendered truth-telling in Guatemala. *Journal of International Women's Studies, 13*(4), 82–99. Retrieved from http://vc.bridgew.edu/jiws/vol13/iss4/6

Pavlovsky, E., Martinez Bouquet, C., & Moccio, F. (1985). *Psicodrama: Cuándo y por qué dramatizar* [Psychodrama: When and why to dramatize]. Buenos Aires, Argentina: Ediciones Busqueda.

Paz y Paz Bailey, C. (2006). Guatemala: Gender and reparations for human rights violations. In R. Rubio-Marín (Ed.), *What happened to the women? Gender and reparations for human rights violations* (pp. 92–135). New York, NY: Social Science Research Council. Retrieved from http://www.ssrc.org/publications/view/D6D99C02-EA4A-DE11-AFAC-001CC477EC70/

People's Institute for Survival and Beyond. (n.d). *Our principles.* Retrieved from http://www .pisab.org/our-principles

Pershey, M. G. (2000) African American spiritual music: A historical perspective. *Dragon Lode, 18*(2), 24–29.

Philipose, E. (2008). On Euro-colonial sovereignty: Decolonizing the racial grammar of international law. In R. L. Riley, C. T. Mohanty, & M. B. Pratt (Eds.). *Feminism and war: Confronting US imperialism* (pp. 103–116). New York, NY: ZED Books.

PNR—Programa Nacional de Resarcimiento [National Reparations Program]. (n.d.). *Manual para la calificación de beneficiarios del Programa Nacional de Resarcimiento* [Manual for the qualification of beneficiaries in the National Reparations Program]. Guatemala City, Guatemala: Author.

PNR. (2003). *El libro azul: Política pública de resarcimiento* [The blue book: Reparations public policy]. Guatemala City, Guatemala: Author.

PNR. (2007). *La vida no tiene precio: Acciones y omisiones de resarcimiento en Guatemala. Primer Informe Temático 2006–2007* [Life is priceless: Actions and omissions in reparation in Guatemala. First Thematic Report 2006–2007]. Guatemala City, Guatemala: Magna Terra. Retrieved from http://memoriavirtualguatemala.org:8080/xmlui/bitstream/handle/123456789/119/La%20vida%20no%20tiene%20precio.pdf?sequence=1&isAllowed=y

Puar, J. (2008). Feminists and queers in the service of empire. In R. L. Riley, C. T. Mohanty, & M. B. Pratt (Eds.). *Feminism and war: Confronting US imperialism* (pp. 47–55). New York, NY: ZED Books.

Qiu, P., Zhiliang, S., & Lifei, C. (2013). *Chinese comfort women: Testimonies from imperial Japan's sex slaves.* Vancouver: University of British Columbia Press.

Radford, J., & Russell, D. E. (1992). *Femicide: The politics of woman killing.* Woodbridge, CT: Twayne Publishing.

Rahman, A. (2004). Globalization: The emerging ideology in the popular protests and grassroots action research. *Action Research, 2*(1), 9–23. doi:10.1177/1476750304040495

Ramos, J. (2016, July 28). Juez abre proceso contra 53 en el caso cooptación [Judge opens process against 53 in cooptation case]. *Prensa Libre.* Retrieved from http://www.prensalibre.com/guatemala/justicia/juez-galvez-dicta-resolucion-en-caso-cooptacion-del-estado

Razack, S. H. (2007). Stealing the pain of others: Reflections on Canadian humanitarian responses. *Review of Education, Pedagogy, and Cultural Studies, 29*(4), 375–394. doi:10.1080/10714410701454198

Reason, P., & Bradbury, H. (Eds.). (2008). *The SAGE handbook of action research: Participative inquiry and practice.* Thousand Oaks, CA: SAGE.

Remijnse, S. (2002). *Memories of violence: Civil patrols and the legacy of conflict in Joyabaj, Guatemala.* Lafayette, IN: Purdue University Press.

Riessman, C. K. (2015). Entering a hall of mirrors: Reflexivity and narrative research. In A. De Fina & A. Georgakopoulou (Eds.), *The handbook of narrative research* (pp. 219–238). Malden, MA: Wiley-Blackwell. doi:10.1002/9781118458204.ch11

Rodari, G. (1996). *The grammar of fantasy: An introduction to the art of inventing stories.* (J. Zipes, Trans. with introduction). New York, NY: Teachers & Writers Collaborative.

Roht-Arriaza, N., & Kemp, S. (2013). *The Ríos Montt judgment in light of international law.* Retrieved from International Justice Monitor website: http://www.ijmonitor.org/2013/06/the-rios-montt-judgment-in-light-of-international-law/

Rojas-Perez, I. (2017). *Mourning remains: State atrocity, exhumations, and governing the disappeared in Peru's postwar Andes.* Stanford, CA: Stanford University Press.

Rome Statute of the International Criminal Court, July 17, 1998 (last amended 2010), 2187 U.N.T.S. 90. Retrieved from http://www.refworld.org/docid/3ae6b3a84.html

Ross, F. (2003). *Bearing witness: Women and the Truth and Reconciliation Commission in South Africa.* London, UK: Pluto Press.

Rubio-Marín, R. (Ed.). (2006). *What happened to the women? Gender and reparations for human rights violations* (pp. 92–135). New York, NY: Social Science Research Council. Retrieved from http://www.ssrc.org/publications/view/D6D99C02-EA4A-DE11-AFAC-001CC477EC70/

Rubio-Marín, R. (Ed.). (2009). *The gender of reparations: Unsettling sexual hierarchies while redressing human rights violations.* New York, NY: Cambridge University Press.

Russell, G. (2010). *Gang rapes, forced evictions, and the endless nightmare of nickel mining in Guatemala*. Washington, DC: Rights Action.

St. Louis, K., & Barton, A. C. (2002). Tales from the science education crypt: A critical reflection of positionality, subjectivity, and reflexivity in research. *FQS Forum: Qualitative Social Research, 3*(3). doi:10.17169/fqs-3.3.832

Sakamoto, R. (2001). The women's international war crimes tribunal on Japan's military sexual slavery: A legal and feminist approach to the 'comfort women' issue. *New Zealand Journal of Asian Studies, 3*(1), 49–58. Retrieved from http://www.nzasia.org.nz/downloads/NZJAS-June01/Comfortwomen.pdf

Sanford, V. (2008). From genocide to feminicide: Impunity and human rights in twenty-first century Guatemala. *Journal of Human Rights 7*(2), 104–122. doi:10.1080/14754830802070192

Sanford, V. (2009). *La masacre de Panzós: Etnicidad, tierra y violencia en Guatemala.* [The massacre of Panzós: Ethnicity, land, and violence in Guatemala]. Guatemala: F&G Editores.

Sankey, D. (2014). Towards recognition of subsistence harms: Reassessing approaches to socioeconomic forms of violence in transitional justice. *International Journal of Transitional Justice, 8*(1), 121–140. doi:10.1093/ijtj/ijt027

Sarkar, A. (2016, February 27). Guatemala: 2 former soldiers sentenced to 120 and 240 years for forcing indigenous women into sexual slavery. *International Business Times*. Retrieved from http://www.ibtimes.co.in/guatemala-2-former-soldiers-sentenced-120-240-years-forcing-indigenous-women-into-sexual-slavery-668442

Scarry, E. (1985). *The body in pain: The making and unmaking of the world*. New York, NY: Oxford University Press.

"Sembramos justicia, estamos esperando sus frutos" ["We sowed justice, we are waiting for its fruit"]. (2016, February 26). *Federación Guatemalteca de Escuelas Radiofónicas*. Retrieved from http://fger.org/2018/02/26/sembramos-justicia-estamos-esperando-sus-frutos/

Sepur Zarco: 33 years for justice. (2016, February 8). Retrieved from Breaking the Silence blog: http://www.breakingthesilenceblog.com/general/sepur-zarco-33-years-for-justice/

Shaw, R. L. (2010). Embedding reflexivity within experiential qualitative psychology. *Qualitative Research in Psychology, 7*(3), 233–243. doi: 10.1080/14780880802699092

Shaw, R., Waldorf, L., & Hazan, P. (Eds.). (2010). *Localizing transitional justice: Interventions and priorities after mass violence*. Stanford, CA: Stanford University Press.

Sherwood, H. (2014, June 11). International protocol launched to deal with sexual violence in conflict. *The Guardian*. Retrieved from http://www.theguardian.com/global-development/2014/jun/11/protocol-launched-sexual-violence-in-conflict

Sholock, A. (2012). Methodology of the privileged: White anti-racist feminism, systematic ignorance, and epistemic uncertainty. *Hypatia, 27*(4), 701–714. doi:10.1111/j.1527-2001.2012.01275.x

Sieder, R. (2011). Building Mayan authority and autonomy: The "recovery" of indigenous law in post-peace Guatemala. *Studies in Law, Politics, and Society, 55*, 43–75.

Sieder, R. (Ed.). (2017). *Demanding justice and security: Indigenous women and legal pluralities in Latin America*. New Brunswick, NJ: Rutgers University Press.

Sieder, R., & Flores, C. (2011). *Vergüenza: Autoridad, autonomía y derecho indígena en la Guatemala de posguerra* [Shame: Authority, autonomy, and indigenous law in postwar Guatemala]. Guatemala City, Guatemala: F&G Editores.

Sieder, R., & Macleod, M. (2009). Género, derecho y cosmovisión maya en Guatemala [Gender, law and the Mayan cosmovision]. *Desacatos, 31*, 51–79.

Sieder, R., & Sierra, M. T. (2010). *Indigenous women's access to justice in Latin America*. Bergen, Norway: Chr. Michelsen Institute.

Smith, A. (2004). Boarding school abuses, human rights, and reparations. *Social Justice, 31*(4), 89–102. Retrieved from https://www.jstor.org/stable/29768278

Smith, A. (2005). *Conquest: Sexual violence and American Indian genocide*. Cambridge, MA: South End Press.

Solano, L. (2013). Development and/as dispossession: Elite networks and extractive industry in the Franja Transversal del Norte. In C. McAllister & D. Nelson (Eds.), *War by other means: Aftermath in post-genocide Guatemala* (pp. 119–142). Durham, NC: Duke University Press.

Sontag, S. (2003) *Regarding the pain of others*. New York, NY: Farrar, Straus and Giroux.

Spivak, G. (1998). *Other worlds: Essays in cultural politics*. New York, NY: Routledge.

Stanley, E. (2002). What next? The aftermath of organized truth telling. *Race & Class, 44*(1), 1–15. doi:10.1177/0306396802441002

Stoudt, B. G., Cahill, C., X, D., Belmonte, K., Djokovic, S., Lopez, J., Matles, A., . . . & Torre, M. E. (2016). Participatory action research as youth activism. In J. Conner & S. M. Rosen (Eds.), *Contemporary youth activism: Advancing social justice in the United States* (pp. 327–346). Santa Barbara, CA: Praeger.

Távara, G., Lykes, M. B., & Crosby, A. (2018). Standing in between: The healing praxis of Mayan women intermediaries in post genocide Guatemala. *Women and Therapy, 41*(1–2), 30–51. doi:10.1080/02703149.2017.1323477

Taylor, D. (2003). *The archive and the repertoire: Performing cultural memory in the Americas*. Durham, NC: Duke University Press.

Teitel, R. (2000). *Transitional justice*. New York, NY: Oxford University Press.

Terrell, F. (2005). Unofficial accountability: A proposal for the permanent women's tribunal on sexual violence in armed conflict. *Texas Journal of Women in the Law, 15*, 107–145. Retrieved from http://heinonline.org/HOL/LandingPage?handle=hein.journals/tjwl15&div=9&id=&page

Theidon, K. (2007). Gender in transition: Common sense, women, and war. *Journal of Human Rights, 6*(4), 453–478. Retrieved from http://wcfia.harvard.edu/publications/gender-transition-common-sense-women-and-war

Theidon, K. (2012). *Intimate enemies: Violence and reconciliation in Peru*. Philadelphia: University of Pennsylvania Press.

Thomas, D. A. (2011). *Exceptional violence: Embodied citizenship in transnational Jamaica*. Durham NC: Duke University Press.

Tiemessen, A. E. (2004). After Arusha: Gacaca justice in post-genocide Rwanda. *African Studies Quarterly, 8*(1), 57–76. Retrieved from http://sites.clas.ufl.edu/africa-asq/files/Tiemessen-Vol8Issue1.pdf

Tijerina, R. (2009). *What did they say? Interpreting for social justice: An introductory curriculum*. New Market, TN: Highlander Research Education Center. Retrieved from http://www.intergroupresources.com/rc/Highlander%20curric.pdf

Torre, M. E. (2009). Participatory action research and critical race theory: Fueling spaces for Nos-otras to research. *Urban Review, 41*(1), 106–120. doi:10.1007/s11256-008-0097-7

Townsend, M. (2015, June 15). Revealed: How the world turned its back on rape victims of Congo. *The Guardian*. Retrieved from http://www.theguardian.com/world/2015/jun/13/rape-victims-congo-world-turned-away

Tribunal Primero de Sentencia Penal, Narcoactividad y Delitos contra el Ambiente [Criminal, Narcoactivity, and Crimes against the Environment Trial Court], Guatemala. (2016, February 26). Sentencia C-01076-2012-00021 [Sentence C-01076-2012-00021]. Retrieved from http://www.mujerestransformandoelmundo.org/sites/www.mujerestransformandoel mundo.org/files/descargas/sentencia_caso_sepur_zarco.pdf

Tuck, E. (2009). Suspending damage: A letter to communities. *Harvard Educational Review, 79*(3), 409–428. Retrieved from http://hepg.org/her-home/issues/harvard-educational-review-volume-79-issue-3/herarticle/a-letter-to-communities_739

Tuck, E. & Yang, K.W. (2012). Decolonization is not a metaphor. *Decolonization: Indigeneity, Education & Society, 1*(1), 2012, 1–40. Retrieved from https://jps.library.utoronto.ca/index .php/des/article/view/18630

UDEFEGUA—Unidad de Protección a Defensoras y Defensores de Derechos Humanos- Guatemala [Protection unit for human rights defenders-Guatemala]. (2010, December). *Informe anual 2010: Agresiones, el precio que debemos pagar: Informe sobre situación de defensoras y defensores de derechos humanos* [2010 annual report: Aggressions, the price we must pay: Report on the situation of human rights defenders]. Retrieved from http://udefegua .org/wp-content/uploads/2015/08/informe_final.pdf

UN Development Fund for Women. (2010). Gacaca and transitional justice in Rwanda. In *Progress of the world's women 2008/2009: Who answers to women? Gender and accountability*, (p. 84). Retrieved from http://www2.unwomen.org/~/media/headquarters/media /publications/unifem/powwo8reportfulltext.pdf?v=1&d=20140917T101016

UN General Assembly Resolution 60/147, *Basic Principles and Guidelines on the Right to Remedy and Reparation for Victims of Gross Violations of International Human Rights Law and Serious Violations of International Humanitarian Law*, 16 December 2005, A/60/147. Retrieved from: https://daccess-ods.un.org/TMP/7882725.59642792.html

UN Office for the Coordination of Humanitarian Affairs. (2008). *Sexual and gender-based violence in conflict: A framework for prevention and response.* New York, NY: Author.

UNAMG—Unión Nacional de Mujeres Guatemaltecas [National Union of Guatemalan Women]. (2017). *La luz que vuelve: Juicio Sepur Zarco. Historieta: Nivel de educación media* [The light that came back: The Sepur Zarco trial. Comic book: Middle school education level]. Guatemala City, Guatemala: Author.

Vargas, R. (2017). *Pewmas/Sueños de justicia. Lonkos y dirigentes mapuche versus Chile en la Corte Interamericana* [*Pewmas*/Dreams of Justice. *Lonkos* and Mapuche leaders versus Chile in the Inter-American Court]. Santiago, Chile: LOM Ediciones.

Vásquez, D. (with Yagenova, S.). (2011). Solidarity is a characteristic of the Maya People. In G. Grandin, D. Levenson, & E. Oglesby (Eds.), *The Guatemala reader: History, politics, culture* (pp. 537–540). Durham, NC: Duke University Press.

Velásquez Nimatuj, I. A. (2012). Peritaje cultural [Expert witness testimony on culture]. In I. Mendia Azkue & G. Guzmán Orellana (Eds.), *Ni olvido, ni silencio: Tribunal de Conciencia contra la violencia sexual hacia las mujeres durante el conflicto armado en Guatemala* [No forgetting, no silence: Tribunal of Conscience against violence against women during the armed conflict in Guatemala] (pp. 119–126). Bilbao, Spain: Universidad de País Vasco, Hegoa, & UNAMG.

Velásquez Nimatuj, I. A. (2016). *Peritaje cultural: Violaciones sexuales a mujeres q'eqchi' en el marco del conflict armado interno (1960–1996) de Guatemala, caso Sepur Zarco, municipio de El Estor, departamento de Izabal* [Expert witness report on culture: Sexual violations of Q'eqchi' women in the context of the internal armed conflict (1960–1996) in Guatemala, Sepur Zarco case, municipality of El Estor, department of Izabal]. Unpublished manuscript.

Viaene, L., (2010a). The internal logic of the cosmos as 'justice' and 'reconciliation': Micro-level perceptions in post-conflict Guatemala. *Critique of Anthropology, 30*(3), 287–312. doi:10 .1177/0308275X10372462

Viaene, L. (2010b). Life is priceless: Maya Q'eqchi' voices on the Guatemalan National Reparations Program. *International Journal of Transitional Justice, 4*(1), 4–25. doi:10.1093/ijtj/ijp024

Viaene, L. (2015). *Voces desde las sombras: El dolor nunca saldrá de nuestros corazones. Visiones indígenas q'eqchi' sobre justicia transicional en Guatemala.* [Voices from the shadows: The pain will never leave our hearts. Q'eqchi' indigenous visions of transitional justice in Guatemala]. Cóban, Guatemala: Ak'kutan Centro Bartolomé de las Casas.

Villatoro García, D. (2016, June 9). Otra brasa en manos de Yassmín Barrios [Another ember in Yassmín Barrios's hands], *Plaza Pública*. Retrieved from https://www.plazapublica.com.gt/content/otra-brasa-en-manos-de-yassmin-barrios.

Vizenor, G. (1994). *Manifest manners: Postindian warriors of survivance.* Hanover, NH: University Press of New England.

Vizenor, G. (Ed.). (2008). *Survivance: Narratives of Native presence.* Lincoln: University of Nebraska Press.

Warren, K. B. (1998). *Indigenous movements and their critics: Pan-Maya activism in Guatemala.* Princeton, NJ: Princeton University Press.

Watkins, M. (2015). Psychosocial accompaniment. *Journal of Social and Political Psychology, 3*(1), 324–341, doi:10.5964/jspp.v3i1.103

Weis, L., & Fine, M. (2012). Critical bifocality and circuits of privilege: Expanding critical ethnographic theory and design. *Harvard Educational Review, 82*(2), 173–201. doi:10.17763/haer.82.2.v1jx34n441532242

Wilson, R. A. (2001). *The politics of truth and reconciliation in South Africa: Legitimizing the post-apartheid state.* New York, NY: Cambridge University Press.

Women of PhotoVoice/ADMI & Lykes, M. B. (2000). *Voces e imágenes: Mujeres Mayas Ixiles de Chajul/Voices and images: Mayan Ixil women of Chajul.* Guatemala City, Guatemala: Magna Terra.

Woodman, S. (2011). Law, translation and voice: Transformation of a struggle for social justice in a Chinese village. *Critical Asian Studies, 43*(2), 185–210. doi:10.1080/14672715.2011.570566

Yaeger, P. (2006). Testimony without intimacy. *Poetics Today, 27*(2), 399–423. doi:10.1215/03335372-2005-010

Yoshiaki, Y. (2002). *Comfort women: Sexual slavery in the Japanese military during World War II* (revised ed.). (S. O'Brien, Trans.). New York, NY: Columbia University Press.

Yuyachkani. (n.d.). Retrieved from www.yuyachkani.org

Zipes, J. D. (1995). *Creative storytelling: Building community, changing lives.* New York, NY: Routledge.

Zur, J. (1998). *Violent memories: Mayan war widows in Guatemala.* Boulder, CO: Westview Press.

INDEX

ABOUT THE AUTHORS

ALISON CROSBY, PhD, is an associate professor in the School of Gender, Sexuality and Women's Studies and director of the Centre for Feminist Research at York University, Toronto, Canada. Her research projects and publications in refereed journals and edited volumes use an antiracist, anticolonial and transnational feminist lens and participatory methodologies to explore protagonists' multifaceted struggles to redress and memorialize harm in the aftermath of political violence. Her current project, *The Inhabitance of Loss: A Transnational Feminist Project on Memorialization*, a collaboration with Dr. Malathi de Alwis, explores memorialization as a site of contestation in Guatemala and Sri Lanka and is funded by a grant from the Social Sciences and Humanities Research Council of Canada (SSHRC).

M. BRINTON LYKES, PhD, is professor of Community-Cultural Psychology and co-director of the Center for Human Rights and International Justice at Boston College in Boston, Massachusetts. Her accompaniment of survivors of war and of gross violations of human rights draws on cultural resources, the creative arts, and participatory action research methodologies. Her current antiracist feminist participatory and action research focuses on violence against women in armed conflict and postconflict transitions and on migration and postdeportation human rights violations. She has published more than 100 articles in refereed journals and edited volumes; coauthored three books and coedited four others, including most recently, *The New Deportations Delirium: Interdisciplinary Responses* (with Daniel Kanstroom). Her activist scholarship has been recognized with multiple awards, including the Ignacio Martín-Baró Lifetime Peace Practitioner Award, the American Psychological Association's International Humanitarian Award, the Florence L. Denmark and Mary E. Reuder Award for Outstanding International Contributions to the Psychology of Women and Gender, and the Seymour B. Sarason Award for Community Research and Action.